G000053772

INFORMATION SYSTEMS REQUIREM
DETERMINATION AND ANALYSIS 2nd E......

Information Systems Requirements

Determination and Analysis 2nd Edition

Donal J. Flynn

Department of Computation
University of Manchester Institute of Science and Technology

The McGraw-Hill Companies

London · New York · St Louis · San Francisco · Auckland · Bogotá · Caracas
Lisbon · Madrid · Mexico · Milan · Montreal · New Delhi · Panama · Paris
San Juan · São Paulo · Singapore · Sydney · Tokyo · Toronto

Published by
McGRAW-HILL Publishing Company
Shoppenhangers Road, Maidenhead, Berkshire, S16 2Q1, England
Telephone 01628 502500
Fax: 01628 770224

The LOC data for this book has been applied for and may be obtained
from the Library of Congress, Washington, D.C.

A Catalogue record for this book is available from the British Library.

Further information on this and other McGraw-Hill titles is to be found
at http://www.mcgraw-hill.co.uk
Authors Website address: http://www.co.umist.ac.uk/~djflynn

Copyright © 1998 McGraw-Hill Publishing Company. All rights reserved.
No part of this publication may be reproduced, stored in a retrieval system,
or transmitted, in any form or by any means, electronic or otherwise without
the prior permission of McGraw-Hill Publishing Company.

McGraw-Hill

*A Division of The **McGraw·Hill** Companies*

Typset by WestKey Limited, Falmouth, Cornwall
and printed and bound in Great Britain at the University Press, Cambridge
Printed on permanent paper in compliance with the ISO Standard 9706

This book is dedicated to Penny, Alex and Clare
for all the love and encouragement they have given to me

CONTENTS

Preface   **xiii**

Part One: Information systems basics   **1**

1.   What is an information system?   **3**
Introduction   3
The MacAdam fast-food takeaway   3
Types of activities and information   7
Benefits of information systems   10
Problems with information systems   12
Problem analysis   18
Summary   22
Discussion questions   23
References   23

2.   Perspectives on information systems   **25**
Introduction   25
Types of information system   26
Contents of an information system   33
Information   40
Information systems in practice   45
Summary   48
Discussion questions   48
References   48

Part Two: Understanding information systems in organizations   **51**

3.   **The systems approach**   **53**
      Introduction   53
      Systems concepts   54
      Systems on different levels: sub-systems   56
      Predictability of systems   57
      Control systems   58
      Design system   59
      State space approach   60
      Classification of systems   61
      The systems approach – discussion   61
      Summary   64
      Discussion questions   64
      References   65

4.   **Analysing organizations and information systems –**
      the OMNIS model   **66**
      Applying the systems approach   66
      Functional system   68
      Eurobells⌂ production system example   68
      Control system   73
      Information system   75
      Interaction of functional and control systems   77
      Information system representation   78
      OMNIS model   81
      Summary   82
      Discussion questions   83
      References   83
      Case study 1 – the fishing fleet 'La Perle'   84

5.   **Management system**   **88**
      Introduction   88
      Classical model of management activities   89
      Mintzberg model of managerial roles   89
      Wide concept of management system   91
      Relative importance of different management roles   92
      Anthony's classification of decisions   93
      Combining activities and levels   93
      Management information requirements   94
      Summary   95
      Discussion questions   96
      References   96

Part Three: Hard approach to information systems   **97**

6.   The systems development process   **99**
       Introduction   99
       Traditional approach   99
       Requirements determination   101
       Analysis   103
       Logical design   105
       Physical design   106
       Implementation and testing   108
       Maintenance   110
       Summary of the traditional approach   112
       Dissatisfaction with the traditional approach   113
       Alternative approaches to systems development   118
       Summary   128
       Discussion questions   129
       References   129

7.   Requirements determination   **131**
       Introduction   131
       Problem definition   132
       Feasibility study   133
       Requirements acquisition   136
       Requirements modelling   139
       Problems with requirements determination   139
       Requirements Engineering   142
       Recent RE approaches   143
       Case study 2 – Eurobells⌂ stock room   148
       Requirements acquisition – case study 2   149
       Requirements modelling – case study 2   158
       Summary   160
       Discussion questions   160
       References   161

8.   Analysis I – entity and rule modelling   **164**
       Introduction   164
       Entity modelling   165
       Entity   166
       Relationship   167
       Relationship constraints   169
       Cardinality constraint   169
       Participation constraint   172
       Attribute   173
       Further topics   175

Eurobells⌂ example   180
Abstraction   181
Rule modelling – introduction and definition   182
Traditional problems of rule modelling   183
Recent approaches to modelling rules   184
Guidance for analysis   186
Summary   188
Discussion questions   188
References   189

9.   Analysis II – process modelling   **191**
Introduction   191
Process decomposition diagram   193
Data flow diagram   194
State transition diagram   197
Flowchart   199
Decision tree   199
Decision table   201
Summary of process phase products   202
Summary   202
Discussion questions   203
References   203

10.   Analysis III – object-oriented modelling   **204**
Introduction   204
Object model   204
Summary of object modelling   214
Dynamic modelling   214
Functional model   221
Relationship between object, dynamic and functional models 222
Summary   222
Further reading   223
Discussion questions   223
References   223

11.   Methods   **225**
Introduction   225
Brief history of methods   226
Description of methods   235
Case study 3 – the university library   235
Information Engineering   235
Structured systems analysis and design (SSAAD)   243
JSD   249
SSADM   258

OMT   270
Comparison of methods   276
Results of comparison   277
Technical trends   279
Problems addressed and solutions provided   279
CASE tools   282
Summary   288
Discussion questions   289
References   289

Part Four: Standardization   **295**

12.   The movement to method standardization   **297**
Introduction   297
Euromethod   299
SPICE   307
ISO 12207 – software life-cycle processes   315
DSDM   319
Summary   321
Discussion questions   323
References   323

Part Five: Soft approach to information systems   **325**

13.   Hard and soft approaches   **327**
Introduction   327
Problems with information systems   327
Hard approach   333
Soft approach   333
Soft approach—conclusions   349
Contingency approach to method use   351
Summary   353
Discussion questions   353
References   354

14.   Socio-organizational factors and information systems   **359**
Introduction   359
Organization structure and information systems   360
Task-technology   362
Technology   363
Task   367
Environment   369
Norms   371
Power   373

Practical recommendations   375
Critical systems thinking   377
Summary   380
Discussion questions   381
References   382

15.   Society and information systems   384
Introduction   384
Information systems evolution   384
Information systems and organizational structure   387
Software as a resource   388
Computers in the economy and the home   390
Computers and crime   390
Reliability   391
Privacy   391
Data Protection Act   392
Security   399
Human threats   402
Software threats   405
Summary   407
Discussion questions   408
References   408

Glossary   410

Author index   416

Subject Index   421

Preface

Overview

A central criticism of information systems today is that many systems do not do what their users require, and consequently fall into disuse. A major reason for this is perceived to be a 'computer-centred' emphasis on technical issues in the development process, at the expense of the 'requirements-centred' conceptual issues, related to problem definition and analysis, which are much more important for the correct modelling of user requirements.

The aim of this book is to describe the requirements-centred view, which places the emphasis on the early stages of systems development, where user requirements are determined and analysed, presenting a new, object-oriented, overview model for information systems analysis and describing relevant conceptual issues and models. The application of these to requirements modelling is fully illustrated, using case studies in addition to examples in the text. To reinforce this view, the organizational and social contexts within which information systems are commonly located are also described. The requirements-centred view is basic for an introductory book such as this, as it needs to be developed right from the start of the study of information systems.

A feature of the book is that it addresses the major problems found with information systems and discusses how different approaches provide solutions. This has three advantages:

1. It integrates the book around one theme, as chapters present relevant problems, and discuss how approaches attempt to solve these problems.
2. The problem-solution theme itself is one that serves a reminder of the book's basic message – that information systems should only be introduced where it can be shown that they are a solution to a problem and that technology is not a solution in its own right.

3. It allows the development of a line of argument that, beginning with a statement of problems found with the traditional approach to information systems development, shows, as the book progresses, how modern approaches to requirements modelling provide solutions to some, although not all, of these problems. This is particularly shown in the contrast between hard and soft approaches to systems development.

The basic message of this book is to convince the reader that information systems should serve a useful purpose in the organization and in the community, and that the use of technology for technology's sake is undesirable, as it may have negative effects.

Information systems face three key challenges in the future. Firstly, as has been stated above, many problems are reported with current information systems, and it is necessary for solutions to be found to these problems. Secondly, while information systems have traditionally been limited to processing data for organizational efficiency, future users are going to require such systems to process graphics and speech as well as data. Thirdly, users will also expect information systems to be able to demonstrate, more clearly than before, how they are improving aspects of the organization, such as effectiveness and competitiveness, as these aspects are becoming increasingly important in determining the success or failure of a system.

I use this book as a basis for my Introduction to Information Systems course at UMIST, a first-year course given to BSc Computation, Information Engineering and Joint Honours students. It assumes only an elementary knowledge of programming, the basic hardware components of an information system, and no knowledge whatsoever of the business environment.

Plan of the book

PART ONE: INFORMATION SYSTEMS BASICS

We define an information system and give an example. Various perspectives on information systems are introduced to motivate and explain the background to the area. The main problems found in information systems development are described.

Chapter 1 defines an information system, using a fast-food takeaway example, and develops a general view, emphasizing the organizational context of information systems and the types of activities assisted. The benefits of information systems are contrasted with their problems. Chapter 2 discusses different types of information system and their contents.

PART TWO: UNDERSTANDING INFORMATION SYSTEMS IN ORGANIZATIONS

We develop and describe the OMNIS model, which is an overview model of an information system in its organizational context, and we use this to illustrate the more detailed aspects of information systems.

Chapter 3 introduces many system concepts that are fundamental to the description of information systems, and Chapter 4 builds on these to define the OMNIS model. This will be used later in the requirements determination phase of systems development. A case study is used to illustrate the model. Chapter 5 discusses management activities and information systems, emphasizing the different types of activities and their information needs.

PART THREE: HARD APPROACH TO INFORMATION SYSTEMS

Here the aim is to describe the requirements and analysis phases of the systems development process, showing the early stages of how an information system is built. The chapter on methods and tools shows how a common requirement is developed by some well-known methods.

Chapter 6 begins with a description of the traditional approach to the process, discusses problems with the approach, and considers alternative approaches, including the iterative, evolutionary, user validation and prototyping approaches. In Chapter 7, requirements determination is examined, beginning with problem definition and feasibility study. The application of the OMNIS model developed earlier is then shown with a stock room case study in the Eurobells△ organization.

Chapter 8, Analysis I, illustrates the use of entities and rules in the analysis phase, using aspects of earlier case study user requirements held in OMNIS. Chapter 9, Analysis II, describes the traditional techniques for analysing processes, while Chapter 10 describes the object-oriented (OO) approach to analysis. Chapter 11 discusses some well-known methods used for systems development and briefly describes CASE tools.

PART FOUR: STANDARDIZATION

Chapter 12 outlines four recent proposals or standards that attempt to integrate some of the techniques and methods described in previous chapters into a set of procedures for the management of the systems development process.

PART FIVE: SOFT APPROACH TO INFORMATION SYSTEMS

The basic approach to development described in Parts Three and Four is criticized by describing the problems that arise when information systems are developed according to this approach, termed the 'hard' approach, and we put forward some ideas for improvements, which are collectively termed the 'soft' approach.

Chapter 13 contrasts the hard and soft approaches, showing how the soft approach addresses problems caused by the assumptions of the hard approach, and Chapter 14 describes an organization theory point of view, considering how information systems can be designed to 'fit' with social factors in the organization. Chapter 15 discusses the impact of information systems on the individual, organization and society.

Preface to the second edition

The plan of the second edition has been to build on the success of the first edition by bringing certain parts up to date to take account of changes over the past four or five years, and by adding some new material which I feel will be influential in the future. I have changed the chapter contents and numbers in the preface to the first edition to reflect the new edition.

The trend to the 'requirements-centred' view identified in the first edition has continued and I have not altered the basic structure of the book, with the result that the main changes consist of two new chapters. Chapter 10 reflects the increasing interest that has developed in the object-oriented approach and Chapter 12 looks at four emerging standards, Euromethod, SPICE, ISO 12207 and DSDM, which broadly focus on the problems of integrating techniques for systems development within an overall management process.

The other most important changes are now briefly described. The requirements-centred trend has led to the emergence of many requirements engineering methods, and some of these are discussed in Chapters 7 and 13; Chapter 8, dealing with entity and rule modelling has been totally revised and expanded; the OMT object-oriented method has been added to the method comparison in Chapter 11; and the previous chapter on CASE tools has been generalized and added to Chapter 11 (Methods). Finally, more recent research on social factors and their relationship with information systems, as well as systems development, is described in Chapter 14.

I am grateful to all the many individuals who have contacted me with suggestions for improvement and criticisms; I have not incorporated all of these but I have endeavoured to maintain a balanced view.

Part One

Information Systems Basics

The first part of this book, in Chapter 1, shows how a simple information system works, using the example of the MacAdam fast-food takeaway, and then describes some important features of the system that need to be clearly understood.

Benefits are mentioned and then certain problems with information systems are described. Problems of quality and productivity are discussed in detail and examples are given of how these problems might relate to the MacAdam takeaway. Chapter 2 discusses different types of information systems and shows how they fit the definition given in Chapter 1.

1

What is an information system?

Introduction

Our definition of an information system is:

> An information system provides procedures to record and make available information, concerning part of an organization, to assist organization-related activities.

The aim of an information system is to provide a means for processing information to improve the efficiency and effectiveness of the organization. We will see that this definition falls into two parts: the first emphasizing system structure and functioning, the second concerned with the organizational context of the system.

We shall use the term 'information system' to refer to a computer-based information system, and, in addition, we shall be mainly concerned with commercial information systems, characterized by the fact that people are the main suppliers and receivers of information. These are the types of system that we find in organizations such as banks, insurance companies, and retail, distribution and manufacturing organizations.

The MacAdam fast-food takeaway

MAIN POINTS

We now present a simple information system which will illustrate the components of our definition. Figure 1.1 shows an information system that is used in a branch of the MacAdam fast-food takeaway, selling food such as beefburgers, French fries and soft drinks. The system has been in full use for six months and all staff report general satisfaction with its operation, finding

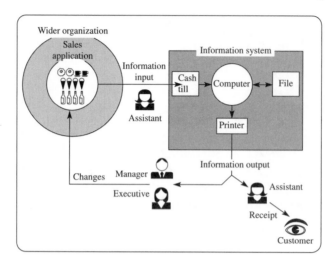

Figure 1.1 Information system in the MacAdam takeaway.

that it helps them to do their jobs better, that it is easy to use and that system reliability is good, with few problems.

The main points of the system are:

1. When items are sold, a sales assistant enters information into a cash till connected to the computer. An entry consists of data identifying the item and the quantity for example, six chocolate milk shakes.
2. The system knows the price of each item and calculates the total price.
3. Each entry is stored on a computer file.
4. Information concerning the sale is produced by the system, in the form of a printed receipt, which is given to the customer by the sales assistant.
5. Sales information is available for the takeaway manager, John Silver, who can obtain a printed report from the computer file showing, for example, sales yesterday or this month, and numbers of customers.
6. Information is also available for Sally Cuthbertson, the sales director, who is based at Head Office in Glasgow, consisting of quarterly sales to date, number of customers weekly and quarterly, and sales for each product.

   In addition, an analysis program can present Sally with predictions of the profiles of proposed products, in terms of business factors such as likely market share and short-term (1 to 6 months) and medium-term (6 months to 2 years) earnings, based on existing product consumption.

STRUCTURE AND FUNCTIONING OF THE INFORMATION SYSTEM

The basic features of the information system in Fig. 1.1, in relation to the first part of our definition, are as follows. First of all, *information* is recorded in the system, on a computer file. The information *concerns a part of the organization* as it relates to the sales function, recording information such as items sold, their quantities and their price. There are *procedures to record and make available* the information as the assistant is helped to enter information into the computer and receives a printed receipt, and managers and executives can obtain reports that present the recorded sales information in different ways.

The human procedures related to recording and making information available initiate procedures carried out by programs (software), such as price finding, item totalling, data storage and report production, which in turn control hardware devices (computer, cash till, printer and file).

The information system in this example supports the sales function of the takeaway, and we term this a *sales application*. There may be other applications, for example the purchase of food from suppliers.

When items are sold, each sale constitutes a *transaction*, which is a basic, everyday process in the organization. Another example of a transaction might be the delivery of a quantity of food, such as a thousand frozen beefburgers, from a supplier.

ORGANIZATIONAL CONTEXT OF THE INFORMATION SYSTEM

Turning our attention to the second part of the definition, we want to emphasize that the information system is used *to assist organization-related activities*. This means that there is a close relationship between the information system and the organization of which it is a part.

This relationship is characterized by the fact that, firstly, the information system satisfies the *information needs* of the required activities. Secondly, it provides automated *procedures* which assist or replace some activities. Thirdly, the system is *usable* by and *acceptable* to the organization.

Information needs

- *Sales assistants*. The sales assistants are provided with item prices by the system, which also provides information concerning the sale on a receipt to give to customers.
- *Takeaway manager*. John uses information from the system to check that the takeaway is performing to expectation. There are targets for numbers of customers, for sales and for staff costs, and if targets are not being achieved then he must take decisions to reduce costs or lower profits on certain items to stimulate more business. In this way he uses the system to control the business.
- *Sales director*. Sally uses information from the system to help her decide if any changes are required to the products sold by the takeaway. For example, pomegranate-flavoured milk shake may be discontinued if its sales are down for six successive months. Using the basic sales information,

the system can accumulate and analyse the figures to present the information she requires to take such product decisions.

Procedures

- *Sales assistants.* Procedures are provided for recording information that allow sales details to be entered, check that the details are valid, calculate total prices and store the entries on the file. Procedures for making information available are also provided, as the system prints the sales receipt automatically, so the assistants do not have to take time to write it out manually.
- *Manager and director.* For John and Sally, the relevant procedures produce the information mentioned above to assist their activities.

Usability and acceptability

The third characteristic of the relationship between the information system and the organization is that the information system is *acceptable* to the users, as they report that they need the information from the system and feel that it helps them to organize their jobs better. In addition, the information system is *usable*, in the sense that the system is not hard to operate, it is reliable and it allows information to be input and output in as simple a fashion as possible.

INFORMATION SYSTEMS DEVELOPMENT

The development of the information system for MacAdam's followed the traditional life-cycle path. This generally consists of several phases, as follows:

1. *Requirements.* The requirements for the system are obtained from the users. These set out what the system should do and how it should fit in to the organization.
2. *Analysis.* The requirements are analysed and a detailed specification is produced.
3. *Design.* This is often separated into logical and physical design, and it is the phase where the detail of the system is worked out, including computer and manual processes.
4. *Implementation.* Programs are written, the system is tested and it is put into operation.
5. *Maintenance.* Users request changes to the system, which are analysed, designed and implemented.

The MacAdam sales information system was developed over a period of twelve months by the takeaway Head Office, underwent a pilot test in several selected branches and is now installed in all branches.

Types of activities and information

We now present a more general view of an information system, focusing on the main types of organizational activity, their information needs and related procedures. Figure 1.2 shows the context implied by the above discussion, where an information system provides automated procedures and information to assist organization-related activities for an application.

ACTIVITIES

The activities in an organization are usually classified into two broad types:

1. Functional activities.
2. Management activities.

Functional activities are performed by junior employees in an organization, such as the sales assistants in MacAdam's. These activities transform different types of input, such as raw materials, money and information, into the goods or services of the organization, as well as carrying out related tasks such as processing customer orders, accepting payments and processing organizational information. In contrast, *management activities* are performed by different levels of management, from supervisors to senior executives, such as John and Sally at MacAdam's. Management activities plan and control the organization and direct its functional activities.

A distinction that may be drawn between these two broad types of activity is the degree of structuring of the decisions that may be made. Management have considerable freedom in the decisions they make, while junior employees can only make very restricted types of decision. For example, a sales assistant in MacAdam's might not be allowed to accept a cheque in payment without authorization from the supervisor.

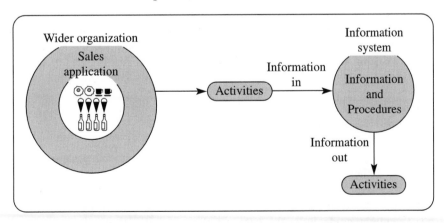

Figure 1.2 A general view of an information system in its organizational context.

A consequence of this is that many functional activities, being more routine, are more easily automated, and hence can be partially replaced by information system procedures.

INFORMATION NEEDS, ACTIVITIES AND PROCEDURES

We shall briefly look at typical management and functional activities and consider their information needs which are satisfied, as well as the activities that are assisted or replaced, by an information system.

Functional activities

Many functional activities contain *information processing activities*, which may record information in and receive information from an information system. For example, in a manufacturing organization the activity that manufactures a part will be accompanied by information processing activities that record details of the part and its manufacture. In a service organization, such as an insurance company, the activity that creates a policy will consist almost exclusively of information processing activities. Examples of information processing activities are:

- *Processing a shipment order*. The customer name and order number is entered; the system checks the order number, supplies the customer address and prints the despatch note. The shipping clerk sends the despatch note with the order.
- *Paying employee wages*. The employee name and code is entered and the system checks the code, supplies information concerning the rate of pay, calculates the total pay and prints the pay slip. The wages clerk gives the pay slip to the employee with the wages.
- *Processing a MacAdam sale*. The sale details are entered and the system supplies the price and calculates the total. The amount tendered by the customer is entered, the change is displayed and the receipt is printed. The assistant gives the customer the receipt and change with the customer's food.

Some activities do not record but only receive information from the information system. For example:

- *Locate warehouse part*. The part code is entered and the system checks to see if there are any in stock. If there are, it displays the location of the part together with the quantity remaining. If out of stock, it displays an appropriate message.

  We may include under this category those activities that only disseminate information to other employees.

A characteristic of information processing activities is that they are typically a mixture of computer procedures and human activities.

Management activities

These include scheduling jobs, hiring and firing staff, managing departmental budgets, checking organizational performance against objectives, or deciding on new markets or strategies. Information is needed for all these controlling and planning activities, and in MacAdam's information is required for controlling costs and planning new products. Such information is typically used to assist the management decision-making process.

TYPES OF INFORMATION

The types of information are directly related to the activities that use the information. *Functional information* is used by functional activities and is the most detailed. *Management information* is less detailed and is typically, as in MacAdam, an accumulation of functional information, although it may also be analysed in a more complex manner.

Another distinguishing characteristic of the types is the time interval to which they relate. Functional information concerns a short time interval, often that occupied by a transaction, while management information concerns a longer interval, such as an hour, a week or a year.

EXTERNAL INFORMATION

Some of the functional activities may send functional information, in the form of, for example, receipts and despatch notes for customers, to external individuals or organizations. In addition, it is common for management information to be sent externally. For example, amounts of income tax deducted from employees' pay may be accumulated monthly and sent to government organizations, and annual accounts may be produced for shareholders. Such external users may, on the basis of this information, act as managers and bring about organizational changes.

External information may also be input into the organization. For example, information concerning the competitive position of other organizations might be required by management activities.

INFORMATION SYSTEM AND ACTIVITIES

We may summarize our discussion with the diagram in Fig. 1.3. The figure shows that information may be used by management activities to result in changes to the application, such as hiring extra staff, or changes to the plans or objectives of the organization, which might eventually result in more fundamental organizational or application changes. Functional information is used by functional activities and may be sent externally. Functional activities also supply detailed information to the information system. Some procedures in the information system are automated and take over activities that were previously human.

The figure shows the two types of information from one system as an illustration only, as different information systems may provide different types of information. There is, however, often a relationship between the systems, as management activities frequently use functional information that has been aggregated or analysed in some way.

The part of Fig. 1.3 labelled 'Information system' refers to the computer part of the information system; we shall see later that the description of an information system may also include the information processing activities which input and output information.

Benefits of information systems

Why have people considered introducing information systems into organizations? Two important reasons are to improve the *efficiency* or the *effectiveness* of the organization.

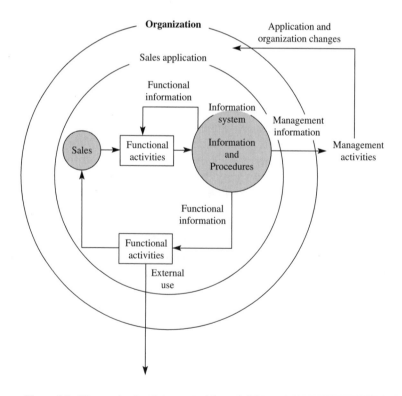

Figure 1.3 IS organizational context with two different types of information.

EFFICIENCY

An activity consumes resources, such as people, time, money, raw materials and information itself. If the activity uses fewer resources, for example, it can be performed more quickly or with fewer people, then efficiency, and therefore productivity, is improved. Three aspects of efficiency that result from automating activities are:

1. *Cost.* A computer system can be considerably cheaper than a corresponding manual system. This is mainly because computers replace jobs formerly held by people.
2. *Accuracy.* A computer is error-free while humans are not. As long as data and software are correct, a computer is capable of performing tedious and complicated functions without error.
3. *Speed.* Computers offer savings in time. They can process large quantities of data in a short time compared with humans. A business cycle of processing orders, making deliveries, sending invoices and receiving payment can thus be shortened, improving cash flow and customer service.

In MacAdam's, the system has improved efficiency as the computer stores accurate information about each sale transaction more cheaply, and prints each receipt, using fewer staff than a corresponding manual operation. The speed of a sale, as well as productivity, has thus increased. In addition, financial accuracy is improved (and fraud reduced), as assistants do not enter prices. For management activities, John is able to find out last week's sales for items much more quickly and accurately than before, improving his decision-making concerning takeaway efficiency.

Another example concerns improved communication of information. Computer systems allow the capability of common access to information within the organization over networks from physically separate locations. In MacAdam's, information on sales at all branches could be available to Head Office if branches are networked.

EFFECTIVENESS

In contrast to efficiency, emphasizing internal organizational factors, effectiveness stresses external factors, such as market share and customer wants. Systems may provide management information to assist decisions concerned with effectiveness. For example, Sally can run the product analysis program on the information to suggest likely implications of new products. Neither the information nor the analysis may have been available before, or available at the right time. External information which is, for example, publicly available (census, telephone directory) may also be accessed.

TRENDS IN BENEFITS

Traditionally, benefits have come from the efficiency and productivity advantages that result from reducing the human and mechanical elements in manual information systems. However, these 'back-office' applications, consisting mainly of functional activities, are becoming increasingly computerized. The trend is more recently towards 'front-office' systems that assist (or even, as some suggest, improve on) the effectiveness of human decision-making processes, typically found in management activities, by making available information of a higher quality than before or by improving reasoning capabilities (Ernst and Young, 1989).

However, improvements in effectiveness are more subjective than improvements in efficiency, and cost-benefit estimates for systems are therefore harder to justify.

Brynjolfsson (1993) discusses how information systems may assist productivity, while Pitt *et al.* (1995) consider one aspect of effectiveness by determining the quality of the service provided by an information system.

SUCCESS STORIES

The *Successes* panel describes some recent system successes. The Sleepezee system also improves effectiveness, as customers receive a bespoke bed more quickly. The police system has led to greater effectiveness by gathering external data and improving reasoning capabilities, while the project described by the Public Accounts Committee aims to improve efficiency. The report concerning speech-based systems assists efficiency and flexibility and the RSPB's digital image system provides access to a wider audience than before.

Problems with information systems

FAILURE STORIES

Some recent systems failures are described in the *Failures* panel. The majority of the stories concern public sector organizations, as their finances are examined by publicly accountable bodies which report on their findings. Failures are probably just as frequent in the private sector, which does not have to report in this way. More stories concerning failures than successes are presented to reflect their incidence in the news media. It may be seen that, in some cases, system failure can lead to consequences such as legal action and business loss.

SURVEYS AND REPORTS

In a national survey of public and private sector IT developments, called Managing Information & System Risks, management consultancy Coopers & Lybrand found that more than 60 per cent of large UK organizations had

Successes

'Sales Talk', *Computing*, 8 June 1995

Bed manufacturer Sleepezee has saved more than £450,000 by improving its order and delivery systems . . . Sleepezee has been able to narrow the time between production and delivery, and, as a result, cut raw material and stock holdings by 30%. Sleepezee can now deliver bespoke beds within 14 days of receiving an order.

'The digital detective', *Computing*, 27 September 1995

. . . Crime figures are coming down over the country. Over the past two years, police forces from Margate to Stirling have announced falls in the overall crime rate, varying from 7% to 20%, while detected crime is up by around 3% a year.

Central Police in Stirling, Scotland has chosen a crime-detection solution from Memex, a company formed to develop the ideas of Professor Fred Heath, chair of computing at Heriot-Watt University. Inspector Peter Watson . . . claims: 'It is no coincidence that, in the last two years, our detection rate has taken a massive hike. There is no doubt that the technology helps. A good deal of detection is based on intelligence, planning and good old-fashioned police work, underpinned by new technology.' . . . George Smith, chief executive of Memex, says: '. . . The force uses information collected from the crime system, the scene of crime and from the various databases available to the police. The real trick is to compare crimes with individuals.'

'Late News', *Computing*, 17 August 1995

The Public Accounts Committee has drawn attention to a public sector IT project which is six months ahead of schedule and sticking to its budget. The Crown Office in Scotland is implementing a £6.8m IBM-based network. . . . The network is expected to save more than £9m in staff costs when completed next year.

'Voice boxes', *Computing*, 13 June 1996

Advances in speech-based software systems are beginning to deliver real business benefits. Malcolm Dove, IT director for Miller Insurance Group Services, recalls . . . 'It enables me to dictate my own reports, letters and faxes, rather than getting my secretary to type the first draft. . . . This improves overall efficiency and shows huge potential . . . when secretarial support is not available.'

lost control of information systems projects ('Project flaws hit firms',*Computing*, 21 September 1995). In addition, 85 per cent of those questioned suffered delays or budget overruns during projects, or failed to achieve their objectives.

A UK survey by the consultants KPMG Peat Marwick McLintock (KPMG, 1990) found that '30% of the UK's biggest computer projects were massively over budget, over time, and, if ever completed, fail to do the job they were meant to'. It is suspected that unsuccessful systems may also lose customers and eventually threaten organizational survival.

More than 70 per cent of New Zealand organizations ('NZ pays price for high failure rate', *Computing*, 15 June 1995) have experienced one or more IT failures in the past three years. The losses which businesses incur often stretch beyond monetary loss and can affect the competitiveness of an organization. They may delay or interrupt the delivery of products or services or dominate management focus when they go wrong. Findings indicated that there is not a clear, single reason for project failure.

Chartered accountancy firm Robson Rhodes quizzed 312 UK legal practices for its sixth annual *Legal IT Survey* ('User satisfaction with legal sector plummets', *Computing*, 6 July 1995). A mere 20 per cent of respondents feel they get a good or excellent service from their suppliers.

In an interview in IEEE Software (Sims, 1995), James Sims, the US-based president of Cambridge Technology Partners, who provide rapid application development for more than 250 clients, quotes an industry report which surveyed application development worldwide. Projects were rated as successful if they were on time, on budget and had the right functionality. The report found that only 16 per cent of the $250 billion spent each year is classed as successful. Thirty one per cent of projects are cancelled and 51 per cent are either late or over budget. The four top reasons for failure were lack of user input, changes in requirements, incomplete requirements and lack of executive support.

GOVERNMENT REPORTS

An often-quoted US Government report, described in Davis (1990), examined nine software development projects in 1979 that had recently completed. Although the project size was quite small (less than $7m in total), 47 per cent of this sum was spent on software that was never used. In addition, 29 per cent was spent on software that was never delivered and 19 per cent went on software that was either extensively reworked after delivery or was subsequently abandoned. Of the remaining $317 000, additional modifications were required, leaving only $119 000 worth, or less than 2 per cent, of delivered software that met requirements!

For 'front-office' systems, a 1986 survey by the DTI in the UK (DTI, 1986) showed that, on average, of 20 pilot office automation projects, only half worked as the users expected, were fully accepted or brought positive benefits to the organization, and 20 per cent were rejected.

RESEARCH

Many information systems are never delivered or are never used, with a figure in the region of 40 per cent being suggested (Eason, 1988). In addition, perhaps only 20 per cent of systems have a positive effect on organizations, the remaining 40 per cent having only a neutral effect. Lyttinen and Hirschheim (1987) estimate that up to 50 per cent of information system projects may be failures.

Lederer and Prasad (1993) surveyed 115 IT professionals and found that 63 per cent of large projects (> $50 000) substantially overspend. The top four reasons found are frequent change requests by users, overlooked tasks, users don't understand their requirements and poor user–developer communication and understanding. About 40 per cent of these projects were not justified with a cost–benefit analysis.

Brynjolfsson (1993) discusses how investment in IT and delivered computing power has increased since 1970 in the USA but, at the same time, productivity (that is worker productivity), especially in the service sector, has not followed this pattern, but has in fact stagnated. In a review of researchers' findings on the relationship between IT investment in manufacturing and services and worker productivity, he concludes that no firm judgement can be made at the moment, on account of problems such as suspected mismeasurement and time lags in measuring productivity.

Robinson (1994) gives an account of a notorious failure concerning a system for the London Ambulance Service and Myers (1993) analyses the reasons for a failed information systems project. Kemerer and Sosa (1991) discuss major failures in information systems.

Neumann (1995, 1996) collects and classifies many 'risks to the public' from computer systems and Capers Jones (1995) presents a view of project success or failure from inside industry, suggesting several contributory factors. Lyytinen and Hirschheim (1987) and Sauer (1993) discuss frameworks for failure analysis and Beynon-Davies (1996) provides a good overview of the topic of failure, discussing several case studies in detail; these include well-publicized failures such as the London Ambulance Service CAD system, the Taurus Stock Exchange system and the Wessex Regional Health Authority regional information systems plan.

OTHER INDICATORS

An analysis (Humphrey, 1988) by the US Government-funded Software Engineering Institute, based at Carnegie-Mellon University in the US, evaluated approximately 150 of the leading software producers in the US and found that over 80 per cent of producers had a development process considered to

'Parliament lights fire under GEC's Phoenix', *Computing*, **13 July 1995**

The Commons Defence Committee has strongly criticized the development of three key military systems which have been dogged by upsets and delays. . . . GEC Marconi was singled out for criticism of its work on the £170m Phoenix project, which is lagging at least eight years behind deadline and is now threatened with cancellation.

'DSS sues ICL over failed benefit analysis software', *Computing*, **25 May 1995**

The Department of Social Security (DSS) has broken with Whitehall tradition by launching legal action against ICL over the 'failed' £25m Analytical Services Statistical Information System (ASSIST). . . . The department wants to . . . gain 'full reimbursement' of £3.6m costs it has already paid ICL for the project, abandoned last October amid claims that the software was inadequate.

'Late News', *Computing*, **17 August 1995**

Two reports from the National Audit Office (NAO) have strongly criticized government computer operations. An examination of Customs & Excise use of computer credibility checks . . . said cutting false queries could save up to £10m. The second report blamed a failure to integrate the computer software development of the Eurofighter's . . . system for contributing to a £1bn overrun in the cost of development.

'PRS keeps legal option open', *Computing*, **8 June 1995**

Last week, the PRS (Performing Right Society) and software supplier LBMS reached an out-of-court settlement in the long-running dispute over the collapse of the Society's attempt to downsize its mainframe-based membership system. . . . The . . . system was abandoned in November 1992 after four years of painful development. The decision was taken following an independent report which said the system could not be made to work as configured and would need 'considerable further investment' if it were to work at all. . . . No-one is admitting liability for the project's failure and the damages paid out are way short of the £16m claimed by the Society. The terms of the settlement leave the PRS with a £5.6m shortfall from the £8m it says it had to write off following the collapse of PROMS.

Failures

'Brighter future for finance systems', *Computing*, **24 August 1995**
The collapse of systems such as the London Stock Exchange's failed Taurus project . . . has made the financial markets nervous about IT. . . . By the time Taurus was abandoned in 1993, the cost had ballooned to £100m – twice the original estimates.

'RAF gives IBM 90 days to curb sky-high costs', *Computing*, **28 September 1995**
The RAF has issued IBM with a 90-day ultimatum to save its £400m Logistics IT Strategy (Lits) from massive cost overruns. Ministry of Defence sources said officials have discussed cutting their losses and writing off development costs to date, after IBM's estimates for completing the current phase of development were three times the RAF budget. . . . A spokesman for the RAF's Lits programme management team described talk of IBM not completing the project as 'premature'.

'Facing the firing squad', *Computing*, **2 November 1995**
James Champy, a top management guru, told last month's Business Intelligence BPR 95 (business process re-engineering) conference that fewer than 1% of corporations are fully re-engineered organisations. Mark Maletz, an up-and-coming young expert, added that only a miserable 5% of BPR projects succeed. Neither seemed shocked by these statistics. . . . Like psychoanalysts offering a cure that never arrives, BPR advocates portray the failure of most of its practitioners as success.
. . . Julian Stainton, chief executive of Western Provident Assurance was scathing about the role of technology. 'I spent £10m on IT, we had hardly any noticeable improvement in service and productivity actually fell,' he recalls. 'The biggest problem in our case was definitely the IT people,' he adds. 'The IT people in organisations are only interested in preserving their own jobs. IT suppliers just want to sell more hardware and software – and they haven't got the slightest interest in other businesses.'

'Late News', *Computing*, **13 June 1996**
Faulty computer software has been blamed by experts investigating the failure of the Ariane-5 space rocket. . . . Daniel Mugnier, launch operations director of the $7bn (£4.5bn) flopped venture, said preliminary checks suggested computers had sent the wrong data to the rocket.

be 'chaotic', with problems in the areas of progress planning and change control.

Problem analysis

MAJOR PROBLEMS

Despite the fact that some information systems, such as the system at MacAdam's, are successful, there have also been a significant number of failures, as shown above. The major problems found are as follows:

1. *Quality*. Information systems are often of poor quality, as they do not have a beneficial effect on the organization. Systems are frequently proposed as solutions to problems of efficiency or effectiveness, but they may not solve the right problem, they may not address the real information processing needs of the users or they may conflict with other parts of the organization. It is often said that 'they do the thing right rather than do the right thing'. Their effect on the organization may be neutral or, at worst, it may be destructive, affecting employees or customers.
2. *Productivity*. Many complaints are concerned with cost and time overruns in the systems development process. Both types of problem may cause systems to be abandoned during development. Real costs may also be hidden, due to the fact that a major rework of systems is often left to the maintenance phase.
3. *Maintainability*. Systems are often costly and time-consuming to change in the maintenance phase if changes occur in the requirements or in the technology. This is because specifications often do not exist. If they do exist, then they are inflexible, as a small change may cause many related, unpredictable, changes.
4. *Reliability*. This concerns the ability of a system to behave consistently in the environment for which it is intended. This might be regarded as a particular type of quality problem in the context of safety-critical systems, important financial systems or systems whose incorrect functioning might cause great embarrassment. Examples of safety-critical systems are nuclear power stations (for example, Chernobyl), railways, aircraft and missile early warning systems. Recent cases of banking systems have involved incorrect transfers of hundreds of millions of pounds.
5. *Security*. Reports are increasing of computer fraud, where information is accessed that is available over networks vulnerable to intervention by unauthorized individuals (such as hackers). There is also a growing problem caused by illegally introduced software (such as viruses) which corrupts systems.
6. *Big Brother*. This problem concerns the fear that information concerning individuals may be used for personal surveillance by government or related bodies.

QUALITY

Reasons for poor quality

It is, unfortunately, only too easy to develop an information system that does not have a beneficial effect on the organization. This may occur for several reasons:

1. The information system may address the wrong problem, in that it may not help (or may help only marginally) the organization become more efficient or effective. There may be a more important problem that is missed. Alternatively, the information system may conflict with organizational aims. In many cases, the wrong activities to assist are chosen.
2. Wider social or psychological factors may be neglected, such as the existing reporting structure of the organization or the extent to which the information system will be acceptable to or usable by its intended users.
3. Even if the right activities are identified, the organization may be incorrectly analysed for its information needs, due to organizational or technical ignorance on the part of users or analysts.
4. The system may be developed for the wrong reasons, such as technology push from technical experts or political pull from ambitious managers.

The majority of these problems are due to a lack of attention to the nature of the relationship between the information system and the organization.

Existing MacAdam system

In the takeaway, the users report that the system has a beneficial effect, so it may be assumed that the problem solved by their system is the correct problem. Firstly, the activities identified, which are concerned with controlling costs and identifying slow-selling products, are activities that are agreed upon as being important for the success of the organization. Secondly, users are happy with the integration of the system into the organization. Thirdly, the activities have had their information needs correctly analysed and, fourthly, the cost and sophistication of the technology chosen for the system is commensurate with the benefits expected.

Overall, the performance of the activities is improved by computerized provision of the specified information.

Poor quality MacAdam system

However, MacAdam might not have been so fortunate in the quality of its information system, and we may now imagine the sort of problems that might have occurred.

- *Wrong problem.* This problem might have been caused by the selection of management activities that were not important for organizational success. Such a selection might have been made due to a lack of understanding of the organization. A more important activity might have been, for example, to closely monitor the age and gender profile of customers to be able to offer new products that are suitable to the different groups. Alternatively, it might have been better to decentralize decision making from Sally to John for new products, as he is on the spot and can respond more quickly. Another possibility is that wider organizational strategy may emphasize the goal of increased product sales through improved product quality, rather than extending the product range. Hence, the information system would be in conflict with this strategy.

  It is probably clear from the above that the choice of organizational activities to be supported by an information system may not be obvious and may depend on intuitive business knowledge. If a mistake is made, then an expensive investment is wasted.

- *Neglect of wider organization.* A problem of this type might have been caused if the existing system had not been piloted in some of the branches. As a result of comments from the pilot, changes were made to the system interface, and a training programme was established in every branch to discuss features and the potential for organizational improvements resulting from the system. Had this not been done, users might have been reluctant to use the system fully, especially as it was devised and imposed by Head Office, and its acceptability would have been low. Such systems often fall into disuse.

- *Incorrect analysis.* The information needs might have been incorrectly analysed, so that sales were only shown by category of product, for example by milk shake, instead of each type of milk shake. Reports might therefore be useless, and delay would occur while a change request was examined for its implications.

- *Wrong reasons.* An example of this problem might have occurred if the MacAdam technical experts had been allowed to acquire the latest type of database for the system. It would probably have been unsuitable, as it was more expensive than the industry standard, and it was a new product which had not been tested properly and might continually break down, threatening system acceptability and cost.

Solutions

Many solutions concern modifications to the basic systems development process. The first problem is addressed by several different approaches, including the requirements engineering approach, described in Chapter 7, and the soft systems approach discussed in Chapter 13 which aims to identify the right problem to be solved.

Solutions for the second type of problem employ an organization theory approach, discussed in Chapter 14, which, with the user-centred approaches described in Chapter 13, aims to involve the users more actively as participants in the development process, including acceptability and usability factors as part of the system requirements.

To address the third problem, there is a growth of methods, such as the OMNIS model discussed in Chapters 4 and 7, and those in Chapters 10, 11 and 12, although most of these require domain knowledge concerning the application to increase their effectiveness.

There is no specific approach for the fourth problem, although group sessions are often used in requirements acquisition (discussed in Chapter 7) to identify and resolve disagreements between users over requirements.

PRODUCTIVITY

Cost overruns of several times the original estimates for development are not uncommon. Such overruns will affect cost–benefit justifications made for the system. If the estimated delivery time extends from 18 months to three years, for example, it is possible that the system may not be useful, as events in the market may move so quickly that it is out of date when delivered. Both these factors may cause systems to be cancelled or never used, once delivered.

Although some of these problems are due to poor estimation techniques and project management, the most important factor is changing requirements. It is a well-known phenomenon that requirements for an information system may be in a state of flux throughout the systems development process. If the specification of a system is always changing in this way then new work must be done and completed work redone, both factors causing costs to grow and delivery times to lengthen. The problem of changing requirements takes place within the context of a shortage of experienced development staff.

Reasons for changing requirements

There are three main reasons why requirements change:

1. Users often have only a vague notion of requirements at the beginning of a project, learning them more thoroughly as the project progresses.
2. Changes in external factors, such as technology, legislation and the market, will change requirements for systems.
3. Requirements may have implications for implementation which are not feasible, but which are realized only at implementation time.

Problems of quality and productivity will interact, as, for example, the discovery during testing that a system is of poor quality may mean a delay while the system is put right.

Existing MacAdam system

The way in which the information system was developed at MacAdam was only discussed briefly. However, the fact that the system is operating successfully does not mean that it met its cost or time development targets. In fact, as it is difficult to estimate the benefits a system brings, it is only rarely that it is possible to measure whether a system is actually of financial benefit to an organization.

Solutions to the productivity problem are discussed in Chapters 6, 12 and 13 and include the prototyping approach, to assist users in learning about their requirements, CASE tools, which automate the more routine aspects of systems development, and project management techniques.

OTHER PROBLEMS

The problem of maintainability has been raised in the discussion on productivity where change was considered. It concerns the maintenance phase. When system changes are required, a process that occupies about 80 per cent of the life of a system, these are often very costly and time-consuming, owing to poor documentation and the way in which many programs are written, where one change often means many dependent changes. A significant proportion of new systems are in fact replacements for old systems that have grown too inflexible to maintain (Swanson and Beath, 1989).

The last three problems mentioned, Big Brother, reliability and security, apply to all computer-based systems. For the Big Brother problem, the Data Protection Act has been introduced to reduce this possibility. However, organizations are increasingly under attack by viruses and hacking, and Chapter 15 deals with these from the point of view of social impact, mentioning the Computer Misuse Act which has been introduced to prevent these problems.

Chapter 13 contrasts the hard and soft approaches to developing information systems, and discusses in more detail the problems found in traditional 'hard' approaches to development, describing the solutions that are brought by the 'soft' approach.

Summary

In this chapter we began by defining an information system, and we then introduced the MacAdam takeaway as a simple example of an information system. Basic features of this example which illustrated the first part of the definition were then briefly discussed. The MacAdam organizational context in which the information system existed was then described, emphasizing three important factors in the relationship between the information system and the organization: (a) information needs, (b) procedures and (c) usability and acceptability. The main phases of the systems development process used to build the information system were then briefly described.

The different types of activities in organizations were then classified into two main types, management and functional activities, as were the types of information needed by the activities. We showed how the information system may provide automated procedures to replace or assist some of these activities, particularly the functional activities, as well as information.

The next section began by describing the benefits resulting from information systems, but this was contrasted with several problems that frequently arise. Successes and failures were discussed. Two of these problems in particular, quality and productivity, have a serious effect on the impact of information systems on organizations, and the problems were discussed in some detail, with later chapters in the book that address the problems being mentioned.

Discussion questions

1. What are the two types of activity in an organization? Give examples of the matching types of information.
2. Describe three benefits that an information system can bring to an organization.
3. What do we mean by a quality problem in an information system? Describe four reasons for poor quality systems.
4. Discuss the three main reasons for productivity problems when developing information systems.
5. Explain the causes of inflexible information systems and possible solutions.

References

Ahituv, N. and Neumann, S. (1990) *Principles of Information Systems for Management*, 3rd edn, Wm. C. Brown, Dubuque, IA.

Beynon-Davies, P. (1996) *Analysing IS Failures*, Technical Communications (Publishing), Hitchin, UK.

Brynjolfsson, E. (1993) The productivity paradox of information technology, *Communications of the ACM*, **36**(12), 67–77.

Capers Jones, T. (1995) *Patterns of Software Systems Failure and Success*, Thomson, London.

Davis, A. M. (1990) *Software Requirements: Analysis and Specification*, Prentice-Hall International, London.

DTI (1986) *Profiting from Office Automation* (2 vols). Available from Library and Information Centre, Department of Trade and Industry, 1–19 Victoria Street, London SW1H 0ET.

Earl, M. J. (1990) *Management Strategies for Information Technology*, Prentice-Hall, London.

Eason, K. (1988) *Information Technology and Organisational Change*, Taylor & Francis, London.

Ernst and Young (1989) *The Landmark MIT Study: Management in the 1990s.* Available from Ernst and Young Ltd, 7 Rolls Buildings, Fetter Lane, London EC4A 1NH.

Humphrey, W. S. (1988) Characterizing the software process: a maturity framework, *IEEE Software*, **5**, 73–79.

Kemerer, C. F. and Sosa, G. L. (1991) Systems development risks in strategic information systems, *Information Software Technology*, **33**(3), 212–13.

KPMG (1990) *Runaway Computer Systems—A Business Issue for the 1990s.* Available from KPMG Peat Marwick McLintock, 1 Puddle Dock, Blackfriars, London EC4V 3PD.

Lyttinen, K. and Hirschheim, R. (1987) Information systems failures – a survey and classification of the empirical literature, *Oxford Surveys in Information Technology*, **4**, 257–309.

Lederer, A. L. and Prasad, J. (1993) Systems development and cost estimating: challenges and guidelines, *Information Systems Management*, **10**(4), 37–45.

Myers, M. (1993) A disaster for everyone to see: an interpretive analysis of a failed IS project, *Proceedings of the 4th Australian Conference on Information Systems*, 596–611.

Neumann, P. G. (1995) *Computer-Related Risks*, Addison-Wesley, New York.

Neumann, P. G. (1996) http://catless.ncl.ac.uk/Risks/I.J.html (*where I = volume no. and J = issue no. of Software Engineering Notes*). Six issues annually, where 1996 is volume 21. Alternatively, email risks-request@csl.sri.com with single text line 'info'.

Pitt, L. F., Watson, R. T. and Kavan, C. B. (1995) Service quality: a measure of information systems effectiveness, *MIS Quarterly*, June, 173–84.

Robinson, B. (1994) Social context and conflicting interests in participant understanding of information systems failure, *Proceedings of the Second Conference on Information Systems Methodologies* (eds. Lissoni, C. *et al.*), 31 August–2 September, Edinburgh, British Computer Society, Swindon, UK, 235–47.

Sauer, C. (1993) *Why Information Systems Fail: a Case Study Approach*, Alfred Waller, Henley-on-Thames, UK.

Sims, J. (1995) In the news, *IEEE Software*, **12**, 92–5.

Swanson, E. B. and Beath, C. M. (1989) *Maintaining Information Systems in Organizations*, Wiley, Chichester.

2

Perspectives on information systems

Introduction

We shall consider information systems from three perspectives in this chapter:

1. Types of information system
2. Contents – people and information
3. Examples of applications

The discussion concerning information system types considers some of the uses for information systems in organizations and differentiates between the main types. We then look at the contents of an information system from the viewpoints of people, procedures and information. The third perspective integrates the discussion concerning systems and contents, describing examples of information systems in practice.

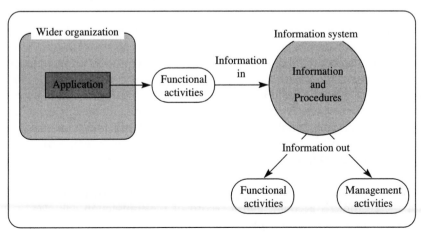

Figure 2.1 General view of information system in its organizational context.

Figure 2.1 contains a diagram that shows the organizational context of an information system, where functional and management activities are assisted by the procedures and information in the system.

Types of information system

TRANSACTION PROCESSING SYSTEMS

In Chapter 1, we met the concept of *transaction* when we were discussing the MacAdam takeaway system. We may define a transaction as follows:

> A transaction is a self-contained event that is a fundamental unit of the main area of concern of the organization.

Examples of transactions are bank withdrawals or deposits, theatre seat reservations and patient appointments in a doctor's surgery. In such trans-action-based applications, many transactions will occur within a given period compared to other types of events, such as requests for information.

We may define a transaction processing system as follows:

> A transaction processing system provides procedures to record and make available information concerning the occurrence of transactions in the application.

In contrast, the more generic information system, as defined in Chapter 1, may concern applications that do not involve transactions, for example a delivery scheduling application concerned with the efficient movement of vehicles between warehouses and customers.

Activities assisted

The transaction processing system will make information available to employees and provide automated procedures to assist them in the functional activities, as defined in Chapter 1, concerned with processing transactions. For example, a system for bank withdrawals and deposits on current accounts may consist of several million transactions daily. The system will provide information that will help employees to process a transaction, for example a request for cash withdrawal, and it may also provide procedures to automatically carry out some of the activities. The system might automatically check the bank account number to see if it exists and then determine whether the current balance is adequate for the withdrawal.

The amount of the withdrawal will be recorded and used to automatically debit the customer's account, and a record of the transaction will eventually appear on the customer statement. In this example, the employee has very little to do, other than to input transaction details to the system. If the

Transaction processing system

'Late News', *Computing,* **8 June 1995 and 'Benefits shortlist leaves three-horse race',** *Computing,* **3 August 1995**

The Post Office is going ahead with a multimillion pound automation project which will allow it to handle the full range of benefit payments . . . post offices nationwide will have computer terminals to deal with 940 million order book payments and 82 million girocheque encashments a year. . . . After initial tests next summer, the system will eventually be installed in all 20,000 UK post offices.

Management information system

'NHS body prescribes HDS Unix', *Computing,* **25 May 1995**

The PPA (Prescription Pricing Authority), which is responsible for drug payments worth more than £3.2bn a year, chose Hitachi Data Systems' (HDS) Osiris Unix operating system running on a GX6210 mainframe in a deal worth £3.5m . . . the new system will handle 480 million transactions a year and issue 27,000 reports each month.

Decision support system

'Mercury One-2-One buys box for Pandora', *Computing,*
25 May 1995

Mobile phone operator Mercury One-2-One has begun installation of a decision support system . . . Pandora . . . intended to make it easier for managers to gather customers and market data for analysis, and is expected to go live in the next couple of months. Pandora will use the Oracle 7 database . . . a Sequent Symmetry 5000 model SE60 will provide a separate data warehouse for information downloaded from the company's various operational systems. Managers will use Pandora to build up a database of call profiles and produce a more accurate picture of customer activity. . . . The decision support system will take data from a number of in-house systems, check it for accuracy, and allow for fast access and complex comparison of information.

withdrawal is taking place through an automatic cash dispenser, no individual is involved at all, and a receipt may be produced, showing information such as the date and amount withdrawn.

Organizational improvements

This system thus assists the functional activities of the application by checking and recording transaction details, debiting accounts, printing statements and issuing receipts. Transaction processing systems usually improve efficiency in the organization by greater speed of operation, reduced numbers of employees and increased accuracy.

Such systems usually contain additional procedures, which can present the basic functional information in different ways to management. The procedures are often fairly straightforward, performing simple transformations such as aggregating the data, sorting it into different sequences or averaging. Such systems are often termed *management information systems* (MIS). Two examples are shown in the previous panel. The MacAdam sales system in Chapter 1 is a management information system.

Where the additional processes become more complex, such systems merge into the type known as decision support systems.

DECISION SUPPORT SYSTEMS

The management activities of an organization are often assisted by systems termed *decision support systems* (DSS) for middle management or *executive (enterprise) information systems* (EIS) for senior management. They contain computer processes that typically apply mathematical (particularly algebraic or statistical) techniques to the analysis of information and the generation of solutions to problems to assist managers in the decision-making elements of management activities.

Such systems are often built on the Simon model of the decision-making process (Simon, 1960). This is a three-stage process, consisting firstly of intelligence, involving searching data for conditions relating to a problem; design, where possible courses of action to solve the problem are generated and tested; and finally choice, where a particular course of action is selected.

Activities assisted

In some cases, information concerning the relevant area of the organization exists in a transaction processing system, and this information may be input to the DSS/EIS. For example, a banking DSS analysing customer spending for deciding credit limits may use information concerning customers and transactions, built by the transaction processing system discussed above, which records deposits and withdrawals.

In other cases, DSS/EIS information may come from other sources. Examples of such systems are delivery scheduling, where the user wishes to minimize travel costs by scheduling deliveries more efficiently, and economic forecasting, where information concerning exports, imports, interest rates and so on is input to a model of, for example, the British economy.

Another example is a share-dealing system where the computer analyses stocks and their prices against expert criteria, but must present a list for a final decision to a human, who uses intuition and 'seat-of-the-pants' expertise. Not all of the human processes may be precisely specified in this system.

Typically, such systems are information systems for individuals or small groups in an organization, used to plan for the future. In contrast, transaction processing systems are designed to monitor daily operations. DSS/EIS are often difficult to design as they need to be closely integrated with the decision-making activities of managers. An example is shown in the previous panel.

REAL-TIME SYSTEMS

Real-time information systems are commonly met in organizations specializing in defence, producing aircraft, tanks and submarines; embedded processing, producing washing machines, car electronics and security alarms; and industrial control systems, concerned with power stations, refineries and so on. Some computer systems used in real-time systems form part of a product that is being made, and most of their inputs and outputs are typically in non-character

---

Real-time system

'BA cuts flight times with on-board navigation tool', *Computing,*
29 June 1995
The first flight controlled by a computer-based, satellite navigation system took off from Heathrow last week in a move which British Airways (BA) hopes will save it £20m a year and reduce journey times on long-haul flights. Last month, the BA board approved a plan to fit all its 747–200s and 400s with the Automatic Dependence Surveillance (ADS) system . . . ADS uses satellites to keep a plane on course, in contrast to the current ground-based navigational system which forces planes to fly a route dictated by the physical location of radar installations.

The £3m plan . . . is expected to pay for itself in the first year of operation. It will, for example, shorten the route between Hong Kong and London by 500 miles, cutting the $12\frac{1}{2}$-hour journey time by an hour . . . . Martyn Thomas, chairman of Bristol-based software house Praxis . . . believes the greater accuracy which ADS offers will improve safety. "The skies over the oceans this year are a hell of a lot safer than they have ever been," he said.

form and are transmitted to and from control devices, as opposed to people. This contrasts with the commercial information system, which stores and makes available character-based information, almost exclusively to people, concerning the product or service of the organization; that is, it is not part of the delivered product or service. However, a real-time system in a chemical plant, a nuclear power station or a railway network will invariably provide information for individuals to check system functioning.

The use of the term 'real time' probably arose in the early days of commercial information systems, which did not operate in real time but which used input devices such as punched cards and magnetic tape for information storage, both of which caused delay in capturing, processing and presenting information. The hallmark of a real-time system is that the computer must be able to respond to input signals immediately. For example, if a car wheel sensor signals an approaching skid to an automatic braking system, a five second delay may mean the system will not survive!

A real-time system will usually combine a transaction processing system with a decision support system for analysing the basic data and an example is shown in the previous panel.

Database system

'MasterCard to use Oracle7 for huge data warehouse project',
Computing, **3 August 1995**
MasterCard International has chosen Oracle7 . . . as the basis for one of the world's biggest data warehouses. The credit card company's global online service . . . will allow MasterCard partners, including financial companies, retail outlets and restaurants worldwide to gain desktop access to transaction, customer and performance-related information.

When completed, the data warehouse is expected to handle approximately 8.5 million cardholder transactions a day, as well as supporting almost 30,000 members worldwide. Internal testing of the one terabyte database will take place during the summer, with a planned roll-out in the autumn.

. . . Butler Bloor . . . said such warehouses would lead to more targeted marketing. "The point of competition is getting finer, and once data warehouses are in place it will get finer still."

'V & A files state of the art records', *Computing*, **2 November 1995**
The Victoria & Albert Museum (V & A) is preparing to take history into the 21st century by putting the records of its 1.5 million artefacts onto a multimedia database. . . . Alan Seal . . . said the museum needed a database which could handle both text and images.

DATABASE SYSTEMS

Most organizations contain information that is used by more than one application, for example information concerning departments and employees that is required by a personnel as well as a project management application. Traditionally, each system would have duplicated some or all of this information on its own files. The trend is for applications that use large amounts of shared information to use *database systems.*

These contain an integrated collection of files (the database) for recording the information, as well as software for providing fast access, often with a user-oriented interface. They are integrated as they remove the redundancy that often occurs when separate files exist, as well as containing links between related items, for example the links between departments and employees that record the department in which an employee works. Typically, they are used to store a large amount of functional data centrally, for sharing by several transaction processing systems, so that users in the different systems can access the data at the same time. Two examples may be seen in the adjacent panel.

EXPERT OR KNOWLEDGE-BASED SYSTEMS

It is rather more difficult to distinguish knowledge-based applications from those discussed above, as they are a more recent development and general agreement does not exist on their contents. However, *knowledge-based systems* (or *expert systems*) share similarities with decision support systems in that they are not based on transactions, although they may use transaction data.

Knowledge-based systems emphasize the separation of knowledge about the application from the processing of that knowledge. Processing typically uses different types of reasoning, such as analogical or qualitative reasoning, in addition to the classical logical type. A successful application of this type of system is to fault diagnosis, where, for example, large generators of electricity have their mechanical vibration patterns continuously analysed. The system is able to compare certain patterns of vibration against others and can issue a warning to avert damage or a breakdown. Two examples are given in the next panel.

OFFICE INFORMATION SYSTEMS

Office information systems are oriented towards traditional paper-based activities found in offices and can include word processing, email, fax, telephone answering and message recording, document management, personal diaries, meetings and conferences.

Groupware systems specifically support the work of office staff as members of a team and usually provide a shared, text-oriented database facility as well as email for team members to communicate with each other. Four examples of office information systems are shown in the panel on pages 34–35.

Expert/knowledge-based system

'Expert analysis', Computing, 1 June 1995

Every day, Barclaycard's knowledge-based system detects 19 attempts at fraud, mainly as shopfloor staff ring in for authorisation. It does this by applying customer buying rules. If a card is suddenly presented in an unusual location for a high-value item which seems out of character for the card holder, the transaction is flagged and, if necessary, the police are alerted instantly.

David Porter . . . was on the Touche Ross team that developed it . . . "One way to spot a stolen card is to look at the way transactions are done, but this involved getting people to sift through mountains of data. They tried a statistical process, but that didn't work well – you need a more sensitive approach." An expert system was chosen for its relative simplicity and reliability. But it wasn't publicized because of the current low image of the technology....

The system, known as Fraud 2000, was written by nine people over a year, and cost about £2m to develop. It went live almost exactly two years ago and, since then, it has saved Barclaycard an estimated £4m.

'Expert analysis', Computing, 1 June 1995

. . . Rob Milne, managing director of expert systems developer Intelligent Applications in Edinburgh, uses expert systems in process control. He points out that an expert system does not take breaks or let its attention wander and, if things go drastically wrong, it doesn't panic.

"We have just completed an online gas turbine monitoring system which takes readings at one-second intervals and does an analysis of engine performance and operation. It can analyse problems quickly where a human expert might be overwhelmed," he says.

SPECTRUM OF SYSTEMS

It may be useful to think of transaction processing systems and executive information systems as being at the extremes of a spectrum of information systems. This would allow an application such as a personnel application, where there is neither a high transaction frequency nor a great deal of very sophisticated processing, to be located somewhere in the middle.

ORGANIZATIONS AND APPLICATIONS – HISTORY AND TRENDS

The first users of computers, in the 1940s in the USA, Germany and the UK, were government-owned or sponsored organizations, involved mainly in mathematical processing with a small amount of input information, solving equations for missile trajectories and decrypting secret messages. Other 'scientific' applications such as weather forecasting, by using a model of the Earth's weather system, encouraged the development of FORTRAN in 1956 as the first high-level programming language.

Early information systems were in large commercial organizations, who could afford the relatively high computer prices, and were used for transaction processing. IBM installed its first business computer, for a payroll application, in 1954 (Davis and Olson, 1985). Such systems (for example payroll, stock control) were often termed data processing systems, as they consisted of simple processes that moved information from file to file and changed it from one format to another, for example, accumulating sales figures and presenting them by region, by salesman or by product type. Such systems produced a requirement for a business-oriented programming language with strong file-handling capabilities, which was met in 1959 by the COBOL language. For a history, see Friedman and Cornford (1989).

A characteristic of these systems was the high frequency of transactions occurring within a given period, with a correspondingly large quantity of input and output information. For example, a payroll system for a firm of 30 000 employees, or a banking system with 1 000 000 transactions daily required a substantial amount of information to be entered.

The trend has been for the price/performance ratio of hardware to fall rapidly, and many small information systems are growing in large organizations. In addition, smaller enterprises can afford systems, and portable computers now contain information systems that manage an individual's diary, telephone numbers, travel arrangements and so on.

Three current trends may be observed in many of the larger organizations. Firstly, there is a need to access separate files or databases which are geographically distributed. Secondly, the move towards electronic data interchange (EDI) is slowly removing the need for paper-based transaction information. For example, an organization may send invoices not by printing and posting them but by producing them in machine-readable form and transmitting them electronically to customers' computers. Thirdly, there is an interest in using information for more rational management by an emphasis on DSS and EIS.

Contents of an information system

An information system contains people and procedures, information, software and hardware. We shall only discuss the first two of these.

People such as clerks and managers carry out procedures in an information system, including, for example, arranging for information to be input to the system, collecting it on output and using it for decision making. However, it is not possible to discuss such procedures on a level other than the most

Office information system

'Sales Talk', *Computing*, 25 May 1995

Teachers Assurance has awarded a . . . contract to Hugh Symons Services to image scan 1.8 million documents in its life and pensions department. Hugh Symons will complete the . . . operation in July, by which time Teachers' document image processing and workflow automation system should be fully implemented. In support of this strategy, Hugh Symons has installed a five-station network using . . . PCs and file servers . . . scanners and monitors.

'City law firm chooses Novell for foreign links', *Computing*, 28 September 1995

Sinclair Roche & Temperley is upgrading its word-processing software to Wordperfect for Windows from a DOS-based version. It has also implemented Novell's document management software . . . to store more than 500,000 documents. . . . messaging software will link 300 staff at offices. . . . Simon Keefe . . . told Computing: "We have rather far-flung offices and one of the driving forces for us was to bring them together under one messaging technology. Before this, international communication was not really possible."

'Mail bonding', *Computing*, 29 June 1995

3i: Investing in Integration – . . . this year, as part of a policy of integrating services at the desktop, the company (3i) has rolled out Novell GroupWise to all its 500-plus UK staff. . . . The email features are more sophisticated than the previous software, and users like the audit trail which tells them who has read a message and when. Documents can also be circulated for comment in a predefined sequence.

Apart from email, the major benefit is scheduling, including personal diaries, booking meeting rooms and sharing resources such as portable PCs. An initial pilot scheme found people didn't like others being able to book time in their diaries, so write access is usually restricted to managers' secretaries and one or two close colleagues.

Office information system

But teams of people have read access to each others' diaries and staff can perform a 'busy search' (finding a mutually convenient slot in several diaries) for anyone in the company, although others are not obliged to accept. This has simplified the process of arranging meetings so that, in future, managers may need less secretarial support. "The roles have changed, and executives will be doing more of that than they did in the past."

'Mail bonding', *Computing*, **29 June 1995**
Price Waterhouse: Population Control – Roger Tilley, a partner at consultancy Price Waterhouse . . . and his team have spent £6m building up an interrelated set of knowledge databases aimed at providing better management information and improving communications between the firm's semi-autonomous groups. The first was Sales Activity Management, which records current proposals and projects, providing a snapshot of the practice's current business position and an aid to tracking opportunities for further sales. It proved to be a good choice because it helped to overcome that bete noir of starting groupware – the "what's in it for me?" syndrome.

One great benefit of groupware has been to support remote team working. "It's a fantastic system for us, with a workforce that's out of the office most of the time. I find it difficult to imagine how we'd survive without it," says Tilley. "We had a computer audit team working in New York, who 'Notesed' a report outline back to the UK. They went to bed, we worked on it in London and the following morning all they had to do was print it out and give it to the client."

The knowledge base provided by groupware is proving increasingly beneficial in optimising the running of the practice. "The system is very powerful in identifying what products we're selling, who we're selling them to and whether we're selling them to the right people". Thanks to the (Lotus) Notes system, Price Waterhouse can target a smaller number of top clients for a much larger proportion of its revenue.

general, as they vary greatly between applications. These will be discussed in later chapters.

CONSUMERS AND PRODUCERS

In an information system, there are many different types of people involved, and we may distinguish broadly between the consumers and the producers of a system. The consumers of a system are the people for whom the system has been built. The producers develop an information system for an application according to the requirements of the users. To understand these roles we need to know a little about the 'life' of an information system.

An information system has two main phases of existence in an organization: building and maintenance. In the building phase, the producers are traditionally the most active, as they are engaged in analysing, designing and developing the system. Consumers usually play a secondary role. However, after the system has been developed, it enters the maintenance phase, where it is in operation and where changes may be made to accommodate, for example, new technology or errors made during development. In this phase, users play the dominant role, both in operating the system and in initiating change proposals for the producers to modify the system. About 80 per cent of the life of a system is spent in the maintenance phase.

CONSUMERS IN INFORMATION SYSTEMS

The departments in organizations that were generally the first to acquire information systems are the accounting, manufacturing and distribution departments. Some employees in these departments will be concerned with the day-to-day information processing activities that make up the running of an information system. For example, junior employees such as data entry clerks will be concerned with the input of functional information and will enter details concerning wages, invoices and product delivery details. This data will be checked by system procedures and, if valid, will be recorded on file. Similarly, despatch clerks may receive printed despatch notes from the system which need to be included with goods being delivered to customers. Other employees, such as warehouse clerks, may only use the system for information concerning, for example, the location of a manufacturing part.

There will also be managers who may have a terminal on their desks for requesting and receiving management information in the form of reports. These individuals participate in the application, whereas some have a stake in the system but do not use it, such as more senior management, who may have commissioned the system. All these people are known as users, or end users, if we want to emphasize the fact that some users have no computing knowledge.

We may consider users as operators of an information system; that is, the individuals who enter information into or receive information from the system and who operate input and output devices, and their management. Operators

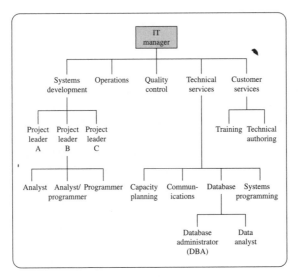

Figure 2.2 Activities and job titles within a typical computer or IT department.

will use functional information to assist in the functional activities of the application, and management will use management information to carry out management activities.

During the building phase, both types of user will usually work with the producers, at least in the initial stages, to define the type of information system that is required. However, information systems may have many levels of user. For example, it is reported in Curtis *et al.* (1988) that up to six levels of user in different organizations may exist in Department of Defense systems in the USA.

PRODUCERS

The employees in an organization who develop new systems and operate current systems are generally located in the computer or information technology (IT) department. Figure 2.2 shows the different types of activity that occur within such a department, as well as some of the more well-known job titles.

Systems development

Systems development is responsible for the development of new and the maintenance of old (legacy) computer systems, and it is often structured on a project basis, with project leaders leading teams of systems analysts and programmers. Project teams are typically grouped on functional areas within the organization, such as accounts, sales and manufacturing.

The *project leader* is responsible for the planning, implementation and completion of a project from start to finish. This may involve budgeting, cost control and organizing project activities and teams. It also involves substantial knowledge about the application area in addition to technical knowledge.

Analysts (also termed *systems analysts* or *business analysts*) investigate the requirements for a system that the users want and produce a specification for the system. They should be aware of organizational practices and be skilled at understanding how to obtain requirements and how to translate them into a specification for an information system.

Programmers are engaged in taking a specification and coding programs that will implement the specification. They should be skilled in program languages and machine capabilities. *Analyst/programmers* combine some of the skills of both the analyst and programmer.

Analysts are supposed to be extrovert and user oriented – perhaps Aries or Leo. Programmers are traditionally seen as introverted and technically oriented – perhaps Virgo or Cancer. All students should aim to combine the qualities!

The term *software engineer* usually refers to a role where extensive use of engineering methods is made to produce both a system specification and a program.

Operations

This is responsible for the day-to-day operation of the hardware on which systems are implemented. This involves the management of shifts of computer operators as well as periodic machine maintenance, looking after tape and disk libraries, scheduling and monitoring work to be run on the computer, and maintaining a help desk for user queries about the progress of their work.

Traditionally, operations has also had data preparation sections, where user input is transferred from paper forms to a computer-readable form such as punched cards or a magnetic disk. However, there is less need for data preparation as on-line systems have become more prevalent, where employees typically key data into a computer terminal or PC (personal computer). Computer operators are also becoming rarer, as computer systems require less manual intervention, but they perform the tasks necessary to operate system hardware, such as changing disks and tapes, and operating printers.

Quality control

This is emerging as a new area within computer departments as the importance of quality standards increases. Such an area might define department-wide standards for documents produced by systems development, and will also define methods for applying the standards. Another task might be to conduct tests on software and ensure compliance with relevant legislation, such as the Data Protection or Computer Misuse Acts.

Technical services

This area contains specialist functions for the infrastructure of the computer department. Capacity planning is concerned with planning future hardware requirements, monitoring current hardware performance and carrying out benchmarking and acceptance tests for potential systems. The communications area is concerned with the technology of communication between, for example, user terminals and central computers, over the public switched telephone network or via private packet-switching networks. An alternative is using satellite transmission. Another area concerns short distance connections between devices, typically within a building, using local area networks (LANs).

The systems programming area has several responsibilities, namely hardware and software commissioning and monitoring the technical performance of computer systems. Systems programmers do not write programs that will form part of an information system, but instead install and tune the systems software supplied with the computer by its manufacturer or other packaged software used by many information systems.

The database area contains two specialists who affect other areas. The database administrator is responsible for data design and standards for databases shared by many organization users, while the data analyst performs a systems development task concerned with representing objects in user applications by data. This area has emerged only recently and is interesting as it is a specialist task that impinges directly on some activities in systems development.

Customer services

Two activities may be mentioned here, training and technical authoring. Training involves the development and presentation of courses to users on computer systems that they will use. This might involve educating and supporting users in connection with packaged PC software they have bought. Technical authoring concerns the design, development and maintenance of manuals describing how users should operate systems, how they should report faults or suspected errors, procedures to follow for back-up of data and similar topics.

ORGANIZATION OF PRODUCERS

Traditionally, for commercial information systems, the producers were organized into a DP (data processing) department within the organization, often coming under the accounting function. This was due to the fact that the earliest applications were primarily financial. All of the development work was undertaken by this department, which also possessed all of the computing resources.

However, this situation has been changing, due to the price/performance ratio of PCs and the availability of standard software, and systems development is sometimes decentralized to users in other departments in the organization who wish to develop their applications themselves. Many organizations have moved to end-user computing to implement this concept, and hope thereby to develop applications that are relevant to their needs and to develop them more quickly than the DP department. Systems that will be shared by many departments are still developed in the computer department, and computer staff are expected to develop standards for, or to coordinate the work of, the users in the different departments. It is still too early to say whether this form of organization has been successful.

Some large organizations, which may have many regional offices, factories or depots, often decentralize or distribute various functions of the computer department to such local facilities.

Where an organization produces its own information systems, the systems are said to have been developed in-house. The larger organizations still maintain large numbers of computer staff for this purpose. However, smaller organizations often approach software houses or management consultancies to develop information systems for them to their specification. Such software is termed bespoke software. Alternatively, organizations may buy a licence to use pre-written software, termed software packages, if the computing part of their desired system is fairly standard.

Outsourcing

Outsourcing is the term given to the process whereby an organization disposes of some or all of its IT services, aiming to receive these services from external sources. Services provided by parts of the IT department, such as hardware or network maintenance, or all services, are contracted out to another organization. The IT department may be transferred to a bidder, including staff, or set up as a separate organization perhaps under management buy-out.

There is a trend among the larger companies to outsourcing and it may be seen as a device to introduce a more commercial, competitive environment into the provision of IT services, whereby an 'outsourced' department, as well as other interested parties, have to submit bids in response to tenders for IT services. Another model is that an organization may sign a contract with a supplier for IT services over a fixed period for a fixed sum. The article by Lacity *et al.* (1994), as well as other articles in the same issue, discuss several aspects of outsourcing. The panel on pages 42–43 gives examples of recent outsourcing.

Information

It will not have escaped the reader that we are already in Chapter 2 and we have not yet defined what we mean by the term information, although we have defined information system, so this section will briefly discuss some problems with a definition of information.

DATA AND INFORMATION

Introduction

We could express the relationship between data and information in the following way:

$$\text{Data} + \text{meaning} = \text{information}$$

What we mean by this is that an item of data only becomes information when it is given a meaning. For example, the data 'UMIST' becomes information concerning the University of Manchester Institute of Science and Technology if an individual gives this meaning to the data.

How certain can we be that individuals give the same meaning to the same items of data? We shall briefly look at two contrasting paradigms of information that explore this question (Harrington, 1991).

Two paradigms of information

- *Resource-driven paradigm.* This assumes that information is a vital organizational resource, to be managed with other resources such as capital and machinery. Information is basically unchanging, it is objective, it exists independently of its receiver and it does not change during transmission. The value of information is constant throughout the organization.
- *Perception-driven paradigm.* In contrast, this assumes that information does not exist beyond the perceptions of the receiver. It emphasizes that data is interpreted by individuals to become information and that interpretations will thus vary, on account of the different psychological and social factors inherent in individuals. The meaning of a data item also extends to its value, and perceptions of the value of information will also vary. The implication of this is that information systems cannot exist, as information is transient and subjectivity determines information. An information system is only a data system.

Formal and informal information systems

Although these two paradigms seem at opposite poles, they are reconciled in actual organizations as individuals are trained to interpret data in information systems consistently; that is an item of transmitted information will be interpreted consistently by different receivers. Information in information systems is often termed *formal*, or structured, information.

Outsourcing

'J Menzies books CSC for support', *Computing*, **29 June 1995**
Computer Sciences (CSC) has increased its presence . . . with a
£40m outsourcing deal with high-street newsagent and bookseller
John Menzies. . . . The 10-year deal . . . involves supplying systems,
development and support for the 274 stores run by John Menzies
Retail (JMR).

Phil Matthews, IT director of JMR, told *Computing* . . . 'The
main reason for outsourcing is so John Menzies can gain access
to a wider IT skills base . . . this will help develop IT systems
much quicker than we could in-house.'

'Data centre spend falls', *Computing*, **7 September 1995**
According to Bob Aylott, principal consultant at KPMG, in-house
IT departments will also find it increasingly difficult to compete
against outsourcing companies. 'Outsourced deals tend to be 30%
better than in-house departments,' he said. 'It is due to a
combination of better economies of scale and a single-minded focus
on giving a professional service and only that.'

. . . Aylott explained that in-house departments often engage in
non-essential work which is regarded as being 'for the good of the
company' rather than meeting business targets.

'Outsourcing profits head overseas', *Computing*, **15 June 1995**
The UK computer services and software industry . . . has grown
to record size on the back of the outsourcing boom. . . . Richard
Holway, author of the report, said: 'We are seeing a significant
shift of business from in-house staff teams to all aspects of

Outsourcing

outsourcing behaviour, not just facilities management'. . . . Japanese-owned ICL is the single biggest supplier, with revenues of £455m, but IBM (£365m) and EDS (£310m) are eroding its lead. . . . When EDS' £1bn Inland Revenue outsourcing deal is taken into account . . . it is sure to take the number one slot.

'Sun Alliance signs BT for £15m', *Computing,* **6 July 1995**
One of UK's largest insurance firms, Sun Alliance, is to outsource its network management and communications needs in a five-year, £15m contract with BT. BT will supply . . . a high-speed network which will connect more than 77 sites in the UK and act as the infrastructure for Sun Alliance's plans to offer insurance services electronically to the home. . . . John Seymour, manager of Sun Alliance's information services department, said: 'We have a network which was installed in the mid-1980s, but with the growth of local area network and image traffic, we saw those limitations becoming more severe. It was cheaper to go outside than to do it ourselves.'

'British Gas staff snub Hoskyns', *Computing,* **25 May 1995**
British Gas staff have issued a vote of no confidence in Hoskyns, named last week as winner of a £55m outsourcing deal at the utility. . . . The survey . . . found that half the 1,500 IT staff at British Gas' 12 regional data centres did not want to join Hoskyns. The centres are being run down during the course of the 18-month outsourcing deal . . . Hoskyns dismissed the survey's conclusions as 'far from black and white'.

However, it is not clear to what extent such training may be successful. In work on management activities, for example, Mintzberg found that although managers were constantly receiving and transmitting information, the great proportion of this was *informal* information, as opposed to formal information (Mintzberg, 1973). One conclusion that may be drawn is that formal information, which is 'public' in that there is organizational agreement on its interpretation, may be of only limited use to managers.

VALUE OF INFORMATION

Relative value

One consequence of our awareness of the perception-driven paradigm is to realize that the *value* of information is perhaps as subjective as its meaning. This is clearly important if we are attempting to build an information system by determining information needs, and we find that perceptions vary widely as to the value of different types of information.

A problem also to be faced is that the value of information is never absolute, but always relative to changing circumstances, such as the availability of other types of information or the situation the organization is in (such as profitable or not profitable). For example, what value should be placed on information concerning the economic state of MacAdam's competitors? Is this more important than information concerning the types of customers they have? Which information system should we build first?

Normative and realistic values

The normative value of information is based on decision theory, and measures the value of information based on the benefits that will be realized by possession of the information. Probability theory is used, as all benefits have to be estimated. In practice, however, except for very structured situations, a normative value cannot be obtained as the probabilities cannot be estimated with any degree of accuracy.

A realistic value of information can, in theory, be obtained by estimating the difference in organizational performance based on the absence or presence of the information. Although one of the attractions of this approach is that it solves the problem of measuring information value by using economic indicators of organizational performance, it is very difficult in practice to set up an experimental situation in an organization that keeps all factors constant except those related to the information.

Reduction of uncertainty

Another approach to information value holds that the key factor in deciding what information is useful in an organization is the extent to which the information reduces uncertainty about an aspect of the organization. For example, Lucas states that 'information is some tangible or intangible entity that reduces uncertainty about a state or event' (Lucas, 1985). A problem with this idea is that there is no way of telling how detailed the information should be, as uncertainty is a continuous variable. For example, should a stock control manager know about all stock levels every week, or every hour?

SUMMARY

The practical conclusions of this discussion on information are that it may not be quite so easy to obtain agreement between users over the meanings to attribute to data. The analyst should in fact expect that different individuals will interpret data differently, although there is less scope for such variations in interpretation with functional information, where employees may be more easily trained. It is not so clear that the problems of subjectivity, both over meaning and value, will be overcome as easily with managers, who use less structured management information.

Information systems in practice

This section presents short descriptions of actual information systems by size of business and then by type of application.

DIFFERENT SIZE OF BUSINESS

Small business

A toy shop uses sales analysis and stock control applications software and has a PC with a Pentium chip, 500 Mbyte hard disk, a floppy disk drive for back-up and a low-speed laser printer. When toys are sold, the assistant uses a bar-code reader to scan bar codes printed on the toy packaging. The bar code contains information such as the toy description and price, and the pen transmits this to the applications software, which uses it to change the sales and stock files on the hard disk. Later, reports on sales and stock levels may be obtained on the printer using the relevant programs.

Medium business

An oil company sells heating oil products to about 250 000 customers country-wide for domestic use. An information system is used to handle order processing, which maintains customer details and orders in a database held on a disk of 380 Mbyte. There are approximately thirty 14-inch terminals connected to an IBM 3090 mainframe computer on which the system runs. The terminals allow orders and queries for customer details to be input. Requests for reports may be processed at the same time and the reports are usually obtained almost immediately. A fast line printer is used for printing delivery advices and reports, and is shared with other applications running on the computer.

Large business

A UK clearing bank is introducing an on-line system for clearing cheques. The system hardware budget is £30m and involves installing on-line item processors for electronic cheque reading in over 2000 bank branches connected to central computers. Up to nine disk drives are attached (each with five gigabytes of data) and six tape drives for data archiving and batch processing.

The project to automate the processing of NHS prescriptions received from various sources such as chemists and hospitals involves data collection from a total of 1500 terminals in nine regional centres, linked to a network of 39 minis connected to four central mainframes.

The IT department of a UK high street bank supports 3000 bank branches, has over 3000 IT staff, consumes an annual budget of £353m, has a total processing capability of 380 mips (million instructions per second) and manages 1.8 terabytes (1 terabyte = 1 million megabytes) of data.

DIFFERENT TYPES OF APPLICATION

Distribution application

Distribution involves the daily transport of many thousands of consignments from the pick-up point to the delivery address. Consignments may include car components for a manufacturer, canned food for a supermarket or electronic parts for a service organization. Distributors may be specialists or may be the distribution division of a retail or manufacturing organization.

Specialist distributor

This organization has a turnover of £100m and moves 35 000 consignments (100 000 parcels) daily. Parcels are picked up in the day by a fleet of 1300 vehicles and brought to one of 20 main collection depots for sorting and overnight delivery. At the depot, details from the consignment note accompanying the consignment are read using a bar-code reader into the computer, which checks details such as customer credit limit. The system creates invoices in an overnight batch process. Two mainframes are used, one for systems development and the other connected via a British Telecom leased line to the collection depots, each with 7 to 11 terminals and a printer.

Current systems allow for the return and forwarding of goods, and customers may, using a PC system containing a database of all customers to whom consignments are sent, produce the consignment note themselves. A future step is to use EDI, where a customer computer will electronically transfer a standard form of consignment note to the distributor's computer. Another project will allow a customer access to the computer so that they may track progress of a consignment, for example when it was delivered and to whom. The present alternative involves telephoning the organization, checking the database for the relevant information and sending a paper copy of the signed consignment note.

Retailer

A large supermarket-based retailer needs to control the supply chain for goods from the supplier to distribution centres and finally stores. However, it also needs to predict what goods supermarket customers will want. It operates its own fleet of vehicles.

The systems it uses are based on two mainframes, one for disaster and development use and one for daily operation based at head office, which are both on a British Telecom leased line network, connecting 24 distribution centres and several hundred country-wide stores. A database maintains not only information concerning store sales but also external data such as census data and data from market research.

Many stores now have scanning systems at checkout tills, termed point of sale (POS) systems, which collect data concerning goods sold, providing information for stock control and marketing. At head office, the stock control system uses packaged software to forecast demand for non-perishable goods, as well as software developed in-house incorporating a forecasting model for perishable goods. Knowing product demand and what is in stock at distribution centres, the system drives what and when suppliers should deliver to the distribution centres. The system thus provides software assistance for management decisions and is a type of decision support system.

The weak link in the system is the suppliers—can they meet organization demands? To address this problem, EDI is being used to communicate more closely with the suppliers, for fast ordering, as well as to keep them informed about future intentions. The aim is to reduce stock held to a minimum.

The distribution centres have software that controls incoming and outgoing goods, showing where incoming goods should be stored, quantities of goods in stock and so on. A database is used for recording information to which common access is available. This also enables staff to ask *ad hoc* questions with immediate response; for example, does any centre have a thousand cartons of yoghurt?

Production control application

This organization has the aim of maintaining the rolling stock for a large city metro system. Car body maintenance is carried out at engineering depots for each of the metro lines, but electrical, electronic and mechanical work to equipment is done at a central factory.

The functions covered by the central system are purchasing, stores and materials control, production engineering and control, time and attendance recording, and management accounting. Previously, many different hardware and software systems existed which were unintegrated. This meant entering the same data many times into different systems. Having one system means that information such as wrong part numbers or delivery quantities that are over-ordered can be detected easily. The new system will, using time/attendance devices situated on the shop floor, allow for work in progress to be tracked and costed. However, progress is slow as union agreement on new operating times for jobs is still to be negotiated.

Hardware consists of a central minicomputer networked to 60 terminals in the factory via two leased lines (one is a back-up). Hardware cost is £500 000. Packaged software was not considered appropriate and bespoke software was commissioned from a third-party developer at a cost of £300 000. The IT department consists of 170 people.

Summary

This chapter has discussed information systems from three perspectives. Different types of system with their related applications were briefly described. The contents of an information system were then discussed under the headings of people and procedures, and information. Some information system case studies and examples then brought together many points made earlier.

Discussion questions

1. Describe the notion of a transaction and give examples of a transaction in an insurance office, in an amusement park, in a garage and in a building society.
2. Discuss the type of information recorded and made available by a transaction processing system in each of the organizations mentioned in Question 1 above.
3. Identify the distinction between transaction processing systems and decision support systems.
4. What is the distinction between data and information? What are the problems and significance in determining the value of information?

References

Curtis, W., Krasner, H., and Iscoe, N. (1988) A field study of the software design process for large systems, *Communications of the ACM*, **31**(11), 1268–87.

Davis, G. B. and Olson, M. H. (1985) *Management Information Systems: Conceptual Foundations, Structure, Development*, 2nd edn, McGraw-Hill, New York.

Friedman, A. L. and Cornford, D. S. (1989) *Computer Systems Development: History, Organization and Implementation*, Wiley, Chichester.

Harrington, J. (1991) *Organizational Structure and Information Technology*, Prentice-Hall, London.

Lacity, M., Hirschheim, R. and Willcocks, L. (1994) Realizing outsourcing expectations, *Information Systems Management*, **11**(4), 7–18.

Lucas, Jr, H. C. (1985) *The Analysis, Design and Implementation of Information Systems*, McGraw-Hill, New York.

Mintzberg, H. (1973) *The Nature of Managerial Work*, Harper & Row, New York.

Simon, H. A. (1960) *The New Science of Management Decision*, Harper and Brothers, New York.

Part Two

Understanding Information Systems in Organizations

The second part of the book aims to develop a model that is useful for providing an overview of information systems in organizations. The aim of this is to familiarize the reader with the types of components that information systems have and the way in which they work within the organizational context.

Chapter 3 describes some systems concepts, which are useful for basic understanding, and Chapter 4 develops the overview model, termed OMNIS, for describing information systems. Chapter 5 shows how management activities in an organization fit in with the information available in the information system.

3

The systems approach

Introduction

When discussing and describing information systems, a systems approach employing ideas from general systems theory is widely used. General systems theory is the name given to a set of writings by systems theorists, including Von Bertalanffy (1968), Churchman (1968) and Ackoff (1971). It will be helpful to define the terms used and to gain some familiarity with the concepts employed in an abstract context before applying them to information systems. We will use the systems approach mainly as a basis to provide a descriptive model for analysing and describing information systems.

DEFINITION

1. A system is an assembly of parts or components existing together in an organized way.
2. The assembly is of particular human interest.
3. Parts are affected by being in the system – they change if they leave.
4. The assembly does something – it has an aim.

This four-point definition is based on an Open University definition (Open University, 1980). You can use this definition yourselves and see if familiar systems fit, for example a human being, a library, or a school or college.

ABSTRACT AND PHYSICAL SYSTEMS

A problem of the above definition is that it is only concerned with systems that do things; that is, systems that exhibit behaviour. These are often termed *physical systems*. However, *abstract systems* also exist, which consist only of ideas and which do not physically exist, instead existing in a conceptual world. For example, Buddhism or Marxism, which are systems of thought, may be regarded as abstract systems.

We may notice that the chief distinction between an abstract system and a physical system is that an abstract system does not do anything, even though it has an aim (which may be to act as a description for a physical system). We must therefore modify point 4 of the definition, as otherwise it only really applies to physical systems. It thus becomes:

4.   The assembly has an aim.

This revised definition may be tested against a plausible abstract system – the rules of chess:

1.   Is it an organized assembly of parts? Yes: parts are squares, legal moves and pieces, all of which are related.
2.   Is the assembly of interest? Yes: to chess players.
3.   Are parts affected if they leave? Yes: removing a single rule would make the rule meaningless without the context of the other rules and pieces.
4.   Do the rules have an aim? Yes: rules regulate the game and resolve disputes.

MODELS AS ABSTRACT SYSTEMS

We are particularly interested in abstract systems in the field of computing, as they are widely used to represent, describe or specify (these terms are, somewhat loosely, equivalent) applications in organizations as well as computer-based systems. Such an abstract system is usually referred to as a model. We shall discuss types of model in more detail at the end of this chapter.

There are many different types of abstract system that we use in everyday life. For example, we use a map (abstract system) to help us understand the town (physical system) that it represents (one-way system in Manchester).

The first step in building an information system generally is the construction of an abstract system which is a model of a part of an organization. The next steps add more detail in a progressive manner, so that a series of models are constructed which become closer and closer to the desired physical system. Once the system is built, the models are available as a specification, on different levels of detail, of the contents and functioning of the system.

A similar procedure exists in other engineering disciplines, where, for example, a set of bridge or building designs are drawn up to define how the bridge or building is to be constructed. Here, again, the contents of the abstract system represent the contents of the desired physical system.

Systems concepts

OPEN SYSTEMS

An *open system* is the commonest type of system, and is shown in Fig. 3.1. The figure shows that an open system consists of *processes* which receive

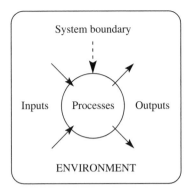

Figure 3.1 Open system components showing boundary and environment.

inputs from the *environment*, producing *outputs*. Internal inputs and outputs are also produced in intermediate stages of the processes. The *system boundary* separates the system from the environment, and it may be set by the processes or by the inputs and outputs of the system. Inputs and outputs are often regarded as static by nature, compared to processes, which are regarded as dynamic.

An example is a post room in an organization. This receives letters, packets and so on as input. They are processed (sorted by building, put into department bins for the post collectors) and finally sent to their destination. The environment therefore is the organization and the system boundary is set by the processes, if no other section performs these processes. Another example is a car, where input it fuel, output is exhaust gases, processes are the steering, gears and motive force, and the boundary is set by the physical parts of which the car consists.

This type of system is termed an open system as it interacts with its environment by receiving inputs and producing outputs.

CLOSED SYSTEMS

Theoretically, a *closed system* is one that does not interact with its environment, and a frequently cited example is that of a chemical reaction in a sealed container. However, perfectly closed systems probably do not exist outside a laboratory, if at all, and it is more useful to consider closed systems as those able to minimize the uncertainty of exchanges with the environment, by accepting only previously defined inputs and processing them into previously defined outputs. In contrast, an open system must be able to cope with uncertain inputs, and it needs therefore to be very adaptive to survive, for example, people or some social organizations.

Systems can thus be located along a spectrum of closed and open systems, depending on the degree of uncertainty of their inputs. The systems we shall encounter are at neither extreme but are to be found somewhere in the middle.

Systems on different levels: sub-systems

ABSTRACTIONS OF SYSTEMS

We may describe a system in one sentence or diagram, or in a thousand-page document. A description with a lot of detail is termed a description on a *low level of abstraction*, while a description on a *high level of abstraction* contains only a small amount of detail. A system is often described in a systematic way by subdividing, decomposing or refining (the terms are equivalent) a high-level description of its processes into a lower level description, consisting of *sub-systems*.

We do this because some systems are large and contain many processes. Such systems are normally too complex and detailed to be described or comprehended as a whole, so a system may be divided into sub-systems that are small enough to be understood. These, in turn, may then be refined into greater detail. A hierarchical diagram is often drawn showing the relationship between systems and their sub-systems, as in Fig. 3.2. Some sub-systems may belong to more than one parent system, constituting a network as opposed to a tree.

Each sub-system is itself a system and may be decomposed. The decomposition of the post room system in Fig. 3.2 shows three levels of abstraction.

COMMUNICATING SUB-SYSTEMS

We simplify a large system by refining it, but we have a price to pay, as we must now define interfaces between the sub-systems that communicate. An interface is an input or an output shared by more than one system. An example might be where objects such as letters in the post room are output from the sorting sub-system and then input to the depositing sub-system. Obviously, the description of the objects must exist in both systems and must

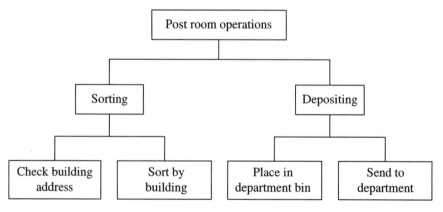

Figure 3.2 Refinement of post room processes.

be identical. This becomes an important issue where processes are computer programs, and many programs may share common interfaces.

COUPLING BETWEEN SUB-SYSTEMS

When we consider system interaction in more detail, we might find that output from sorting is input to depositing immediately. Such close coordination is referred to as tight coupling. However, it may not be desirable or possible for depositing to be so responsive to sorting. For example, sorting might output continually throughout the day, while depositing might only accept input at specified times. Another reason might be due to the fact that the speed of sending or receiving between sorting and depositing is not the same.

The solution adopted is to decouple the two systems so that they can operate independently, at least for a time. One way to achieve this is to use a *buffer*, where output from sorting waits in a buffer (which might be a bag outside the depositing room) until it is collected by the depositing system at the next input time.

Predictability of systems

DETERMINISTIC SYSTEMS

Some systems are predictable in their behaviour. By this we mean that we know what output will be produced, given a certain input, as there is a rule that relates outputs to inputs. These systems are termed *deterministic systems.*

Such systems usually consist of simple processes, and to achieve the aim of the system it is necessary only to provide the appropriate input. For example, we may consider an electric fire as a predictable system, whose aim is to provide a certain quantity of heat. The rule is that for input current I and resistance R, heat output will be I^2R. This is obviously a simple process and we only have to provide the requisite level of current for the system to achieve the aim.

NON-DETERMINISTIC SYSTEMS

Non-deterministic (or *stochastic*) *systems* are unpredictable, in that we do not know for sure how to make them achieve their aim, or we do not even know what output will result from a given input. This is due to complex or poorly understood processes, or unknown or indeterminable inputs or combinations of inputs. For example, unpredictable systems include the weather, the British economy or a garden. A cricket match is unpredictable in that we do not know the result for a given input, but as long as a result is achieved, it will have achieved its aim. Unpredictable systems are characterized by the fact that they display uncertainty.

However, as we increasingly require systems upon which we depend in everyday life (such as nuclear power and airline systems) to behave predictably, some form of control is required to make sure that systems achieve their aims. In our example of the electric fire we simplified the discussion, as a guard against unknown inputs in the form of excessive current is required, and a fuse in the plug or in the building circuit usually exists which acts as a control system.

Control systems

CONTROLLING SYSTEM BEHAVIOUR

We have to check systems to make sure that they are achieving their aims. Inputs may be incorrect or little-understood processes may be conflicting, so we must add a *control system*, which checks that the system being controlled (which now may be termed the functional system) is behaving correctly. Figure 3.3 shows the main components of a control system, together with the related functional system.

OUTPUT CHECKING

The control loop shown in Fig. 3.3 senses system output using the sensor component. The control device then compares some characteristic of the output to a desired standard. In its simplest form, any difference causes a corrective input to be generated by the activating unit to the functional system process so that the output will be nearer the standard. However, control systems may also alter processes or, for self-organizing systems, may alter system aims.

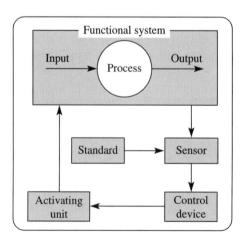

Figure 3.3 Control system components and related functional system.

A common example is where the temperature of a heated room is checked against a standard temperature and any difference initiates a process to bring the room nearer to the standard. A central heating thermostat constitutes a control system that senses the temperature of the air warmed by the boiler and radiators, compares that temperature with a desired standard (usually manually set in the thermostat) and sends an input to the system to start heating if the temperature falls below the desired standard.

An example where processes are altered is in the post room, where the number of items output per hour is monitored. If it is less than some standard figure the control device takes action and extra staff can be assigned to processes.

This type of control system is termed a negative feedback system, as it samples the output of the functional system and seeks to reduce fluctuations around a standard. A positive feedback system does the opposite – if the output characteristic deviates from the standard then the system processes are repeated or increased so that the deviation increases. We will be concerned only with negative feedback control systems.

INPUT CHECKING

Control systems frequently check the validity of system input as well as system output. This may be termed filtering. For example, in the post room, a check will be made that each input item has an address. If it has none, it cannot be processed and may be rejected.

DIFFICULTIES OF CONTROL

A control system may be seen as one that reduces the amount of uncertainty in the system. However, controlling complex systems may be a problem, as the law of requisite variety, in a simplified form, says that to control each possible state of the system elements, there must be a corresponding control state. In addition, it is necessary to receive and transmit control information to and from system elements, imposing a substantial information processing task. To predict all system states may not be possible, especially if the system under consideration is relatively open, with unpredictable inputs.

A solution often adopted is to use a human–computer system for the control system, where the computer can generate control responses for expected cases and where a human decision maker generates responses for unexpected situations.

Design system

As many systems are continuously under review and are being redesigned, then to give a wider picture we may include a design sub-system, shown in Fig. 3.4, as both functional and control sub-systems interact with it. The

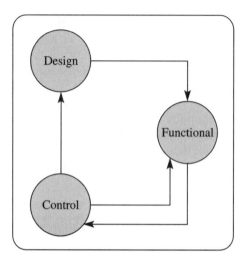

Figure 3.4 Design, functional and control systems.

control system detects discrepancies between functional system output and objectives, and will produce input to the design system to change the functional system's processes, inputs/outputs or objectives. The design system will be producing outputs that are designs for a new process or control system.

State space approach

The *state space approach* is an additional concept for describing system behaviour, and considers objects and processes. Under this approach, at any given instant a system is considered to exist in a certain state. This state is defined or characterized by the relevant objects that exist in the system at that instant. For example, in the post room, the state at a given instant will be determined by objects such as the letters, packages, numbers and types of staff, and so on. An object need not only be a physical object, but may be, for example, a person's age.

Such an approach is only applicable to *discrete* systems; that is, systems that exist in separately identifiable states, and information systems are discrete systems. For example, in a system that models deposits and withdrawals from bank deposit accounts, a separately identifiable state occurs each time a deposit or withdrawal is made. In contrast, many other types of system are *continuous* systems, which are continually changing, often extremely rapidly. For such systems, it may not be possible to determine their states before the state has changed, for example the level of water in a reservoir.

An important type of process termed an *update process*, is viewed by this approach as a transformation of the system from one state to another. An update process is a process that makes changes to the system, for example adding a staff member to the post room, as opposed to a process that reports on the system state. For example, in a football match, an initial state could consist of 22 players and a score of 0–0. A subsequent state (achieved by the update process of goal scoring) could consist of the same number of players but a score of 1–0.

The state space approach is a useful extension to the basic systems approach which we shall use in our analysis of information systems.

Classification of systems

Many different attempts have been made to classify systems. For example, general systems theory considers open and closed systems, deterministic and non-deterministic systems, discrete and continuous systems, and abstract and physical systems, as we have seen.

The Open University definition (Open University, 1980) also discusses three types of systems, evolved, designed and model systems. Evolved systems have objectives that emerge from the evolutionary process. Although biological systems are prime examples, some social systems might fall into this category. Designed systems are designed by people specifically to achieve certain objectives, for example a telephone network.

Finally, model systems are systems embedded in 'messes' (complex situations that are poorly understood) that we can identify as an aid to structuring our thinking about the mess. Model systems are similar to the type of abstract system we identified at the beginning of this chapter. The first two types are termed recognized systems and the third type unrecognized or invisible systems.

The last classification we shall consider is taken from Checkland (1981). Checkland proposes four types of system:

1. *Natural systems.* For example, a human being.
2. *Designed physical systems.* For example, a washing machine.
3. *Designed abstract systems.* For example, philosophical or scientific systems such as utilitarianism or Darwinism.
4. *Human activity systems.* For example, a post room.

An information system under this classification would be a human activity system, while it would be a designed system under the Open University classification above. Existing classifications are thus based on different viewpoints, and no one classification is regarded as superior.

The systems approach – discussion

TYPES OF MODEL

The systems approach provides a *model*, based on systems concepts, which is claimed to be applicable to an unrestricted set of situations. We may define a model as *an abstract representation of reality*. The model is usually on a level of abstraction that is of interest, and there are three general types of model:

1. *Predictive* models are used for predicting the future and are therefore useful for planning. Given input concerning, for example, an event, they will determine the consequences of that event. A predictive model is also termed an analytic model, and many scientific models are predictive. For example, Newton's model of the laws of motion predicts that, if you drop an object from rest, its velocity at any time t will be ft, where f is the acceleration due to gravity. In a computing context, an analytic model of the performance of a certain type of file might be that the rate of access A to the file varied inversely with the square of the number of records N, so that $A = 1/N^2$.
2. *Normative* or optimizing models suggest the best action to be taken in a given situation. They contain norms or suggestions as to how systems ought to behave. Linear programming problems may be solved with normative models.
3. The systems approach provides the open systems model, which is the last type of model, the *descriptive* model. As its name implies, such a model allows for a description which is useful for leading to deeper understanding of a situation under investigation. This model is based on the classic 'divide and conquer' principle, where a situation is divided into smaller parts using the concepts of input/output and process and partitioned from other systems using the concepts of systems boundary and environment. The model further provides a typology of systems, from open to closed, depending on the degree of interaction with the environment.

It is important to realize that the model underlying the systems approach does not predict anything; that is, it cannot predict that certain system behaviour will occur for a given input, for example. It is merely an approach for a description of situations in systems terms for clearer understanding. We shall use descriptive models almost exclusively for describing and specifying information systems.

PROBLEMS

The first problem with the systems approach is that, although individual understanding may be improved by using systems concepts, the analysis of a given situation by different individuals may result in quite different systems. This is a consequence both of the extreme level of generality of the underlying model and the fact that, in situations involving humans, it is difficult to agree on the facts of the situation. It is thus obviously a problem if the situation cannot be described precisely and objectively.

Contrast this 'soft' situation with a 'hard' situation, for example, the forces acting on a train going uphill. Here the situation may be described objectively by a predictive model incorporating the laws of motion. We are not so fortunate with the systems approach, as the systems we wish to describe are not governed by such laws.

The main problem with multiple views of a problem situation is: which one is the correct view? Is there more than one correct view? The resolution of multiple views into one common, acceptable-to-all view is often a difficult process. A particular aspect of this problem is that a system may be decomposed in different ways into sub-systems. These may be so different that it would appear that different systems are being described. This is often due to different individuals decomposing a system to different levels of abstraction. An associated problem is that the ease of obtaining widely differing descriptions does not lead to confidence in the approach.

A second problem is that a process is always considered to involve transformation of inputs into outputs. However, inputs that control or affect the process are often required and are not transformed. The approach might refute this criticism on the ground that the approach is sufficiently general to include these different types of input or processes.

A third problem is that processes and objects may be shared by more than one system and the system boundary is often arbitrarily defined, so it may be difficult to know whether to include a process or object. For example, should machinery used in the post room be included in the post room system if it is also used by others for training purposes? Should the delivery process whereby letters are input to the post room be included? Sometimes there is a problem about including what may be termed general knowledge. For example, should the location of the post room be kept in the system description, as everyone knows it?

The fourth problem is that no fixed method is available for applying the concepts to the real world. Should we determine inputs and outputs first, or processes? How do we set the boundary? A different system might result, depending on the way in which we proceed.

DISADVANTAGES OF SYSTEMS APPROACH

1. Its application to the real world results in a non-unique description; that is different applications of the approach give different results. There are problems with objective descriptions of processes and boundaries.
2. The model may be incomplete or inaccurate when applied, as there is no guidance to the level of detail required for a description.
3. No method is suggested to apply the approach.

ADVANTAGES OF SYSTEMS APPROACH

1. The approach provides an informal start to understand and describe a situation, using intuitively familiar notions of input, output and process.

2. The decomposition of processes is a useful method of analysing complex processes.
3. The notion of the importance of a control system often highlights the fact that one is missing or ineffective.
4. A system description is often simple enough for it to be used as a tool for communication between individuals, accompanied by a suitable explanation.

Summary

The systems approach described in this chapter is based upon the following concepts and assumptions.

Firstly, basic systems concepts are that:

1. A system may be described in terms of these components: input, output, process, boundary and environment.
2. Input and output are regarded as consisting of static objects, transformed by dynamic processes. Examples of objects are letters, people and so on.

Secondly, we note the need for a control and a functional system:

3. A control system, for checking input, comparing output and adjusting functional system behaviour, if required, is essential for controlling unpredictable systems. Information systems are a major type of unpredictable system.

Thirdly, we add the state space approach:

4. The state space approach views processes (update processes) as transformations between one state and another. A state at a given instant consists of the objects in the system at that instant.

The systems approach may be criticized, chiefly for its subjectivity and its high level of generality, but it possesses certain advantages, such as providing an informal start to understanding and analysis.

Discussion questions

1. Describe briefly, using an example, the components of an open system.
2. Give the Open University definition of a system. How would you criticize the Open University definition?
3. Are the examples below systems according to the Open University definition? Explain your answer.
    (a) A briefcase
    (b) Set theory
    (c) A firework

4. How would you classify the following systems, using the classification due to the Open University?
   (a) A map of England
   (b) A filing cabinet
   (c) A water molecule
   (d) An end-of-term party
5. Describe the main elements of the state space approach. Why is this important for analysing information systems?
6. Give some examples of information systems that are relatively closed and some that are relatively open. Do you agree that these are characterized by their inherent degree of uncertainty?
7. Explain why it is necessary to control information systems. What problems are there in trying to do this?
8. How would the following examples be classified, using Checkland's four-point systems classification?
   (a) PASCAL programming language definition
   (b) A television set
   (c) A hydrogen atom

References

Ackoff, R. L. (1971) Towards a system of system concepts, *Management Science*, **17**(11), 661–71.

Checkland, P. (1981) *Systems Thinking, Systems Practice*, Wiley, Chichester.

Checkland, P. and Scholes, J. (1990) *Soft Systems Methodology in Action*, Wiley, Chichester.

Churchman, C. W. (1968) *The Systems Approach*, Dell Publishing Co., New York.

Open University (1980) *Systems Organization: The Management of Complexity*, Block 1, The Open University Press, Milton Keynes.

Von Bertalanffy L. (1968) *General System Theory: Foundations, Development, Applications*, Penguin, London.

4

Analysing organizations and information systems – the OMNIS model

Applying the systems approach

FUNCTIONAL SYSTEM AND CONTROL SYSTEMS

In Chapter 1, we used the terms application, information system and organization-related activities to gain an intuitive feel for information systems in organizations. However, these terms are widely used and are capable of many interpretations. In this chapter, we want to present a more precise description of information systems, so we will use instead the terms *functional system* and *control system*, with the general meaning given to them in the chapter on the systems approach. This is shown in Fig. 4.1.

The functional system is roughly equivalent to the application, and the control system contains the *information system* and the *management system*,

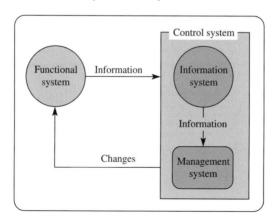

Figure 4.1 Functional and control systems, showing control system components.

consisting of management activities. We will show later how the information processing type of functional activities discussed in Chapter 1, concerned with information input and output, are usually considered as part of the information system. The view we are taking here emphasizes the use of information in the information system to assist management activities.

ORGANIZATIONAL MODELLING – THE OMNIS MODEL

We shall apply the systems approach to organizations to develop a model, based on Fig. 4.1, for describing information systems in a social and organizational context. The model is termed OMNIS – *o*rganizational *m*odelling of *i*nformation *s*ystems and is shown in Fig. 4.2

The model is a descriptive, generic model, and allows us to analyse and describe an information system in an organization in more detail than the basic open systems model. We will use the model later, in the systems development process, for building a description or specification of an information system. The scope of the model is wide, as it includes individuals and organizations external to the organization in which the information system is situated.

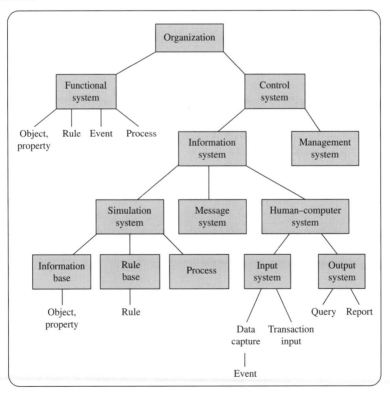

Figure 4.2 The OMNIS model.

We shall first of all describe the functional system of OMNIS in more detail and then the information system. The management system will be described more fully in the next chapter.

Functional system

INTRODUCTION

If we consider an organization such as an insurance company or a manufacturing organization making cars, we can easily apply the concepts of the systems approach. The environment of the organization will be, for example, government and local laws, market demand for the products of the organization, share price, value of sterling and other currencies, competitive position of similar organizations and so on. The system boundary separating the organization from the environment may change if new departments are added or changed, new products are produced or takeovers occur.

Typical processes of the organization are the activities that attempt to meet its objectives, for example, receiving orders, manufacturing cars, providing life and other insurance services, delivering cars, arranging mortgages or pensions. These processes have inputs in the form of human, financial and physical resources as well as relevant information, such as marketing or sales information, to help produce outputs that consumers want, such as cars, insurance, pensions or mortgages. A group of such processes, in a part of an organization that is of interest, often forms the focus of a functional system.

If we take another example, that of a doctor's practice, the outputs are slightly more abstract, as an input may be considered to be a sick or unwell patient and an output, taken over a period of time, is hopefully a healthy patient. The environment consists of the National Health Service with Regional and District Health Authorities, local hospitals and consultants, the relative prosperity of the local area and so on. Processes include consultations with patients, injections and other treatment by the nurse belonging to the practice, calls at patients' homes, ordering and receiving medical equipment and writing reports on patients' health.

Eurobells⌂ production system example

INTRODUCTION

We shall now discuss an example using an organization called Eurobells⌂, which makes, markets and sells bells in different shapes and sizes. We will show details of a production system that performs a crucial function within the organization. This system produces, from different types of bronze, the bells from which the organization earns its main income. Such a system, termed an 'operating core' in Mintzberg (1979), is often the base functional system for a transaction processing system.

STATIC AND DYNAMIC COMPONENTS

The functional system in Eurobells⌂ is concerned mainly with processing physical resources for the production of its two main products, bells and clappers of different shapes and sizes. For example, it receives raw bronze from suppliers; subjects this to various processes such as melting, casting and cooling to produce bells and clappers; tunes bells; assembles bells and clappers into products; packages the products into containers; and finally ships the products to customers.

We can regard this system initially as being made up of a static and a dynamic component where inputs and outputs are static and processes are dynamic, and we show inputs, outputs and related processes in a simple table, as in Table 4.1. The table shows some of the steps that make up the production and shipping of bells, the main product, omitting details of the production of clappers.

Table 4.1 Inputs, outputs and related processes for Eurobells⌂ production system

Inputs	Processes	Outputs
Raw bronze	Receive	Raw material
Raw material	Melt	Molten bronze
Molten bronzes	Mix	Mixed bronze
Mixed bronzes	Cast bell	Bell
Bell	Tune	Tuned bell
Bell, clapper	Assemble	Product
Container, bell, clapper	Package product	Packaged product
Packaged product	Ship	Delivered product

OBJECT AND PROPERTY

We now want to consider inputs and outputs in more detail as *objects* and *properties*. An *object* is something of interest to the organization that is static, not dynamic, and may be, for example, a bell or a customer. A *property* describes an object, and may be the address of a customer or the price of a bell. We can describe the static component of the production system using these concepts. Examples of the types of objects and properties that exist are shown in Table 4.2.

Table 4.2 Objects and properties in Eurobells⌂

Object	Property
Customer	Name, address, telephone number, credit limit
Supplier	Name, address, telephone number
Bell	Type (treble, soprano, tenor), quantity, mass, pitch, price
Clapper	Type, mass, price, quantity
Raw material	Type (bronze, copper), material code, quantity, supplier
Mixed bronze	Type, quantity
Product	Product number, type (bell, clapper), price

We can also use these concepts to describe instances of the types, such as individual objects that exist in the production system. At a given moment, there may be, for example, 42 individual suppliers, a quantity of 20 bells of the treble type and a quantity of 400 kilograms of raw material of the bronze type.

SYSTEM STATE

In Chapter 3, when we discussed the state space approach, we defined a system state as being described by the relevant objects that exist in the system. It can be seen from Table 4.2 that we can use objects and properties such as product and raw material quantity to describe, in a static manner, the different, discrete, stages produced by the dynamic component of the production system, caused by receiving raw bronze, casting bells, assembling products and so on. We will thus use, in general, objects and properties to define states of the production system.

PROCESS

Update processes that change the system state

If we examine the processes shown in Table 4.1, we see that they are basically *update processes*, where we define an update process as one that changes a system from one state to another. Hence, these production system processes change the objects and properties of the production system from one state to another.

For example, before a cast bell process starts, the state of the production system might consist of a certain quantity of mixed bronze, and a certain quantity of bells. After the cast bell process finishes, the quantity of mixed bronze has decreased, while the quantity of bells has increased. Hence, the cast bell process has changed the production system from one state to another. A simpler example may be seen by considering the receive process. This changes the system state by increasing the quantity of raw material.

Refining update processes

- *Primitive process.* The primitive process is an important type of update process refinement. As an example, consider the tune process from Table 4.1. This process tunes a bell to the desired pitch, as a set of bells may be required to be in the key of D major. We can refine the tune process into the removal of bell material, to make it lighter and hence have a higher pitch, and the addition of material, to produce a lower pitch, as shown in Fig. 4.3.

  The tune process is refined into two change processes, which change the values of the mass property of the bell object. A *change* process is

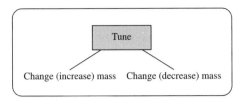

Figure 4.3 Refinement of the tune process.

termed a *primitive* process, and the two other primitive processes are *create* and *delete*. A create process may add a new object or property to a system, while the delete process may remove them. All update processes may be refined into primitive processes that affect objects or properties. However, many will require more than the one level of refinement shown in Fig. 4.3, because, for example, a primitive process on an object may be refined into a set of primitive processes on the object properties.

- *Support processes.* These are grouped separately in the application. They are termed support processes as they are only indirectly concerned with actual production activities, but they operate on the objects and properties in the production system. For example, new customers are acquired, suppliers are discontinued, properties of products may be changed and so on. We show examples of such processes in Table 4.3.

    When Eurobells△ acquires a new customer or supplier, this may be regarded as a create process, adding the new object to the system. From time to time, properties of customers and suppliers, such as addresses and telephone numbers, will require a change process, and the organization may acquire a new supplier of a particular type of raw bronze (perhaps at a cheaper price). In this way the supplier property of raw material will be changed.

Report processes that report on the system state

Report processes do not change the state of the system but only report on it. They are read-only processes which may test a state for a given value, transmit the value of a state to a destination, perform a calculation on a state value and so on.

Table 4.3 Support processes affecting system objects and properties

Component	Type	Process
Customer	Object	Create
Supplier	Object	Delete
Bell pitch	Property	Change
Supplier address	Property	Change
Raw material supplier	Property	Change

They may be refinements of a higher level report process or of an update process. For example, the tune process will contain an initial report process to test the pitch of a bell, to determine whether an increase or decrease mass update process is required.

EVENT

An *event* is an important occurrence that provides information or initiates a process, for example, the arrival of a consignment of raw bronze or a customer placing an order.

In contrast to a process, which takes place during a time interval, an event is instantaneous. In the functional system, processes are not continuously active, and the importance of events is that they are the triggers for groups of related processes. For example, when a customer rings with an order, this event triggers the package products process, and when a bell is out of tune, the tune process is triggered. As events and processes are closely related to each other in the system, we consider them jointly as constituting system *behaviour*.

RULE

Description

We have seen that an important part of describing a process is to define its inputs and outputs. However, in addition, processes must obey *rules*. For example, there might be a rule that the cast bell process is not allowed to produce a bell with a mass greater than 1500 kg. This rule governs an output, and an example of a rule governing input might be where the tune process is not allowed to take place on a bell (for quality control reasons) if the pitch of the bell is out of true by more than 1 per cent.

We express rules only in terms of object and property, and the type of expression we use is, for example: mass of bell ≤ 1500 kg. Many rules restrict property values or the numbers of instances of objects.

The main advantage to separating rules from processes is that we simplify both the description of processes and rules. When a process refers to an object or property, it must not violate any rule associated with the object or property.

Definition

A rule is a restriction on the system states (expressed in terms of objects and properties) that may exist.

Rules (together with the definition of objects and properties) thus define allowed system states. It is easier to define the allowable states by general assertions in the form of rules than by enumerating all the object and property instances that may exist.

The above is a static view of a rule, and a dynamic view is that it is a restriction on the inputs or outputs of a process. This view is obviously implied by the static view, as processes obeying the rules will have only allowed system states as input and will produce only allowed system states as output.

It can sometimes be difficult to identify rules, as they may only be implicit, being embedded in the detail of the way in which processes are actually carried out. For example, the bell moulds in Eurobells⌂ may be such that they can only hold so much mixed bronze, so the cast bell process is physically prevented from ever violating the rule that the mass of bell ≤ 1500 kg.

SUMMARY

Figure 4.4 summarizes our analysis of the functional system.

Control system

NEED FOR A CONTROL SYSTEM

For a large and complex social organization, no theory of organization exists that will allow us to predict its behaviour. When we discussed the systems approach in Chapter 3, we saw that such unpredictable systems need a control system to ensure that they function correctly.

CONTROL WITH AN INFORMATION SYSTEM

In the simple example of a control system given in Chapter 3, a thermostat controlled the temperature of a room. An important aspect of its operation was that it sensed a part of the functional system (the output room temperature) directly. However, in organizations, it is generally more efficient to have available relevant information about the functional system in an information system than it is to check the functional system directly. The reason for this may be illustrated by an example from Eurobells⌂ concerning its control

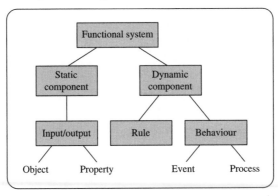

Figure 4.4 Functional system components.

over the amount of stock (raw material, products) it keeps in its stores. This is affected by processes, such as receive raw bronze and ship packaged product, from Table 4.1.

If the stock manager wants to know how many of these items are in stock at the end of every day, he or she can walk round the stores and count each item directly. However, this is a tedious, inefficient and error-prone job if the stock quantity is large.

A more efficient way, using an information system, is to start with an initial count of items, kept perhaps on card index or computer file, and to have procedures that record the stock items in and out of the store. These figures may then be added to or subtracted from the initial count, giving an up-to-date total of the amount of stock. The key to this approach is that the information in the information system is checked, rather than the items in the store. We assume that procedures have been carefully designed so that the information accurately represents the relevant part of the functional system.

CONTROL REQUIRES INFORMATION AND MANAGEMENT

Naturally, it is not enough to have only an information system. For control, the information in the information system is used to monitor the behaviour of the functional system, and changes are then proposed and made, if required. Such management activities take place in what we term a *management system*, shown in outline in Fig. 4.1. In the example above, a manager may use the stock control information in the information system to order an increase in production of treble bells if their quantity has fallen below a certain point.

This example has concerned checking the state of the organization against a standard, and taking appropriate action. We shall see in the next chapter that other types of management activities exist which also use information from the information system; for example hiring and training staff or deciding on new products. As such activities are intended to have a positive effect on the organization, we may see them as control activities, in the broad sense of the word.

We therefore define the control system as consisting of an *information* and a *management system*, as shown in Fig. 4.5. The management system will be discussed in more detail in the next chapter.

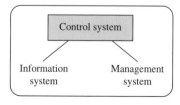

Figure 4.5 Components of the control system.

Information system

THREE SUB-SYSTEMS

The information system discussed above in the Eurobells⌂ stock control problem is a transaction processing system, as discussed in Chapter 2. We can identify three important features of this system:

1. It stores and maintains information that represents the state of the stock in the functional system. Information is stored on the cards or on the computer file, and update processes exist that keep the stock totals up to date.
2. It contains processes that allow users to obtain information they want.
3. It provides a means for synchronizing the functional and control systems so that the functional system may be kept up to date with the control system and information may be received when required from the control system.

We can refine the information system into three sub-systems, shown in Fig. 4.6.

SIMULATION SYSTEM

This consists of (a) *processes* (update processes), (b) *rules* and (c) *objects and properties* which represent those of interest in the functional system – hence the name *simulation system*. It is a 'working' model of the relevant part of the functional system.

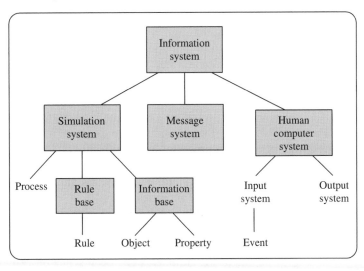

Figure 4.6 Refinement of the information system.

The objects and properties in the simulation system are stored in an *information base*. It is the different states of the information base that represent the different states of the functional system.

We saw earlier that the cast bell process in the production system was prevented from violating a rule (mass of bell $\leq$ 1500 kg) by the details of the manufacturing process. When we simulate this process, we have no such physical restriction to stop the process violating this rule. We therefore need to simulate the rule in a rule base, with the knowledge that the cast bell process must obey this (and any other relevant) rule.

In the dynamic component, the processes maintain the information base by changing the state of the information base (under control of the rules) whenever the state of the functional system changes.

MESSAGE SYSTEM

The purpose of this system is to transmit information, in the form of messages concerning the states of the information base, to the management system users, who will use the information to perform their activities. The *message system* processes are *report* processes and only read the information base. They are not update processes, so they do not alter the information base.

HUMAN COMPUTER SYSTEM

We use the term *human computer system* as we are mainly interested in computer-based information systems, although a more general term might be interface system, as it serves as an interface between the functional system and the simulation and message systems. The information processing activities discussed in Chapter 1, concerned with the input and output of functional information, are placed in this system and not the management system. This is because they are non-management activities, closely related to the physical information system, using its hardware and software.

Input system

In order for the states of the information base to be kept up to date, the execution of the simulation system processes needs to be linked to the triggering of the functional system processes which they represent. The link between these two systems is achieved by the *input system*, using the *event*.

The input system has two main activities. Firstly, it responds to the occurrence of an event in the functional system and records relevant information associated with the event. For example, if the arrival of raw bronze from a supplier constitutes an event, the type and quantity of bronze is recorded, together with details of the supplier. (The occurrence of a functional system event may be made known to the input system by user intervention. For example, a user may select the receive raw bronze menu on a terminal.

Alternatively, an event may be time-related, where no human intervention is required.)

Secondly, the input system initiates the simulation processes, corresponding to the functional system processes triggered by the event, which will use the recorded information to update the information base.

Output system

The function of the *output system* is to provide an interface between the message system and the management system. It responds to a request for a message system process and initiates the appropriate process and information formats, which receive any information the user supplies in relation to the information required. For example, if a user requests the address of a customer, the customer name must be supplied. It then initiates the appropriate message system process, which receives the information and searches the information base for the information required and then sends this back to the user. The request for information is similar to the event concept discussed above, but the concept is normally used only in the input system.

Interaction of functional and control systems

The interaction between the functional and control systems constitutes an information cycle. As the system in this example is a transaction processing

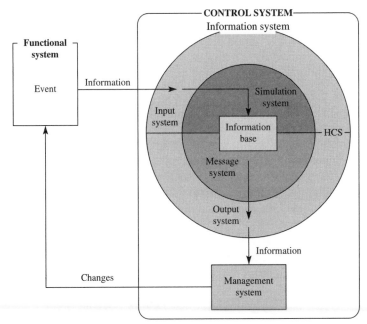

Figure 4.7 Interaction between functional and control systems.

system, cycle input is likely to occur many times in a given period. Figure 4.7 shows the information cycle and the different sub-systems of the control system that are involved. The cycle consists of:

1. The event occurs in the functional system.
2. The human computer system (input system) records details concerned with the functional system event.
3. The input system initiates the appropriate simulation system process.
4. The simulation system process updates the information base.
5. The user initiates the human computer system (output system) process to start the appropriate message system process to obtain information from the information base.
6. The user performs the management system activity using the information obtained.
7. Possible change is made to the functional system.

Information system representation

The discussion up till now has necessarily been rather abstract, so in this section we shall describe the organization and contents of an information system in Eurobells△ in a little more detail, by focusing on how objects and processes are represented. This will reveal one further level of detail necessary to complete our description of the components of the OMNIS model.

SIMULATION SYSTEM

Information base

Instances of objects and properties in the functional system are represented by *data* in the information base. The data can be stored on paper, filing cards, computer storage or some other medium.

An instance of an object is usually represented by a unique name, and the values of properties for a given object are usually stored together in a record, along with the object name. Sometimes a code is used instead of a name. A

Table 4.4 Data records representing objects and properties of two customers – the London Symphony Orchestra and Campanile Priory – and of the supplier Bronze Age

Object name	Properties (address, credit limit, . . .)
LSO	Barbican, London, 20 000, . . .
Campanile Priory	Paean Park, Berkshire, 1000, . . .

Object name	Properties (address, telephone number, . . .)
Bronze Age	Bronze Buildings, Brasilia, 09 23 45 63, . . .

collection of these records is termed a file, which we may visualize as a particular area of the information base. Table 4.4 shows how some of the objects and properties from Eurobells⌂ are represented by data.

Processes

To represent the functional system processes, simulation system processes create, change and delete the objects and properties in the information base. The processes may be performed by humans or by computers, depending on the type of information system being used. Table 4.5 shows some processes together with the effect on the relevant objects.

MESSAGE SYSTEM

This system is concerned with retrieving information, in the form of messages, from the information base. It reports on the state of the simulation system and contains processes that provide the user with the required information, in terms of objects and properties. Information may also be derived if it is not held explicitly in the information base. For example, the average credit limit of customers may be obtained by adding all customer credit limits and dividing by the number of customers. Processes may be human processes, manually obtaining information and typing reports, or computer processes that search files and send information to computer screens.

Information needs

The type of information that can be obtained from the information base is, for example:

- *Objects.* How many customers does Eurobells⌂ have currently? How many treble bells do we have in stock or on order? Is Bronzecheek a current supplier?
- *Properties.* What is the order date of Clapper CC13? How many products will be finished this year? What is the address of Crazy Casting? Is the

Table 4.5 Representing processes in the simulation system

Functional system	Simulation system
Tune bell	Change the mass property of bell
Receive raw bronze	Add to quantity of raw material
Create a new customer	Create process creates a customer record and inserts values for properties
Delete product	The record representing that product is deleted
Delete supplier of raw material	Delete supplier property value on raw material record

credit limit of Oedipus' orchestra £300? What supplier(s) supply raw material type F56/P7? Have we ever supplied Boinnng! Monastery with a product?

HUMAN COMPUTER SYSTEM

Input system

This system keeps the simulation system in step with the functional system, and we can distinguish two types of processes within the input system, *data capture* and *transaction input*:

- *Data capture*. The occurrence of an event in the functional system initiates a data capture process. For example, when the receive raw bronze event occurs at Eurobells△, the event causes a data capture process to start, recording relevant details about the event, such as the supplier and the quantity.
- *Transaction input*. The next stage is to initiate the process in the simulation system that represents the corresponding functional system process. This is done by a transaction input process, which uses the data 'captured' by the data capture process to provide input to the simulation system process.
- *Coupling between functional and simulation systems*. Coupling refers to the degree of time synchronization that exists between these two systems. A simulation system process need not occur instantaneously (or as soon afterwards as possible) with its corresponding event. The user requirements will determine how up to date the simulation system is to be. Thus, the data capture and transaction input processes could, at one extreme, be merged. At another extreme, they might be separated by a time factor of hours, days or even weeks.

Output system

In a computer-based information system, message system processes will be computer processes. In order to interact with these processes, procedures for humans as well as computers will exist. In addition, message formats will be required: for example, screen formats for input and output, menus, report layouts and so on. We may distinguish broadly between two types of output system process: the *query* and the *report*.

A query is an inquiry for a small amount of information that may be made at any time, and expects a result after a short interval, for example within a minute. The query is generated by human intervention. A report is usually a planned request for a larger amount of information that takes place periodically, such as at the end of the day or week. Human intervention may not be necessary and a report may be produced automatically from a computer-based information system. For example, a query will find out a supplier address, given a supplier name, while a monthly printed list of all current suppliers and their properties would be produced by a report.

OMNIS model

We shall use the OMNIS model both to analyse organizations and as a base to design and build computer-based information systems that operate within an organizational context.

OMNIS AIMS

The basic aim of OMNIS is to analyse a description of an organization so that relevant facts are separated out using the 'pigeon-holes' or categories of the model, such as functional system, simulation system, information base and so on. The structured description that results is a simpler description than the original as irrelevant material has been ignored. The description may be used to detect incompleteness or inconsistencies, and may also be used as the basis for checking, with the users, that the analysis is correct. We deliberately avoid the use of a precise language for the analysis.

To apply OMNIS properly, you should understand the following principles and method.

OMNIS PRINCIPLES

1. *Non-redundancy*. Model a fact only once. Do not duplicate facts.
2. *Completeness*. Model all the relevant facts.
3. *Accuracy*. This principle is the corollary of the preceding principle. Do not 'invent' facts. Model only what is in a description.
4. *Clarity*. Model a fact as an object, rather than a property, as an object is easier to see in the result. Only model important properties, as others will be added later.

OMNIS METHOD

1. Read the description of the organization. Broadly identify the scope of the functional and control systems.
2. If message system (MES) processes are fairly obvious, then proceed as follows:
   2.1 List and number MES processes.
   2.2 Identify information base (IB) elements referenced by the MES processes and classify as objects and their properties.
   2.3 Identify simulation system (SIS) processes that update the IB elements:

      2.3.1 List and number processes.

      2.3.2 Refine processes where necessary.

      2.3.3 Identify support processes.

  2.4 Identify human computer system (HCS) processes:

      2.4.1 Input system (IS) processes: list and number events and associated SIS processes.

      2.4.2 Output system (OS) processes: refer to MES processes initiated, and specify whether they are query or report.

3. If IB elements are fairly obvious then proceed as follows:

  3.1 Classify IB elements as objects and their properties.

  3.2 Identify, list and number MES processes that reference the IB elements.

  3.3 As 2.3 above.

  3.4 As 2.4 above.

4. Verification. Check your result as follows:

  4.1 SIS and MES processes must not reference elements that are not in the IB.

  4.2 If any IB element is not referenced, check the description again.

  4.3 All MES processes should be referenced by HCS(OS) processes.

  4.4 All SIS processes should be referenced by HCS(IS) events and processes.

Summary

This chapter has focused on the structure of the OMNIS model, which is described as follows:

1. In the functional system, the static component is refined into object and property. The states of the functional system are defined in these terms.

2. In the functional system, there are update processes, which change the system state, and report processes, which do not. Update processes are refined into primitive processes, which consist of create, change and delete processes and which carry out the changes to the system state at the lowest level. Support processes are update processes that operate on the objects constituting the system state. Events trigger processes.

3. The control system consists of two systems, the information system and the management system. Broadly, the control system controls the functional system, using the information and management systems.

4. The management system consists of management activities, performed by users. These activities require information in the information system.

5. The information system consists of three systems, the simulation system, the message system and the human computer system.

6. The simulation system maintains and stores information representing the states of the functional system and consists of processes representing the

functional system processes, while the functional system states are represented by the objects stored in the information base.

7. The message system contains processes that only read the contents of the information base, transmitting messages concerning system states to the management system.
8. The human computer system consists of the input system and the output system.
9. The input system keeps the simulation system up to date with the functional system, using the concept of event. The time coupling between the two systems may not be instantaneous.
10. The output system allows users access to the message system.
11. Objects are represented in the information base with data, while processes are represented by human, computer or some other type of process.

Discussion questions

1. Explain why a model such as the OMNIS model is useful for describing information systems.
2. Without consulting the text, list the constituent sub-systems into which OMNIS analyses the organization.
3. Describe the relationship between the functional, information and management systems.
4. Describe the relationship between objects and properties, system state and update processes.
5. What is an update process and what are the three types of primitive process into which it may be refined?
6. Explain how rules are related to (a) objects and properties, (b) processes. Are rules used by message system processes?
7. Explain the concept of event and how it is used to synchronize the functional and information systems.
8. What type of process is a support process?
9. Describe the functions of the input and output systems within the human computer system.
10. What relationship does the information system have to the control system?

References

Mintzberg, H. (1979) *The Structure of Organizations*, Prentice-Hall, Englewood Cliffs, NJ.

Rock-Evans, R. (1989) *A Simple Introduction to Data and Activity Analysis*, Computer Weekly Press, London.

Case Study 1 – the fishing fleet 'La Perle'

INTRODUCTION

The case study has been designed as a worked example for demonstrating how OMNIS is applied to the analysis of information systems in organizations. The input to the analysis that we shall use is a descriptive organizational document written in English.

This case study concerns an organization that contains an information system. Such documents are commonly used when new systems are required, and are expressed from the point of view of a user (or potential user) of the system who works for the organization concerned. From the case study you will become familiar with (a) how organizations and information systems are described from a user viewpoint, (b) how to apply the model to the organization and (c) which format to use for presenting the results.

BACKGROUND

The fishing fleet 'La Perle' consists of a fleet of modern boats based on the port of St Quay-Portrieux, on the northern coast of Brittany in France. The fleet is interested in two main sea products, fish and seaweed. The fish is sold to humans while the seaweed is finding increasing favour as an organic fertilizer for the artichoke-growing area around Roscoff. The owner of the fleet, Capitaine Yeux d'Oiseau, is a young woman who has inherited the business from her father, and, as a recent engineering graduate in fish processing and informatics from the University of Brest, has developed an information system to make the business more efficient. She uses a new portable PC.

The quantity of fish caught and sold is recorded on a daily basis and accumulated to a monthly total. Owing to the rapid decomposition of fish, no stocks are kept after the day of the catch. The quantity of seaweed caught and sold is recorded daily only. It is also important to record which customers buy fish and seaweed and in what quantities, again on a daily basis. A monthly total of fish sales to customers is provided. Customer details such as name and address are also included.

A large percentage of costs involves maintenance of the fleet. Each boat has a record kept of its name, last maintenance date and cost. The cost has a limit of FF 50 000. Information is kept concerning the docks where boats have been maintained. The names and addresses of the docks are also kept. In addition, information relating to repairs to nets is kept, including net number, date of purchase and number of repairs.

The way the system works is that each boat captain writes down the quantity of fish and seaweed caught every day and sends these details to the office staff in the harbour. Staff who sell the catch in the daily market note the quantities of the various items sold and to whom.

The type of information that the Capitaine has available includes: How many fish were caught and sold today and last month? What customers bought seaweed today? Who is my biggest customer this month for fish? When did we last maintain the boat *Pisces*? How many times have we repaired net number 14?

With the information, she is able to offer the best customers a discount if they guarantee to buy a certain quantity of the catch on a regular basis. Staff decide when boats should be maintained, based on yearly maintenance intervals, and when nets should be repaired. After ten repairs, a net is discarded.

Using this description of the organization and the information system you are required to apply the OMNIS model and produce a description of the information system.

SOLUTION – INFORMATION SYSTEM

SIMULATION SYSTEM

Information base

Object	*Properties*
FISH	Quantity caught (daily)
	Quantity sold (daily)
	Quantity caught (monthly)
	Quantity sold (monthly)
SEAWEED	Quantity caught (daily)
	Quantity sold (daily)
DOCK	Name
BOAT	Name
	Last maintenance cost
	Last maintenance date
	Dock name
NET	Number
	Number of repairs
	Date of purchase
CUSTOMER	Name
	Quantity fish bought (daily)
	Quantity seaweed bought (daily)
	Quantity fish bought (monthly)

Rule base

Number of repairs of NET ≤ 10
Last maintenance cost of BOAT ≤ 50 000

Process	*Refinement*
1. Catch fish	Replace quantity caught (daily) property of FISH
	Replace quantity caught (monthly) property of FISH
2. Sell fish	Replace quantity sold (daily) property of FISH
	Replace quantity fish bought (daily) property of CUSTOMER
	Add to quantity sold (monthly) property of FISH
	Add to quantity fish bought (monthly) property of CUSTOMER
3. Catch seaweed	Replace quantity caught (daily) property of SEAWEED
4. Sell seaweed	Replace quantity sold (daily) property of SEAWEED
	Replace quantity seaweed bought (daily) property of CUSTOMER
5. Maintain boat	Replace last maintenance date property of BOAT
	Replace last maintenance cost property of BOAT
	Replace dock name property of BOAT
6. Repair net	Add to number of repairs property of NET
7. Set monthly totals	Set to zero monthly totals on FISH and CUSTOMER
Create, change, delete	Dock, customer, net, boat

MESSAGE SYSTEM

1. List FISH quantity sold and caught
2. List name of CUSTOMER with quantity seaweed bought (daily) > 0
3. List name of CUSTOMER with largest quantity fish bought (monthly)
4. List last maintenance date of BOAT with name 'BOATNAME'
5. List number of repairs of NET with number 'NETNUMBER'

HUMAN COMPUTER SYSTEM

Input system

Event	*Process*
1. After all catch is landed	Catch fish (1) and Catch seaweed (3)
2. At end of day	Sell fish (2) and Sell seaweed (4)
3. Boat returns from dock	Maintain boat (5)
4. When net is old	Repair net (6)
5. At month end	Set monthly totals (7)

Output system

1. Daily report process for MES processes 1 and 2
2. Query process for MES processes 3, 4 and 5

NOTES

1. The harbour, staff, Capitaine, artichokes and so on are not modelled in the information system, as we do not wish to record information about them. The Capitaine, staff and the boat captains are users – they perform activities in the HCS and the management system. However, this part of the description is indispensable for understanding the social and organizational context into which the information system will fit, and will be used to plan the management system.

   Management system activities might be, for example: (a) offer best customers a discount in return for guaranteed purchase, (b) send boats for maintenance at yearly intervals, (c) send nets for repair, (d) discard nets after ten repairs.

   The PC hardware and software is not modelled in the system, as it is only an implementation vehicle.
2. Objects FISH and SEAWEED are 'abstract' objects and have only one instance each. In contrast, BOAT or CUSTOMER are more typical and have many instances, representing the physical instances of boat and customer.
3. The model is incomplete, as no distinction is made between data capture and transaction input processes. Users should be queried about this.

5

Management system

Introduction

In the previous chapter, we formed a picture of the interaction between a functional system and a control system, which may be represented by the diagram in Fig. 5.1. This shows information from the information system being used in a management system to assist users with management activities. Many of these activities will result in changes to the functional system.

The production system example from Eurobells⌂ that we used gives a rather narrow view of the use of a control system, as it shows information being used only to monitor and control organizational behaviour. There are other types of management activity performed by users in the management system, which we shall discuss below. This will give us an insight into the kind of information that users require from the information system.

The management system is not as easily visible within an organization as the information system, which has a physical presence of its own, normally

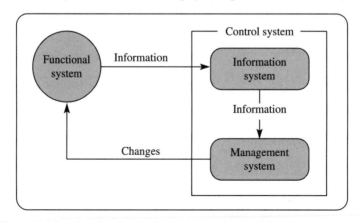

Figure 5.1 Functional and control systems showing control system components.

being located on computers, disks, printers, terminals and so on. This is because there may be many different individuals, in different departments or locations, who use the information for activities which themselves are not necessarily explicit.

Classical model of management activities

There are several models of management activities, but we shall examine only two contrasting ones. The classical model of management activities derives from the turn of the century French engineer and manager Henri Fayol (Fayol, 1949; Pugh *et al.*, 1983), and is a normative model, that is, a model that sets out what it thinks managers ought to do. Fayol thought managers ought to:

1. *Plan.* Goal selection and policy definition for achieving goals for the future.
2. *Organize.* Creating organizational forms and structures from materials and humans.
3. *Direct* (originally, command). Leading and motivating employees and organizing their activities.
4. *Coordinate.* Ensuring that different organizational components are working together efficiently and harmoniously, for example synchronizing the work of two different departments, such as the production and packaging departments in Eurobells⌂.
5. *Control.* Ensuring that the organization behaves in accordance with established rules and expressed commands. In OMNIS terms, monitoring functional system behaviour, comparing the outputs with system objectives and adjusting the system if necessary.
6. *Staff.* Selecting and training employees.

The sixth activity, the staff activity, has been added more recently (Davis, 1974). These activities are general for all organizations.

Mintzberg model of managerial roles

Henry Mintzberg has produced a descriptive model of managerial roles, based on empirical research, where he 'shadowed' five senior executives in all aspects of their work (Mintzberg, 1973). In comparison with the classical model, the Mintzberg model is descriptive and is based on his empirical studies.

He found ten roles, each role characterized by a set of similar managerial activities, and suggested that the roles be grouped into three areas, informational, interpersonal and decisional.

INFORMATIONAL

Managers are often key figures at the centre of networks of information; and there are three informational roles where the manager receives information as input and supplies it to others as output. In the *monitor* role, the manager obtains information, mostly current. In the *disseminator* role, information is transmitted to others in the organization. The information may concern areas outside as well as within the organization and may consist of fact or opinion. The third role is that of *spokesperson*, where the manager provides information concerning the organization to outsiders, such as the general public and those in influential positions.

INTERPERSONAL

Three interpersonal roles exist, all characterized by the involvement of the manager with people, internal as well as external to the organization. Firstly, managers may act as a *figurehead*, performing symbolic duties such as speaking at an annual dinner or a party given for a departing employee. The second role is that of a *leader*, concerned with staffing and motivation and training of individuals. Finally, the *liaison* role involves maintenance of contacts with individuals, for information acquisition purposes, both inside and outside the organization.

DECISIONAL

In the first of these roles, the manager is an *entrepreneur*, seeking and initiating change in the organization to improve it in some way. Secondly, there is the *disturbance handler* role, where the manager responds to problems that arise. Thirdly, *resource allocation* involves deciding on the distribution of resources such as people, time and money to organizational tasks. Finally, disputes arise from time to time, perhaps between a manager's subordinates or between managers and subordinates; as a *negotiator*, the manager needs to resolve the disputes.

ROLES AND INFORMATION REQUIREMENTS

As we remarked in the introduction, we can see that management activities span a wider range than those of the production system example, which only focused on an activity that was a type of disturbance handling, using the Mintzberg classification. In addition, it is clear that, in this model, information processing is at the heart of all management activities.

We may consider some examples of how the roles make use of information from an information system.

Informational

An example of an important dissemination activity is to send information, such as an annual balance sheet, to external individuals and bodies such as shareholders and investors. For example, Eurobells⌂ has to send a monthly profit and loss account to Eurobank$, who have loaned it £2 000 000 for recent expansion.

Interpersonal

A manager may, based on employment history, send employees on appropriate training courses if their history indicates that they need a certain skill. For example, Eurobells⌂ sends its more musical employees to different levels of campanology classes, so that the bell-ringing demonstrations used on marketing drives may maintain a high standard.

Decisional

Many examples may be seen here. As entrepreneur, a manager needs information on, for example, public response to a planned product. An early step in the marketing plans for a new size of bell at Eurobells⌂ is the generation, maintenance and analysis of survey data, from prospective and current customers, regarding their views on the planned bell. As a disturbance handler, managers may measure organization performance against objectives, as discussed earlier. As a resource allocator, a manager requires information about current organizational resources, to decide, for example, on funding for a project to produce a prototype of a new bell.

FEATURES OF THE MINTZBERG MODEL

One of the useful aspects of the model, for our study of information systems, is that the different types of role that are defined give us an intuitive understanding of the kind of information required to carry out the roles. We may note in passing, as a comment on the model, that the first informational role, where the manager monitors information, seems to overlap partially with the disturbance handler role.

The model emphasizes management activities, internal to an organization, that use the information for a purpose. Human computer system activities that merely retrieve the information from the information system to pass on to managers are not covered by the model.

Wide concept of management system

EXTERNAL USERS

We can extend the concept of management activities to external users also, as their actions may have an effect on the organization. This is shown in Fig. 5.2. External bodies such as Customs, Income Tax, shareholding institutions, banks, customers and suppliers may act as disturbance handlers to check some aspect of the organization against their own standard. Such a standard might be, for example, competitors' prices for similar products or the annual dividend for shareholders. In this way, the market-place may constitute an external control system.

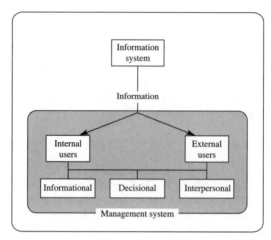

Figure 5.2 Management system components, showing external and internal users.

Decisions and actions taken as a result of this checking process will often have an effect on the organization. An example of an indirect effect might be a slackening in demand for an organization's products when prices become too high, forcing organization management to consider a change. Direct effects may occur where there is more at stake. For example, the major partner in a loan consortium may demand changes to the board if a loss is declared in the annual accounts.

Not all information may be used in decisional roles. An example of an informational activity might be where information concerning the proportion of different ethnic groups among organizational employees is sent to an external body, for compilation and publication of a survey on organizational policy in the area of job discrimination.

The last point we may make is that not all individuals who fulfil a managerial role in fact have the job title manager, or even supervisor. There are many jobs entailing responsibility for close supervision of organizational affairs that may be performed by non-managerial employees.

DEFINITION OF MANAGEMENT SYSTEM

After our discussion, we can define a management system as follows:

> A management system consists of individuals or bodies, internal or external to the organization, who use information from the information system to assist in their management activities.

Relative importance of different management roles

Comparing the classical model with the Mintzberg model, activities 3 and 6 fit the interpersonal category and activities 1, 2, 4 and 5 are in the decisional category, while informational activities are not mentioned.

It is traditional that the information required and functions performed by management for decisional activities have received the most attention, as they have the greatest potential for bringing about improvements to organizations. However, a more modern view also emphasizes the importance of the informational activities.

Anthony's classification of decisions

Three types of decisions are made in organizations, according to Anthony (1965). These are:

1. *Strategic planning.* Strategic planning decisions are concerned with setting organizational objectives and deciding the type of business that the organization should be in. They are decisions with long-term implications which may require a substantial amount of organizational resources.
2. *Management control.* Management control decisions concern the acquisition of new resources, ensuring that they are used efficiently and effectively, to accomplish organizational objectives.
3. *Operational control.* Operational control decisions use existing facilities and resources to check that specific organizational activities are carried out properly.

Although these decision types are not related to types of user by Anthony, it is generally assumed that strategic planning is carried out at the highest level of management, for example, by boards of directors in British organizations. Management control (often termed tactical management) is in the hands of middle managers, while overseers or supervisors form the lowest level of management, the operational control level.

Combining activities and levels

To illustrate the applicability of the discussions above, we may combine the Mintzberg model with Anthony's three levels of decision. For example:

1. *Operational control level*
   Decisional (entrepreneur)   An overseer checks the quantity of certain raw materials and decides to reorder some that are known will be in demand soon.
   Decisional (disturbance handler)   Production line A is critical and is falling behind schedule. The overseer transfers workers from a non-critical line to line A.
   Interpersonal (leader)   An overseer assigns a new employee to an experienced workman to learn a specific job
2. *Management control level*
   Decisional (disturbance handler)   A manager analyses weekly production figures.

| Decisional (resource allocation) | A manager analyses monthly costs of the profit centre by product and by production line. As a result, workers may be hired/fired or cheaper/more expensive raw materials may be ordered. |
| Informational (dissemination) | Every month, Eurobells⌂ has to send figures for industrial effluent dumped in the nearby river to the National Rivers Authority. |

3. *Strategic planning level*

| Decisional (entrepreneur) | Analyse product sales and initiate new products. |

Management information requirements

INTRODUCTION

We may now attempt to systematize the different types of information required for management activities.

BASED ON THREE LEVELS OF DECISION

Information may be characterized in terms of its level of detail and its timeliness, on the basis that different levels of management activity require different levels of detail of information, concerning shorter or longer periods of time. According to this view, the lowest, operational control level of management requires very detailed information that is very up to date, for example, information concerning the system that is less than a day old; we may term this *operational information.*

Middle management would require information concerning a longer time scale, for example weekly or monthly, and would only require, for example, transaction levels to be summarized for that week or month. This can be termed *managerial information.* Finally, the strategic planning level would require information to be summarized at a higher level of abstraction, concerning a quarterly or half-yearly period, and we will term this *strategic information.*

For external information, reports such as yearly balance sheets for shareholders and institutional investors are a good example of strategic information, perhaps at its most condensed, and managerial information might be produced for the tax authorities, such as annual earnings and deductions for each employee.

FUNCTIONAL INFORMATION AS A TYPE OF MANAGEMENT INFORMATION

We should note that functional information, discussed in Chapter 1, may also have a management use, as it is required in this role by some external users. For example, information relating to a single transaction in the form of an invoice, remittance advice, despatch note or receipt may be input to external decisional activities. External users use a despatch note to check that goods delivered are the right goods or they can use a receipt to compare prices with other organizations.

This information is typically disseminated by clerical employees, and, as we have seen, such information processing activities are carried out in the human computer system. With increasing use of electronic data interchange (EDI), involving, for example, the transmission of invoice information directly to information systems belonging to customers, no individual may be involved at all.

FOUR TYPES OF INFORMATION

To summarize, we identify four types of information, which are hierarchically related:

1. Strategic
2. Managerial
3. Operational
4. Functional

Table 5.1 shows characteristics of information that are required for each level of management decision, as suggested by Anthony. The importance of this type of table is the help it gives us, when designing information and related management systems, in choosing the right type of information for the right type of decision. A common error, for example, is for a designer to provide a senior manager, required to make control decisions, with information that is too detailed.

Summary

This chapter looked at two models of activities performed by managers in organizations, the classical and the Mintzberg models. The classical model

Table 5.1 Four types of information required by the management system (adapted from Lucas, 1985)

Information characteristic	Information type			
	Strategic	*Managerial*	*Operational*	*Functional*
Source	External	Internal	Internal	Internal
Accuracy	Less important	Important	Very important	Vital
Level of detail	Very summarized	Summarized	Detailed (high volume)	Detailed (low volume)
Time interval covered	Long	Medium	Short	Very short
Timeliness	Not so recent	Fairly recent	Up to date	Up to date
Effect of resulting decision	Long term	Medium term	Short term	Short term

consisted of six types of normative management activity, while the more recent Mintzberg model described ten different types of management system activity in three role categories. We used this to produce a model of management system activities that differentiates between internal and external users, also defining a management system.

We then discussed the three levels of management decision, according to Anthony, and showed how these could be combined with the Mintzberg activities, giving a matrix of activities on different levels. On the basis of this discussion, we made some inferences about the types of information and their characteristics required for management activities, including functional information, and we presented a table showing the four different types of information, based on six information characteristics, required for different management system activities.

Discussion questions

1. Of the ten managerial roles identified by Mintzberg, to what extent do you think they process informal, as opposed to formal, information?
2. Apart from transaction processing systems, what other sources of information are implied by Mintzberg's managerial roles?
3. Looking at Table 5.1, could you use this to determine whether a given item of information was strategic as opposed to managerial?

References

Anthony, R. N. (1965) *Planning and Control Systems: A Framework for Analysis*, Harvard University Press, Boston, MA.

Davis, G. B. (1974) *Management Information Systems: Conceptual Foundations, Structure, and Development*, McGraw-Hill, London.

Fayol, H. (1949) *General and Industrial Management* (Translated by C. Storrs), Pitman, London.

Lucas, Jr, H. C. (1985) *The Analysis, Design and Implementation of Information Systems*, McGraw-Hill, New York.

Mintzberg, H. (1973) *The Nature of Managerial Work*, Harper & Row, New York.

Pugh, D. S., Hickson, D. J. and Hinings, C. R. (1983) *Writers on Organizations*, 3rd edn, Penguin Books, Harmondsworth, Middlesex.

Part Three
Hard Approach to Information Systems

Part three describes methods and techniques that are representative of what has come to be known as the *hard* approach to systems development. Broadly, this means that the methods and techniques assume that a problem to be solved has a logical or mathematical basis and that a computer system, which has its functions specified very clearly and in great detail, is in most cases a suitable solution.

Chapter 6 describes the traditional variant of the hard approach, discusses problems and shows how alternative approaches attempt to address these problems, while Chapter 7 describes the requirements determination phase, and again discusses the problems found with traditional approaches. It then mentions several methods that provide partial problem solutions.

Chapters 8 and 9 describe the analysis phase in detail, illustrating the structured approach to modelling entities, rules and processes while Chapter 10 describes the object-oriented (OO) approach to analysis.

Chapter 11 describes five well-known methods, structured systems analysis and design, Information Engineering, JSD, SSADM and OMT, all of which use some of the techniques described so far, and then discusses the solutions these methods provide to a library case study. A brief method comparison is described as well as some remarks concerning the differences between structured and OO methods. Chapter 11 ends with a brief discussion of software (CASE) tools for method support. The problems posed and addressed are described.

6

The systems development process

Introduction

SYSTEMS DEVELOPMENT PROCESS

To bring an information system into existence, many different activities need to be undertaken. For all but the smallest systems, a team process is involved, where many different individuals, users and computer specialists work together to define user requirements, produce a system specification, select and integrate computer hardware, write computer software, test the system, train users, operate the system and so on. This process is known generally as the *systems development process*, which we shall subsequently refer to as the *process*.

As organizations are always changing, for example, by responding to changes in the environment or by acquiring improved technology, it is usual for information systems to be in a state of frequent modification, requiring replanning, software rewriting, retesting and so on. Hence, another name for the process is the *systems life-cycle*.

HARD AND SOFT APPROACHES

There are several different views concerning the nature of the process, and in this book we identify two broad approaches, commonly termed the *hard* and the *soft* approaches. This chapter will discuss variants of the hard approach, with the soft approach being discussed in a later chapter.

Traditional approach

The *traditional approach* to the development process is perhaps the best known, and a version of this may be seen in Fig. 6.1. The process, in its first phase, attempts to determine the scope and type of system the user wants. This may involve a wide-ranging investigation into different kinds of application and

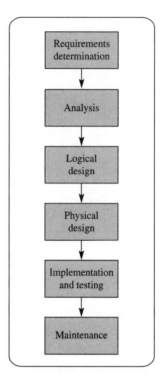

Figure 6.1 Traditional approach to systems development.

system possibilities. The next phase analyses the system requirement into smaller parts, so that it can be understood and checked in detail, and then the system is designed and implemented.

It is useful to identify two important constituents, *phase tasks* and *phase products*, which we may define very generally as follows:

- A phase task is an activity within a phase of the systems development process which produces a phase product.
- A phase product is a description of a system on a certain level of detail.

The majority of approaches to the process consist of distinct activities separated into phases where each phase usually contains many stages, each producing one or more phase products. Most of the phase products are input to different stages in successive phases, so the process may be seen as a transformation process, separated into phases, each of which adds further detail to an evolving description of the information system.

The terms used to describe the phases, as well as their content, are not yet fully standardized. Different authors will employ different names and draw the boundaries between the phases differently. This particularly applies to the first two phases.

Requirements determination

The *requirements determination* phase consists of several stages: *problem definition, feasibility study, requirements acquisition* and *requirements modelling.* The aim is to obtain a description of the user requirements which are expressed in terms of user concepts. In the problem definition and feasibility study stages, the outline of the desired system is defined. The requirements acquisition stage obtains user requirements in an unstructured form, while the requirements modelling stage uses a method such as OMNIS, introduced in Chapter 4, to analyse the requirements and to produce a phase product termed the *requirements model.*

PROBLEM DEFINITION

The starting point for deciding to build a system is often the perception of a problem in an existing system which the user feels can be improved by the introduction of a computer-based information system. However, another reason might be to improve some aspect of the organization, for example, the speed of customer service, in the hope that this will put the organization ahead of the competition.

The aim of this stage is to define, on a high level of detail, the application for the desired information system and an indication of the advantages that will result. The problem definition is drawn up mainly by user management, although a computer specialist may be consulted, especially if the organization has a strategic IT plan into which new system proposals must fit.

FEASIBILITY STUDY

The feasibility study takes the problem definition and examines different alternatives that may exist for the desired system. For example, it may become apparent that computerization will bring no advantages and that a manual system will be more effective! More typically, there will be several alternatives for drawing the boundary between human and computer activities.

This activity is essential as it attempts to establish whether the proposed system will in fact bring about the advantages that are expected. It does this by anticipating costs and benefits of different kinds. An important aspect of this is to determine whether the cost of the system will be contained within the budget set by user management. Another important part is to set a boundary to the desired system. For example, a stock control system may be required for just one regional depot as a pilot study. Non-functional requirements, which are requirements concerned with, for example, resource constraints, data archiving and security, may be ascertained in this stage and developed in more detail later.

The feasibility study is usually carried out by systems analysts and results in a report containing different options for a proposed system with recommendations.

REQUIREMENTS ACQUISITION

Assuming that the feasibility study has identified and approved the type of system required, the next step is to acquire the system requirements in more detail. Requirements acquisition methods are used for obtaining the requirements about the desired system from users, and they are normally used by analysts or analyst/programmers. The four traditional methods are: (a) observation, (b) analysis of existing system, (c) analysis of desired system documentation, (d) interview or questionnaire.

The next chapter describes these methods and others that address some method problems, in more detail. Any of the methods may be used, separately or in combination, in this phase.

REQUIREMENTS MODELLING

It is becoming increasingly common to use a model to organize the facts that result from requirements acquisition into a more structured form. This makes it easier for analysts to check the requirements for properties such as completeness and inconsistency and to refer back queries to the users. The OMNIS model addresses this problem area, as it is on a user level, and we may use it in this stage.

PHASE TASKS AND PRODUCTS

We will term the phase product from the requirements acquisition stage the *statement of requirements*. This is a description, on a user level of abstraction, of the desired system, and is typically in an unstructured, natural language form.

The requirements modelling stage produces the *requirements model* phase product, using the statement of requirements as the main input. The aim of the requirements model is to act as an overview of the desired system, in a structured form but using natural language.

NO STANDARD APPROACH

It should be noted that although the four methods for requirements acquisition are widely used, their results may be expressed differently. In addition, a feasibility study does not occur in all approaches to systems development. No agreement exists in terms of the contents of the statement of requirements for components that should be included or the level of detail required.

One of the reasons for this is that the methods used to analyse organizations and evaluate proposed projects involve management techniques and managers, rather than computer techniques and computer experts, and the study of these techniques has not, until recently, been undertaken from within the computer community.

Analysis

AIMS

The product of the analysis phase is the *specification*, an abstract, precise and high-level definition of the desired information system. The aims of analysis are to produce a specification that is:

1. Suitable for communication between users and developers as well as between developers.
2. Suitable for use as a basis for mapping through lower levels to an implemented system.

The structure of the specification has been strongly influenced by the conceptual modelling approach, discussed in Nijssen and Halpin (1989) and Boman *et al.* (1997).

CONCEPTUAL MODELLING APPROACH

Levels

The specification consists of three levels: conceptual, external and internal.

- *Conceptual level.* On this level, the part of the organization that will be modelled in the computer system is represented by the conceptual model.
- *External level.* The organizational context of the computer system is represented on this level.
- *Internal level.* This concerns the logical and physical design phases, describing how the information system will be implemented.

Conceptual modelling principles

These include the following:

1. To model the organization *precisely*.
2. To model the organization on an *abstract* level; that is, with no details concerning representation, presentation or computer implementation.
3. To model the organization *naturally*. This means that constructs in the modelling language or method correspond on a one-to-one basis with user concepts of the components of the organization.

To summarize, conceptual modelling aims to add more detail while retaining user terms and concepts (the user semantics), so that the description is recognizable to a user. It differs from requirements determination as, to avoid ambiguity and to assist the detection of inconsistency and incompleteness, it uses more precise languages, some of which are mathematically based.

CONCEPTUAL LEVEL

The conceptual model consists of three components: structure, process and rule.

Structure component

The structure component typically consists of entities, attributes and relationships, which are specified diagrammatically using a method such as entity modelling. The term 'structure' is used, as these elements are the basis for other parts of the conceptual model. They are refined from the requirements model, which, so as not to obscure its basic nature as a system overview, contains only the most important objects and properties.

Rule component

Rules are restrictions in the organization which are modelled in terms of restrictions on the entities, attributes and relationships in the structure component. For example, in Case Study 1 in Chapter 4, there is a restriction on the number of repairs that a net may undergo, and this is modelled by restricting the values of the number of repairs attribute of the net entity.

Rules are specified non-procedurally, that is declaratively, with the elements of the structure component to which they refer, using a precise language usually based on logic or sets.

Process component

Processes from the requirements specification are refined into more detail, down to the level of primitive processes operating on elements of the structure component. All events are specified. Process control structure is also modelled, as well as the structure elements operated on.

There are a variety of forms for specifying processes; for example, process decomposition diagrams for showing detailed process refinement and events, data flow diagrams for process sequence and entity life histories showing processes which operate on objects.

EXTERNAL LEVEL

Here, the organizational context of the computer system is defined, usually in terms of user procedures. These consist of processes performed by users which involve the computer system, such as OMNIS data capture and transaction input processes, grouped into related units. In a transaction processing system, for example, a procedure will typically consist of processes grouped by a particular event. Relevant objects, such as screens, reports and forms, may also be defined on an abstract level.

User procedures may be defined quite broadly, or may only focus on the direct user interface to the computer system, for example defining the navigation of a screen-based menu. State transition diagrams may be used for specifying these procedures.

Logical design

The aim of the *logical design* phase is to produce a design of the desired system that will serve as a basis for a computer implementation. Hence we begin to place the emphasis not on producing a specification whose components correspond closely to user concepts (such as entity, process and so on), but on transforming the user-oriented components from the analysis phase into integrated components which incorporate factors such as non-redundancy of data, speed of access, and suitability for acting as the basis of a computer program, which are important for a computer-based system.

The two major tasks of logical design, using the specification produced by the analysis phase, are to: (1) transform the conceptual model into the design for the computer system and (2) design the human computer system from the external level.

CONCEPTUAL MODEL TRANSFORMATION

Structure

The significant difference in this phase is that the structure component is now represented by data. We may also group several attributes together and represent them with one item of data. For example, a street name, a city name, and a postcode may be grouped into a data item termed an address. There will often be several possible ways of representing relationships. We may use the normalization technique based on the relational data model in this phase. We also decide on detail, such as what data types are required for representation and how many characters are required for each data item, and we design records, files and databases to store the data, taking into account the type of processes that will operate on the data.

Rule

Rules are integrated with the processes that operate on the constrained objects, and their form is transformed from declarative into procedural.

Process

Processes are now expressed in terms of operations on data. An abstract programming language form is often used here, such as structured English,

JSP diagrams or action diagrams. In addition, data flow diagrams may be drawn showing the processes that occur, the data input to and output from each process and data stores. Processes are grouped into logical units, such as transactions and procedures, and they are integrated into the human computer system.

DESIGNING THE HUMAN COMPUTER SYSTEM

Two levels of detail are normally considered here: firstly, the design of user procedures and, secondly, the design of the user interface. For user procedure design, defined in the analysis phase, the way in which the procedures are to be carried out is specified in more detail. Basic procedure types normally considered are: (a) human procedures, such as filing, writing and information searching; (b) automatic procedures, which may be mechanical (for example, folding letters and filling envelopes) or computer procedures; and (c) joint human–automatic procedures, such as entering data into a computer and responding to messages. Procedures with a human element should be designed to be satisfactory for human use. The procedures will be integrated with the user interface processes.

User interface design considers processes and the objects on which these processes operate, and may involve considerations related to interaction style (screen and report layouts, dialogues), specifications of human or automatic operations, and off- or on-line processing. These processes are designed using the data objects defined elsewhere in logical design.

Physical design

INTRODUCTION

Physical design is the last of the design phases, and we may consider it as consisting of three components: hardware, software and the human computer system.

The logical design from the previous phase may be used as a basis for the design of a system consisting of many different types of hardware, software and human procedures. For example, we may decide that software will be written in Visual Basic, will execute on a small PC and, from the example in Case Study 1, will require boat captains to total the daily catch.

Alternatively, we may choose a 4th-generation language such as Microsoft Access for the software, an IBM for the machine and let the harbour staff total the catch. The reasons influencing the choice will not be discussed here, but they will obviously take account of factors such as project estimated cost, process response time, storage capacity, number of users and so on. If a feasibility study has taken place in requirements determination, then it will need to be consulted. An obvious point is that the system components chosen, particularly the hardware and software, must be capable of working together.

The order in which we discuss the three components does not reflect the sequence in which they are considered at design time, as choices affect each other.

HARDWARE DESIGN

The hardware design consists of a description of the computers, storage devices, input/output devices and possibly networking devices required for the desired system. The hardware used for implementation and testing, and for operation may be different. This is often the case when a system is being built that will be sold to many different users who will run it in different hardware/software environments. The terms 'development' and 'delivery' environments are often used to distinguish the two.

Factors to be taken into account include: storage capacity and access times for storage devices, memory capacity and response time for processors and networks, cost of hardware, support for desired software, programmability of interface devices, and quality and speed of printer required.

SOFTWARE DESIGN

Software consists of the programs that run on the hardware. We shall include decisions about the physical design of data under this heading as the kind of data invariably affects the programs that process the data. Data is used by the programs in computer memory and 'persistent' data (data which has a life longer than the execution of a program) is stored on storage devices. It will be necessary to decide on the appropriate types of applications software, including languages and packages, as well as the systems software required to support the eventual system.

Process design

Traditionally, most applications software would be written in-house. However, there are now four options for process design:

1. For standard processes, we can buy packaged software. For example, accounting software is largely standardized. (An equivalent process is to contract out the software development to a third party, such as a software house or consultant).
2. Use an application generator or 4th-generation language.
3. Generate code using a CASE tool (see Chapter 11).
4. Write our own code.

If we write our own code, data structures are chosen for the representation of data in the programs, together with decisions as to the programming language required, for example COBOL, BASIC or C.

Detail is added to the logical design to take account of the data structures and data storage types chosen, and input and output data are designed for the processes. Issues such as execution speed and ease of maintainability of program code are considered, and processes are grouped into program modules.

Data design

The structure component, represented by data in the logical design phase, has decisions made for data storage and access on storage devices. Many different designs are possible and the feasibility of choices is determined. These will partly depend on the decisions for processes discussed in the previous section. We may use manual means, or CASE tools, to design sequential or indexed sequential files, or databases. The maximum number of expected records will determine the file or database sizes required.

HUMAN COMPUTER SYSTEM DESIGN

The human computer system consists of hardware, software and processes. Processes will be carried out both by people and the hardware/software environment, and some processes will be manual processes that will not involve the computer.

Some of the design of this system has had to wait until the physical design phase, as the procedures are hardware and software dependent, specifying the activities to be followed when communicating with the computer: for example, detail of dialogue between computer and operator, procedures for starting up and shutting down the system and screen contents such as windows or colours.

On the periphery of the system, data capture processes may not involve computers at all if they are off-line processes: for example, the data capture procedures in Case Study 1. Such processes may be assigned to certain departments, job roles or individuals.

Implementation and testing

MAJOR TASKS

The main output of the *implementation and testing* phase is a physical information system and not merely a design. Of course, the physical (and earlier) designs remain available for reference, as they form the specification.

The major tasks consist, firstly, of acquiring and integrating hardware, producing software, generating data for the files or databases and producing the human computer system. Secondly, the system is tested, and user comments are evaluated and perhaps used to redesign part of the system. Thirdly, in a stage termed post-implementation, the operation of the implemented system in the user organization is monitored closely for a limited period.

IMPLEMENTATION

Human computer system

The HCS processes require a clear definition for the humans who will carry out these processes. This definition should consist of natural language descriptions of procedures to be followed, and are typically written in manuals. They will cover details such as input preparation, how to request reports and so on. They are generally aimed at two levels: user management and users who will be concerned with functional information. Training for users will also be given.

Software and data

In-house implementation may consist of writing computer programs from the physical design, that is, producing source code or programming language statements. Alternatively, application generators may require forms to be filled in rather than program code to be written.

Programming development environments contain language-sensitive editors, compilers and interpreters, debuggers and other facilities such as version control to assist in this area. Data is generated for all entity, attribute and relationship instances and is used to populate the empty files and databases on the storage devices. This may be done manually or with the help of CASE tools.

TESTING

System testing, as the term is usually understood, refers to the demonstration of an implemented system's behaviour, with the aim of establishing that it behaves according to specification; that is, it should behave in the way intended for the desired system.

System testing is rarely a structured procedure. However, a three-stage process may be identified. The first stage concerns individual programmers and designers who test individual units of the implemented system to their own satisfaction, supplying their own test data and procedures. In the second stage, the work of several people may be integrated and tested as a whole. Often, users may be asked to supply test data or even test procedures to provide a degree of objectivity.

It is only in the third and last stage that users are usually involved in evaluating a system. Typically, whole sub-systems will be demonstrated to users, usually with live data and performing tests designed by the users to assure them that the system does what they intended. The testing of the human computer system often takes place rather earlier than above, as factors such as the usability of the system for the intended system operators are crucial to eventual user acceptance.

It should be said that system testing is often a rather neglected task, with system developers anxious to obtain quick user acceptance and users unsure as to how thoroughly they should test the system.

POST-IMPLEMENTATION

Here the implemented system has been tested and is operating in the organization. It is often the case that where there is an existing system, both this and the new system run in parallel for a few months. This is in case teething troubles with the new system should cause it to break down.

In some cases, a post-implementation review may be carried out after an interval such as six months or a year of operation. The procedure evaluates the behaviour of the implemented system against the original objectives, recommending changes if necessary to both the system and the process that developed it.

Maintenance

NEED FOR MAINTENANCE

Inevitably, some errors will exist in the system, or the human computer system will require adjustment after practical experience. However, in addition, real-world changes will occur, which mean that objects or processes may be required to change also. Another source of change is technological, in that upgrades to hardware or the availability of improved software may necessitate radical system change. *Maintenance* is thus a re-execution of earlier phases of the process for the parts of the system that are evolving.

This phase has traditionally had little attention devoted to it. One reason may be that it is concerned with old applications, whereas new applications are more glamorous. Another reason may be that specialists find it hard to change old programs, often with no documentation, and prefer new applications with new technology.

However, recent work has emphasized the importance of maintenance, and various figures have been used to underline the fact. For example, Rock-Evans and Hales (1990) estimate that maintenance uses in excess of 50 per cent of systems development budgets, then amounting to expenditure of over $30 billion per year worldwide. Howard and Potter (1994) have a figure of 67 per cent of the budget, based on a survey conducted in the mid-1980s. According to Pressman (1992), 80 per cent of software costs occur in the maintenance phase. This means that, over all systems, more resources are consumed on maintenance than on all the previous phases in systems development. A typical system takes between 1 and 2 years to develop, and has a lifespan of over ten years before it is replaced. Thus, its maintenance life accounts for around 80 per cent of its lifespan.

Again, there are estimated to be about 75 billion lines of code in use, world-wide, some or all of which require maintenance attention. Of the estimated population of 10 million programmers by the year 2000, the great majority of these will be performing maintenance tasks.

TYPES OF MAINTENANCE ACTIVITY

Three basic types of maintenance activity have been identified:

1. *Corrective maintenance* is performed in response to processing, performance or implementation failures. It corresponds most closely to the traditional, narrow, view of maintenance whereby systems must be kept up and running. It involves 'firefighting' in response to emergencies, such as program failure in the middle of execution, as well as more routine tasks, concerned with bringing code into conformity with specifications or standards.
2. *Adaptive maintenance* is performed in response to anticipated changes in the data or processing environments, for example payroll changes due to new legislation.
3. *Perfective maintenance* is performed to eliminate processing inefficiencies, enhance performance or improve maintainability. Providing user enhancements is the major portion of this task, keeping in step with the evolving needs of users.

Of the three types, perfective maintenance accounts for more than half the total effort (Howard and Potter, 1994).

PROBLEMS OF MAINTENANCE

Problems in performing maintenance activities have been found (Swanson and Beath, 1989) to depend on the following factors:

1. *User knowledge.* This factor includes seemingly insatiable demands from users for system changes, lack of understanding of current systems and unrealistic expectations.
2. *Programmer time availability.* This concerns the normally high programmer turnover rate and the preference of programmers for development rather than maintenance work.
3. *Product quality.* In many cases, the installed systems that are to be maintained have many errors or the documentation is inadequate.
4. *Programmer effectiveness.* This factor relates to the skills, knowledge of the installed systems and motivation of maintenance programmers.

REASONS FOR PROBLEMS

The third factor, *product quality*, is usually regarded as the most important, as this drives the other three. Poor product quality is due to:

1. Errors made during requirements and design phases.

2. Requirements changes occurring during development but not incorporated in the system.
3. Lack of, or inadequate, documentation of systems, necessitating detailed effort to understand often obscurely written programs.

The fact that perfective maintenance requires more effort than other types may conceal the fact that what computer management term 'providing user enhancements' may in fact be fixing errors or omissions made during development. According to Pressman (1992), 80 per cent of maintenance costs are due to unforeseen or unmet user requirements.

Although it is often assumed that maintenance tasks are analysis and design tasks, this is not the case. For example, an initial step is to check an existing program to see how it works. This involves system familiarity and diagnostic skills that are not required during systems development. In many cases, it may take longer to understand the program than it does to make a change.

SOLUTIONS

To alleviate maintenance problems it is suggested that maintenance should be separated from development, a maintenance career path for staff designed, more knowledge of maintenance (including statistics) should be accumulated and maintenance aids should be used.

Maintenance aids are methods or software tools that aim to improve productivity or quality of the maintenance activities. *Reverse engineering* tools have recently become available that analyse poorly documented systems and provide high-level descriptions, making the systems easier to maintain. For example, a type of data analysis may be performed on program code to show control flow and the flow of data. Another example uses file declarations to build an entity–relationship model.

Summary of the traditional approach

LINEAR MODEL

The traditional approach may be termed a *linear model*, as it regards phases, and stages within phases, as executing in a sequential fashion. The model rather oversimplifies actual practice, although it is useful as a framework within which the main activities may be discussed. We may summarize the advantages and disadvantages of the linear model as follows.

Advantages

1. The phases are clear-cut, with a beginning and end, making them easy to manage.

2.   All the analysis and design is done before coding starts. If this were not the case, some parts of the system might not fit with others, requiring redesign or recoding.

Disadvantages

1.   The assumption is that requirements are perfectly known before the project starts. However, requirements usually change as the project progresses and as the user understands the implications of the requirements.
2.   There is no guidance for understanding the organization in which the information system is to be situated. For all but the simplest systems, there is a danger that the wrong activities to assist will be chosen.

Most suitable use

The most suitable use is for projects with fixed requirements based on an existing system.

Dissatisfaction with the traditional approach

PROBLEMS

Although the process described above is well known, it is not ideal. Information systems development has been under pressure for some years to come up with an improved process that removes, or at least alleviates, some of the major problems that users experience in the development, operation and evolution of their systems.

Increasingly, development is taking place against a background of documented dissatisfaction with many aspects of the process. For example, a UK survey by the consultants KPMG Peat Marwick McLintock (*Computing*, 11 October 1990) found that '30 per cent of the UK's biggest computer projects were massively over budget, over time, and, if ever completed, fail to do the job they were meant to'.

More specifically, many users question the *productivity* of the process, feeling that development is too slow and expensive. Alternatively, they question the *quality* of the product, as they find that the eventual system does not do what they want. Another aspect of quality is that many users find that systems have been designed for computer experts, rather than organization users, and they question the usability of their system. In addition, many job changes may result from the introduction of a system, which, when fully known, may seriously affect the acceptability of the system to users or unions in the organization.

It is common for more effort to be spent during system evolution, in the phase often termed maintenance, than in the previous development phases.

However, this phase has been neglected until recently, and the *maintainability* of systems is a key problem. How can existing systems, which are always growing in size and complexity, be easily changed to incorporate, for example, changes to old functions or the addition of new functions?

Another problem is *reliability*, where systems in safety-critical areas such as nuclear power stations and aeroplanes, as well as in organizations that carry out large financial transactions where errors are costly, are becoming increasingly dependent on computer-based information systems. Finally, *security* of systems is increasingly under threat from human agents (for example via hacking) or software agents such as viruses. We will attempt to show later how improvements in information systems development are being made in an attempt to address these problems.

Quality and productivity are the two problems that are emphasized currently, and we shall therefore examine their main causes in more detail.

QUALITY PROBLEM

A poor quality system is one that, for example, does not conform to its specification, does not have a positive effect on the organization or is not used by its intended users. The main reasons for poor quality are:

1. The information system may address the wrong problem, as it may not improve organizational efficiency or effectiveness, as discussed in Chapter 1. Alternatively, the system may conflict with organizational aims or strategies. In general, the wrong activities to assist are chosen, which may be due to lack of business knowledge or ignorance of wider organizational strategy.
2. Wider social or psychological factors may be neglected, such as the degree of decentralization or centralization of the organization or the extent to which the information system will be acceptable to or usable by its intended users. Systems that have low acceptability often fall into disuse.
3. The right activities may be identified, but errors may be made by users or analysts in analysing information needs. This is often due to the use of poor development techniques or the degree of complexity inherent in the development process.
4. The system may be developed for the wrong reasons, such as technology push from technical experts or political pull from ambitious managers. There are often problems with technocrats, keen to work with new hardware and software, as well as those who seek to extend their power or influence with a state of the art computer system, whether it is necessary for the organization or not.

The majority of these problems are due to the fact that the linear model does not pay enough attention to the nature of the relationship, discussed in

Chapter 1, between the information system and the organization, and relies too heavily on analyst intuition, providing little guidance for the process.

PRODUCTIVITY PROBLEM

It is common for system development costs to be underestimated by a factor of two or more. This obviously affects the cost–benefit justifications made for the system in the feasibility study stage. It is also common for systems to be delivered later than planned, perhaps by a year or more. In this case, it is possible that the system may not be useful to the organization, as events in the market or environment may move so quickly that the system is out of date when delivered. Both these factors may cause system development to be cancelled or, if the system is delivered, never used.

An important factor causing poor productivity is *changing requirements*. The linear model assumes that requirements are known before the project begins. However, it is usually the case that information system requirements are changing continuously throughout the systems development process. If the specification of a system is always changing in this way, then new work must be done and completed work redone, both factors causing costs to grow and delivery times to lengthen.

Reasons for changing requirements

Three main reasons why requirements change are:

1. Users are often not sure of their requirements at the beginning of a project, and they only discover what they really want as the project progresses and as they learn what they can realistically expect from a computer-based information system, with the existing budget, time-scale and development staff. There may also be conflict between multiple users.
2. Changes in external factors such as technology, legislation, the market or the political environment often change requirements.
3. There may be implementation implications contained in requirements that are not feasible and are recognized only during implementation and testing.

Poor project control

A fourth reason for low productivity is that the estimation and tracking techniques used for project control may be inadequate:

4. Many projects have no means for their status to be measured at any given point, in relation to the work already completed or remaining to be done. In addition, at the start of a project, techniques for estimating the resources required are inadequate, based only on previous experience, and often give rise to over-optimistic predictions for delivery dates and

costs. For example, it is common practice not to include maintenance costs in the cost estimates for a system.

In addition, the problem of low productivity takes place within the context of a shortage of experienced development staff. Problems of quality and productivity will interact, as, for example, the discovery during testing that a system is of poor quality may mean a delay while the system is changed, and changing requirements that are not taken into account result in a system of low quality.

IMPLICATIONS OF PROBLEMS FOR THE ORGANIZATION

It should be emphasized that there may be serious repercussions from these problems, such as a simple increase in costs, a write-off of all development costs for a system amounting perhaps to millions or tens of millions of pounds, poor staff morale owing to an unwanted system, missed commercial opportunity due to late delivery or a threat to organizational survival if a system contains many errors and existing customers are lost.

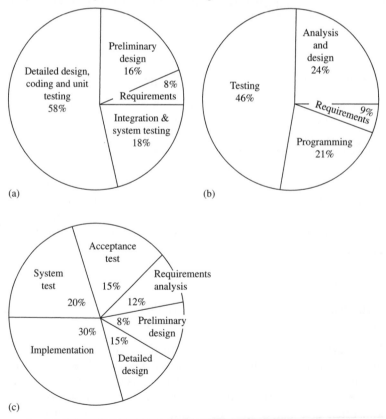

Figure 6.2 Resources spent on each phase as a proportion of all (non-maintenance) phases: (a) Boehm (1981); (b) Howard and Potter (1994); (c) Basili *et al.* (1995).

DIRECTIONS FOR IMPROVEMENTS

The main alternatives to the linear model that we shall discuss are based on the assumption that the above problems are best addressed by emphasizing the correct definition of requirements within the development process. The justification for this is as follows.

Figure 6.2 shows the resources estimated to be spent on each phase, as a proportion of all non-maintenance phases. Three sets of results are shown, where Fig. 6.2(a) is adapted from Boehm (1981), based on 63 projects compiled in the 1970s and undertaken in the USA, mostly in the real-time processing area. Figure 6.2(b) is based on a more recent survey conducted in the mid-1980s. These percentages refer to the total costs of the projects and not time taken. Figure 6.2(c) shows effort distribution (in time taken, not total costs) of 11 FORTRAN-based development projects with which the authors were involved in the Software Engineering Laboratory, associated with the NASA Goddard Space Flight Center. It is interesting to note that slightly more attention is being paid to requirements in the recent surveys.

Figure 6.3, based on surveys undertaken by de Marco (1982), quoted in Finkelstein (1989), shows the sources of system errors and the relative cost of their correction. Figure 6.3(a) shows the causes of errors in systems, with

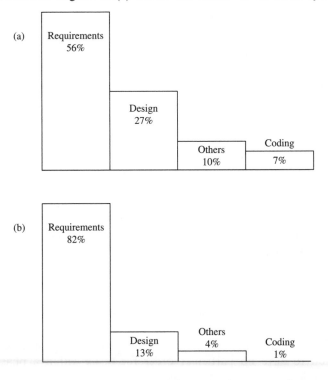

Figure 6.3 Error detection and correction in maintenance: (a) sources of errors; (b) proportion of effort to correct errors depending on error source (from Finkelstein, 1989).

errors in program coding contributing to only 7 per cent of errors found. The major problem is due to errors in the early, requirements phase (56 per cent). Comparable figures are also reported in Boehm *et al.* (1975), although their figure for the coding phase is higher, at 16 per cent.

Figure 6.3(b) shows the maintenance cost of eliminating errors, depending on the phase in which the errors were made. The coding errors (7 per cent) require 1 per cent of the cost, the design errors (27 per cent) require 13 per cent, while the requirements errors (56 per cent) require 82 per cent of the cost! Howard and Potter (1994) suggest that an error made in the requirements phase will, if not detected immediately, be one hundred times more expensive to correct if it is not noticed until maintenance.

Most errors are thus introduced long before coding begins, and hence are the most expensive to eliminate, as they will clearly have a great impact on designs and software based upon them, all of which will have to be changed.

Linear model alternatives thus mostly aim to redistribute the proportion of effort shown in Fig. 6.2 away from later phases, such as implementation and testing, and into the early phases. However, they do not address all the problems discussed above, concentrating mainly on the third quality problem and the productivity problem.

Alternative approaches to systems development

We shall discuss the *iterative, user validation, evolutionary* and *prototyping* approaches, which are all basically variants of the linear model.

ITERATIVE APPROACH

An important modification to the linear model incorporates *iteration*, and we shall briefly explore the concept. The term 'iteration' is applied to rather a wide set of activities. We may define it, within the context of models of the systems development process, as the process of performing a task in a phase more than once. It may be seen as the process whereby we go back over ground which we have covered before, repeating or reiterating that task. In practice, due to the interrelatedness of the specification components, we usually have to iterate many tasks at once. We shall discuss this topic from two viewpoints, iteration within a phase and iteration between phases.

Iteration within a phase

The discussion concerning the phase tasks of the traditional approach may have given the impression that when the first task finished, the second was begun, and so on. In other words, the tasks were totally ordered. In fact, it is common to have no particular order for tasks within a phase, and it is often necessary to iterate tasks before the phase product produced is satisfactory.

This applies particularly in requirements determination, which is not a phase that can be executed only once. It normally requires several repeated attempts, which refine the requirements obtained by analysing them and then checking them with the users, until a satisfactory requirements specification is obtained. This is partly because early requirements tend to be incomplete and inconsistent, and partly because requirements often change as the project progresses.

Study of a particular phase product in requirements modelling may reveal, for example, that a certain part is incomplete or that one part conflicts with another. In this case, the requirements acquisition task which obtains information must be repeated until the situation is clarified. A similar problem may occur in later phases where, for example, a data structure might be found to be incomplete, when the information required by all queries on that structure is cross-checked with the information in the structure. It is not possible to say how many times a particular task should be executed until it results in a satisfactory product, and there is no general model of the process that attempts to take account of this type of iteration.

Iteration between phases

Another implicit assumption of the linear model is that work only begins on the tasks of phase 2 when all the products of phase 1 have been completed, and so on. This is a management perspective of the process. However, we often need to repeat the work of earlier phases, particularly if we discover that a part of the evolving specification is incomplete and should have been captured earlier.

Figure 6.4 shows a model that takes account of iteration between phases. This model only assumes iteration to the previous phase. Variants of the model that allow iteration between any phase have been termed 'loopy linear' (Hawryszkiewycz, 1988). An example might be that an overlooked process comes to light in analysis, so we have to go back to requirements determination to redo the requirements model. An early non-functional requirement concerning, for example, system performance, may not be possible, and it is not until physical design or testing that we find out.

Incorporating iteration into the systems development process is more a reflection of the real situation that occurs when systems are built, rather than a modification to the process itself. It aims to address the problem of incorrect requirements and changing requirements due to user uncertainty.

Advantages

1.   The evolving system becomes closer to the desired system, as reworking is allowed.

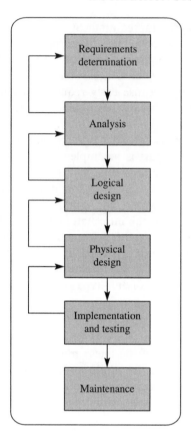

Figure 6.4 Iterative approach to systems development.

Disadvantages

1. Uncontrolled iteration can cause a significant amount of wasted resources, owing to the need to redo earlier specifications. Where the span of iteration between phases is very great, for example, between the testing stage and analysis, then project progress and costs may be significantly affected.

Most suitable use

All types of project are suitable, but particularly those where the developers may be unfamiliar with either the application or the technology.

USER VALIDATION

The *user validation* approach aims to restrict iteration to the previous phase only, and involves the users in the *validation* activity of the development process. We may define validation as follows:

Validation is an activity that checks that a product produced by the systems development process is correct, where the notion of correctness is that of correspondence to the user requirement.

An assumption of linear models is that users are rather passive 'consumers' in the process and that analysts and designers only 'empty' them of their knowledge. To counteract this, the user validation approach incorporates validation into the basic process by allowing phase products to be checked by the user. The general aim is to intercept any errors before work begins on the next phase, and so avoid iteration over many phases.

Of course, designers do perform this activity in practice, but only on an informal basis. Validation has also tended to be restricted to the design and implementation and testing phases, where it is often termed verification or program verification. Structured techniques termed walkthroughs (Gane and Sarson, 1979), desk checking, chief programmer teams, and Fagan's inspec-method (Fagan, 1976) are sometimes used in practice, and may be employed to check program designs and code. In some computer departments, there may be a quality assurance section that performs such project checking. More analytical methods have been used recently.

However, it has been found more satisfactory for users, rather than designers, to evaluate phase products, as their knowledge of the desired system is naturally greater than that of the designers. However, the approach requires extra resources (project time, user time) which may be difficult to schedule with the normal jobs of users. In addition, users often find it difficult to understand specifications.

A common type of user validation is to provide the products for the user to check at the end of every phase. These must be of sufficient quality to attract a 'sign-off' by the users before work is allowed to begin on the next phase.

The user validation model of the systems development process in Fig. 6.5 shows the different phases augmented by a feedback loop for validation. At the end of each phase, phase products go through a validation process V, which may require some part of the phase to be iterated if the products do not correspond to the user requirement. Otherwise, the next phase is begun. The diagram also may be used to represent iteration between many phases.

A feature shown on the diagram is the user requirement. The line from this to the phases represents information concerning the desired system being input to the phases. In traditional models, the user requirement is shown as being input only to the requirements determination phase. However, this is clearly an over-simplification, because, although the majority of information is obtained in this phase, there still remains lower-level detail, for example concerning human–computer interfaces, that may not be gathered in the first phase but is left to later phases.

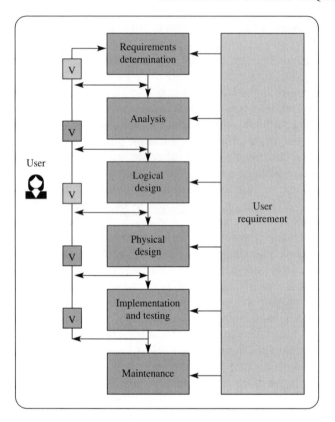

Figure 6.5   User validation model of systems development.

User validation aims to cope with users changing their requirements, to increase system acceptability and usability, and to address the right problem.

Advantages

1. It takes into account changing, incomplete or uncertain requirements, or designer errors, as users check phase products.
2. User involvement in the process is increased. This may make the eventual system more acceptable to the user.
3. There is a natural emphasis on the early stages, where any errors made will have significant impact on later designs.

Disadvantages

1. Users do not feel comfortable with specifications, as they are typically expressed in computer-oriented languages. Therefore systems may not be validated satisfactorily.

2. The process consumes more development resources than the linear model.
3. Users may not have the time for validation.
4. The process is harder to manage, as more individuals are involved, and it is not possible to tell how often iteration is required.

Most suitable use

It is used for projects with requirements that are likely to change.

EVOLUTIONARY APPROACH

The *evolutionary* approach to systems development, illustrated in Fig. 6.6, breaks up a project into separate parts, and then, one by one, each of the parts is taken through the development process. Each part either adds to the functionality of one of the earlier parts or integrates into the system with

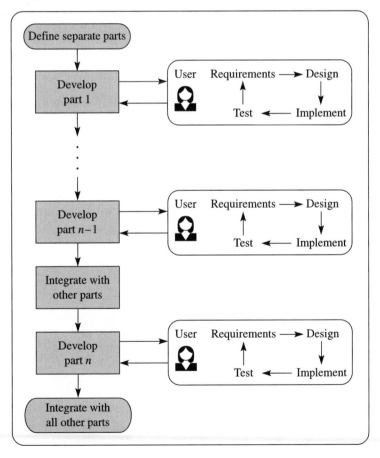

Figure 6.6 Evolutionary approach to systems development.

other parts. The emphasis is on a learning process, whereby users and developers refine the requirements or learn more about the possibilities of the technology, from the experience of developing and testing a given part, and then use this knowledge to shape the development of the next part. The maintenance phase is as normal but is not shown on the diagram. The *incremental* approach, which also divides a system into a number of parts, implementing and delivering each separately, does not have this emphasis on one part influencing succeeding parts. More detail on an evolutionary approach may be found in Gilb (1988).

In Fig. 6.6, the initial 'define separate parts' phase must consider the overall architecture, as well as the hardware requirements for the whole project, to ensure that the parts will fit together without the need for rework. It is recommended (Longworth, 1989) that the first part to be developed should include most of the really necessary functionality and should cost not more than 5 per cent of the total cost. The figure shows that each part, once developed, is integrated into the evolving system, but there are variations on the approach which might integrate parts at later stages. The aim is that each part should deliver something tangible and useful.

Advantages

1. Compared with the traditional approach, requirements do not have to be frozen for the whole project soon after project commencement. Each individual part will be developed relatively quickly, so that if requirements change during this period only the part being developed may require changing.
2. Users can try out an implemented system before all the system is developed. This enables them to learn the implications of their requirements, which they can apply to influence later parts of the system.
3. Project control is easier as the parts, being small, are less complex.

Disadvantages

1. Later parts may be seriously affected by mistakes made in earlier phases.
2. If the most important part of the system is done first, there is a risk that requirements may have changed significantly by the end of the project, requiring major changes to this part.
3. It usually takes a longer time, overall, to complete a project carried out in this manner.

Most suitable use

The use of this approach might be decided by project management or during the feasibility study, and it is normally used for complex projects, to simplify them, as well as to enable users to learn their requirements in more detail.

PROTOTYPING

The basic elements of the *prototyping* approach are to design and code a key part of the desired system and to test this implemented part (the prototype) with the user. After it meets with the user's satisfaction, the prototype may be discarded or, alternatively, it may be used as a nucleus to build the complete system.

Prototyping is thus a type of validation and addresses a central problem found in validation, which is the difficulty users have in understanding, and therefore validating, specifications. It also recognizes the fact that many users do not actually have a fixed requirement before the process begins.

User difficulty in understanding specifications

There is a problem that runs through all of systems development, but which perhaps is experienced most acutely in the first phase. The problem is that there is a tension between a description of a system that is understandable to computer experts such as analysts and designers and a description that is meaningful and understandable to the user. This is probably based on the two different roles of a specification: the need to be a precise description of the desired system and the need to communicate the nature of that system to the eventual user of the system.

There are two aspects to this. Firstly, precise system descriptions by computer experts tend to use unfamiliar, computer-oriented languages. Secondly, a user tends to visualize a system as a physical system, that is in terms of processes executing, receiving inputs and producing outputs. A user finds it hard to tell from an abstract system description what the physical system will be like, even if the language is user oriented. Users feel happiest when they are validating an implemented system, so that they can experience its operation for themselves.

The danger of developing a system in abstract is that it may not be until the implementation and testing phase that users find out what the physical system is really like. If the users require major changes, then extensive and costly iteration must take place.

Features of prototyping

The linear model is modified by the prototyping approach, as shown in Fig. 6.7, where a prototyping cycle is taking place during the requirements determination and analysis phases, although it may be used in principle in any phase.

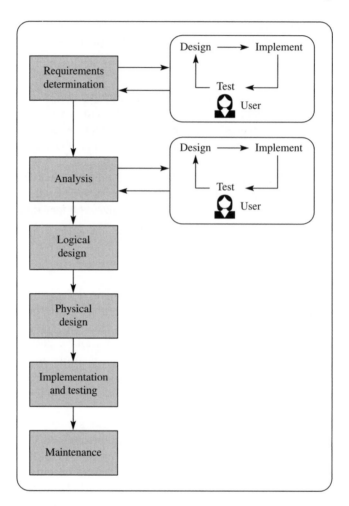

Figure 6.7 Prototyping modification to the linear model.

The approach provides users with an implemented system that they can try out, and that serves as a basis for improvements which can ideally be incorporated in the prototype and re-presented to the users. Hence, this avoids the problem discussed above of presenting only an abstract specification. The approach also takes into account the fact that many users do not in fact have a fixed requirement, as many approaches imply, and that experimentation with a real system enables users to better define, refine and communicate their requirements to the designers. Prototyping languages are also available which help to produce a prototype more quickly than conventional languages.

Advantages

1. The availability of a real system, as opposed to a specification, allows for more effective validation in the early stages, addressing:
   (a) error correction by users
   (b) definition of requirements, as it is easier to suggest changes based on experience of a real system, if the requirements are uncertain at the beginning
   (c) incorporation of changes to an evolving requirement, due, for example, to changing environment or technology
2. Fast production of prototypes is possible using prototyping languages.

Disadvantages

1. It has been found expensive to produce prototypes, in terms of programmer effort.
2. Projects can be hard to control, as users continually retune their requirements; that is they spend a lot of time making changes that appear to be only 'cosmetic'.

Most suitable use

An early use of prototyping was only for naive users with little or no experience of systems development, where the requirements were likely to change as users learnt their requirement. However, it is now used more widely, typically for prototyping screen dialogues and input/output forms, as it is increasingly recognized that validation is more effective with a real system than with specifications.

An early claimed advantage of prototyping was the fact that it did not produce documentation. Although this was always a doubtful advantage (for example, how could a prototype be maintained if no documentation existed?), it was claimed in a context of linear manual development methods which produced excessive documentation that quickly became out of date. However, this has been improved by the recent trend to CASE tools, which automate the storage and maintenance of the specification.

An improvement on the prototyping approach, termed *specification execution*, uses a specification language that can generate code to form a working prototype of the desired system. This combines the benefits of checking an actual system with the existence of a specification.

Another variation on the prototyping approach is to combine it with the evolutionary approach discussed above, whereby prototyping languages are used to produce parts of the implemented system for testing. An example of this is the Systemscraft method (Crinnion, 1991).

Summary

TRADITIONAL APPROACH

In this chapter we have given an overview of the traditional approach to information systems development. The terminology of phase task and phase product was introduced, and then the main phases of the approach were described in outline, finishing with a summary of its main characteristics, advantages and disadvantages. The phases are:

- *Requirements determination.* This is the phase where we attempt to determine what is often termed the user requirement for the information system. We may define the user requirement as 'the user perception of a system that the user wants, interacting with his or her organization, together with the expected benefits that the user hopes will materialize from the introduction of the system'. We refer to this system as the *desired system.*
- *Analysis.* This phase analyses the requirements into components which are used to build a specification of the desired system. This is more precisely expressed than in the previous phase, and computer-oriented specification languages are used. However, a conceptual modelling approach is often used which emphasizes user terms and concepts. The analysis phase is important as it establishes a precise specification which is used as the basis for producing the eventual system.
- *Logical design.* Logical design builds on the previous phase by designing the desired system, deciding on the data representation of objects, the detailed way in which processes will be carried out and the integration of the separate analysis components.
- *Physical design.* This is the last of the design phases and targets the phase product from logical design onto a set of specific hardware and software components. Individuals and groups who are to be involved with system processes may also be identified here.
- *Implementation and testing.* This phase produces a physical system, as opposed to a design. Computer hardware is obtained, software is acquired or written, and user training takes place. In the testing activity, expected behaviour of the system is evaluated against actual behaviour by the users. This may result in some modifications to earlier phases.
- *Maintenance.* The maintenance phase consists of correcting errors in the system or responding to changes in the user requirement, due, for example, to environmental changes or personal preference for system operation, and it may require all the previous phases to be performed for the part of the system that requires changing.

However, the background of problems that users experience with the process was then described, and two particular problems, quality and productivity, were discussed at some length, together with the main reasons for these problems. Problem implications were briefly mentioned. Several alternative approaches to systems development were then described, all being variations on the traditional approach, and the ways in which they addressed the problems were briefly discussed. Iteration within and between phases was discussed, as well as user validation, the evolutionary approach and prototyping.

Although a perceived disadvantage of the alternative approaches is that they consume more resources than the traditional approach, their advocates justify this on the basis that resources are simply being transferred from the maintenance phase. Their argument is that an emphasis on better quality requirements will produce software that contains fewer errors and that is accompanied by good, matching documentation. Demands on maintenance resources should therefore be lessened.

At the present time, this argument appears plausible, but it is difficult to set up a proper study to investigate whether in fact the predicted maintenance savings do occur. In addition, there is pressure to produce systems in a shorter, rather than a longer time.

Discussion questions

1. Draw a diagram summarizing the main phase tasks and products of the traditional approach to systems development. Which of the products do you think are suitable for validating with users?
2. Contrast the aims of the requirements determination, analysis and logical design phases.
3. Why do you think, as suggested by Fig. 6.3, that most errors are made in the requirements phase?
4. If you were a project manager, how do you think you would try to control iteration in your systems development project?
5. What are the reasons for calling the model in Fig. 6.5 user validation?
6. What are the significant differences between validation and prototyping?

References

Basili, V., Zelkowitz, M., McGarry, F., Page, J., Waligora, S. and Pajerski, R. (1995) SEL's software process-improvement program, *IEEE Software*, November, 83–7.

Boehm, B. W. (1981) *Software Engineering Economics*, Prentice-Hall, Englewood Cliffs, NJ.

Boehm, P. W., McClean, R. K. and Urfrig, D. B. (1975) Some experience with automated aids to the design of large-scale reliable software, *IEEE Transactions on Software Engineering*, **SE-1**(1), 125–33.

Boman, M., Bubenko, Jr, J. A., Johanneson, P. and Wangler, B. (1997) *Conceptual Modelling*, Prentice-Hall, London.

Crinnion, J. (1991) *Evolutionary Systems Development: A Practical Guide to the Use of Prototyping within a Structured Systems Methodology*, Pitman, London.

Davis, G. B. (1974) *Management Information Systems: Conceptual Foundations, Structure and Development*, McGraw-Hill, London.

de Marco, T. (1982) *Software Systems Development*, Yourdon Press, New York.

Fagan, M. E. (1976) Design and code inspections to reduce errors in program development, *IBM Systems Journal*, **15**(3), 182–211.

Finkelstein, C. (1989) *An Introduction to Information Engineering*, Addison-Wesley, Wokingham.

Gane, C. and Sarson, T. (1979) *Structured Systems Analysis*, Prentice-Hall, Englewood Cliffs, NJ.

Gilb, T. (1988) *Principles of Software Engineering Management*, Addison-Wesley, Wokingham.

Hawryszkiewycz, I. T. (1988) *Introduction to Systems Analysis and Design*, Prentice-Hall, London.

Howard, P. and Potter, C. (1994) *CASE & Methods Based Development Tools: An Evaluation and Comparison*, ButlerBloor Ltd, Challenge House, Sherwood Drive, Bletchley, Milton Keynes, MK3 6DP.

KPMG (1990) *Runaway Computer Systems – A Business Issue for the 1990s*. Available from KPMG Peat Marwick McLintock, 1 Puddle Dock, Blackfriars, London EC4V 3PD.

Longworth, G. (1989) *Getting the System You Want: A User's Guide to SSADM*, NCC Publications, Manchester.

Nijssen, G. M. and Halpin, T. A. (1989) *Conceptual Schema and Relational Database Design – a Fact Oriented Approach*, Prentice-Hall, London.

Pressman, R. S. (1992) *Software Engineering – A Practitioner's Approach*, McGraw-Hill, New York.

Rock-Evans, R. and Hales, K. (1990) *Reverse Engineering: Markets, Methods and Tools*, Ovum Ltd., 7 Rathbone Street, London W1P 1AF.

Swanson, E. B. and Beath, C. M. (1989) *Maintaining Information Systems in Organizations*, Wiley, Chichester.

7

Requirements determination

Introduction

Requirements determination is the least well-defined phase in the systems development process. One reason for this is that it is the least technical, and therefore the most organization dependent. This means that procedures and products are likely to vary greatly from organization to organization. In addition, many organizations are realizing the advantages that result from strategic planning, which analyses the information needs of an organization and produces an information systems plan to match. If a strategic plan exists, then some of the early activities described in this chapter will have already been done.

Another reason lies in the nature of the requirements themselves, which, as discussed in the previous chapter, are by no means as clearly defined and fixed as is commonly supposed. Requirements frequently change once systems development is under way, for a variety of reasons, and, in addition, it is often difficult to be sure that the system whose requirements are being obtained is the best system. Different ways of coping with these problems cause differences between organizations in the way in which requirements determination is carried out.

Four stages frequently found in requirements determination are:

1. Problem definition
2. Feasibility study
3. Requirements acquisition
4. Requirements modelling

We will use a case study, based on Eurobells⌂, to demonstrate the use of the interview method as well as the iterative nature of requirements acquisition and to illustrate the application of the OMNIS model to requirements modelling.

Problem definition

REASONS FOR A SYSTEM

The original idea for a desired system often originates in a *system proposal*, which is typically an informal document concerned only with system scope and its justification. A system proposal may originate to achieve one or more objectives:

1. To solve a problem
2. To take advantage of an opportunity
3. To respond to a directive

To illustrate objective 1, in Case Study 1 in Chapter 4 a rather informal manual system may have existed for some time, recording the customers who buy fish on a daily basis. This has meant laboriously adding daily totals (many of which were incomplete and missing) to obtain monthly totals for individual customers. Also, daily totals were often exaggerated and incomplete, and it was felt that a computer-based system would help accuracy and provide information not available before.

Objective 2 concerns expanding or improving organizational performance, for example offering customers access to organizational databases so that they get a better service. An example of objective 3 is where legislation such as the Data Protection Act may necessitate changes to the way customer information is stored or accessed.

These are rather abstract and high-level objectives, and a proposed system should normally describe how it will contribute towards the efficiency or effectiveness of the organization. Projects may be undertaken for five general reasons (Senn, 1989), which we may classify as follows:

- *Efficiency improvements*:
  1. *Capability*. This concerns an increase in processing speed, volume or faster information retrieval, compared to manual equivalents.
  2. *Communication*. This is concerned with communication both within and between organizations, mainly to increase the transmission speed of messages, for example EDI or electronic funds transfer (EFT). Also covered is integration of business areas.
- *Effectiveness improvements*:
  3. *Control*. This aims to improve management controlling functions, and includes procedures for greater accuracy and consistency, and improved security.
  4. *Cost*. This covers cost monitoring for labour, goods or overheads and their relationship to departments or individuals.
  5. *Competitive advantage*. Factors here are locking in customers, locking out competitors, improving arrangements with suppliers and developing new products.

Projects concerned with communication may contribute towards effectiveness as well as efficiency.

A system proposal usually originates from a section manager, senior executive or analyst, and should not take any longer than a few days to compile. After the problem definition report has been prepared, which is generally in a standard organizational format, it has to be accepted by a committee in order for it to pass to the feasibility study stage, which is an exercise that consumes more resources than problem definition.

Project selection committees are usually one of three types: (a) a steering committee, which usually contains a majority of senior departmental managers, (b) an information systems committee, whose membership is usually drawn from the computer department, or (c) a user group committee, a departmental committee consisting mainly of users together with department computer specialists. If the organization has a strategic plan, as mentioned in the introduction, then the relationship of the project to that plan should be determined here.

REPORT

The form and content of the problem definition report will vary between organizations, but its contents are typically:

1. A statement of the problem to be solved and its significance, or a justification for the system.
2. The suggested solution, how an information system will help and the benefits expected.
3. The scope of the desired system.

The system may be a simple upgrade to an existing system or a multimillion pound organization-wide system involving a major change in hardware supplier. The detail required in reports in these early stages will obviously depend on the size of the system.

Feasibility study

The committee will have narrowed down the number of potential projects to pass a proposal to the *feasibility study* stage. The aim here is to evaluate the feasibility of the proposal, involving an analysis of the problem and the determination of the best solution within the context of the organizational situation. It is usual for several alternative solutions to be prepared from a proposal, usually ranging in the scope of their functionality; that is, in the size of the proposed system.

This stage will prepare a high-level set of non-functional, as well as functional, requirements for each of the alternative systems. Functional requirements concern the functions of the system; that is, what the system will do. Non-functional requirements concern, for example, resource restrictions on the system, such as the maximum number of users and factors such as future expandability, security and reliability.

To pass this stage and to go through to systems development, a proposal must demonstrate (Kendall and Kendall, 1988):

1. That it will help attain organization objectives
2. Economic feasibility
3. Technical feasibility
4. Operational feasibility

ORGANIZATION OBJECTIVES

A topic that may be investigated here concerns the nature of the problem asserted in the problem definition. Has the problem been defined correctly? Another issue that may arise concerns the motivation for the proposal, which may be due to internal organizational power battles, prestige of the computer department or similar reasons.

If the organization has a strategic plan, the proposal should be checked for conformity to this. For example, an organization may have a five-year plan for IT development, which has an overall budget and has, as a priority, horizontal integration over different departments, such as, for example, sales, marketing and manufacturing. Another element in a strategy might be to give priority to systems for automating areas that are still largely manual. The priority of the system as a whole, and different parts of it, should be described.

ECONOMIC FEASIBILITY

The aim here is to estimate the costs required for alternative systems and set them against the expected benefits. Obviously, a successful system will aim to benefit the organization! The types of alternatives that are frequently considered are the placing of the manual/computer boundary, as some tasks may benefit more than others from being computerized, and non-functional requirements such as the time delay between the real world and different parts of the information system, which may be batch, on-line or real-time. Such decisions will also have an impact on technical feasibility, discussed below.

The systems also have their costs estimated in terms of the basic resources of money, people and time. For example, the following must be costed:

1. Systems development, involving, for example, analysts and programmers for systems development, or consultancy costs
2. User time for requirements, testing and training
3. Hardware and software acquisition

To set against the costs, the expected benefits should be quantified, for example, reduced costs, improved customer service or a predicted increase in business.

This area is rather unsatisfactorily served at the moment, because apart from transaction processing systems, which may result in quantifiable efficiency increases, it is very difficult to predict with any certainty whether a given system will in fact benefit the organization, as many factors are involved in system success. This point will be developed later in Chapter 13. In addition, on the costs side, the cost for maintenance (which may be several times the cost of developing the system) is rarely included.

TECHNICAL FEASIBILITY

Technical feasibility is concerned with determining whether a solution can be implemented on existing technology. If it can, then current technical resources may require upgrading or adding to. Some solutions might require the use of very new equipment or software that have not been integrated before.

Non-functional requirements are taken into consideration here, such as on- or off-line processing, maximum response times for user–computer interaction, estimated hourly or daily frequency of transactions, maximum record and file sizes for storage, networking loads and typical numbers of users at one time. In addition, requirements for system expandability, security, data archiving and reliability are considered.

OPERATIONAL FEASIBILITY

This investigates factors such as the likely reaction of organizational employees and union representatives to job and other proposed organizational changes. The main aim is to assess whether the solution will operate and be used after installation. For example, if users are happy with their current system and see no need to change, there might be a high degree of resistance to the new proposal.

Relevant factors here concern whether the solution has general management support and whether or not proposed system users have been involved with the development of the proposal. In general, a project without management support is unlikely to succeed, and projects with a high degree of user involvement are more likely to be acceptable to the users.

OUTPUT FROM THE FEASIBILITY STUDY

A problem of the feasibility study is that many questions cannot be properly answered at such an early stage of the project. In addition, a key factor in successful development which is not covered is the availability of sufficiently experienced systems development staff. In general, the study often adopts a rough and ready approach, whereby it rejects proposals that do not fit in with the organization strategy, that appear technically impossible or improbable, where the cost–benefit equation looks wrong or where no user seems to want the system.

The study is typically carried out by analysts, who interview proposed users and review documentation; they will produce a report with recommendations. The report should contain a description of the functional requirements, as well as the important non-functional requirements, for the proposed system, and should cover the four points concerned with organizational objectives and feasibility discussed above. A recommendation might be to commission software from a software house, in preference to in-house systems development, for cost reasons. A recommendation with an operational reservation might be to install a proposed system in two stages, a pilot system followed by the full system.

PROJECT PLAN

For successful proposals, a plan for the systems development project, including a budget, time-scale and an estimate of different kinds of personnel required, will usually be based on the feasibility study. Project planning is a wide topic, which we cannot develop here, but an important element comprises a set of detailed activities for the project, usually broken down into a hierarchy. For example, the top level will often be in terms of the sequence and duration of the systems development phases that will be required. These may vary considerably from project to project as, for example, prototyping or incremental development may be used. Major deliverables will be identified for each phase and the extent of validation or quality control will usually be set.

The next level down will refine each phase into a set of ideal activities, based upon the resources (financial costs, person-days, elapsed time) available. Budget limitations are crucial here, especially when considering project team costs such as salaries or fees. Diagrammatic aids may be used, such as the Gantt chart, which is a bar chart showing the duration scheduled for activities and whether or not they have been completed. The PERT diagram is used for showing the sequence of activities and their scheduled duration, and is also used to derive the critical path of those activities whose completion is critical to on-time project completion.

Requirements acquisition

When the proposed system has been approved as a result of the feasibility study, the detailed requirements of the users are then acquired. We shall discuss the four traditional *requirements acquisition* methods and later present a case study resulting in the production of the statement of requirements.

OBSERVATION

Observation may focus either on an individual's behaviour or the physical environment of the individual. Observation of an individual's behaviour consists of observing how that individual operates as part of an existing system, so as to find out, for example, the main inputs and outputs or the type of information that individuals are using. Observation of a physical environment is used to make inferences about the relative power (and hence information requirement) of an individual. For example, a manager might effectively delegate important decisions to a subordinate not shown on an organization chart.

This method is used chiefly where information about the system cannot be obtained by another method, or where conflict or doubt about the system is apparent from other sources and observation can help to confirm a particular issue.

A variety of techniques may be used. These include participative observation, where you may ask individuals in a system questions about some part of its functioning. Another technique is to avoid being present in the system, in case you affect its behaviour, by using a technique such as video or tape recording. For observation of the physical environment, an approach termed STROBE (structured observation of the environment) may be used (Kendall and Kendall, 1988).

ANALYSIS OF EXISTING SYSTEM

This method analyses available data concerning a system. It may be divided into quantitative data, consisting of, for example, output report formats, input documents, program listings with comments, procedure manuals and reports such as financial statements. Qualitative data includes documents concerning organizational culture, for example annual reports, publicity documents, memos and noticeboards. An organization is likely to be centralized and authoritarian where there are many notices signed by senior managers setting rules or giving warnings. In contrast, an organization with noticeboards advertising support groups and requesting employee participation is likely to be less centralized. This may help to decide whether management reports should be directed only to senior management or to lower-level management also.

ANALYSIS OF DESIRED SYSTEM DOCUMENTATION

By desired system documentation we mean documents that state a part of the requirements. They are generally in a narrative form, giving an outline only of the sort of system required. As such, they may give information about how the parts of the desired system are to work together. Such documents include strategic plans, problem definition reports and feasibility study reports.

INTERVIEW AND QUESTIONNAIRE

Interview

A frequently used method of acquiring requirements is to question the user in an interview. This is popular with users as they can, for example, express their plan for a desired system in their own language, and they can control the amount of time the interview takes.

There are five steps in interview preparation: read background material (understand organization), establish interview objectives (what kind of information you want), decide who to interview (which users are important), prepare the interviewee (schedule appointment and interview length) and decide on question types and structure. Closed questions limit the response options available to the respondent, while open questions leave all possible response options open. Three structures for interviews are the pyramid, funnel and diamond structures.

A pyramid structure begins with questions that are very specific, leading up to general questions nearer the interview end, for example beginning with 'I understand there's a . . . problem with your system for bell tuning' and ending with 'Tell me what you think of the different approaches to bell tuning'. The pyramid structure is used if the interviewee does not seem keen to address the topic and it is necessary to lead up to it.

The funnel structure is the inverse of the pyramid structure: you begin generally by leading up to the specific points, for example 'Has the development team done a good job?' leading to 'I heard that you experience delays with . . .'. This approach is useful for putting interviewees at ease or for eliciting a large amount of detail.

Finally, the diamond structure combines the two, beginning with specific points, examining general issues and then concluding with specific issues.

Questionnaire

This is typically used where there exists a need to gather information from a number of people in an organization. It may be used where relevant people are widely dispersed, where many people are involved with a project or where exploratory work is necessary before interviews begin to, for example, sense problems.

A problem with a questionnaire is that users may find difficulty in writing down their requirements for open response questions, the process takes them longer than in an interview and the questionnaire may simply not ask the necessary questions. The immediacy of an interview can identify problem areas or conflicts in requirements right away. The design, use and analysis of a questionnaire may require some time.

On the other hand, a problem with the interview is that of assimilation. This involves not only recording all that a user says but understanding what is meant. Tape recording can be used but transcription is a tedious and error-prone task.

SUMMARY

Not all of these methods are appropriate in all problem situations. For example, system documentation can only be considered as a source of knowledge if there is an existing system. Observation may not be possible if staff are not to be disturbed. The methods are basic methods and may be used at any point within the systems development process. The fact that they are termed requirements acquisition methods is a relic of the times when it was believed that requirements from the user were only obtained in the early phase. Although most requirements should be obtained here, more detailed requirements are also required in subsequent phases.

Requirements modelling

Traditional methods tend to use computer-oriented analysis and specification techniques, such as data flow diagrams, to be discussed in later chapters, which are not suited for user validation and which show only a partial view of the requirements.

Problems with requirements determination

PRODUCTIVITY PROBLEM

This problem is due to the assumption that requirements are an objective set of facts, that they are all known at the beginning of systems development and that they are fixed and will not change. Another assumption is that development resources can be estimated in advance.

Changing requirements

Requirements change, for the following reasons:

1. *Users change their minds*
   (a) Users refine their requirement by interacting with the investigative process that constitutes systems development. What seemed a good idea when the project was proposed seems naïve or limiting after a while. Users may learn more about their organization or more about the capability of the technology, by interaction with developers, by thinking over problems or by coming into contact with other users. In other words, the process of defining requirements for an information system often leads to changes in the way information is used or in the types of information required, thus creating a circular relationship between requirements and the information system (Orman, 1987).

   For example, an initial requirement, consisting of a simple stock control application, monitoring levels of products and supplies, might expand into a system supporting the sales and accounts departments. This may occur when users realize that each transaction, consisting of the sale of a product or the purchase of

supplies, can be recorded, with information such as supplier, customer, price, date and so on.

(b) The requirement may have been fluid at the start, perhaps subject
to disagreements between users or at the mercy of political forces.
It is common for different users to disagree about requirements,
especially where information is to be shared between different departments. The prevailing view at the beginning of the project may
change as users resolve their differences. In addition, system requirements may be largely determined by constantly shifting political
pressure involving users and managers. Users thus only rarely possess
an objective requirement which can simply be tapped by the application of the appropriate acquisition method.

For example, in Eurobells⌂, the accounts department may have
a rule, to safeguard cash flow, that customer credit limits may not
exceed £10 000, but the sales department, to encourage sales, frequently lets customers go above this limit for a limited period.

An example of political pressures might be where different department managers may be competing to be the first to have an on-line
system. Depending on the waxing and waning of their arguments
and influence, the position may change several times.

2. *External events may occur that change the requirements.* Many systems
take up to two or more years to develop, and during this time there may
be changes to legislation (for example, tax changes), the organization
may merge with another and be required to integrate systems, or the
original competitive impetus for the system may have passed.

Another possibility is that more attractive (on cost or facilities grounds)
hardware or software may become available during the lifetime of the
project, or the planned hardware and software environment may become
unobtainable or unattractive.

3. *Implementation may not be feasible.* There may be explicit or implicit
non-functional requirements, for example, concerned with system response
time under typical transaction loads, that are revealed by the implementation and testing phase to be infeasible. This may necessitate a return
to the requirements phase.

The conclusion is that obtaining requirements is a process that must be
iterative, and requirements acquisition will take place several times before
users have a requirement definite enough with which to proceed. Having to
repeat activities will cause delays and increase costs. However, external changes
and hidden implementation problems may undermine existing requirements
at any stage of development. Such changes increase the problems of project
control.

Poor project control

Experience has shown that it is difficult to estimate necessary project resources and keep track of how resources are being used once a project begins.

4. *Poor project control.* There is an assumption that project resources, including development costs, costs of buying hardware and software, the number and quality of individuals required in the development team and project duration, can all be estimated at the start of the project in the feasibility study.

   However, although there are some rules of thumb for estimating implementation time, for example, using lines of code, there are no such metrics that may be used at the beginning of a project, and very few heuristics are available. In addition, standard practices such as not including predicted maintenance costs in estimated system development costs may be misleading.

Project control thus proceeds with much reliance on personal experience and intuition, and as users are usually pressing for early delivery dates at the lowest cost, resource estimates are often overly optimistic. Such estimates are usually revised several times as the project proceeds.

QUALITY PROBLEMS

Traditional methods of requirements determination discussed earlier may be considered to be neutral with respect to the application, as they are very general, aimed for use in any situation. They therefore assume that requirements can be successfully obtained with no knowledge of the organization or of the application. However, this assumption may produce a poor quality system, as:

1. *Methods address the wrong problem by ignoring organizational or application knowledge that is part of the requirements.* Such knowledge concerns factors that are critical for organizational success, such as important goals and activities, structure (roles and organizational units), function (work procedures) or knowledge about the particular application area, for example knowledge of industrial best practice.

   It is assumed that the user knows best, and that the developer does not need expert domain knowledge. But it is becoming clearer that knowledge of this type is possessed by experienced developers, in intuitive form, and does help in determining requirements.

   For example, knowledge concerning the relative importance of the stock room functions to the rest of Eurobells⌂, and the level of computer-related training and attitudes among stock room staff, may be helpful in deciding on the requirements for the case study discussed above.

2. *Wider social or psychological factors are neglected.* Organizational behaviour, such as conflict between organizational units, attitudes of staff and organizational politics should be taken into account to ensure that a computer system will fit into its social context. Qualitative measures of success or failure standards, concerning factors such as usability and acceptability of the eventual system may not be included in the requirements.

3. *Errors are made in modelling the requirements.* Methods often employ inadequate techniques and languages that only address part of the requirements, or may not be accompanied by a systematic method to guide the developer, instead relying upon developer intuition. For example, it is common for narrative, unstructured techniques to be used, with the associated problems of ambiguity and redundancy.

Owing to the communications gap between user and developer, misunderstandings about requirements are bound to occur, and in general there are few requirements modelling languages that correspond to the ways in which users view their organization. In addition, validating requirements effectively with users is generally poor, who usually have to resort to scanning lengthy requirements documents and imagining what the eventual system will be like.

It is likely that users will hold differing viewpoints of requirements, as an organization is not an objective 'reality'. This is especially true if requirements are changing. Such viewpoints, which may be partially or totally inconsistent, should ideally be detected and highlighted, but they are often ignored or merged in such a way that satisfies none of the users.

Requirements Engineering

Requirements Engineering (RE) is a term applied to recent research directed at the problems in requirements determination (El Emam and Madhavji, 1995). The chief areas addressed by RE are the requirements acquisition and modelling stages, as shown in Fig. 7.1. The figure also shows that a new validation stage, requirements validation, is present in RE, taking account of experience which shows that iteration and validation are required to get requirements right.

Some recent RE approaches, aimed at different problems, will be briefly described. Very few, if any, of these approaches have been exposed to a significant amount of real use and they should therefore be regarded primarily as research approaches. They are grouped by the RE stage they most concern.

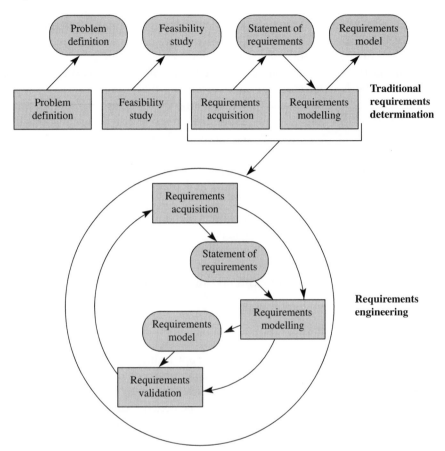

Figure 7.1 Requirements determination and requirements engineering.

Recent RE approaches

REQUIREMENTS MODELLING

How to model

Natural language processing. Natural language processing (NLP) approaches aim to improve requirements modelling by providing software to assist the process of transforming the natural language statement of requirements into the requirements model. For example, Knight and Flynn (1992) and Ishihara *et al.* (1993) describe how a model of organizational objects may be built from a statement of requirements.

NLP approaches are centred on a lexicon, a highly structured knowledge base containing the allowable terms in the statement of requirements; there may also be information which helps to establish the meaning of phrases and sentences. In addition, there are knowledge bases defining the structure of the target requirements models. The software is based on a grammar, that is a theory of the structure of natural languages, and it analyses the requirements using the knowledge bases to produce the output. The structure of the lexicon usually is determined to some extent by the grammar.

This type of approach aims to reduce the communications gap between user and developer and also to reduce the errors which occur in modelling due to the intuitive nature of the process. There are several difficulties, however, one being that the languages in which the models are expressed are usually more suited for the later, analysis phase rather than for the requirements phase. In addition, there are theoretical and practical difficulties in building a lexicon that is sophisticated enough to cope with the wide range of possible natural language statements, in a variety of domains, especially given the inherent ambiguity in natural language.

A wide range of grammars also means that research in this area is not very cohesive. More research is needed to take the NLP approach forward from small, very restricted applications, and Ryan (1993) provides a critique of the area.

What to model

Design decisions and goals. While NLP approaches are aimed at 'how' to carry out requirements modelling, Greenspan and Feblowitz (1993) are concerned with 'what' is modelled. They consider the main idea of requirements modelling is '. . . to capture assumptions, goals and design decisions about behaviour, function and structure of existing and proposed systems, in the context of knowledge about the system environment and other domain knowledge'.

They outline a high-level generic type of organization they term a service providing enterprise (SPE) which is viewed in terms of four models: the services, workflow, organization and systems models. The services model is not a definition of behaviour but a statement of the SPE and its contractual-level customer relationships. The workflow model defines the abstract activities carried out by the SPE, incorporating quality targets, for example friendliness or cost-effectiveness. The organization model describes roles and organizational units while the systems models define requirements for the information systems in the SPE that carry out detailed organizational activities.

The first three models, expressed in a semi-structured language, thus describe the organization on an abstract level, and the intention is that the requirements for a particular information system should be consistent with these models, which may have to be built or which may already exist.

Yu and Mylopoulos (1994) focus on dependency relationships between agents (actors and roles). Using a formal language, a model is built of relationships between organizational agents in terms of goal, task and resource dependencies. This shows, for example, goals and tasks that are to be achieved and the means of achieving them, and it is intended to guide requirements or select requirements options.

The above proposals in effect establish a hierarchical structure within a requirements model, with goals, dependencies and assumptions on a (possibly global) high level and requirements for individual systems on a lower level. The high-level information, emphasizing *why* agents perform the activities that they do, often contains quality indicators for evaluating the final system and is usually omitted in traditional requirements modelling.

This may help requirements address the right problem or expose inconsistencies between requirements and higher level goals. For example, high-level organizational goals (such as an organizational mission statement) may be used to check aspects of the requirements for proposed information systems. Traceability mechanisms which explicitly link requirements to the higher level make design decisions visible, also useful for later re-engineering. Van Lamsweerde *et al.* (1995) describe a language, KAOS, which integrates both levels of requirements modelling.

However, the scope of what should be modelled is difficult to decide (should all organizational goals be modelled?), the higher level needs to be continually updated and the modelling languages currently used are difficult for users to validate.

Non-functional requirements. Requirements modelling is also widened by considering non-functional requirements (NFRs), for example performance, confidentiality and security, traditionally viewed as global properties of a system. These have been only informally addressed in the past. Nixon (1993) describes a modelling framework for NFRs expressed in a formal language and shows how to model performance goals: for example responsiveness (time) and storage (space) goals. These can represent design alternatives and may be used to influence a design to be consistent with these requirements. Harrison and Barnard (1993) describe how the usability of a system may be formally represented at the requirements stage, while Wright *et al.* (1994) model human error tolerance requirements as system properties. NFR modelling addresses the second quality problem described above, but it is not clear how NFRs may be validated with users.

REQUIREMENTS VALIDATION

In general, requirements validation approaches help to bridge the user–developer communications gap and allow changes to be incorporated in requirements, for example where the user is unsure about the requirements at the beginning of a project.

Natural language processing

The validation stage may also be assisted by NLP, and Wu and Flynn (1995) describe the software assistant NALABA, which compares a model of organizational business rules against an English language statement of requirements from which the rules have been manually derived, reporting missing, duplicate or inconsistent rules.

From the direction of generating natural language as opposed to its understanding, Salek *et al.* (1994) describe REVIEW, which is a natural language generation system for paraphrasing a model expressed in a formal language. As users face difficulties in understanding such models, REVIEW will generate English sentences from the model.

Prototyping

The CARD system (Ohnishi and Agusa, 1993) is an RE environment which allows for the modelling, verification and prototyping of a set of requirements. When executing requirements, the prototyper asks for control and data flow data to be input and, at a branch, asks which route to take. The emphasis in prototyping is on showing the data flow through the system.

Prototyping is a valuable aid to user validation, but it often shows only a limited part of the computer system; this is compounded by the fact that there is not much detail given on the requirements level. In addition, current prototyping tools do not show the impact of the computer system on the projected information system or on the wider organization.

Inspection

Structured validation sessions with users based on small 'chunks' of requirements, termed scenarios, are described by Gough *et al.* (1995).

Explanation

Gulla *et al.* (1994) describe PPP, an integrated software environment for modelling and validation. A conceptual modelling approach is taken to modelling using a structured language and three techniques are used for validating the resulting conceptual models: complexity reduction, prototyping and explanation. The complexity reduction component produces abstracted views of the model, the prototype component can be exercised (that is, executed) and the explanation component allows users to request individualized explanations to clarify model properties or to explain, for example, why an error message occurred during prototyping.

Verification

Easterbrook and Nuseibeh (1995) describe, using a mix of formal and structured languages, how a set of requirements may be partitioned into viewpoints and then consistency rules defined between viewpoints. A software tool partially implements consistency checking and documents the results of the checks in each relevant viewpoint, providing a later record when inconsistencies need to be resolved. Inconsistency detection can be used as a tool by the developer in a pre-validation stage to select relevant parts of the requirements for users in validation sessions.

This addresses an aspect of the third quality problem described above and may provide a useful aid to focus requirements validation. However, its success is highly dependent on the extent to which important, non-trivial inconsistencies that arise in the application may be detected and traced to their origin by the software tool. Work in this area has not been very successful for real applications in the past.

REQUIREMENTS ACQUISITION

Domain knowledge and reuse

Domain knowledge is knowledge about the particular domain or application area to which the required information system belongs, and this type of knowledge may be (re)used to assist requirements acquisition, as the developer often has insufficient knowledge of the domain.

Ryan and Matthews (1993) describe the ReqColl system, which contains hierarchically organized generic knowledge of application areas (the example provided concerns the inventory area). The knowledge, stored in a knowledge base as entity and action types, provides a framework to help developers acquire the requirements for particular inventory applications. It is argued that, similarly, experienced developers gradually accumulate mental design plans which they use to solve recurring problems.

User problem statements are translated into a conceptual graph form and compared by software against the conceptual graph in which the generic knowledge is expressed. Either an exact match, close match or no match may be found. A match of either type means that some part of the generic knowledge may be reused. If a new component has to be defined for a particular application this is stored in the knowledge base for future reuse.

Similar approaches exist where the level of abstraction and scope of the generic knowledge varies. Maiden and Sutcliffe (1993) describe a method based on 35 abstractions which aim to cover all domains, while Castano and De Antonellis (1993) store application-independent conceptual schema abstractions.

This approach to requirements acquisition has promise, and it may help requirements address the right problem, but there are major difficulties in conceptualizing the level of abstraction at which domain knowledge is most effective and then populating this level with the required knowledge. User interface and search matching problems also exist in accessing and retrieving only the knowledge relevant for any particular application. It is not clear as to whether the scenario of use is that of a user or a developer using such a system.

MODELLING LANGUAGES

A variety of different types of languages have been proposed for requirements engineering, mainly to alleviate the third quality problem discussed above, and an important characteristic is the formal or informal nature of the language. A language may be (a) *formal*, with precisely defined syntax and semantics; (b) *structured*, for example a diagrammatic language with a defined syntax; (c) *semi-structured*, for example OMNIS which categorizes natural language expressions; or (d) *informal*, for example unrestricted natural language.

Jackson and Zave (1993) propose a formal, logic-based language which focuses on the organizational domain, while Lefering (1993), in the IPSEN project, emphasizes the integration of steps to map downwards from the requirements to the implementation level, using structured languages for the requirements model. In the CARD project, Ohnishi and Agusa (1993) use a semi-structured language, termed the requirements frame model. Van Schouwen *et al.* (1993) describe a formal language used for specifying requirements for domains that can be described with predictive or normative models; systems that implement such requirements are often embedded real-time systems. Kent *et al.* (1993) describe a logic-based language which focuses on the declarative specification of behaviour with time constraints.

Regnell *et al.* (1995) describe the UORE language, providing improvements to the use case approach, which defines scenarios of system usage from the perspective of a single agent, using a mixture of semi-structured and structured languages that may be suitable for users to understand. Leite and Oliveira (1995) describe a semi-structured language, intended to be understood by users, that has facilities for recording and tracing model changes.

Requirements are often vague, expressed in high-level terms and incomplete, and these characteristics do not suit a formal language. Another problem of using formal languages on the requirements level is that without validation assistance users cannot understand models expressed in such languages and so cannot validate them. Although users are more likely to be able to understand models expressed in less formal languages, there is no agreement about the characteristics of these languages, such as level of detail or scope.

Case study 2 – Eurobells⌂ stock room

This case study shows how we might proceed in requirements acquisition and modelling to obtain information about a problem situation in Eurobells⌂, a feasibility study having already taken place. A condensed account of an investigation will be given, followed by the resulting statement of requirements, and then OMNIS, a model which you have already met in Chapter 4, will be used for the requirements modelling stage.

Requirements acquisition – case study 2

PROJECT ASSIGNMENT

Orelie Gallo is a consultant analyst in the information technology department at the consulting firm Spiel-Jouet-Ludus. She has recently been promoted and is at this moment being told about her next project by Evelyn Ludus, the IS director.

Tuesday 13 October, 9.32 a.m.

'The stock room manager at Eurobells⌂ has a problem, Orelie,' Evelyn Ludus said. Orelie looked expectant. 'They need a system to take care of their stock control. The Finance Director has been on to me as well – but don't tell the stock room that.'

'What's the problem?' Orelie enquired.

'They're losing money', Evelyn said, wryly. 'They've got a lot of old bells down there but they're not sure how many. They never seem to have the right type when they get a rush order, even a normal order!'

'What do you want me to do?' asked Orelie.

'Go down there and talk to them,' Evelyn smiled.

'Who shall I contact?' Orelie wanted to know, 'Shall I start with Ken Campana?'

'Yes, start with Ken', Evelyn looked into the mirror. 'Ken's a good manager, and he'll help you to find out how things work. He's the one who wants changes – he just took over recently. This is what we've got.' Evelyn handed Orelie a folder. 'In here you'll find an overview of the main departments at Eurobells⌂, together with a sequence diagram for processing customer orders, and the feasibility study Eurobells⌂ have completed. It's not much, is it?'

'It's not,' Orelie was looking at the diagram.

'Spend a few days there,' Evelyn told her. 'Get to find out things. Talk to Ken, use any method you like. Produce a statement of requirements outlining a plan for a simple computer-based stock control system. Get Ken's approval and bring the plan back to me. Then we'll cost it. OK?'

Orelie had already gone by the time Evelyn's gaze returned to the room from the mirror. She went to her office and opened the folder. It contained a feasibility study report, a description of the functions of departments in Eurobells⌂ and a sequence of processes through the departments for the production cycle and for when an order was received. A diagram was also attached. She began to read the background material, shown in Fig. 7.2 and Tables 7.1 to 7.3.

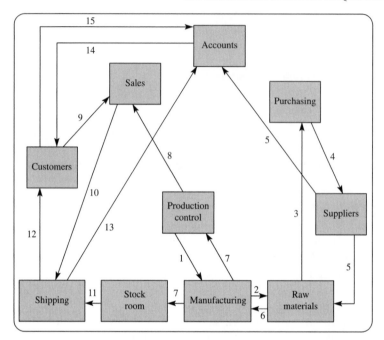

Figure 7.2 Sequence of processes through Eurobells⌂ departments on receipt of an order.

THE FIRST INTERVIEW AT EUROBELLS⌂

Wednesday 14 October, 11.05 a.m. Ken Campana's office

'Yes, you're right, the order we processed last week had to await manufacture. In the ideal situation of course there will be sufficient finished products in stock to meet any order. It is necessary for speedy dispatch to keep the stock levels for each product as high as possible.'

Orelie Gallo was having her first interview with Ken Campana at Eurobells⌂. She had assimilated the departmental description and had decided to use the interview method with Ken Campana to find out more about the problems in the stock room. She had scheduled the 45-minute interview yesterday afternoon.

Table 7.1 Eurobells⌂ feasibility study report – stock room

Objectives	Improved efficiency of some or all stock room activities so that stock levels are maintained at a minimum level
Technical feasibility	Any computer solution must be compatible with current Eurobells⌂ hardware and software strategy
Operational feasibility	Company policy is that there should be no staff redundancies
Economic feasibility	The proposed system budget is £150K capital and £20K recurrent annually

Table 7.2 Description of Eurobells⌂ departments

The Eurobells⌂ organization relies for its income on the process involved in making its bells and clappers. The functions of the various departments are:

Accounts	Deal with Eurobells⌂ finances including customer and supplier accounts, invoices, staff payroll
Sales	Have direct contact with customers through salespeople. They are the customer's link to the company
Purchasing	This is the department that buys raw materials from the suppliers. It is their job to buy as efficiently as possible
Manufacturing	The department that turns raw materials into bells and clappers, and assembles them into products
Production control	It has information regarding current stock levels, orders from customers, staffing figures in manufacturing and so on. They tell manufacturing what and when to manufacture
Stock room	A store room where products and raw materials are kept prior to shipping and manufacture
Shipping	This department packs the products (bells, clappers) into containers and sends to customers by road, rail, sea or air

Table 7.3 Sequence of processes through Eurobells⌂ departments

The sequence of processes through these departments for the production cycle and when a customer order is received is described below (see Fig. 7.1 also):

1. Production control tell manufacturing to make a quantity of bells and clappers.
2. Manufacturing tell the stock room (raw materials) the raw bronze it requires.
3. There is a shortage of raw bronze, so the stock room (raw materials) tells purchasing (note that production control may know and may tell purchasing themselves).
4. Purchasing order the necessary raw materials from suppliers, having chosen the best supplier in terms of cost and delivery time.
5. Suppliers send the raw materials to the stock room (raw materials) and the invoice to accounts.
6. The stock room passes the raw materials to manufacturing.
7. Manufacturing makes the bells and clappers, assembles them into products, sends the products to the stock room and tells production control what products were made.
8. Production control tell sales what products are available.
9. The customer orders 5 tenor bells and 20 soprano bells. Sales receive the order and check:
   (a) Does the customer do business with us?
   (b) Is this customer's credit OK?
10. Sales tell shipping that the products are in the stock room.
11. Shipping obtain the products from the stock room and pack them into containers.
12. The products are sent to the customer by shipping.
13. Shipping tell accounts.
14. Accounts produce an invoice and send it to the customer.
15. The customer sends money to accounts.

'But there are two main problems with this approach, aren't there?' pointed out Orelie.

Ken looked apprehensive, then relaxed. 'You're right there!' he shouted. 'First, there's too much space required. That raises our costs – heat, light, we have to rent space sometimes. Secondly,' he pointed at the laptop on his desk, 'it's costing the company a fortune! Look at my estimate of the value of the current stock. There's just too much capital tied up in unsold goods.'

Orelie joined Ken behind the desk and examined the figures on the screen. She made some notes. 'So,' Ken continued, 'we want to keep stock levels as low as possible to minimize the problems. However, as I guess you also know, keeping very low stock levels causes delays in filling orders and possible loss of customers.'

'That's right,' Orelie agreed. 'Each company therefore has to decide on a balance between very high stock and very low stock. What can happen is that a company can choose a stock level for each product which is a danger level. That's the level below which the stock should not be allowed to drop. But it can be complicated,' she continued, 'as the danger level will vary from product to product, depending on its popularity.'

'And in our field,' chimed in Ken, 'there's also the problem of seasonal factors. Christmas and Easter are our biggest times, and so the danger level will vary throughout the year.'

'What sort of control system do you have right now?' Orelie asked.

Ken looked defiant and then he laughed resoundingly. 'Well,' he said, 'it's like this. Come over to the window.' Orelie walked over to the open casement. 'What do you see?' asked Ken.

'There's a lot of packing cases,' she exclaimed.

'Those are the bells and clappers that we're not sure if anyone wants because we don't know what's in them,' Ken commented sarcastically.

'What are those teams of people doing with notebooks?' Orelie wanted to know.

'That's your control system,' Ken laughed. 'The problem, right, is the problem of monitoring stock levels in order that stock lows and highs can be highlighted,' Ken stated, staring at the shuffling teams. 'We want to keep an up-to-date view of stock levels of individual products. Well, the way it's done here is that there's meant to be a periodic stock check by clerks, who traipse around the store room counting products. The only thing is that it's a full-time job now! Our problem, and I hope you can help us here, Orelie,' Ken suddenly became more business-like, 'is that the current control system, if we may grace it with such a term' (here Orelie grinned), 'is that it's (a) time consuming, (b) boring, (c) useless for monitoring theft or loss as it's never complete, (d) prone to error and (e) always going to produce out of date figures.' Ken pointed at his right hand with its fingers and thumb outstretched. 'Those are my five problems!' he complained, slumping back into his chair dejectedly.

Orelie stood up. 'Thank you, Mr Campana, for an interesting interview. I think I've understood most of the problem. Let me fix another interview with you for Friday. I think I'll have a first proposal for you then.'

'I'll look forward to that, Orelie,' said Ken. 'Just remember, though, we don't want to lay off any staff. We want to keep on good terms with our people.'

Thursday 15 October, 3.40 p.m. Spiel-Jouet-Ludus offices

'Hi Orelie.'

'Oh, hi', smiled Orelie.

Martine was her closest colleague at work. 'So, anything new? Hey, what's that?' She was quizzically examining Orelie's notepad contents.

'Don't touch it, it'll probably fall to dust', Orelie joked.

'Museum piece, is it?' Martine called from the staircase.

Orelie looked at the proposal she was preparing for Eurobells⌂. She had the uneasy feeling that although she had covered the present situation in Eurobells⌂ she did not really know what sort of system Ken Campana had in mind. However, she at least knew that it only concerned the stock room.

THE SECOND INTERVIEW AT EUROBELLS⌂

Friday 16 October, 10.06 a.m. Ken Campana's office

'Thank you very much, Orelie.' Ken had just finished leafing through Orelie's statement of requirements. 'Why don't you give me a quick summary?'

Orelie started nervously. 'Right, Mr Campana. Your problem is that at the moment you have only an informal manual information system.'

'Inherited, Orelie, I inherited that system,' Ken interjected ruefully.

'Your staff,' Orelie continued, 'have no clear procedures and no set way of recording data. They aren't even sure what data to record.'

'In a nutshell, Orelie,' confirmed Ken.

'So, in the statement,' she went on, 'I've set out a proposal for you to consider. Here we go.'

'*Point 1*. Each time an item is added to stock or removed from stock the stock clerk completes a document containing the following information:

Product code or raw material code, quantity (+ or −), date

Each document thus represents an amount in to or out of stock of one of the different sorts of product or raw material, for example different types of bell or different types of bronze.

'*Point 2*. At the end of the day these documents can be accumulated to give totals for each sort of product or raw material. We can use a simple formula:

Current stock level =   old stock level + additions from manufacturing
                        and suppliers − removals from shipping and
                        manufacturing

Where do we get the old stock level from?

'*Point 3*. You keep a file which is altered daily, giving current stock levels
for all items. You can do this in a filing cabinet with a record for each item.
The stock file will contain the following information for each record:

(a) item name and code
(b) stock level
(c) danger level − the clerk checks this at the end of the day to see if reorder
    is required
(d) selling price
(e) cost price

I've included the price fields in case accounts might find the file useful in
future.'

Orelie paused and scrutinized Ken to gauge his reaction to what she had
said so far. He was gazing out of the window. 'Keep going, you're doing
fine,' he said without turning. Encouraged slightly, she continued.

'*Point 4*. At the end of the day, here are the procedures for your staff:

(a) extract each item record
(b) perform the calculation
(c) alter the item record
(d) return the record to the cabinet

'In addition, Mr Campana, if you have this information available to you,
you can send a note to production control when the stock level for an item
drops below danger levels. To summarize' − here Ken faced Orelie − 'I can
provide a formal, manual, information system to assist you with up to date
and accurate stock information.'

Orelie sat down and sipped her Buxton. Ken looked thoughtful and then said,
'Thank you, Orelie. Come back on Monday. I'll have digested it by then.'

'OK, Mr Campana,' said Orelie, 'until Monday then.'

THE THIRD INTERVIEW AT EUROBELLS

Monday 19 October, 9.30 a.m. Ken Campana's office

Ken steepled his fingers behind his head. 'OK, OK,' Ken mused, 'tell me,
Orelie, how your proposal can cope with these issues.' He spread the fingers
of his right hand. Orelie began to feel rather apprehensive.

'*Point 1*. Speed. Your daily procedure can only be performed at the end of the day. If current stock figures are required earlier than tomorrow morning then overtime will be required.

'*Point 2*. Errors. There seem to be a few possibilities for the sorts of error that we're experiencing right now to happen. Errors can be made:

(a) during calculation
(b) during reading of stock levels
(c) during writing new stock levels
(d) if the stock clerk forgets to fill in a slip when a product goes or comes

'*Point 3*. Cost. How many staff is this going to take? How does it square with the costs and benefits in the feasibility study? As your method is time-consuming, people-dependent and error-prone, it is going to be very costly. That's my opinion.' Ken looked out of the window.

'But Mr Campana,' Orelie exclaimed, 'you said that you didn't want to lay off any staff!'

Ken looked embarrassed. 'The thing is, Orelie, that I thought we could just computerize our manual system. You know, leave things as they are – don't upset the staff. But now I've thought this through, I see we can't. Why don't we arrange a meeting for, say, next Tuesday, and we'll have another go?' Ken smiled encouragingly at Orelie.

'Right, Mr Campana,' said Orelie, 'and I'm sorry if . . .'

'Don't worry,' Ken said, 'Just rethink it.'

THE FOURTH INTERVIEW AT EUROBELLS⌂

Tuesday 27 October, 9.30 a.m. Ken Campana's office

'I think that this proposal will be more realistic, Mr Campana.' Orelie was presenting her revised statement of requirements. 'A main feature is that I've reduced the manual intervention as much as possible. The main problem is stock out. Stock in is usually one product at a time in large quantities, but stock out is usually many products at once in small quantities. Here are the main points:

'*Point 1*. At the moment, shipping ask for products by way of a shipping note. We can use this, or a copy. This document contains source data that will be keyed into a computer. Raw materials are requested by manufacturing using a materials request form. On the computer there is a file containing the stock levels for all the different products and raw materials. You can use the source data whenever you want to update this file.

'*Point 2*. We perform the same calculation for my first proposal to calculate stock levels, but the way we hold the data is different.

(a) The current stock level is kept on the computer file
(b) Stock out comes from a copy of the shipping note and the materials request form

(c) Stock in covers raw materials as well as products and comes from one of two document types: supplier's supply document or manufacturing completed worksheets or something similar

'*Point 3*. The system can have software to report automatically when danger levels of items are reached. In addition, we can introduce a stock reorder level field for each item. When this level is reached, the computer can print a report showing you the items to reorder.'

Orelie turned off the projector and closed her file. Ken came round from the other side of the desk and stood in front of her. 'I enjoyed that presentation,' he admitted, 'I think that you've got a good plan for the system here. I like the idea about automatic reordering, too.'

Orelie showed her relief visibly. 'Thanks, Mr Campana,' she said.

'What's the next step?' Ken asked.

'We'll do a study on this proposal,' Orelie went on. 'We'll cost it on a range of computers and produce a plan for operation by your staff. I think it means that you won't need so many people. Oh, and we'll also plan an initial phase of data collection.'

'What's that?' asked Ken.

'You need to count every item of stock you've got as of now so we can initialize the product records on the company,' Orelie explained. 'That'll be the starting old stock level.'

'But that's what we're doing now!' expostulated Ken.

'That's true, but,' Orelie hastened to add, 'you'll only have to do it once.'

'Oh, right,' said Ken, laughing with relief.

'Can I have your signature on the statement of requirements, please, Mr Campana?' Orelie asked politely.

Ken thought for a moment. 'Just leave it with me, Orelie. There is one other item I wanted to talk to you about. The Production Director has been thinking the new system over.'

'Yes?' queried Orelie.

'He thinks that we could easily adapt the system to store containers as well. What do you think about that? Shouldn't be too difficult, should it? I know that Simone Vessel, the Container Manager, is on good terms with him, and, it makes sense, doesn't it? Now the system's going to do more work, it can justify the retention of a few more staff, can't it?'

After a pause, Orelie asked, 'How many staff, Mr Campana?' in an odd tone of voice.

'Oh well,' said Ken, 'I'm not sure right now. I'll let you know next week.'

SUMMARY

From the case study we may note some of the characteristics of the activity of requirements acquisition:

1. The existing control system was inadequate, as it relied on many staff to do an error-prone and time-consuming job. Orelie used this as a model for her first proposal, as the requirement was not to lay off staff. However, the users learnt, by realizing the implication of the first proposal, that no benefits would be obtained by modifying the system as it was. Requirements thus changed after the project started.
2. Iteration. Several (there was only space to show two) attempts were necessary for proposing a solution to the user. In addition, it seemed that the final proposal might be open to change in the future, owing to the intervention of the Production Director, for reasons that were not clear. The widening of the scope of the system may genuinely require more staff, or it may be just a political decision.
3. The requirements acquisition methods used were the interview and analysis of existing system documentation.

The statement of requirements for Eurobells⌂ may be seen in Table 7.4.

Table 7.4 Statement of requirements – Eurobells⌂ stock control system

Current situation
Only an informal, manual information system exists. Staff have no clear procedures and no set way of recording data. It is not clear what data to record.

Proposed system
1. *Stock file.* A computer stock file is kept, altered daily, giving current stock levels for the different kinds of products and raw materials. The stock file will contain the following information for each item type:
   (a) Product/raw material code
   (b) Stock level
   (c) Danger level
   (d) Selling price
   (e) Cost price
2. *Stock in.* This covers raw materials as well as products and comes from one of two document types:
   (a) Suppliers supply document
   (b) Manufacturing completed worksheets
3. *Stock out.* Shipping ask for products by way of a shipping note. Raw materials are requested by manufacturing using a materials request form. For stock in and out, the documents contain source data which will be used to update the stock file. Keyed input data will be:
   Product/raw material code, quantity (+ or −), date
4. *At end of day.* These documents can be batched together and keyed into the computer. To give totals we use the formula:
   Current stock level = old stock level + additions from manufacturing and
                                    suppliers − removals from shipping and manufacturing
5. *Reorder.* The system has software to report automatically when danger levels of products are reached. A stock reorder level field for each product is to be introduced. When this level is reached, the computer can print a report showing the items to reorder.
6. *Data collection.* An initial data collection phase is required to create the stock file on the computer.

Requirements modelling – case study 2

For this stage of the case study, the *requirements model* is built from the narrative statement of requirements using OMNIS. An OMNIS model is a structured description of the requirements which has two main purposes. Firstly, the developer can check or reason with a structured model more easily to detect incompleteness or inconsistency, that is missing or contradictory requirements. Secondly, parts of the model can be presented more systematically, and possibly in a variety of ways, to the user for understanding and validation.

The statement of requirements requests a control system with a computer-based stock control information system. In addition, the management system activity of stock reorder, previously a manual activity, is now to become a computer activity.

Figure 7.3 shows that we have simplified the stock control system to consider only four main 'production' processes, as the stock room does not store intermediate states of raw material, produced by the melt or mix processes, nor does it store unassembled bells or clappers, produced by the cast bell and tune processes. Only raw materials and products are stored in the stock room. A product may be either an assembled bell and clapper, or a clapper.

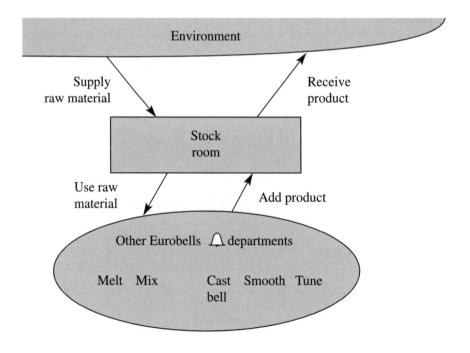

Figure 7.3 Schematic of stock control system.

REQUIREMENTS MODEL

SIMULATION SYSTEM

Information base

Object	Properties
PRODUCT-LEVEL	Product-code, stock-level, danger-level, price, reorder-level, reorder-quantity
RAW MATERIAL	Material-code, stock-level, danger-level, price, reorder-level, reorder-quantity

Rule base

stock-level ≥ danger-level

Process

Process	Refinement
1. Supply raw material	Increase stock-level of raw material
2. Use raw material	Decrease stock-level of raw material
	Initiate message system process 2
3. Add product	Increase stock-level of product-level
4. Receive product	Decrease stock-level of product-level
	Initiate message system process 1
5. Create, modify, delete	Product-level, raw material

MESSAGE SYSTEM

1. Check product-level stock-levels.
2. Check raw material stock-levels.

For the above processes, generate a list of codes and reorder quantities where stock-level < reorder-level.

3. Allow for reports on stock-level for all products and raw materials.

HUMAN COMPUTER SYSTEM

Input system

- *Data capture system.* Use copies of supplier documents, worksheets, material requests and shipping notes as source data. Batch until day end.
- *Transaction input system*

Event	Process
1. At day end	Use batched information to initiate simulation system processes 1 to 4
2. On request	Initiate simulation system process 5

Output system

1. MES processes 1 and 2 started by simulation system processes.
2. MES process 3 to be run at day end.

MANAGEMENT SYSTEM

Obtain the stock reorder list and send it to production control.

Summary

The chapter began by describing typical activities in the first two stages of requirements determination: problem definition and feasibility study. The four traditional methods of requirements acquisition were then described, followed by a brief description of the methods used in requirements modelling.

Quality and productivity problems with requirements determination were then described, which were largely due to assumptions being made about the fixed nature of the requirements, the ability to estimate resources, and the knowledge required concerning the organization or the application. Such assumptions date back to the days when computer systems were simply computerized versions of existing manual systems, where the requirements remained the same.

The requirements engineering (RE) approach was introduced, showing the areas of requirements determination that are addressed, and several recent RE methods were then described which attempt to meet the above problems. Case study 2 was then presented, illustrating some of the principles of requirements acquisition, followed by the requirements modelling stage, which modelled the statement of requirements using OMNIS.

A major problem, concerned with the analysis of information needs, is that there are no accepted methods or languages for building or expressing requirements in a structured form in this first requirements phase. It is thus hard to detect properties such as incompleteness and inconsistency early on, which might indicate error by the developer or a changing requirement.

However, the emergence of modelling languages such as OMNIS are improving this situation, as they are both user-oriented and capable of providing a structure within which requirements may be expressed more precisely, allowing errors or changes to be detected more easily than in narrative form. Such a language is particularly suitable as a basis for prototyping.

This first phase is a crucial phase in the process, as any errors made become magnified in the succeeding phases. It is estimated that an error in the requirements phase that costs £1 to correct when detected immediately costs £100 to correct in the maintenance phase (Boehm, 1987; Howard and Potter, 1994), due to the length of time required to understand and 'decode' programs, and the knock-on effects of changing systems which contain dependent parts.

Discussion questions

1. What question types did Orelie use in her interviews and how did she structure the interviews – funnel, diamond or pyramid?
2. What do you think Orelie could have done to avoid or anticipate the change in requirements proposed by the Production Director?
3. Do you think it is necessary to distinguish between requirements acquisition and requirements modelling? Why do you think the distinction is made?

4. How do you think you could begin to address the problem of changing requirements?

References

Boehm, B. W. (1987) Industrial software metrics top 10 list, *IEEE Software*, 4(5), 84–5.

Castano, S. and De Antonellis, V. (1993) Reuse of conceptual requirement specifications, *Proceedings of the IEEE International Symposium on Requirements Engineering*, 4–6 January, San Diego, California, IEEE Computer Society Press, Los Alamitos, California, 121–5.

Easterbrook, S. and Nuseibeh, B. (1995) Managing inconsistencies in an evolving specification, *Proceedings of the Second IEEE International Symposium on Requirements Engineering*, 27–29 March, York, UK, IEEE Computer Society Press, Los Alamitos, California, 48–55.

El Emam, K. and Madhavji, N. H. (1995) A field study of requirements engineering practices in information systems development, *Proceedings of the Second IEEE International Symposium on Requirements Engineering*, 27–29 March, York, UK, IEEE Computer Society Press, Los Alamitos, California, 68–80.

Gough, P. A., Fodemski, F. T., Higgins, S. A. and Ray, S. J. (1995) Scenarios – an industrial case study and hypermedia enhancements, *Proceedings of the Second IEEE International Symposium on Requirements Engineering*, 27–29 March, York, UK, IEEE Computer Society Press, Los Alamitos, California, 10–17.

Greenspan, S. and Feblowitz, M. (1993) Requirements engineering using the SOS paradigm, *Proceedings of the IEEE International Symposium on Requirements Engineering*, 4–6 January, San Diego, California, IEEE Computer Society Press, Los Alamitos, California, 260–3.

Gulla, J. A., Lindland, O. I., Willumsen, G. and Solvberg, A. (1994) Executing, viewing and explaining conceptual models, *Proceedings of the First International Conference on Requirements Engineering*, 18–22 April, Colorado Springs, Colorado, IEEE Computer Society Press, Los Alamitos, California, 166–75.

Harrison, M. and Barnard, P. (1993) On defining requirements for interaction, *Proceedings of the IEEE International Symposium on Requirements Engineering*, 4–6 January, San Diego, California, IEEE Computer Society Press, Los Alamitos, California, 50–4.

Howard, P. and Potter, C. (1994) *CASE & Methods Based Development Tools: An Evaluation and Comparison*, ButlerBloor Ltd, Challenge House, Sherwood Drive, Bletchley, Milton Keynes, MK3 6DP.

Ishihara, Y., Seki, H. and Kasami, T. (1993) A translation method from natural language specifications into formal specifications using contextual dependencies, *Proceedings of the IEEE International Symposium on Requirements*

Engineering; 4–6 January, San Diego, California, IEEE Computer Society Press, Los Alamitos, California, 232–9.

Jackson, M. and Zave, P. (1993) Domain descriptions, *Proceedings of the IEEE International Symposium on Requirements Engineering*, 4–6 January, San Diego, California, IEEE Computer Society Press, Los Alamitos, California, 56–64.

Kendall, K. E. and Kendall, J. E. (1988) *Systems Analysis and Design*, Prentice-Hall, Englewood Cliffs NJ.

Kent, S. J. H., Maibaum, T. S. E. and Quirk, W. J. (1993) Formally specifying temporal constraints and error recovery, *Proceedings of the IEEE International Symposium on Requirements Engineering*, 4–6 January, San Diego, California, IEEE Computer Society Press, Los Alamitos, California, 208–15.

Knight, D. R. and Flynn, D. J. (1992) Automatic conceptual model acquisition, *Proceedings of the 3rd International Conference on Information Systems Developer Workbench*, Gdansk, Poland, 22–24 September, 166–75.

Lefering, M. (1993) An incremental integration tool between requirements engineering and programming in the large, *Proceedings of the IEEE International Symposium on Requirements Engineering*, 4–6 January, San Diego, California, IEEE Computer Society Press, Los Alamitos, California, 82–9.

Leite, J. C. S. P. and Oliveira, A. P. (1995) A client oriented requirements baseline, *Proceedings of the Second IEEE International Symposium on Requirements Engineering*, 27–29 March, York, UK, IEEE Computer Society Press, Los Alamitos, California, 108–15.

Maiden, N. and Sutcliffe, A. G. (1993) Requirements engineering by example: an empirical study, *Proceedings of the IEEE International Symposium on Requirements Engineering*, 4–6 January, San Diego, California, IEEE Computer Society Press, Los Alamitos, California, 104–11.

Nixon, B. (1993) Dealing with performance requirements during the development of information systems, *Proceedings of the IEEE International Symposium on Requirements Engineering*, 4–6 January, San Diego, California, IEEE Computer Society Press, Los Alamitos, California, 42–9.

Ohnishi, A. and Agusa, K. (1993) CARD: a software requirements definition environment, *Proceedings of the IEEE International Symposium on Requirements Engineering*, 4–6 January, San Diego, California, IEEE Computer Society Press, Los Alamitos, California, 90–3.

Orman, L. (1987) Information intensive modeling, *MIS Quarterly*, **11**(1), 73–84.

Regnell, B., Kimbler, K. and Wesslen, A. (1995) Improving the use case driven approach to requirements engineering, *Proceedings of the Second IEEE International Symposium on Requirements Engineering*, 27–29 March, York, UK, IEEE Computer Society Press, Los Alamitos, California, 40–7.

Ryan, K. (1993) The role of natural language in requirements engineering, *Proceedings of the IEEE International Symposium on Requirements Engineering*, 4–6 January, San Diego, California, IEEE Computer Society Press, Los Alamitos, California, 240–2.

Ryan, K. and Matthews, B. (1993) Matching conceptual graphs as an aid to requirements re-use, *Proceedings of the IEEE International Symposium on Requirements Engineering*, 4–6 January, San Diego, California, IEEE Computer Society Press, Los Alamitos, California, 112–20.

Salek, A., Sorenson, P. G., Tremblay, J. P. and Punshon, J. M. (1994) The REVIEW system: from formal specifications to natural language, *Proceedings of the First International Conference on Requirements Engineering*, 18–22 April, Colorado Springs, Colorado, IEEE Computer Society Press, Los Alamitos, California, 220–9.

Senn, J. A. (1989) *Analysis and Design of Information Systems*, 2nd edn, McGraw-Hill, London.

Van Lamsweerde, A., Darimont, R. and Massonet, P. (1995) Goal-directed elaboration of requirements for a meeting scheduler: problems and lessons learnt, *Proceedings of the Second IEEE International Symposium on Requirements Engineering*, 27–29 March, York, UK, IEEE Computer Society Press, Los Alamitos, California, 194–203.

Van Schouwen, A. J., Parnas, D. L. and Madey, J. (1993) Documentation of requirements for computer systems, *Proceedings of the IEEE International Symposium on Requirements Engineering*, 4–6 January, San Diego, California, IEEE Computer Society Press, Los Alamitos, California, 198–207.

Wright, P., Fields, B. and Harrison, M. (1994) Deriving human-error tolerance requirements from tasks, *Proceedings of the First International Conference on Requirements Engineering*, 18–22 April, Colorado Springs, Colorado, IEEE Computer Society Press, Los Alamitos, California, 135–42.

Wu, C.-H. and Flynn, D. J. (1995) NALABA: a natural language based integrity requirements validation system, *First Workshop on Applications of Natural Language to Data Bases NLDB'95*, 28–29 June, Versailles, France.

Yu, E. S. K. and Mylopoulos, J. (1994) From E-R to 'A-R' – modelling strategic actor relationships for business process reengineering, in *Entity-Relationship Approach – ER '94* (ed. Loucopoulos, P.), Springer-Verlag, Berlin, 548–65.

8
Analysis I – entity and rule modelling

Introduction

CONCEPTUAL MODELLING APPROACH

Modern approaches to the analysis phase are founded on the *conceptual modelling approach* (ISO, 1982; Loucopoulos and Zicari, 1992; Nijssen and Halpin, 1989), in turn based on an influential report defining the structure of database systems (ANSI/SPARC, 1975; Tsichritzis and Klug, 1977).

The approach distinguishes three levels of description of an information system: external, conceptual and internal. While the internal level is the level of logical and physical design the notions of external and conceptual levels are now found in the specification, the product of the analysis phase. The most recent version of the SSADM method (SSADM, 1995) adopts this approach.

On the external level, the organizational context of the computer system is modelled. This may have a broad scope, describing work procedures within which the computer system will operate, or it may be narrow, only defining the human–computer interface.

The conceptual model is on the conceptual level and it represents the part of the organization that will be modelled in the computer system. It has three components: structure, process and rule (Brodie *et al.*, 1984; Tsichritzis and Lochovsky, 1982). There is an emphasis on the modelling of structure that has evolved from database design from the late 1960s (Navathe, 1992) and that views structure as a framework to support other parts of the specification.

More recently, the rule and process components have had a lot of attention (Winter, 1994) particularly as the conceptual model has been broadened to apply to information system specification (Rochfeld, 1987).

The conceptual modelling approach has a static and a dynamic view of the organization. The dynamic view is concerned with the processes of the organization, while the static view considers the structure objects and their states that are involved in the processes. There are usually restrictions, termed rules, on the states that objects may assume.

Processes are of two broad kinds: update processes, which change the state of objects, as in the state space approach discussed in Chapter 3, and report processes, which simply report on object states. Update processes must obey the rules, as otherwise object states might be changed into invalid states.

This chapter will discuss the modelling of the structure component, using the entity modelling method, in some detail, and will also briefly describe how the rule component may be modelled. The next chapter will discuss process modelling.

AIMS OF ANALYSIS PHASE

In analysis, we use a precisely defined language to build a precise specification of the desired system, adding more detail to the requirements model from the previous requirements determination phase. The specification should be:

1. Suitable for communication between users and developers as well as between developers.
2. Suitable for use as a basis for mapping through lower levels to an implemented system.

We must use a precisely defined language if we wish to minimize ambiguity, and although a model such as an OMNIS model used in requirements determination is helpful, it is expressed in natural language or informal diagrams. Although this may help user communication, such means of expression are inherently ambiguous, and in analysis we wish to expose inconsistencies and incompleteness more thoroughly.

Entity modelling

The entity modelling method is widely used for modelling the static part of an organization, using the basic concepts of entity, attribute and relationship to build the structure component. There are many variants of this method, originating from the entity–relationship (ER) model (Chen, 1976), and we shall use one based on SSADM (SSADM, 1995). An example of the way in which entity modelling may be applied to model organizations may be found in Rock-Evans (1987) and Halpin (1995), who describes the NIAM method. Other relevant books in this area include Batini *et al.* (1992), Elmasri and Navathe (1994), Flynn and Fragoso Diaz (1996), Teorey (1990) and Wintraecken (1990).

Entity

DESCRIPTION

An *entity* is an object of interest in an organization that may be concrete or abstract, and which is static rather than dynamic.

In Eurobells⌂, customers buy products and managers manage projects. In this case, customer, product and manager are concrete objects and project is an abstract object.

For a more precise definition the terms *entity type* and *entity instance* are used:

> *An entity type is a set or class of entities that share the same characteristics. An entity instance is a particular entity that is a member of an entity set or class.*

ENTITY INSTANCE AND ENTITY TYPE

The structure component usually models only entity types, although some methods allow entity instances to be modelled. The entity instance concept is necessary to define entity modelling semantics. It is normal practise to use the shorter term 'entity' to refer to an entity type unless the meaning is unclear. An entity is represented graphically by a soft box containing its name, as in Fig. 8.1.

Figure 8.1 Entity product

DETERMINATION OF ENTITIES

It can be a difficult task to decide on the 'objects of interest' that are entities. There are problems concerned with the different views of users, who place different importance on objects, and difficulties with distinguishing between entity, attribute and relationship. Some guidelines for entity determination are now discussed.

Firstly, any kind of object may be regarded as an entity, and it may be concrete or abstract as shown above. Secondly, only those objects about which information is to be recorded, to satisfy the information requirement of users, should be regarded as entities.

Thirdly, objects should be distinguishable from each other and should be capable of being individually identified.

Fourthly, an instance of an abstract entity may represent a particular level of granularity of a set of real world objects, depending on the level about which the user wishes to record information. For example, an instance of the entity raw material in Eurobells⌂ represents a medium level of granularity of the set of real world raw material objects, as it represents a *collection* of a particular sort of raw material, for example low-quality bronze. The reason for this is that the user is not interested in recording information about a lower level, for example each separate 'lump' of low-quality bronze, but is only interested in information about the collection of this sort of bronze, for example its quantity.

It is common for beginners to make two basic mistakes when deciding on objects that appear to be entities. Firstly, objects which are concerned with *internal* representation of any part of the desired system should not be considered as entities. This includes objects such as file, program, computer and system. Users are not interested in recording information about programs or computer files.

Secondly, objects which are concerned with *external* representation of the desired system, such as invoices, reports, input forms and screen maps, should not be considered as entities. These should be modelled on the external level within the specification, and the major reason for excluding these representations is that they will duplicate information already in the model. For example, an entity invoice, containing information such as customer name and address, product number, description and quantity, would duplicate the name and address of the entity customer and the number and description of the entity product.

Relationship

DESCRIPTION

A *relationship* is a meaningful association between entity instances. For example, when customers buy products and managers manage projects, relationships occur between instances of customer and product and between instances of manager and project.

The more precise term *relationship instance* refers to a particular association between entity instances, while the term *relationship type* refers to an association between entity types. As for entities, the structure component usually models only relationship types. The term relationship will be used to refer to a relationship type. A relationship is represented graphically by an edge between the relevant entities as shown in Fig. 8.2.

RELATIONSHIP NAME AND ASSOCIATED ENTITIES

Different entities

In Fig. 8.2, a relationship is shown between two different entities customer and product, with the meaning that a customer samples a product. The name of the relationship, in this example, samples, is termed a *role name*.

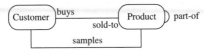

Figure 8.2 Examples of relationships showing role names.

Same entity

Figure 8.2 shows that instances of the entity product may relate to instances of the same entity. This is termed a *recursive* or *involuted* relationship, and its meaning is that a product (for example a clapper) may be part of another product (a bell).

More than one relationship between entities

Figure 8.2 also shows an example of how more than one relationship may exist between entities, as a customer can buy a product as well as sample it. Role names must be unique between entities so that relationships may be distinguished from one other.

Inverse role name

It is often necessary to name both directions of the relationship, in which case there is an *inverse role name* as well as a role name. It is an arbitrary modelling choice as to which direction either of these refer to. In the figure, the role name might be 'buys' and the inverse role name might be 'sold-to' for the customer : product relationship.

RELATIONSHIP SEMANTICS

In the structure component, a relationship between two entities, for example customer buys product, is modelling the fact that, in the organization, a customer instance may associate with a product instance, with the meaning expressed in the role name, to form an instance of this relationship. However, it may be the case that, at a given point in time, there are entity instances that are not associated together. For example, there may be a new product which no one has bought yet, or there may be customers who are only sampling and who have not bought a product.

We may show relationship instances in a table, often termed an occurrence or population diagram, and the population diagram in Fig. 8.3 shows some of the entity instances that were participating in a customer : product

Customer	Product
Dr Truelove	
Mr Bryan	1235
Ms Frind	4325
Mrs Smith	9845
...	...
...	...
Mr Farnaby	4769

Population diagram at 10 am
Wednesday 21 April 1996

Figure 8.3 Population diagram for customer buys product relationship.

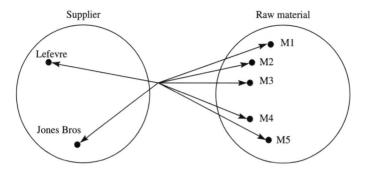

Figure 8.4 Every supplier related to every sort of raw material and vice versa.

relationship at a given point in time. Each row represents an instance of the relationship. Such a diagram may be helpful in understanding the organization when building the structure component, particularly when deciding relationship cardinality, as discussed in the next section.

Relationship constraints

When entities are related, they can do so without restriction. For example, every supplier could be related to every sort of raw material, and vice versa, such that the relationship is the cartesian product of the entity instances. This is shown in Fig. 8.4, where we have had to assume that there are only two suppliers to keep the diagram to a manageable size.

At the other extreme, if no suppliers were related to no raw materials there would be no relationship between the two entities! However, relationships are more normally subsets of the cartesian product.

Two important relationship constraints are the cardinality and participation constraints.

Cardinality constraint

The *cardinality constraint* of an entity A defines the number of instances of the other entity that may associate with one instance of entity A in a relationship. The constraint holds at any time in the life of the entity. The most common cardinality values are *one* and *many*, where 'many' means one or more than one.

CARDINALITY RATIO

It is common practice to combine the cardinality constraints of the two entities in a relationship into a single expression, resulting in the four well-known *cardinality ratios*: *one to one, one to many, many to one* and *many to many*. These are illustrated below for a relationship R(AB) between two entities A and B.

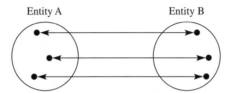

Figure 8.5 1:1 relationship between entities A and B.

One to one (1:1)

For entities A and B:

>   One entity A instance associates with only one entity B instance.

and

>   One entity B instance associates with only one entity A instance.

Figure 8.5 illustrates a 1:1 relationship between entities A and B, for example a relationship between entities customer and account, where a customer has only one account and an account is held by only one customer.

One to many (1:n)/Many to one (n:1)

For entities A and B:

>   One entity A instance associates with many entity B instances.

but

>   One entity B instance associates with only one entity A instance.

- *One to many (1:n)*
  Figure 8.6 illustrates a 1:n relationship between A and B in the A → B direction. An instance of entity A is associated to many instances of entity B (a1 → b1, b2).
- *Many to one (n:1)*
  The inverse of a 1:n relationship is an n:1 relationship, B → A, and Fig. 8.6 shows that an instance of B is associated to only one instance of A (b1 → a1, b2 → a1, b3 → a2, b4 → a4).

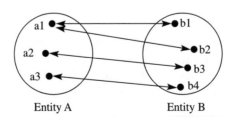

Figure 8.6 1:n relationship between entities A and B (A → B).

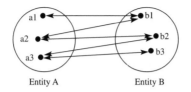

Figure 8.7 *m:n* relationship between entities A and B.

In a 1:*n* relationship between two entities, for example customer and product, there is a hierarchy which is a tree. A customer may buy many products but a product is sold to only one customer.

Many to many (m:n)

For entities A and B:

> One entity A instance associates with many entity B instances.

and

> One entity B instance associates with many entity A instances.

Figure 8.7 shows an *m:n* relationship between entities A and B. In an *m:n* relationship between two entities, for example manager and project, there is a hierarchy which is a network and not a tree. A project may be managed by many managers and a manager may manage many projects.

GRAPHICAL REPRESENTATION OF CARDINALITY

A 'crow's foot' next to an entity on a relationship edge indicates that the cardinality of the other entity is many, while its absence indicates that the

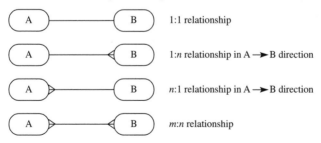

Figure 8.8 Relationship cardinality ratios.

Figure 8.9 Relationship cardinality examples.

cardinality is one. This is shown in Fig. 8.8 for entities A and B and in Fig. 8.9 for the examples given above.

DETERMINING RELATIONSHIP CARDINALITY

Functionality determination

When deciding the cardinality of an entity in a relationship, we must be careful to choose a value that will be true *at any time* in the life of the entity instances.

For example, by inspecting the population diagram in Fig. 8.3, which is at a given time point for the customer and product relationship, one might infer that customers may buy only one product. However, this is just the situation at that particular point in time, and does not accurately reflect the fact that a customer can buy more than one product.

Meaning of 'many' as in 'one to many'

Be careful that you do not equate *many* with *all*. Many means one or more than one.

Symmetric and asymmetric relationships

Note that 1:1 and *m:n* relationships are symmetric, in that the cardinality is the same from either entity direction, but that 1:*n* and *n*:1 relationships are not. This means that care has to be taken in the order of the entities when we refer to a relationship as 1:*n* or *n*:1.

Fixed cardinality

Cardinality may be *fixed*, where the number of instances of the entity that may associate with an instance of another entity may be expressed as an integer or as a range. For example, if a manager can manage a maximum of four projects, the cardinality ratio of the relationship manager:project is *m*:4. This is shown in Fig. 8.10.

Participation constraint

The *participation constraint* specifies whether or not entity instances must participate in a relationship with instances of another entity. The two types of participation are termed *total* and *partial*, and they are defined below considering the participation of instances of entity A in a relationship R(AB).

Figure 8.10 Fixed degree relationship cardinality.

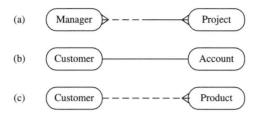

Figure 8.11 Participation constraint examples: (a) partial – total; (b) total – total; (c) partial – partial.

- *Total participation.* Where all instances of entity A must participate in a relationship with instances of entity B, at any time, the participation of A in R(AB) is termed total.
- *Partial participation.* Where some, not necessarily all, instances of entity A may participate in a relationship with instances of entity B, at any time, the participation of A in R(AB) is termed partial.

Alternative terms for total and partial are *mandatory* and *optional* respectively. The participation constraint is graphically represented by a solid relationship edge next to an entity with total participation in the relationship, and a dashed edge next to an entity with partial participation in the relationship.

For example, Fig. 8.11 shows in example (a) that although a project must be associated with a manager, a manager does not have to be associated with a project. Example (b) shows that a customer must have an account and that an account must have a customer, while in example (c) a customer may not buy a product and a product may not be bought by a customer.

Attribute

DESCRIPTION

An *attribute* is a descriptor of an entity instance, such as the name Dr Truelove of a particular customer. The more precise term is *attribute value*, while an *attribute* is a set of entity descriptors. Attributes are most commonly modelled, although attribute values may also be shown.

An attribute is usually considered in relation to the entity it describes. For example:

Entity	*Attribute*
Product	product number, product type, price
Customer	name, address, telephone number, fax number

Product and customer are entities, whereas product number, address and so on are attributes which describe these entities. For example, product is described by its price.

ENTITY–ATTRIBUTE RELATIONSHIPS

Graphical representation

Entity–attribute relationships may be represented graphically in a variety of ways, and one way is to use attribute names connected to the relevant entity by an edge, as in Fig. 8.12.

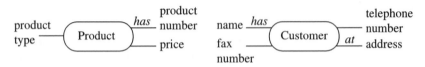

Figure 8.12 Entity–attribute relationships.

As for entity–entity relationships, role names and relationship constraints apply to entity–attribute relationships.

Cardinality constraint

Cardinality constraints also apply to entities and attributes in relationships.

One to one. An attribute in this type of relationship is termed an entity *identifier*, as each attribute value uniquely identifies an entity instance. Each entity instance has only one value of this attribute, and each attribute value is associated with only one entity instance. For example, the identifier of the product entity is the attribute product number. Thus, a product has one product number, and a product number is associated with, and therefore identifies, only one product.

| *Entity* | *Attribute* |
| *Product* | product number |

The identifier is the attribute whose values are used by the user to identify and to refer to entity instances, and it thus constitutes an important link between the real world and the system. Identifiers are useful when determining entities as they give clues to entity semantics, and they are important in logical design as they are used as data items to represent entities.

When building the structure component, care should be taken with identifiers, as many organizations recycle the values. For example, it is common in Europe to recycle car registration numbers after a certain period of years. Many organizations use an artificial attribute as an identifier, which has the benefit of being unique. This partially explains the lengthy customer numbers on UK gas and electricity bills.

Many to one. This is where an entity instance has only one attribute value, but an attribute value may be associated with many entity instances. Most entity–attribute relationships have this cardinality ratio. For example:

Entity	*Attribute*
Customer	address
Product	product type

A customer entity has only one address, but that address may be for many customers.

One to many. In this case each entity instance may have many values of the attribute, while each value uniquely identifies the entity instance. For example, a customer may have many fax numbers:

Entity	*Attribute*
Customer	fax number

We may note that in a one to many relationship the attribute is an identifier, as each value uniquely identifies an entity instance. In this example, each fax number is associated with only one customer and thus uniquely identifies that customer. An entity may thus have several identifying values of the same attribute.

Many to many. For example, a product may have many prices, if different levels of discount are offered, and a price may apply to many products.

Entity	*Attribute*
Product	price

Role names and participation constraint

For the participation constraint, there is often a default assumption that, in the attribute $\rightarrow$ entity direction, attributes always have a partial participation constraint. However, from the entity direction, the participation constraint is important as it specifies, for the later design stages, whether a given attribute value must be input when an entity instance is created.

Role names are not usually specified in detail, as the meaning of the relationship is usually clear from the attribute name. However, they may be required if an entity has more than one relationship with the same attribute. For example, a customer could have two attributes named address, with the role names *home* and *business*.

As the combination of cardinality and participation constraints as well as role names often makes the diagram cluttered, they are usually recorded in a non-diagrammatic part of the structure component. To record an *m:n* cardinality ratio between product and price, where all products must have a price and vice versa, we may write *product:price (m/n, t/t)*.

Further topics

We shall briefly discuss additions to the basic elements discussed above which widen the expressive power of entity modelling.

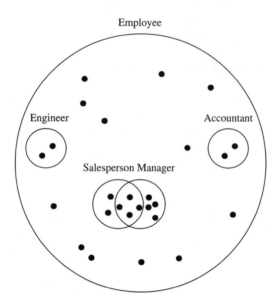

Figure 8.13   Four subsets of entity employee.

SUPERTYPE AND SUBTYPE

Entity subsets

An entity type A consists of a set of entity instances $\{a_1, a_2,..., a_n\}$. These instances may semantically constitute a subset of the instances of another entity type B. For example, the set of instances of entity manager may be a subset of instances of entity employee. In addition, instances of entities engineer, salesperson and accountant may also be subsets of employee. This is shown in Fig. 8.13.

These relationships between entities form what is termed a generalization hierarchy, as a higher level (generic) entity, employee, is the generalization of the lower level entities accountant, salesperson, manager and engineer, which in turn are termed the specialization of employee. In order to form such a hierarchy, entities must have at least one property in common. A subset does not have to be a *proper* subset as it may include all instances of its superset.

The generic entity is termed the *supertype* of the lower level entities which are termed *subtypes*. In a generalization hierarchy with many levels, an entity may be a supertype of lower level entities and a subtype of a higher level entity.

Figure 8.14   Generalization hierarchy of entities.

Graphical representation

Generalization hierarchies are represented as shown in Fig. 8.14, where subtypes are shown enclosed in the supertype entity box. This form of representation is not very adequate where there are more than two levels, and in these cases arrowed edges from subtype to supertype are often used.

Distinguishing properties of entity subsets

The user requirement often contains a name describing a subtype, and this name must be retained to capture the user semantics. We may distinguish two different ways in which entity subtypes may arise in the organization.

- *Grouping*. A subtype may arise if some entity instances are viewed as a set or group, on the basis of a *common attribute value*. For example, if the entity employee has a qualification attribute, that subset of employees with the value engineering degree for the qualification attribute may be viewed as the engineer subtype.
- *Extra property or properties*. A subtype may occur if a subset of instances have an extra property, that is a relationship to an entity or attribute that other instances do not have.

Figure 8.15 shows that some instances of employee have an extra property, as they have a manages association to instances of the entity project. This subset of employee is termed manager. Instances forming the subtype manager may thus be distinguished from other instances of employee, as they have this distinguishing property.

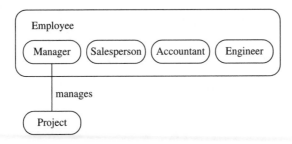

Figure 8.15   Subtype formation by association.

Membership criteria, either by grouping on an attribute value or by the possession of an extra property, are largely in the mind of the developer and cannot be inferred from the diagram.

Subtypes are very useful, as they make the different types of entity more visible on the diagram, and they allow, for example, separate processes to be specified for them. This may mean that processes are more numerous, but they are less complex.

Exclusion and exhaustion

Figure 8.13 shows that subsets may be disjoint (accountant and engineer, accountant and salesperson, and so on) or may overlap (manager and salesperson). Such subsets are referred to as *exclusive* and *non-exclusive* respectively.

In addition, Fig. 8.13 shows that there are some employee instances that are not members of any subset. This is the *non-exhaustive* case, where all the subtypes modelled do not include all instances of the supertype. The *exhaustive* case is where all the subtypes modelled do include all instances of the supertype; that is, where the subtypes exhaust the supertype.

Some methods allow both exclusion and exhaustion to be modelled.

Multiple inheritance

A generalization hierarchy need not be a tree, as multiple inheritance is allowed by some modelling methods. For example, an entity sales controller could have both salesperson and manager as its supertypes.

MULTIPLE RELATIONSHIPS

Implicitly, the discussion concerning relationships has only considered *binary relationships*; that is, relationships between two entities. However, there are many cases where *multiple relationships* occur, which are relationships involving more than two entities. The number of entities participating in a relationship defines its *degree*, and there may be ternary relationships where the degree is three, and higher degree relationships.

For example, let us consider three entities, supplier, raw material and project. The semantics are that a supplier supplies many sorts of raw material,

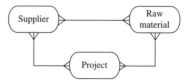

Figure 8.16   Binary relationship modelling of supplier, raw material and project.

and raw material is supplied by many suppliers. In addition, raw material is used in many projects, and a project will use many sorts of raw material. We might begin to model this using binary relationships as in Fig. 8.16.

We now add the additional restriction that a supplier only supplies certain sorts of raw material to certain projects. For example, supplier S1 supplies raw material R1 only to project P1. This last restriction is not modelled by simple binary relationships between the three entities, for the following reason. Suppose that supplier S1 is associated with raw materials R1 and R2, and raw materials R1 and R2 are associated with different projects. In this case, we cannot know from Fig. 8.16, for raw materials R1 and R2, the project(s) to which they were supplied by supplier S1.

To model this multiple relationship successfully we use what is termed an *n*-ary relationship approach. From the participating entities supplier, raw material and project, we create a new, abstract entity that we name SRP. This is then associated with the participating entities via binary associations, as in Fig. 8.17. This type of model allows us to represent the information that we need. For example, supplier S1 may be associated with instances of SRP, each instance of which is associated with an instance of raw material and an instance of project which receives that raw material from that supplier. The relationship constraints in the figure are important to the semantics of the relationship.

The entity SRP may be considered rather artificial, and an example of a more naturally occurring abstract entity which models a multiple relationship is the entity complaint, where a customer complains about a product sold by a salesperson. In this case, Fig. 8.18 shows the modelling.

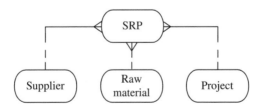

Figure 8.17 *n*-ary relationship modelling of supplier, raw material and project.

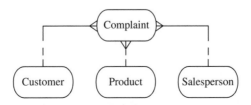

Figure 8.18 *n*-ary relationship modelling of a complaint.

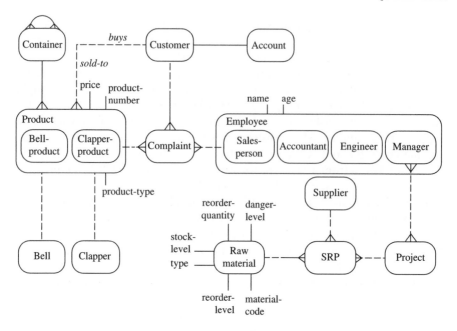

Figure 8.19 Entity diagram for Eurobells⌂ production system.

Eurobells⌂ example

Figure 8.19 shows a partial model of the Eurobells⌂ production system. The product entity, which is the final object produced by assembly, has two subsets, bell-product and clapper-product, which are formed by grouping on values of product-type.

Product, employee and raw material entities have relationships with the attributes as shown, and in addition they have relationships with other entities. Product has relationships with customer (the customer that buys the product), bell (the bell that constitutes the product), clapper (the clapper that constitutes the product) and container (the container designed for the product). Customers do not have to buy products and products do not have to be bought by customers. Relationships with container and customer are all *n*:1, from the product direction, so a product is associated with only one container and customer.

Raw material, supplier and project entities are shown in a multiple relationship, with the abstract entity SRP, while product, customer and salesperson form the abstract entity complaint. Container has an *m*:*n* relationship with itself, reflecting the fact that a container may be made up of many containers. A manager may have many projects, but a project must have at least one manager and possibly several. A customer must have only one account and vice versa. Finally, employee and product subtypes are shown.

Abstraction

As developers, when we build a structure component we make use of three abstraction operations: classification, generalization and aggregation. An abstraction operation is an operation performed on a set or group of objects which results in a simpler object or set of objects. The aim of abstraction is to reduce complexity, and this is done by hiding or reducing the amount of detail that is visible on a diagram. Many entity modelling methods are supported by CASE tools, to be discussed later, which provide different levels of diagram to assist in this process.

CLASSIFICATION

During the entity determination process mentioned at the beginning of this chapter, and probably before we even start initially sketching trial entities, we mentally group similar objects into sets and then classify the ones that seem to coincide with the user view. An important part of the operation is to give the set a name, for example employee. The name should correspond to the name used in the organization, denoting the type of object, and it usually attempts to express the difference between this and other types.

The operation reduces the complexity of many employees to just the employee type, so making the distinction between type and instance. Although the user is often quick to classify concrete entities, developers often use this operation to build abstract entities, as for *n*-ary relationships. In addition, decisions must often be made concerning the level of granularity that is required concerning sets of objects, for example concerning the raw material entity.

GENERALIZATION

The use of generalization to form subtypes and supertypes was mentioned above. Generalization is an abstraction operation whereby instances of different entities (which share a common property or properties) are viewed as instances of a single, generic entity. For example, we may generalize the entities aircraft, land vehicle and boat into the more generic entity vehicle.

Generalization establishes the *is-a* relationship between instances of an entity and a more generic entity, so that an instance of the lower level entity *is-a* instance of the higher level entity, but not vice versa.

An important feature possessed by entities in a generalization hierarchy, from the point of view of reducing detail in the structure component, is that as a lower level instance *is-a* higher level instance, it accordingly inherits all the properties of the higher level entity. This is termed the *inheritance* principle. For example, in Fig. 8.19, salesperson, accountant, engineer and manager inherit properties of employee, in this example the two attributes name and age.

Another way in which detail is reduced is that higher level diagrams may show only supertypes, with subtypes shown on lower level diagrams.

AGGREGATION

Aggregation is an operation whereby entities, attributes or relationships are combined to become *part-of* a higher level, aggregate object. For example, the bell and clapper entities in Fig. 8.19, instead of being related to product with binary relationships, could be aggregated to form an aggregate product entity, if the view is taken that bell and clapper are *part-of* a product.

Aggregate objects behave like entities and they may thus be related to other entities and attributes. An overview diagram may sometimes be produced by aggregating all attributes into their entities, considering attributes as part of their entities, so only entities and relationships are shown.

Rule modelling – introduction and definition

The concept of rule has many different interpretations in an organization. For example, there may be rules concerning no-smoking areas, the unauthorized use of organizational facilities, the frequency of productivity reports to management or the maximum age of employees.

The type of rule we are interested in concerns those rules which restrict, in some way, one or more of the objects in the organization that are modelled in the structure component. These rules, which must hold at any time, are generally termed *conceptual* or *business* rules, and we may define a rule broadly as follows:

> *A rule restricts the allowable states of one or more entities, attributes or relationships.*

The structure component only captures a part of the static requirements, concerned with the entities, attributes and relationships that may exist. However, there are many rules in the requirements which we also wish to capture, which are expressed in terms of the elements of the structure component, and the rule component is designed to do this in a declarative way. A rule is modelled as a restriction on the structure component of the specification. Historically, rules derive from integrity constraints in database systems.

One reason why we need the rule component is that the structure component is only expressed in terms of sets and not individual instances. It cannot therefore capture any of the requirements which refer to individual instances.

In the requirements determination phase, rules are expressed in OMNIS only in natural language. In the rule component, they are expressed in a precise language, usually based on sets or logic, and they are expressed solely in terms of the elements of the structure component to which they refer.

Traditional problems of rules modelling

PROBLEM EXAMPLES

Rules have traditionally been modelled in procedural forms, in application programs, edit routines, update transactions and human–computer systems. However, this brings about two problems: (1) being embedded in procedural forms and (2) being expressed on a low level of abstraction in program code.

Procedural expression

As an example, we consider a rule which restricts the number of customers to 1000. The rule might be specified procedurally as follows:

```
IF customer-numbers < 1000 THEN
    BEGIN
        Insert new customer
    END
ELSE
    BEGIN
        Write "error message – transaction disallowed as too many
        customers"
    END
```

Three specification elements are present here: the rule itself in precondition form, an update transaction and a violation response. The rule is embedded in these three, causing complexity and obscuring the rule to the human reader.

Low level of abstraction

Application program expression often emphasizes the *how* rather than the *what* of the rule. For example, the above rule might be expressed in code as follows:

```
Read customer record
    DO WHILE NOT END-OF-FILE
        COUNT = COUNT + 1
        Read customer record
    END
IF COUNT < 1000 THEN . . .
    (as above)
```

This code fragment shows how rule semantics become hopelessly lost amidst implementation details. In particular, the reference to customer, the structure element with which the rule is concerned, has been removed. Instead, there is a reference to a program variable count.

PROBLEM SUMMARY

The problems of the traditional approach to rules modelling are that:

1. It is hard for the developer to understand a rule specification:
    (a) rules are embedded in updates, error messages and preconditions
    (b) procedural expression allows many different forms in which the same rule may be expressed, adding to complexity
    (c) rules may be expressed on implementation levels of abstraction
    (d) rules are scattered over the specification and are not therefore in one place

    Rules are very similar, in these respects, to the state of entities in specifications before entity modelling became generally used.
2. It is hard to verify or validate rules. This is because rules are scattered, and are embedded in procedural parts of the specification. It is hard to check them against each other, to check for completeness, or to present them to the user for validation.
3. Each application program contains a copy of some of the rules, possibly leading to inconsistency between programs.

The main reason why rules are embedded in procedures is due to the fact that, as rules restrict the states of the structure component, they therefore restrict the kinds of updates that are allowed to transform one state to another. It is more efficient at implementation time for rules to be in the same program, rather than in a central rulebase, for example, and this approach is still applied at the level of rule specification.

Recent approaches to modelling rules

AIMS

To avoid the problems discussed above, more recent approaches to rule modelling aim to:

1. Express as many rules as possible declaratively, not procedurally.
2. Express rules on a conceptual level of abstraction, and only in terms of structure component elements.
3. Express rules separately from other parts of the conceptual model in a central rule component.

We shall briefly describe a more recent approach to rules modelling termed NORMA (Flynn, 1996) which has two parts: a framework based on rule types which occur frequently in the user requirement and a set-based rules modelling language.

RULES FRAMEWORK

The framework in Table 8.1 has rows for the different elements of the structure component that may be restricted, and columns for the different classes of rule that may be applied to the elements. Row 1 rules are on attributes, row 2 rules are on entities, while rules on rows 3 and 4 are in terms of related entities and attributes. There are four classes of rule: cardinality, set, function and order.

Table 8.1 Rules framework

| | Class | | | |
Object	Cardinality	Set	Function	Order
Attribute	1.1	1.2	1.3	1.4
Entity	2.1	2.2	2.3	2.4
Related object	3.1	3.2.1, 3.2.2	3.3.1, 3.3.2	3.4
Related object by value	4.1	4.2.1, 4.2.2	4.3.1, 4.3.2	4.4

The cardinality rule restricts set properties while the other three classes of rule restrict sets. Set members are instances of attributes or entities, and sets are denoted by attribute or entity names or a combination of such names.

We shall not discuss all the different types of rule in Table 8.1, but we shall present two types of rule on row 1, showing rules that involve attributes. In addition, we shall show how the participation constraint discussed earlier may also be modelled as a rule.

Attribute cardinality rule (1.1)

This rule restricts the cardinality (number of values) of a given attribute. For example, we may restrict the cardinality of the material-code attribute to 300. A typical expression would be:

$$CARD(material\text{-}code) \leq 300$$

Attribute set rule (1.2)

Here we want to restrict the actual values that an attribute may possess. For example, to restrict the values of the price attribute to between 50 and 2000, we write:

$$price\ IN\ \{50\ .\ .\ 2000\}$$

Participation rule (3.2.1)

This concerns the participation of set instances in a relationship. Either *all* instances must participate in the relationship or *not all*. For example, from Fig. 8.19, there may be a rule that all instances of product must participate in the relationship product : clapper. In user terms, this means that all products must be associated to a clapper. We express this rule as:

$$product:clapper = product$$

Summary of framework

Rules are specified declaratively, and they are only expressed in terms of elements of the structure component. Rules are modelled separately in a rule component and they are easily related to their elements and to the processes which require them, as structure elements are part of the rule expression. One copy only of rules addresses the later problem of duplication of rules over processes.

Rule specification can help as a check on the contents of the structure component. For example, a rule referring to an object not modelled might indicate either that the object should be modelled or that the rule is outside the system. Rules may also be used to help decide on subtypes or aggregate objects. Another approach to rule modelling may be found in Bassiliades and Vlahavas (1994).

Guidance for analysis

CONCEPTUAL MODELLING PRINCIPLES

This section will present some principles which are useful to bear in mind when carrying out conceptual modelling to help achieve the aims of a correct and complete specification. The principles have been drawn from those found in Batini *et al.* (1992), ISO (1982) and Peckham and Maryanski (1988).

1. To model *completely* – to model in all the detail required on the conceptual level of abstraction.
2. To be *precise* – to expose any ambiguity, redundancy or inconsistency in the requirements (often the case where multiple users exist). A precise language helps to achieve this.
3. To be *abstract* – to avoid any detail regarding design or implementation. Such detail is firmly relegated to lower levels of the development process. User terms and concepts must be retained so that a description based on the specification is recognizable to a user.
4. To be *declarative* – to avoid procedural forms as much as possible. It is not clear to what extent there is a trade-off between the formality and

the declarative nature of a language or technique required for the declarative specification of processes. However, we should postpone to the latest possible stage any descriptions of processes which resemble program code, either by their level of detail or their level of abstraction.

5. To avoid *redundancy* – to model facts in the requirements only once.
6. To be *natural* – to aim for a one to one correspondence with organization objects. This means that if the user is accustomed to regarding certain components of the organization as single concepts, for example a static object or a single process, then the modelling language should preserve this single nature by providing constructs (language concepts) which model these components. We may contrast this approach with one where an organization object may be modelled in many modelling language constructs, or vice versa.

To help with principle 1, we should use a method that supplies the techniques necessary to model all the relevant parts of the requirements. For principle 2, precise languages will be the basis on which techniques are built. Although some limited forms of checking are possible with current techniques (for example checking a structure component for entities with the same name), the intuition of the developer coupled with validation is the chief current means for checking specification content.

To achieve principle 3 is largely the task of the developer, to resist the temptation to build a specification in terms of implementation objects. Principle 4 can be applied if declarative techniques, such as entity and rule modelling, are used. Principles 5 and 6 may be achieved by the use of good techniques that do not allow overlap in the facts they model and that possess natural constructs.

PROBLEMS

There are two main problems in the analysis phase: the quality problem of making errors in analysing information needs and the productivity problem caused by changing requirements.

The first problem is being addressed by the use of more abstract and declarative models which attempt to be more complete and specific in their coverage of the necessary components of a specification on this level. The ER model and its variants have helped with structure modelling in the past few years, and the next advance is expected to be with the modelling of rules, as briefly described in this chapter.

However, developers may make errors or may misunderstand users in such a way that models cannot detect the errors. It is thus essential that there are methods for validating the specification with the users, and it is expected that prototyping or specification execution aids, discussed in Chapter 6, will become more common in the near future.

Although changing requirements, due to users learning about what they really want, is not so much a problem in this phase as it is in requirements determination, validation methods can be expected to help with this problem, as they allow users to define and incorporate their changes into the system which they validate.

Summary

The principles of modelling the structure and rule components in the analysis phase have been described in this chapter in outline only, and their full study would require considerably more space than is available. Entity modelling, for example, is a very well-developed topic, and books are available that deal exclusively with the subject. Rule modelling, on the other hand, is emerging as an area in which it may be possible to make significant progress (using declarative forms such as the framework described), as rules have for so long been specified procedurally, with the attendant problems of complexity and difficulty of validation described above. It is likely that rule modelling will add significantly to the value of the object-oriented approach.

Discussion questions

1. Refer to Fig. 8.9. How would you change this if a supplier could have many accounts and a customer could buy only one product?
2. In Fig. 8.13, what change would you make to add the fact that employees may be full-time or part-time?
3. Produce an entity diagram from the following description:
    Hospitals consist of wards which consist of beds. A hospital has one matron only, who is attached to only one hospital. Each ward has a sister, who may be responsible for many wards.
4. Produce an entity diagram from the following description:
    Schools have different types of teacher: full-time, part-time, peripatetic and trainee. There may be several deputy heads, but only one head. Schools also have a caretaker and a secretary. Pupils attend the school and are administered tests on a regular basis.
5. Produce an entity diagram from the following description:
    A garage has to keep track of cars brought in for repair, its customers, suppliers of spare parts as well as oil and petrol and the government MOT department. Cars have registration numbers, chassis numbers and service histories. Cars are classified as commercial or private. Customers are recorded along with their name, address, telephone numbers and amount owing. All jobs must be recorded, with start and finish dates, customer, car, and items such as spare parts and labour that need to be charged to the customer.

References

ANSI/SPARC (1975) ANSI/X3/SPARC study group on database management systems, *Interim report*, FDT (Bulletin of ACM-SIGMOD), **7**(2).

Bassiliades, N. and Vlahavas, I. (1994) Modelling constraints with exceptions in object-oriented databases, in *Entity–Relationship Approach – ER '94*, Springer-Verlag, Berlin, 189–204.

Batini, C., Ceri, S. and Navathe, S. (1992) *Conceptual Database Design: An Entity–Relationship Approach*, Benjamin/Cummings, California.

Brodie, M. L., Mylopoulos, J. and Schmidt, J. W. (eds.) (1984) *On Conceptual Modelling: Perspectives From Artificial Intelligence, Databases and Programming Languages*, Springer-Verlag, New York.

Chen, P. P. (1976) The entity–relationship model: towards a unified view of data, *ACM Transactions on Database Systems*, **1**(1), 9–36.

Elmasri, R. and Navathe, S. B. (1994) *Fundamentals of Database Systems*, 2nd edn, Benjamin/Cummings, California.

Flynn, D. J. (1996) *NORMA: a conceptual rule modelling framework and language*, Technical report, Department of Computation, UMIST, January.

Flynn, D. J. and Fragoso Diaz, O. (1996) *Information Modelling: An International Perspective*, Prentice-Hall, London.

Halpin, T. (1995) *Conceptual Schema and Relational Database Design*, 2nd edn, Prentice-Hall, Australia.

ISO (1982) *Concepts and Terminology for the Conceptual Schema and the Information Base* (ed. Van Griethuysen, J. J.), ISO/TC97/SC5–N695, March.

Loucopoulos, P. and Zicari, R. (1992) *Conceptual Modelling, Databases and CASE: an Integrated View of Information Systems Development*, Wiley, New York.

Navathe, S. B. (1992) Evolution of data modelling for databases, *Communications of the ACM*, **35**(9), 112–23.

Nijssen, G. M. and Halpin, T. A. (1989) *Conceptual Schema and Relational Database Design – a Fact Oriented Approach*, Prentice-Hall, London.

Peckham, J. and Maryanski, F. (1988) Semantic data models, *ACM Computing Surveys*, **20**(3), September, 153–189.

Rochfeld, A. (1987) MERISE, an information system design and development methodology, in *Entity–Relationship Approach* (ed. Spaccapietra, S.), Elsevier Science Publishers, Amsterdam, 489–528.

Rock-Evans, R. (1987) *Analysis Within the Systems Development Life-cycle. Book 1: Data Analysis – the Deliverables*, Pergamon Infotech, Maidenhead.

SSADM (1995) *SSADM Version 4+*, NCC Blackwell, Oxford.

Teorey, T. J. (1994) *Database Modelling and Design: the Fundamental Principles*, 2nd edn, Morgan Kaufmann, San Francisco.

Tsichritzis, D. and Klug, A. (eds.) (1977) *The ANSI/X3/SPARC DBMS Framework: Report of the Study Group on Database Management Systems*, AFIPS Press, Montvale, NJ (reprinted in *Information Systems*, **3**(3), 1978, 173–91).

Tsichritzis, D. and Lochovsky, F. H. (1982) *Data Models*, Prentice-Hall, Englewood Cliffs, NJ.

Winter, R. (1994) Formalised conceptual models as a foundation of information systems development, in *Entity–Relationship Approach – ER '94*, Springer-Verlag, Berlin, 437–55.

Wintraecken, J. J. V. R. (1990) *The NIAM Information Analysis Method: Theory and Practice*, Kluwer Academic, Utrecht.

9

Analysis II – process modelling

Introduction

AIMS

A process is an activity carried out in an organization, for example, casting a bell or sending an invoice, and several process modelling techniques are described in this chapter. Many of these are used both for modelling processes on the external level, concerning the organizational context of the information system, and for building the process component of the conceptual model.

Process modelling is more complex than entity modelling and this is reflected in the variety of techniques in current use. Some of these have a broad scope, using several concepts to build the process model, while others specialize in one or two.

There are four aims to this chapter:

1. To describe the important concepts of process modelling.
2. To describe some common phase products used for process modelling in the analysis phase.
3. To comment upon the suitability of the products in different situations or at different points in the life-cycle.
4. To show product similarities and differences, using a common example.

PROCESS CONCEPTS AND PHASE PRODUCTS

The concepts are:

1. Process and its decomposition into more detailed processes.
2. Event and the processes initiated by the event.
3. Process control structure:
   (a) sequence – the order in which processes occur

(b) selection – the conditions under which processes occur
(c) iteration – whether a process may be repeated
(d) concurrency – whether a process may occur at the same time as another process
4. Process input and output.

The phase products which we shall describe are:

1. Process decomposition diagram
2. Data flow diagram
3. State transition diagram
4. Flowchart
5. Decision tree
6. Decision table

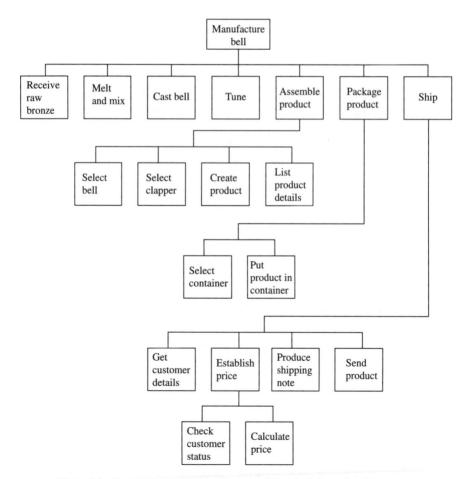

Figure 9.1 Process decomposition diagram of Eurobells⌂ production system.

Process decomposition diagram

The *process decomposition diagram* shows a *process* and its *decomposition* into more detailed processes. The partial refinement of the production system in Eurobells⌂ for manufacturing a bell may be seen in the process decomposition diagram in Fig. 9.1. The diagram is the simplest of the process modelling diagrams and it uses only two graphical symbols. Symbols vary, and Fig. 9.1 uses a rectangle containing a process name to represent a process and an edge to show the hierarchical relationships between processes (Rock-Evans, 1987, 1989).

The root level is usually termed level 0, and this diagram shows four levels of process, with three level 1 processes refined. We shall use this example to illustrate detailed aspects of process specification in the rest of the chapter. The diagrammatic ordering of the processes from left to right often models the sequence in which they occur, as is the case in Fig. 9.1.

The level 1 processes are taken from Table 4.1. The refinement of the assemble product process selects a bell and a clapper to form a product and then lists the details of the product. The package product process selects the correct container for the type of product and then puts the product into the container.

The ship process obtains customer details and then calculates the price for the product, using a range of discount prices, the choice of which is dependent on customer status. A shipping note is produced and this is sent out with the product.

With decomposition, the question often arises: where do we stop? We shall see later, when we discuss methods, that there are different answers for this, but a realistic level at which to stop is when primitive processes (discussed in Chapter 4) refer to attributes of entities. For example, the create product process on level 2 in Fig. 9.1 may be decomposed further, as in Fig. 9.2, where leaf processes (bottom level) are in terms of operations on the attributes shown in the Eurobells⌂ model in Fig. 8.19.

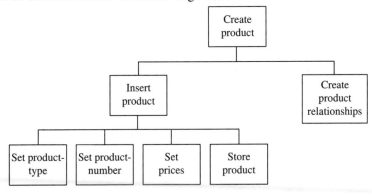

Figure 9.2 Refinement of create product process.

The use of the terms leaf process or node indicates that a decomposition may be a tree. However, it may also be a network if there are common actions. For example, although this is not shown, the get customer details sub-process of the ship process may be used in other systems.

It is also possible to show events (described in the next section) on the process decomposition.

Data flow diagram

We often wish to model *process input and output*, and a widely used technique that shows such process relationships is the DFD or *data flow diagram* (Gane and Sarson, 1979; de Marco, 1979). The DFD can provide a wide overview of a system and is particularly suited to those systems where data is transformed by a series of processes, the sequence forming a logical whole, such as the transaction processing cycle discussed in Chapter 4.

DFD SYMBOLS AND RULES

A common form of DFD uses the five symbols shown in Fig. 9.3. A circle represents a *process*, which has a unique name and number. The number may indicate the level of the process (for example, 2, 2.1, 2.1.1 and so on). All processes must have an input and an output, consisting of a *data flow*, which is shown by an arrowed edge joining the process to other symbols on the diagram. The direction of the flow is shown by the arrow, and the edge is labelled with the name of the data flow. *Events*, which initiate processes, are shown by thick arrows, labelled with the name of event, and the event is placed by the process which it initiates.

External entities, shown by a square, are outside the system in the sense that the developer does not specify their behaviour or record information about them. Typically, they supply system input and receive system output. Input entities are often termed *sources*, while those receiving output are termed *sinks*.

Data may be stored in a *data store*, shown by an open rectangle. This acts as a buffer, as there may be a time delay between processes where, for example, process B, which receives data from process A, may not necessarily start immediately after process A finishes. Processes may input and output data into and from a data store. Data cannot flow directly between stores.

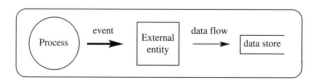

Figure 9.3 Data flow diagram symbols.

If the DFD is being used to build the process component of the conceptual model, then it is an *abstract* DFD, as it is a specification for a computerized system modelling some part of that organization. The DFD models the organization in terms of data, representing the flow of both material and data in the organization. For example, the DFD of a library models the flow of data, for example member names and addresses, and the flow of material, for example books and periodicals.

However, if a DFD is being used on the external level, to build a model of the organizational context of a system, then it is usually a *physical* DFD, as it models the organization in terms not only of data but also material, representing the flow of data and material in the organization. Where both material and data flow occur it may be necessary to annotate, that is to explain in an additional note, whether a given flow is data or material. For example, in such a library DFD, if a flow is labelled *book*, does this model the flow of a book or of data representing that book?

It is important to distinguish the purpose of a given DFD; that is, whether it is on the conceptual or external level. The DFD should be concerned with *what* material or data are used and stored, not how, by whom or where.

EXAMPLE DFD

Figure 9.4 shows a DFD which models the Eurobells⌂ production system, where the processes are the level 1 processes from Fig. 9.1. The DFD is intended for a process component of the conceptual model. A warehouse is an external entity, which sends raw bronze to the organization. This is input to the receive raw bronze process, which adds the bronze to the stock of raw material. The next stage is where the melt and mix process begins, which takes raw material as input, producing mixed bronze, which is input to the cast bell process, which produces a bell.

The tune process takes a bell as input and produces a tuned bell. The assemble product process produces a product from a bell and clapper, also generating product details for production control, which constitutes an external entity sink. The package product process packages a product in a container, and the ship process finally takes a product and sends it to a distribution organization, along with a shipping note for sending to the customer.

The figure also shows five events. The receive raw bronze process is begun when raw bronze arrives, and the melt and mix process begins when product stock is low and more bells and clappers thus need to be made. If a bell is out of tune, the bell is tuned. Products are assembled at the end of the day, and package product is started when a customer order arrives.

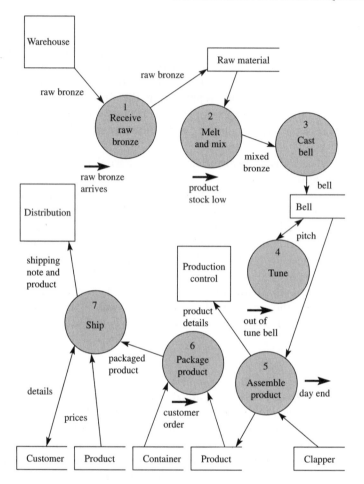

Figure 9.4 DFD of Eurobells⌂ production system.

RELATIONSHIP WITH OTHER PHASE PRODUCTS

It is increasingly the practice to build a DFD after, or in parallel with, the structure component. In this case, many of the objects referred to in the data flows and stores should be defined in the structure component. However, there will be some objects that are not in the structure component, such as external level objects (for example invoices and reports) and derived objects (for example an average price derived from values of a price attribute). This is the case even when the DFD is part of the conceptual model as opposed to being on the external level.

The DFD and the process decomposition diagram normally work closely together, as each level of the process decomposition diagram has a corresponding DFD. In this way, phase products may be used to cross-reference and thus verify each other.

SUMMARY OF DFD

This brief description of the DFD has only outlined the use of the method. In practice, many levels of DFD may be constructed, showing the decomposition of each process and showing the internal data flows. There are also a number of guidelines for good practice when using DFDs, and an important topic concerns whether a DFD should be built using a top-down or a bottom-up method. In practice, it is usually built using a combination of both of these methods.

The main use of the DFD is as an overview of conceptual model processes, which can then be decomposed in a top-down manner to allow detailed analysis if necessary. The DFD is also the medium for the developer to specify the organizational context of the system, including the interface between human and computer.

The DFD is also used extensively on the logical design level, when designing the information system, and it is necessary to be careful not to let lower level design aspects 'creep' into the DFD on the analysis level.

The DFD is possibly the oldest diagrammatic tool used for modelling systems, originating in diagrams that show the flow of paperwork or physical material through an organization. Its main disadvantages are that it can become over-complex and it cannot cope well with error-handling or exceptional situations. It also does not show process control structure.

State transition diagram

A *state transition diagram* shows conditions on transitions between states, and it is used frequently on the external level for specifying an interactive user interface, where users enter commands and data and receive computer responses. It uses three concepts, the state, the transition and the condition/action label, to model *process*, *event* and the *sequence* and *selection* parts of *process control structure*.

A state is shown by a rectangle containing the state name, and a transition is shown by an arrow between states. The condition/action label has two components, separated by a horizontal line. The condition which must be true before the transition may occur is specified above the line, and the actions (processes) which the system may perform in the transition are specified below the line.

For example, Fig. 9.5 shows how to specify a partial data capture system based on the level 1 processes of the production system. Each of the states in Fig. 9.5 might be implemented by a screen containing a menu of options with a form for entering data and a means of initiating a computer system process. The system has been put in the state 'production system initiated' and when an event occurs a transition (consisting of the action 'check event') occurs to the state represented by the empty rectangle. This is empty, as the system may transit to one of a number of states from this state.

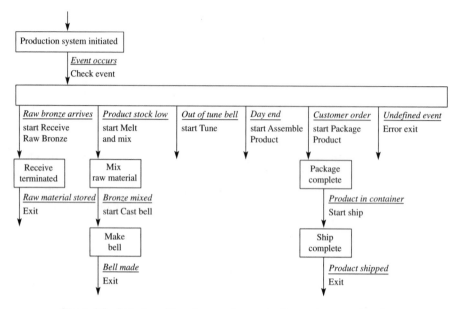

Figure 9.5 State transition diagram for production system user interface.

The figure shows that if a known event occurs then the corresponding process will be started. If an unknown event occurs, an exit to an error routine is taken.

After a transition to one of the next states, for example, 'mix raw material', the bronze will have been mixed by the melt and mix process. Then, a transition to the state 'make bell' occurs by the process cast bell being started. When the bell has been made, an exit is taken.

It is thus possible to show selection, as there may be many transitions from a state, and sequence, as a transition to one state may depend on a transition to a preceding state. A problem of this type of diagram is that rather artificial names may be given to states, and it is easy to slip into informal and therefore imprecise means of expression for the conditions and subsequent actions, by giving names which do not refer to defined components of structure or process.

An important element of a user interface specification is that, as shown in Fig. 9.5, there should be a direct correspondence between the events in the DFD or process decomposition diagram and the states or conditions on the state transition diagram, as the events will eventually be represented by the input of a command or the selection of an icon.

The state transition diagram is useful where the system being specified consists of a set of discrete, easily identifiable states, and where we are not so much concerned with the details of the transitions that take us from one state to another but are interested in the sequence of transitions, as well as the conditions for taking different transitions. As such, it is ideally suited to

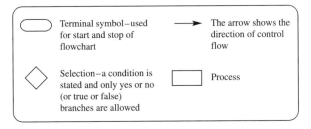

Figure 9.6 Some common flowchart symbols.

user interface specification, where we cannot be too detailed about transitions, as this involves design phase detail that is related to interaction style.

Flowchart

A *flowchart* is a diagrammatic aid which, in its purest form, shows only *processes* and *process control structure*. However, it is often adapted to show data input to and output from processes as well. Some common flowchart symbols are shown in Fig. 9.6, with their meanings. It is commonly used for showing the refinement of a process in greater detail.

Originally a tool for program design, it can show a complex control structure, with many selections for processes and where there is much transfer of control. However, as flowcharts become more complex, they quickly resemble 'spaghetti', with control flow arrows pointing in many directions. They have been superseded, for program design, by several structured methods, which are described below. They are usually restricted nowadays to showing simple process sequence (and possibly data flow as well) for system overview diagrams or user procedures, which involve a mixture of manual and computer processes.

Figure 9.7 shows a flowchart that is a refinement of the insert product process, showing a selection to determine whether the product is a bell or not. It also shows iteration to set the price fields, as there are a range of prices specified for a product, where the final price, determined in the ship process, will depend upon a set of factors such as favoured customer discount.

Decision tree

Decision trees (de Marco, 1979; Davis, 1990) are used to describe a process (or process fragment) that contains a number of alternative actions to be selected. A tree consists of a set of nodes, which are conditions, and a set of unlabelled edges, while the leaves (rightmost nodes) contain the actions. The first (leftmost) node shows the name of the process. Trees are usually shown left to right, although they may be shown top to bottom.

A decision tree for the select container sub-process of the package product process from Fig. 9.1 is shown in Fig. 9.8. Within the process, different types and qualities of bell are determined for matching with different sizes and finish of container.

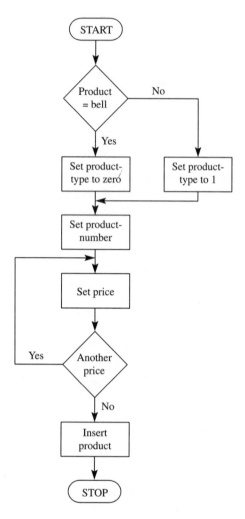

Figure 9.7 Flowchart for the insert product process.

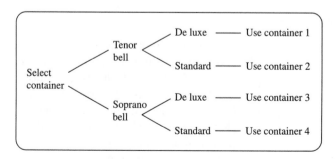

Figure 9.8 Decision tree for the select container process.

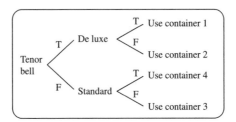

Figure 9.9 Predicate form of decision tree.

Tree styles are not standardized, and an alternative for Fig. 9.8 is to use a predicate form, where edges are labelled only true or false, as in Fig. 9.9. This has fewer nodes, but is not as informative, as only a tenor bell is mentioned, compared with Fig. 9.8, which refers to both soprano and tenor bells.

The tree is normally used for complicated conditions and dependent actions within processes and may be suitable for discussion with users. The tree is used in preference to the decision table (see below) as it shows the likely sequence of events dependent on conditions. It is used where there are a *large number of conditions* that determine the appropriate action.

Decision table

Figure 9.10 shows a *decision table* (de Marco, 1979; Davis, 1990), containing actions in what is termed the action stub in the bottom left-hand part of the table, with the conditions in the condition stub in the top left-hand part. A condition is expressed in predicate form, that is it expects an answer true or false. All possible combinations of true and false responses are recorded in the top right-hand part of the table, termed the condition entry. In the corresponding columns of the bottom right-hand part, the action entry contains an ×, indicating the appropriate action to be taken.

The decision table is more suitable for large numbers of *actions* than the decision tree, and it is also easier to check that all conditions have been catered for. Where there are many conditions, it is inferior to the decision

Condition stub	Condition entry			
Tenor bell	T	T	F	F
De luxe model	T	F	T	F
Use container 1	×			
Use container 2		×		
Use container 3			×	
Use container 4				×

Action stub   Action entry

Figure 9.10 Decision table for select container process.

Table 9.1 Characteristics of different types of process specification.

	Form of expression[1]	Level of detail[2]	Purpose[3]	Components[4]	Suitable for users[5]	Easy to modify[6]
Process decomposition	D	O/M/D	G	P, E	Y	Y
Data flow diagram	D	O/M	G	P, E, D	Y/N	Y
State transition diagram	D	O	H	P, C	Y	N
Flowchart	D	D	G	P, C	Y	N
Decision tree	D	D	S	P, C	Y	N
Decision table	D	D	S	P, C	Y	N

[1] Diagram (D), text (T)
[2] Overview (O), medium (M), detailed (D)
[3] General (G), HCI (H), update (U), selection (S)
[4] Process (P), control structure (C), data (D), event (E)
[5] Yes (Y), moderately suitable (Y/N), not suitable (N)
[6] Yes (Y), no (N)

tree, as, for n conditions, the table requires 2^n condition entries. Four separate conditions would therefore create a table with 16 columns in the condition entry. In general, its use is similar to that of the decision tree.

Summary of process phase products

Table 9.1 summarizes the above discussion with respect to the different means for specifying processes. It can be seen that a detailed process specification may be difficult to validate with users, apart from decision trees and tables.

Summary

In this chapter, we have discussed various techniques for modelling processes. An overview of these techniques may be found in Curtis *et al.* (1992), while more detailed accounts are in Davis (1990) and Flynn and Fragoso Diaz (1996). The *entity life history* is an alternative process modelling technique, which is described in Chapter 11. Process decomposition diagrams and data flow diagrams are the most common forms for use on the overview level, and they are complementary, as the DFD basically adds data flow to the processes modelled in the process decomposition diagram. Events may be shown on both types of diagram and are important, as they identify groups of related processes which will form transactions.

The state transition diagram, emphasizing states and the sequence in which they are reached, is suitable for specifying user interface processes. Flowcharts are used for specifying low-level detail diagrammatically, and are popular with users, while decision trees and tables are used for specifying complex selection conditions which are process fragments. Problems with analysing and specifying processes are similar to those concerned with entities and rules, discussed at the end of the previous chapter.

Discussion questions

1. List the main concepts used to build a process specification.
2. As an exercise in diagram use, show the processes that constitute (a) your normal working day and (b) what you do for fun, on three different levels of detail: (i) overview – DFD; (ii) medium – process decomposition diagram; (iii) detailed – flowchart.

References

Curtis, B., Kellner, M. I. and Over, J. (1992) Process modeling, *Communications of the ACM*, **35**(9), 75–90.

Davis, A. M. (1990) *Software Requirements: Analysis and Specification*, Prentice-Hall, Englewood Cliffs, NJ.

Downs, E., Clare, P. and Coe, I. (1992) *Structured Systems Analysis and Design Method*, 2nd edn, Prentice-Hall, London.

de Marco, T. (1979) *Structured Analysis and System Specification*, Prentice-Hall, Englewood Cliffs, NJ.

Flynn, D. J. and Fragoso Diaz, O. (1996) *Information Modelling: An International Perspective*, Prentice-Hall, London.

Gane, C. and Sarson, T. (1979) *Structured Systems Analysis*, Prentice-Hall, London.

Rock-Evans, R. (1987) *Activity Analysis—the Deliverables*, Pergamon Infotech, Maidenhead.

Rock-Evans, R. (1987) *Activity Analysis—the Methods*, Pergamon Infotech, Maidenhead.

Rock-Evans, R. (1989) *A Simple Introduction to Data and Activity Analysis*, Computer Weekly Press, London.

Warhurst, R. and Flynn, D. J. (1990) Validating JSD specifications by executing them, *Information and Software Technology*, **32**(9), 598–612.

10

Analysis III – object-oriented modelling

Introduction

The modelling approach discussed in the previous two chapters is often referred to as the *structured approach*, and is broadly characterized by the separate specification of structure, rule and process components. In contrast, the *object-oriented (OO)* approach is a more recent approach that attempts to produce a more integrated specification, with the emphasis on structure and process.

This chapter describes an OO approach to modelling the organization in the analysis phase which is used to build the specification on both the conceptual and the external levels.

As the OO approach is fairly recent there are several different techniques and forms of graphical representation. The one we use is taken from the analysis phase of the Object Modelling Technique (OMT) (Rumbaugh *et al.*, 1991) which builds three models: object model, dynamic model and functional model.

The object model corresponds to the structure component and uses very similar concepts, while the dynamic and functional models specify processes. The examples in this chapter are based on the Eurobells⌂ production system in Chapters 8 and 9, and we shall now describe the concepts used to build each of the models.

Object model

OBJECT AND OBJECT CLASS

An *object* is a real-world concept or thing that makes sense in the context of an application. An object may be, for example an individual named Mr Bryan or a particular product. All objects have definite boundaries and are distinguishable.

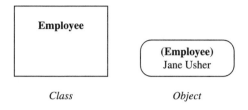

Figure 10.1   Class employee and object Jane Usher.

An *object class* or *class* is a group of objects with similar characteristics, such as similar attributes, common relationships to other objects, common behaviour and common meaning. Classes are, for example, employee and product.

An *object* thus corresponds to the concept of *entity instance* discussed in Chapter 8. The term *instance* is also used to refer to an object. A *class* is broader than our concept of *entity type* as it models behaviour as well. The meaning of the term behaviour will be described later.

Objects as well as classes may be graphically represented. A rounded box represents an object, with the class name in parentheses and emboldened and the object name in normal font, while the symbol for a class is a box with the class name in bold, as shown in Fig. 10.1.

ATTRIBUTE

An *attribute* is a data value held by the objects of a class and it is similar to the concept of attribute type. Attributes of the class customer are, for example name, address, telephone number and fax number, while the value of the telephone number attribute of customer object Alex Stapleton might be '0111–123456'.

Attribute values are not necessarily distinguishable as there may be, for example several values of the telephone number attribute with the above value.

Attributes are graphically represented by specifying their names in the second part of their class box under the class name. Optionally, details such as type and default value may follow the attribute name. Objects may also have their attribute values shown, as in Fig. 10.2. Object identifiers or attribute relationship constraints are not specified.

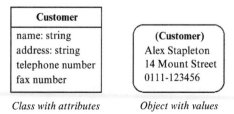

Figure 10.2   Class customer and object Alex Stapleton showing attributes and values.

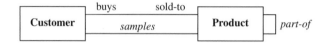

Figure 10.3 Associations involving classes customer and product.

BINARY RELATIONSHIP

Link and association

A *link* is a connection or relationship between objects, while an *association* is a group of links between objects from the same classes. Link is thus equivalent to the concept of relationship, while association is equivalent to the concept of relationship type.

A single association name may optionally be specified; in addition, role names may optionally be specified for the classes at each end of the association. The term inverse role name is not used; the reason for this may be that the designation of any one role name as 'inverse' might imply that both directions of the relationship are not equally important.

Role names should be unique within a class, and they should be used where there is more than one association between the same pair of classes. Their use is also recommended for associations between objects of the same class.

An association between two classes is graphically represented by a line drawn between the relevant classes. Figure 10.3 shows an association between objects of two different classes as well as between objects of the same class.

Links may also be shown graphically, and Fig. 10.4 shows links between customers and products. This diagram is similar to the population diagram of Fig. 8.3. This type of diagram, termed an *instance diagram*, is allowed in the object model.

Component relationship

The term *aggregation* refers to the type of association between classes where the semantics are those of part–whole or component–assembly. Aggregation as an abstraction operation has been briefly discussed in Chapter 8. An *aggregation relationship* may be considered to be a typed binary association,

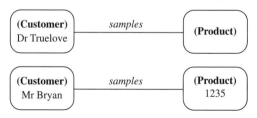

Figure 10.4 Links between classes customer and product.

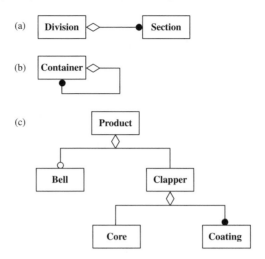

Figure 10.5 Aggregation relationships between classes: (a) division and section, (b) container (recursive aggregation), and (c) product, bell, clapper, core and coating.

which is a normal binary association with the implicit role names 'part of' and 'consists of' from the relevant directions. An aggregation relationship relates an assembly class to only one component class.

An example of an aggregation relationship is parts explosion, where there are links between part objects; for example, a bolt is part of a frame which is part of a door which is part of a car. Another example concerns the relationships between the classes region, area and cooperative in the German wine industry, where a region consists of many areas and an area consists of many cooperatives.

An aggregation relationship is graphically represented by a small diamond symbol at the assembly end of the association, as shown in Fig. 10.5. In Fig. 10.5(a) a division may have many sections, while in (b) an example of *recursive aggregation* is shown, where the component is of the same class as the assembly (container) and where the number of potential levels of objects is unlimited.

Figure 10.5(c) shows an example of an aggregation relationship on three levels, where a product consists of a bell (optional) and a clapper, which in

Figure 10.6 Association between classes showing multiplicity: (a) one to one; (b) one to many; (c) many to many; (d) zero or one and zero or more.

turn consists of a core and many coatings. The solid and hollow ball symbols are explained more fully in the next section.

RELATIONSHIP CONSTRAINTS

The concept of *multiplicity* corresponds, although not fully, to the two relationship constraints of cardinality and participation discussed in Chapter 8. Multiplicity is chiefly specified using graphical symbols as explained below and several examples are shown in Fig. 10.6.

Cardinality constraint

Figure 10.6(a) shows *one to one* multiplicity, corresponding to a 1:1 cardinality ratio, where a customer holds one account and where an account is held by only one customer. This is shown by the absence of multiplicity symbols on the line representing the association.

Figure 10.6(b) shows *one to many* multiplicity, corresponding to a 1:*n* cardinality ratio in the customer → product direction, where the solid ball line terminator next to a class represents a multiplicity of many. The meaning of this type of multiplicity is that zero or more instances of the class may be associated with an instance of the other class in the association. A customer may buy many products, while a product is sold to only one customer.

Figure 10.6(c) shows *many to many* multiplicity, corresponding to the *m*:*n* cardinality ratio. A manager manages many projects, while a project is managed by many managers.

Additionally, it is possible to specify integer cardinality values as well as intervals, including disconnected intervals. For example, 1 (exactly one), + 1 (more than one), 4–6 (four to six inclusive) and 2, 4, 6 (two, four or six) may be specified.

Participation constraint

This constraint is specified in a different, 'lookacross' style to that described in Chapter 8, as it is specified on the *opposite* entity in the association to which it applies. This may be confusing at first.

From the examples given (Rumbaugh *et al.*, 1991), it may be inferred that the classes in an association with one to one multiplicity both have total participation. That is, in Fig. 10.6(a), each customer must hold an account and each account must be held by a customer.

Partial participation of a class opposite a class with a multiplicity of one may be specified as shown in Fig. 10.6(d). This shows *zero to one* multiplicity, where the hollow ball line terminator means zero or one, representing the fact that zero or one instances of customer may buy a product. There is thus a partial participation constraint on product.

There is also an implicit partial participation constraint on customer, as the multiplicity of many on product, meaning zero or more, means that zero instances of product may be sold to a customer.

It does not appear possible to specify total participation for a class opposite a class with a multiplicity of many.

N-ARY ASSOCIATION

Multiple relationships, termed *n*-ary associations, may be modelled directly as two or more objects may be related by a link. This removes the need for the abstract entity as discussed in Chapter 8. An *n*-ary association is graphically represented by a diamond with lines drawn to the participating classes. The name of the association is optional and is written near to the diamond. Where a class participates in more than one *n*-ary association the association name is mandatory.

Figure 10.7 shows the *n*-ary association complaint between three different classes (a ternary association). *N*-ary links may also be shown, similar to the binary links in Fig. 10.4.

{Candidate key: (customer, product, salesperson)}

Figure 10.7   *N*-ary association between customer, product and salesman classes showing candidate key.

N-ary association relationship constraints

The multiplicity symbol shown in Fig. 10.6 is not used to specify the cardinalities of the classes involved in *n*-ary associations, as it may be ambiguous in this context. Instead, the *candidate key* of the *n*-ary association is listed underneath the association. A candidate key is that minimal set of attributes that uniquely identify any link of the association, and Fig. 10.7 shows that the combination of a customer, product and salesperson objects uniquely identifies a link of the complaint association.

RELATIONSHIP ATTRIBUTE

A relationship attribute is termed a *link attribute* and is viewed as a property of the links in an association. Graphically, a link attribute is represented by a box attached to an association by a loop, with the names of one or more link attributes in the box.

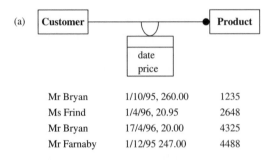

(a)

Mr Bryan	1/10/95, 260.00	1235
Ms Frind	1/4/96, 20.95	2648
Mr Bryan	17/4/96, 20.00	4325
Mr Farnaby	1/12/95 247.00	4488

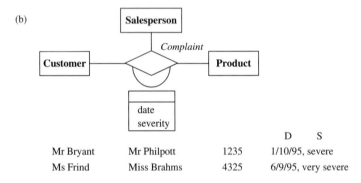

(b)

			D	S
Mr Bryant	Mr Philpott	1235	1/10/95, severe
Ms Frind	Miss Brahms	4325	6/9/95, very severe

Figure 10.8 Link attributes showing sample data for (a) binary and (b) *n*-ary associations.

Figure 10.8 shows link attributes of a binary as well as an *n*-ary association. Also shown are some links together with values for link attributes.

ASSOCIATION AS A CLASS

It is sometimes useful to model an association as a class, where each link becomes a class instance. Figure 10.9 shows that the graphical representation of an association modelled as a class is an extension of the link attribute notation. In this example, the association between project and manager classes is modelled as a class named team, with attributes budget and completion-date, and is associated with an office.

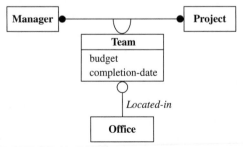

Figure 10.9 Modelling an association as a class.

GENERALIZATION

Generalization hierarchy

Generalization is viewed as a relationship between one class (the *superclass*) and more refined versions (*subclasses*) of the superclass, and it is graphically represented in an *inheritance hierarchy* by a triangle connecting a superclass to its subclasses, with the subclasses connected by lines to a horizontal bar, as shown in Fig. 10.10.

A *discriminator* is the attribute on which class instances may be grouped to form subclasses, and Fig. 10.10 shows that the discriminators for employee and accountant are employee type and specialism respectively.

Property inheritance

Each subclass inherits the properties of its superclasses as well as possessing its own properties. In Fig. 10.10, engineer inherits the two attributes of employee and also has an institution attribute of its own. It is possible for a subclass to override an inherited property by defining a property with the same name.

Multiple inheritance

A class that is allowed to have more than one superclass is termed a *join class*, corresponding to the concept of multiple inheritance discussed in Chapter 8. Join classes inherit properties from all superclasses; where a property from

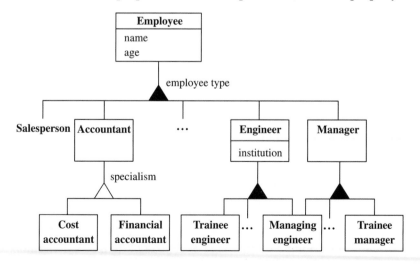

Figure 10.10   Inheritance hierarchy.

the same superclass may be found along more than one path it is inherited only once. Figure 10.10 shows that the class managing engineer is a join class, inheriting properties from both manager and engineer.

Exclusion and exhaustion

The situation where there are additional subclasses that are not shown on the inheritance hierarchy is graphically represented by a triple dot, as shown in Fig. 10.10. The absence of this symbol thus indicates that all subclasses exhaust the superclass.

Disjoint classes, where there is exclusion, are graphically represented by the hollow triangle joining the related classes, while overlapping classes are represented by the solid triangle. Cost and financial accountant are thus disjoint classes whereas manager, salesperson, engineer and accountant are not.

OTHER MODELLING FEATURES

Qualification

A qualified association is an association between two classes with some extra semantics, where a special attribute termed the *qualifier* of one of the classes is specified.

An example of this is where the qualifier is a partial identifier of class A, requiring the identifier of class B to fully identify class A. For example, in an association between department and office, where a department has many offices, the (partial) identifier of office may not be unique over all departments, requiring the identifier of department (class B) as well as the (partial) identifier of office (class A) to form the full identifier of office. This concept is similar to that of 'weak entity' (Chen, 1976), where in this example office is the weak entity.

Constraints

Different kinds of constraint may be specified, and they are similar to the rules discussed in Chapter 8. A precisely defined constraints language is not provided, but three examples are shown in Fig. 10.11, enclosed in parentheses by the classes to which they apply.

One kind restricts the values that entities, attributes or links can assume, and the example shown under the employee class restricts the values of the age attribute of employee. A similar example restricts the values of the product-number attribute. Another kind of constraint, termed a derived object, is shown for raw material, such that the value of the danger-level attribute is derived from 80 per cent of the value of the reorder-level attribute.

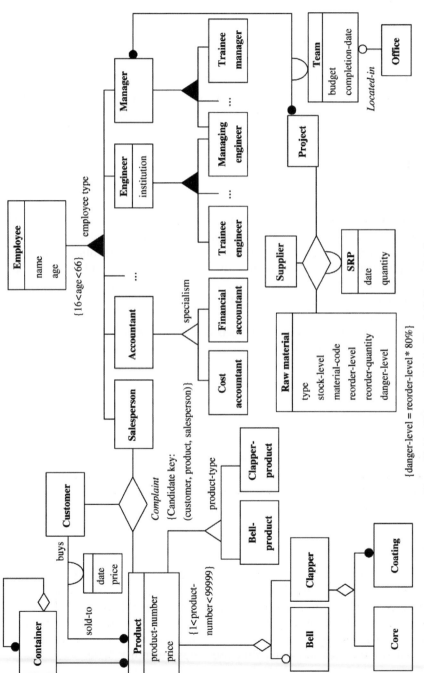

Figure 10.11 Object model for Eurobells⊕ production system.

Data dictionary

An object model will usually be accompanied by a data dictionary, containing descriptions of classes, associations and attributes.

Summary of object modelling

Figure 10.11 brings together the object modelling concepts discussed above and shows an object model for Eurobells⌂, based on the production system diagram in Fig. 8.19.

Dynamic modelling

INTRODUCTION

Dynamic modelling is concerned with the events that occur, over time, to the objects specified in the object model. The effects of the events on the objects are conceptualized in terms of transitions between object states, in which processes occur. The main form for the dynamic model is the *state diagram* for an object. In addition, other types of diagram, such as the event trace, scenario and event flow diagram, may be used to assist in building the state diagrams.

The dynamic model is thus concerned with *event*, *process* (termed operation, activity or action) and all aspects of *process control structure*.

EVENTS AND STATES

Event

An event occurs at a point in time and has no duration. It is a stimulus, such as the order of a soprano bell product from Eurobells⌂, and it also conveys information from one object to another. Events are grouped into event classes with a class name, and usually have attributes, which are data values conveyed by the event.

State

In contrast to an event, a state has duration and represents an interval in time, corresponding to the interval between two events received by an object. A state is an abstraction of the properties (attribute values and links) of an object, often defined by a particular value of one attribute or a group of attributes. For example, a bell may be in the out of tune state, defined by the value of its pitch attribute. Processes occur within a state.

STATE DIAGRAM

The state diagram describes behaviour by showing the relationship between states and events for a given object of a class. The diagram shows the allowable *transitions* that exist between states and the events that cause these transitions. A transition is viewed as a change of state of an object and it is said to *fire* when the object changes from the initial state to the receiving state.

Graphically, a state is represented by a rounded box containing an optional name in bold, a transition is represented by an arrowed line from the receiving state to the target state, and an event is shown as an italicized label on the transition that it causes. Time is implicit in the diagram by the direction of the arrows and thus the event time sequence on a given object is shown. Figure 10.12 shows a part of the state diagram for the product object with state, event and transition.

Figure 10.12   State diagram showing state, event and transition.

The figure shows that a customer order event causes a transition of the product object from a previous state to the packaging product state. The next transition, to the shipping product state, is unlabelled, which means that no explicit event is required, and the transition is made when the operations associated with the packaging product state have been completed. This is termed an *automatic transition*.

ACTIVITY

A state is not a passive interval in the life of an object but is active. It is often the case that an object will 'respond' to an event by performing operations, termed *activities*.

An activity may both change and access object properties, and it takes time to complete. If the activity changes the properties then this should not constitute a change of object state; if it does, an event should be modelled. If an activity is continuous it will start on entry to a state and will stop on exit; if it is a sequential activity it will stop after an interval of time and will complete before the next event is received by the object.

Figure 10.13 State with associated activity.

Graphically, an activity is represented by the notation *do: activity name* within its state box. Figure 10.13 shows the packaging product state with the associated package product activity. When the packaging product state is entered this activity immediately starts. When the activity terminates, this immediately causes a transition (as an automatic transition is shown) to the next state.

Concurrent activities within a state are also modelled, and may also show a merging of control, so that a transition to a succeeding state is only made when all concurrent activities have terminated, in any order.

ACTION, CONDITION AND ATTRIBUTE

Action

An *action* is an operation that is associated with an event, not a state. It may be regarded as instantaneous. It is often useful to associate an action with an event when the event is context-dependent; that is, when its effect depends on the state of an object. For example, depressing a button to call a lift from a floor may cause a lift to go up or come down, depending on whether the current floor for the lift is above or below that of the calling floor.

Figure 10.14 shows that when the customer order event occurs, the action locate product is the response. The notation uses a slash '/' after the name of the event with the action name following it.

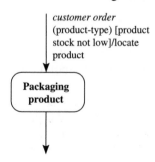

Figure 10.14 Event, attribute, condition and action.

Condition and attribute

Where a transition is governed by a *condition* it will only fire if the condition is true. For example, in Fig. 10.14, when the customer order event occurs, the labelled transition only fires if product stock is not low. A condition is expressed as a boolean function of object values and is enclosed in square brackets after the event name.

Figure 10.14 also shows that the customer order event supplies one attribute value, product-type, shown in parentheses.

ONE-SHOT STATE DIAGRAMS

The one-shot state diagram shows objects with finite as opposed to continuous lives and has initial and final states. The initial state implies creation of the object while the final state implies object deletion, as far as the situation being modelled is concerned. Figure 10.15 shows the initial and final states in the life of a product, where the initial state is represented by a solid circle and the final state is represented by a bull's-eye. These states can be labelled for descriptive purposes.

As a product is not 'created' within Eurobells⌂ until the assembling product state is reached then the initial state in Fig. 10.15 might represent a decision in some other part of the organization that the product is to be created.

NESTED STATE DIAGRAMS

An activity within a state can be expanded as a lower-level state diagram, where each state represents one step of the activity. Figure 10.16 shows a

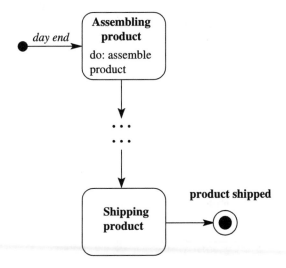

Figure 10.15 One-shot state diagram showing initial and final states.

Figure 10.16   Nested sub-diagram for assembling product state.

sub-diagram for the assemble product activity, which is associated with the assembling product state. Events may also be refined into more detail.

STATE GENERALIZATION

Where there are several states that have a transition to the same target state for the same event, the state diagram may be simplified by considering the initial states as substates, abstracting them into a superstate and allowing the substates to inherit transitions of the superstate. This may be useful when, for example, specifying a common action to be taken when an error event occurs in any one of several states.

A superstate is graphically represented by a large rounded box enclosing all substates and showing the superstate name. For example, Fig. 10.17 shows that when a poor quality product is detected, a transition is made to the rejecting product state from either of two states.

In Fig. 10.17, the states assembling product and packaging product are all substates of the superstate good quality, and as such they inherit the poor quality transition to the rejecting product state.

CONNECTIONS BETWEEN OBJECTS

It is usually the case that the occurrence of an event affects objects of more than one class. This situation is modelled by allowing objects to send events to one another. When an event occurs to an object, the object may

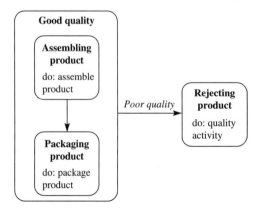

Figure 10.17   State diagram with generalization.

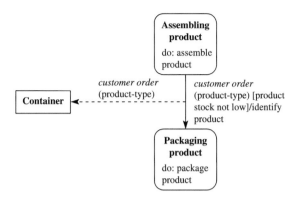

Figure 10.18 Sending an event to another object.

send this event, with attributes if required, to another object or objects. This is considered an instantaneous action rather than an activity. Figure 10.18 shows this, where the customer order event causes a transition of product to the packaging product state. The container object is affected as well as product, as the correct container has to be selected for the type of product. The dotted, arrowed line from the transition to container represents the fact that the event is sent to the container object when the transition fires. The line is labelled with the names of the event and any attributes that accompany it.

The line may also be shown connected directly to a particular transition within the state diagram of the object.

SUMMARY OF DYNAMIC MODELLING

Figure 10.19 shows a dynamic model, emphasizing the states discussed above, which brings together the different concepts discussed in this section. It shows partial state diagrams for the product and container objects. A complete dynamic model would show complete state diagrams for all the relevant objects. All objects shown on a dynamic model behave concurrently.

The day end event causes a product transition to the assembling product state, where the activity assemble product is started. The customer order event causes a guarded transition to the next state; the action associated with this event is locate product.

To show more clearly how interaction between objects is modelled, the packaging product state from Fig. 10.17 has been split into two states on Fig. 10.19, consisting of the activities container selection and containerize product. The customer order event is now shown as being sent, with the product-type attribute, to a particular state of the container object. The activity in this state, select container, uses the value of the product-type attribute to select the correct container for the product.

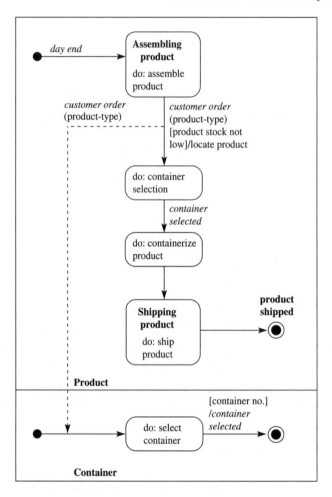

Figure 10.19 Dynamic model for part of Eurobells⌂ production process.

When this activity terminates, an action takes place which sends the container selected event, accompanied by a container number attribute, to any object or objects with a matching event name; that is, with a transition on this event. The effect of this will be to return 'control' to the containerize product state of the product object, as the transition to this state matches the event name. This is an alternative way to specify interaction between objects.

When the containerize product activity terminates, a transition automatically occurs to the next state, shipping product, where the 'life' of the product ends when the ship product activity terminates, causing a transition to the final product shipped state.

Functional model

INTRODUCTION

The aim of the functional model is to specify the computations that are carried out by the operations in the dynamic model. The functional model shows the flow of values from external inputs, through operations and data stores to external outputs, using the data flow diagram (DFD) as its graphical representation.

DATA FLOW DIAGRAM COMPONENTS

The DFD models process, data flow, control flow, data store and actor (external entity), and Fig. 10.20 shows the symbols which are their graphical representation. DFDs may be nested to any depth, and the leaf processes are operations on the objects in the object model. This type of DFD thus covers all the process modelling concepts described in Chapter 9 except event.

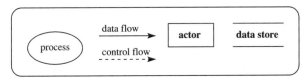

Figure 10.20 Data flow diagram symbols for functional model.

The DFD is similar to that discussed in Chapter 9, with the difference that it allows control flows. These are flows labelled with boolean values that determine whether or not a process is executed, and they are shown with a dotted line from the process producing the value to the process being controlled.

Figure 10.21 shows this with a DFD based on the tune process from the DFD in Fig. 9.4. The output from the verify pitch process consists of two control values: pitch OK and pitch wrong, governing the execution of their target processes.

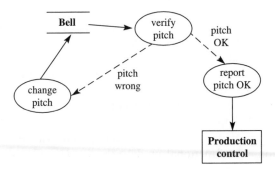

Figure 10.21 Data flow diagram for tune process showing control flow.

Relationship between object, dynamic and functional models

Different applications may place more emphasis on one of these types of model as opposed to another. For example, the dynamic model is very useful for specifying interactive applications, while an application with a simple set of objects would not have a complex object model.

Flows, actors and data stores in the functional model correspond to classes or attributes in the object model. Each leaf process in the functional model is an operation on an object, and will eventually be implemented as a method on that object.

Important processes should be summarized and shown on the object model in the bottom third of the class box. For example, Fig. 10.22 shows two operations that take place on the bell class.

Figure 10.22   Class showing operations.

Classes in the object model should have a state diagram in the dynamic model, showing the events, actions and activities related to each object. Events can be represented as operations on the classes in the object model. The interaction between classes is shown by the information sent from one class to another. The functional model is useful for showing high-level functionality of a system and for showing complex transformations with multiple inputs and outputs, involving different classes. It may also show leaf processes that are not defined on the dynamic model.

Summary

This chapter has discussed the three models which comprise the analysis phase of the OMT object-oriented approach: the object, dynamic and functional models.

The object model has a wider scope than many current entity modelling techniques in commercial use, as it contains advanced concepts such as multiple inheritance, *n*-ary relationships, aggregate relationships and constraints, all of which are diagrammatically represented. It lacks completeness when specifying the participation constraint.

The dynamic model is based on the notion of state diagram and also has a wide scope, modelling event, state and process, condition, state and event generalization. It provides for nested state diagrams and the specification of object interaction. The functional model uses the data flow diagram, without events but with control flow.

The degree of integration between object and dynamic models is good as each class on an object model may be inspected to see whether or not there are relevant events that are required to be specified on a state diagram for that class. However, it is not clear what the correspondence is between the events and operations of the dynamic model and the processes and flows of the functional model. It is possible that there may be extensive duplication. In addition, the functional model does not appear to be well integrated, and may not be included in future versions of OMT.

Further reading

There is a great deal of material concerning the OO approach. In addition to OMT (Rumbaugh *et al.*, 1991), well-known OO approaches which address the analysis phase are given by Shlaer and Mellor (1988), Coad and Yourdon (1991) and Jacobson *et al.* (1992). Booch (1991) is more oriented to the logical design phase. Coad (1992) has interesting remarks on the nature of OO 'objects', while several readable surveys and comparisons of OO and structured approaches may be found in Fichman and Kemerer (1992), Iivari (1994) and Monarchi and Puhr (1992). Finally, Pancake (1995) offers a view of an object-oriented future.

Discussion questions

1. What are the major differences between the object model of Fig. 10.11 and the entity diagram of Fig. 8.19?
2. List the extra modelling features possessed by the object model compared with the entity modelling technique in Chapter 8. Do you think that the benefits provided by the wider scope are outweighed by the greater complexity?
3. Build a state diagram, based on a class person and model (a) your normal working day and (b) what you do in your time off. Compare this to your answer to Question 2 in Chapter 9.
4. Extend the DFD in Fig. 10.21 to cover all the processes in Fig. 9.4. How complex is the resulting diagram? Would you say it was easy for users to understand?

References

Booch, G. (1991) *Object Oriented Design: With Applications*, Benjamin/Cummings, Menlo Park CA.

Chen, P. P. (1976) The entity-relationship model: towards a unified view of data, *ACM Transactions on Database Systems*, **1**(1), 9–36.

Coad, P. (1992) Object-oriented patterns, *Communications of the ACM*, **35**(9), 153–9.

Coad, P. and Yourdon, E. (1991) *Object-Oriented Analysis*, 2nd edn, Prentice-Hall, Englewood Cliffs NJ.

Fichman, R. G. and Kemerer, C. F. (1992) Object-oriented and conventional analysis and design methodologies: comparison and critique, *IEEE Computer*, October, 22–39.

Iivari, J. (1994) Object-oriented information systems analysis: a comparison of six object-oriented analysis methods, in *Methods and Associated Tools for the Information Systems Life Cycle* (eds. Verrijn-Stuart, A. A. and Olle, T. W.), Elsevier Science BV, Amsterdam, 85–109.

Jacobson, I., Christerson, M., Jonsson, P. and Overgaard, G. (1992) *Object-Oriented Software Engineering: A Use Case Driven Approach*, Addison-Wesley, Wokingham.

Monarchi, D. E. and Puhr, G. I. (1992) A research typology for object-oriented analysis and design, *Communications of the ACM*, **35**(9), 35–47.

Pancake, C. M. (1995) The promise and the cost of object technology: a five-year forecast, *Communications of the ACM*, **38**(10), 32–49.

Rumbaugh, J., Blaha, M., Premeriani, W., Eddy, F. and Lorensen, W. (1991) *Object-Oriented Modelling and Design*, Prentice-Hall International, New York.

Shlaer, S. and Mellor, S. J. (1988) *Object-Oriented Systems Analysis: Modelling the World in Data*, Prentice-Hall, Englewood Cliffs NJ.

11

Methods

Introduction

Up until now we have discussed systems development from a rather general point of view, so as to convey the flavour of the kinds of activities that occur and to discuss some of the important issues involved. In this chapter, the aim is to describe some specific methods that are widely used for systems development in organizations. We shall reflect the technical emphasis of current methods by not addressing non-technical issues, such as project planning and control, quality assurance, training and contractual activities.

We shall first of all define a method and discuss associated terminology. A brief history of the evolution of methods will then be given, and we shall then look at five methods: Information Engineering, Structured systems analysis and design, Jackson System Development (JSD), Structured systems analysis and design method (SSADM) and Object Modelling Technique (OMT). These methods cover the main phases of systems development that we have discussed.

The first four are termed structured methods, whereas the fifth method, OMT, is an object-oriented method. We shall use a small case study for the methods to contrast them, and this will be followed by a discussion of the problems addressed and solutions provided.

We close with a short description of CASE (computer-aided software engineering) tools, discussing the support they provide to methods.

DEFINITION

An information systems development method, or *method*, may be defined as follows:

A method is an integrated set of procedures and techniques which, when applied in a certain sequence, result in the specification or generation of an information system.

This definition takes into account the fact that some methods may only cover part of the development cycle and may not generate systems. It is also a very loose definition, as it does not even suggest a basic set of procedures or identify crucial development phases.

TERMINOLOGY

Method and methodology

Certain other terms are in use that approximate to the term *method*. The term *methodology* is often used because it means study of method, the implication being that a method may contain instructions for adapting it to fit a given situation.

The terms *development method* and *systems development method* are equivalent, as is the term *approach*, although an approach may not be as well defined as a method. The distinction is wholly academic, but a *technique* is normally much more specific, referring to a fairly precisely defined set of steps that address a particular (usually small) area of the life-cycle. It is defined (Olle *et al.*, 1991) as 'a part of an information systems methodology which may employ a well-defined set of concepts and a way of handling them in a step of the work'.

Phases and phase products

We shall use the terminology defined in Chapter 6 for describing methods. A method consists of a set of *phases* (usually in a certain sequence), where each phase may be refined into one or more *stages*. Outputs from stages and phases are termed *phase products*, and may be referred to generally as *documentation* or as the *specification*, which often implies a precise, non-narrative description, such as entity diagrams, of the desired system.

Brief history of methods

The way in which methods have evolved historically is a rather interesting subject, and in this short section we shall describe only some of the most important features of methods that have changed significantly. The features are: (a) model of systems development on which the method is based, (b) level of abstraction emphasized by the method; that is, the level on which defined activities exist and (c) project management activities. For additional reading, the following may be consulted: King (1984); Horowitz (1975); Yourdon (1982); Avison and Fitzgerald (1995); Friedman and Cornford (1989); Jayaratna (1994).

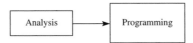

Figure 11.1 Pre-method model of systems development process.

PRE-METHOD ERA (BEFORE 1970)

The model of systems development implicitly used before methods came into use is shown in Fig. 11.1. This concerns, approximately, the period before 1970.

Analysis (which incorporated a form of systems design) was performed by analysts, who gave specifications to programmers to do programming. When the programming was finished, individual programs were tested. The activities within these phases were not defined, varying between individuals, and had no start or end and no defined products existed.

The level of abstraction implicitly emphasized was the programming level, as program execution efficiency, in terms of either execution speed or main memory size, was the overriding consideration. Types of assistance typically available consisted either of efficient algorithms for common programming problems, such as master-detail batch tape update, or diagrammatic techniques such as the program flowchart, which was used to help code the more difficult parts of programs.

Work began with analysis and continued until the system was in operation. The sizes of the boxes in Fig. 11.1 reflect the approximate amount of resources expended on the areas, and the tendency was (and still is) to concentrate resources on programming at the expense of analysis and design, especially if there was pressure for the system to be installed, as code was the only visible product. Documentation had a low priority.

An example of a method of this type, which had a commercial following in the United Kingdom, was that recommended by the National Computing Centre (NCC). The method, which evolved in the 1960s, is described in several publications concerned with the analysis and design of data processing systems (Daniels and Yeates, 1969; Lee, 1979). Although this method contained different phases (analysis, design, implementation, and maintenance and review), they contained few defined activities or techniques and had little or no interdependence. They consisted mainly of advice, such as guidelines for forms design for input and output documents.

PROCESS-ORIENTED METHODS – 1970s

Process-oriented methods mark a significant point in method evolution. They are characterized by the gradual progression from the simple model of systems development to one that increasingly differentiated between the development activities. The problems addressed were discussed at a well-known NATO conference in Garmisch, Germany, where the term software engineering was first used (Naur and Randell, 1968).

Structured programming

- *Programming.* The central principle of structured programming was that only three constructs, sequence, selection and iteration, were sufficient to code programs with one entry and exit point. The principle was the result of the work of two Italian mathematicians, Bohm and Jacopini (Bohm and Jacopini, 1966), and that of Dijkstra, who became famous with his 'Go To statement considered harmful' letter (Dijkstra, 1968). Coding could thus be reduced to the use of these three constructs, and the proliferation of undisciplined 'spaghetti' code reduced.

  The program flowchart was given a structured companion by the Nassi–Shneiderman chart (Nassi and Shneiderman, 1973), which was a type of structured flowchart, only allowing diagrammatic representations of the three structured constructs.

- *Project management.* A project that took place at the *New York Times* (Baker, 1972) introduced elements of project management into the development process. In addition to using structured programming as a project standard, as well as the top-down program structuring approach, a program production library was set up, organized by a program librarian, to centralize documentation and to keep track of programs and program changes. The programmers were also organized according to a concept termed the chief programmer team.

  An activity that distinguished testing from programming, termed code inspection (Fagan, 1976), defined desk-checking aspects of testing by instituting a walkthrough procedure, with defined activities and individuals, to check code before it was tested by execution.

Structured design

The design of programs and files had largely been left to individual intuition until now. General program design techniques began to appear that had the effect of differentiating physical design activities from those of programming. There were two main approaches, the functional and the data structured approach.

- *Functional approach.* This approach, developed in the USA (Stevens *et al.*, 1974), produced a design for a system or program by decomposition into a number of hierarchical functions or modules, expressed these on a structure chart and then applied design rules, using the concepts of coupling and cohesion to determine the quality of the design. The rules were later elaborated in Myers (1975) and in Yourdon and Constantine (1979). Data flow diagrams were used to identify major data transformations and sub-systems and to act as a basis for the production of structure charts.

- *Data structured approach.* This was presented in the work of Jackson (Jackson, 1975) in the UK and Warnier (1974) in France. Under the Jackson Structured Programming (JSP) approach, the structure of input and output data, shown diagrammatically in structure charts, determined the structure of the program; that is, the different hierarchical functions the program should have. The work of Warnier was made more generally available by the development of Warnier–Orr diagrams (Orr, 1977), which used a bracketed type of indented narrative to show function hierarchy similar to action diagrams. Data flow diagrams were not used in this approach.

Structured analysis

The basic principles of structured systems analysis were set forth in several influential publications from the late 1970s (Ross and Schoman, 1977; Gane and Sarson, 1979; de Marco, 1979), and grew from the use of the data flow diagram (DFD) in structured design.

- *Analysis.* The emphasis was on providing a non-technical picture of the user's requirements, and the medium advocated was the DFD, which was used to understand and model the application in terms of the hierarchical decomposition of organizational processes and data flows (although the data flows were usually a secondary consideration), rather than the programs and files of physical design.

   Abstraction away from physical considerations was thus occurring, as the top-level DFD gave an overview of the system, which was considered to assist in the clarification of requirements. Also provided were facilities for more detailed specification, such as minispecifications, data dictionaries, decision tables and trees.
- *Walkthroughs.* Products were more clearly described and walkthroughs setting out checking procedures for the products were also introduced (Yourdon, 1978). Validation with users was thus being introduced into the development process.

   The JSD method (Jackson, 1983) was a later UK method, which also modelled organizational processes and data but which was an early object-oriented approach and did not use hierarchical decomposition.

Summary of process-oriented methods

- *Process emphasis.* Process-oriented methods emphasized the analysis and design of processes as opposed to data. The level of abstraction of processes had been raised from programs to high-level transformations on data, but data was still viewed in physical terms.

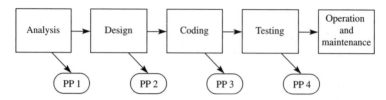

Figure 11.2   Avalanche model of systems development showing the production of phase products (PP).

- *Avalanche model.* By the end of the 1970s, the more widespread use of these methods, involving the emergence of distinct phases and defined phase products, was reflected in the adoption of a process often termed the 'waterfall' (Royce, 1970) or 'avalanche' model, as shown in Fig. 11.2, so called as it tended to create an avalanche of paper documentation as the project progressed. The appearance of maintenance on the model was due to realization of its increasing importance, as its share of the software budget was rising steadily.

   The more precise definition of phase products also allowed the development of walkthrough activities for checking.

DATA-ORIENTED METHODS – 1980s

Deficiencies of process-oriented methods

However, dissatisfaction grew with process-oriented methods, as many errors were still found at the test phase or in operation and maintenance. A study of the main structured analysis methods reveals that, in general, they assumed that users had a current (usually manual) system, which they wanted to computerize for increased efficiency. The user requirement was thus assumed to be fixed, implicitly on the functional organizational level, and improvements would result simply from making the old system more efficient, without the need for a new or extensively modified system.

However, as new systems were required that had not existed before, such as management and strategic information systems, which required significant user participation for establishing requirements, the structured analysis approach ran into difficulties. Methods that were more successful at establishing this new type of user requirement, as well as using terms that users could understand, came to be needed. The analysis phase in Fig. 11.2 had been expressed on a relatively low level and much of it came to be known later as logical design.

New features

We may pick out two key features of the new methods that emerged in the early 1980s to address the deficiencies mentioned above:

- *Conceptual modelling.* The first feature was the differentiation of the analysis phase, with the emphasis on the principles of conceptual modelling, concentrating on the precise modelling of objects on a user level using entity modelling techniques. Such methods were termed *data-oriented.* This type of modelling was useful for new types of applications, as well as for using terms that were more understandable to the user.

  An early type of data orientation was normalization (Date, 1995), which was a data design technique from the late 1970s, taking as input a set of files or input/output documents and 'normalizing' them into a more abstract set of data structures or *relations*, suitable for use in a relational database.

  The CRIS conference series (Olle *et al.*, 1982, 1983, 1986, 1988) encouraged debate and comparison between both commercial and research-based methods, and the terms 'data oriented' and 'process oriented' were used to describe different method emphasis.

  Methods did consider data as well as process, but usually emphasized one or the other, and it was felt that methods should provide techniques to encompass both orientations. This was because the term 'data oriented' usually implied an emphasis on the conceptual level, as many data-oriented methods used entity modelling and some data-oriented methods lacked a satisfactory treatment of process. Data-oriented methods usually pushed a lot of the more low-level detail of process specification down to the next, logical design phase.

  The emphasis on user level modelling also led to the realization that many systems had problems as they did not meet the user requirements, and some attention thus began to be directed to the process of requirements determination.

- *Iterative model.* The second feature was the emphasis on iteration, which meant the reworking of previous phases. This was regarded as an essential ingredient, as it had been gradually realized that it was in the nature of the development process that requirements and subsequent designs were rarely right initially. Phase products needed to be validated, and iteration, at least between successive phases, would take place if any errors, conflicts or misunderstandings were found. This contrasted with the avalanche model, where once a phase was completed it was not revisited.

  The different phase products were now being integrated into one specification, with explicit relationships between the different parts. The review component of walkthroughs was extended to include validation (checking against requirements with the user), as well as verification (reconciliation of different but related parts of the specification within phases and checking against the previous phase product). This often emerged as a separate quality control activity.

  However, the increasing use of verification within phases often meant that there was little or no checking to be done at the phase end. This

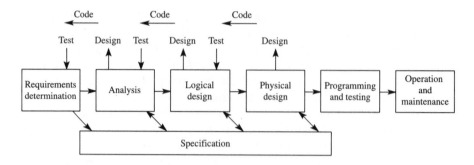

Figure 11.3 Iterative model (incorporating prototyping) of systems development.

meant that project management had to be more flexible, planning for iteration and adapting walkthroughs to project circumstances. Iteration could, however, be difficult to control.

Incorporating iteration soon led to the existence of several models of the development process, intended for use in different situations. For example, prototyping was a new type of validation that was introduced to take account of user unfamiliarity with computer terms or systems. A new type of iteration was incremental development, which might design and implement some parts of a system, leaving the design stage to be revisited later for the remaining parts. This was possible as it was now easier to see different levels and parts of a system.

Figure 11.3 shows an iterative model of the process at this point, incorporating prototyping, with renamed phases and a specification phase product. Methods now tended to cover most or all phases. Two methods that have evolved from this time, and which are used commercially to an increasing extent, are SSADM and Information Engineering, both of which are described later in this chapter.

OBJECT-ORIENTED METHODS – 1990s

The OO approach dates from the 1970s, when programming languages such as Smalltalk were developed, but OO methods have only become widely used in the last few years. Well-known OO methods are Object-Oriented Analysis (OOA) (Coad and Yourdon, 1991), Object-Oriented Design (Booch, 1991), Object Modelling Technique (OMT) (Rumbaugh *et al.*, 1991) and Object-Oriented Software Engineering (OOSE) (Jacobson *et al.*, 1992).

OO methods for analysis, design and programming exist and they continue the emphasis on modelling the static part of the organization, but extend it by grouping the processes that operate on an object into the specification of that object.

One aim of this is to achieve a less procedural and more modular specification, thus reducing complexity, and another is to assist the modelling process by offering an integrated path from analysis through design to the implementation phase, as the concept of object is the same in every phase. This is in contrast to the process- and data-oriented methods discussed above, often referred to as *structured* methods, where, for example, the process of transforming the entities and processes in the analysis phase to the files and transactions of logical design may be accomplished in many ways.

REQUIREMENTS ENGINEERING METHODS – 1990s

The 1990s has seen the appearance and gradual industrial penetration of requirements engineering (RE) methods. This may mark an acceptance of the fact that the early phases are the most important. Most methods address the requirements acquisition and modelling stages of the requirements determination phase and do not tend to be integrated with later phases.

However, some OO methods (for example OOSE (Jacobson *et al.*, 1992) and Object-Oriented Analysis and Design (OOAD) (Martin and Odell, 1992)) have begun to cover some elements of the requirements determination phase and, in addition, more established methods such as SSADM (1995) are attempting to improve their front ends by adding requirements-oriented processes and products.

Many RE methods focus on relationships with the user, and emphasize the need for improved communication between user and developer, employing, for example, user workshops or video techniques.

FUTURE METHODS

Phase emphasis

A key feature of methods in the 1980s was the emphasis on the development of conceptual modelling principles in the analysis phase. However, although entity modelling has become well developed there has been little progress in developing commercially usable techniques for modelling or generating either rules or processes, as discussed in Chapters 8 and 9, in a declarative manner. The human–computer interface, constituting the external level, is now increasingly modelled in the analysis as opposed to the logical design phase.

With the realization of the importance of the early phases of the process, these have been differentiated from the later phases more clearly. This is shown by the emergence of RE approaches in the 1990s, all of which have a strong focus on the requirements determination phase and which are discussed in Chapters 7 and 13. In addition, different types of validation, for helping the user to express and refine the requirement, and iteration, to allow changes to be incorporated in the phase products, are expected to increase in importance.

OO methods have not brought about a significant advance towards the requirements determination phase, but instead focus on a different approach

to the analysis and later phases. It is an open question, which we address at
the end of this chapter, whether the differences between these and structured
methods are as great as is often claimed.

Situational factors

Methods are rigid, as, by and large, they prescribe a process for systems
development that is assumed to fit every situation. However, it is likely that
future methods will incorporate procedures that, based on different situational
factors, allow methods to be tailored to make them more effective for specific
situations. At the moment, however, it is true to say that we do not know
which are the key determining factors, and there are many under consideration,
encompassing cultural (Rachel and Van Hasselt-Lim, 1995) as well as technical
factors. The next chapter will describe some technical situational factors in
its discussion of Euromethod.

Standards

Over the past decade there has been a movement towards the definition of
standards for systems development. For example, SSADM has been a British
standard since 1994 and the Euromethod programme is providing an emerging
standard in Europe.

The ISO 9000-based set of international standards have evolved from the
British standard BS 5750 and prescribe an integrated set of activities that
organizations should follow to ensure the quality of their systems development
process. For example, the UK TickIT scheme (TickIT, 1995) is an assessment
procedure that rates the quality management aspects of the development
process in an organization using the ISO 9001 standard, which is a general
standard for any type of production process, and the ISO 9000–3 standard,
which consists of specific guidelines for applying ISO 9001 to systems
development.

In the USA, the government-sponsored Capability Maturity Model (CMM)
defines five levels of maturity of the systems development process and is used
by organizations for development process assessment (Humphrey, 1989; Paulk
et al., 1993). These standards focus on what we may term non-technical areas
of systems development, such as procurement, contractual, project management
and quality assurance areas. A comparison between ISO 9001 and the CMM
may be found in Bamford and Deibler (1993).

There is likely to be increasing pressure from user organizations and
international bodies, such as the European Commission, to adopt standards
to improve quality and to provide a reference point. The standards are likely
to be on a general level, covering the whole systems development process and
focusing on non-technical areas. Technical areas, such as development phases

and their products, will be defined on a more general level than in current methods. The issue of method standardization is an important one and Chapter 12 will discuss different approaches to these standards.

Method development

The above discussion concerning situational factors and standards is indicative of the trend towards greater awareness of what we may generally refer to as project management, including the choice of different types of method to fit different applications and a focus on the performance and management of non-technical as well as technical aspects of the whole systems development process.

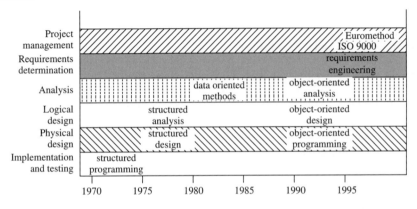

Figure 11.4   Method development in terms of systems development phase emphasis.

Figure 11.4 shows the development of methods in terms of the system development phase they emphasize. The figure clearly shows that the trend is towards the requirements determination and project management phases. However, it may also be seen that this is occurring at a slower rate than the movement through the programming and design phases, although it has accelerated in the last few years.

Description of methods

FIVE METHODS

In the rest of this chapter we will describe five methods, all of which are used currently in industry. They are Information Engineering, Structured systems analysis and design, JSD, SSADM and OMT. The methods are described theoretically by discussing their main points, in terms of phases, products, and techniques, and empirically by showing how they model the same case study. The first four are structured methods, while OMT is an object-oriented method.

> The aim of the library is to serve its members. and other libraries, by providing high quality book services at a fair cost. A member may join and leave the library. Before leaving, the member may loan and renew books. A book reservation may be made (either by title or for a specific book volume) and cancelled. After a member leaves, tidying-up will return any books and cancel any outstanding reservations. Books are obtained either by acquisition or by being borrowed from other libraries (swapped-in), and disposed of by being given to a local charity or swapped-out to their original library. A book may be sent for binding, and received back while in the library. An automated information system is required to improve efficiency.

Figure 11.5 Library case study.

Case study 3 – the university library

The case study adopted is small, given the space available, but it is part of a realistic case study used in commercial courses for method training. The user requirement may be seen in Fig. 11.5 and concerns part of the activities of a library.

Information Engineering

PHASES AND PRODUCTS

Figure 11.6 shows that Information Engineering (IE), following the description given in Finkelstein (1989), consists of three main phases, analysis, design and generation. It also contains a strategic planning phase that is not relevant here. The main products occur in the analysis phase and are different levels of data models, termed strategic, tactical and operational data models.

ANALYSIS PHASE

The analysis phase consists of four stages: project scope, strategic modelling, tactical modelling and operations modelling.

Project scope stage

This first stage is a preliminary stage whose purpose is to scope the project. Its steps are:

- *Identify project area.* The project boundaries are set, identifying the areas to be included and excluded. This prevents the project expanding uncontrollably to other, irrelevant areas, which can jeopardize the success of the project. Organizational priorities relevant to the project must be set,

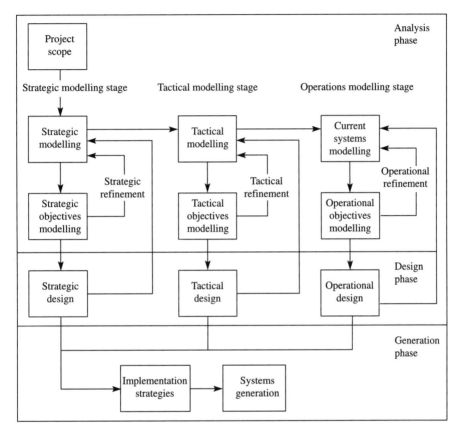

Figure 11.6 Overview of three main phases of Information Engineering. (Adapted from *An Introduction to Information Engineering*, C. Finkelstein, Addison-Wesley, 1989).

which may be defined from the strategic statements obtained from strategic planning. Project aims, deliverables and completion time are set.

- *Select software tools.* The tools to be used for the strategic and tactical modelling stages are selected. IE suggests that these include a data dictionary, a diagramming tool and an integrated word-processing system.
- *Establish initial project plan.* Project planning is based on estimates of the numbers of project areas that are involved. Each project or strategic area typically contains 50 to 90 strategic entities and is refined into tactical areas of 30 to 40 entities each. Estimates of the time needed for each of the stages and phases are then made.
- *Establish project teams.* Of the project teams 80 per cent should be composed of managers and those users with the greatest knowledge of the project areas. Remaining members may be analysts or data administrators. Team size is suggested as six members.
- *Set project budget and funding.* Based on project size, number and size of teams, hardware and software support, the project budget is set.

- *Schedule Information Engineering workshops.* As modelling is mostly done by users, these five-day workshops train the users in IE methods and techniques.

Strategic modelling stage

This stage produces the *strategic model*, which contains entities mainly of interest to senior management.

- *Strategic modelling.* The initial input to this phase is the set of relevant strategic statements from strategic planning. These consist of the mission, purpose, concerns, issues, goals, objectives, policies, strategies and tactics of the project area. These are analysed and used as catalysts to identify strategic organizational data.

  Heuristics are given to assist in mapping organizational features on to data. For example, policies and issues map to entities, goals and objectives to attributes, and strategies and tactics to associations.

  The output, the strategic model, consists of high-level strategic entities, and is produced by applying *business normalization*, which is similar to the normalization technique mentioned earlier in this chapter. The model is expressed in a *data map*, which is similar to an entity diagram, or as an *entity list*.

- *Strategic objectives modelling.* This phase reviews and identifies criteria for performance monitoring using goals, objectives, policies, concerns and issues, and defines strategic data required to measure performance. Performance ranges and controls for early warning systems may be defined. Strategic attributes are added to the strategic model by this phase.

- *Strategic refinement.* This is an iterative step which uses business normalization to refine the strategic model, with the aim of identifying hidden entities. The strategic statements referred to earlier may also change here. Standard terminology and performance rules are identified.

  The final strategic model is used to identify *strategic sub-models*, which will form the basis for the tactical data models in the tactical modelling stage.

Tactical modelling stage

This stage refines the strategic model by producing different *tactical data models* for *key functional areas*, of interest to middle management, which are based upon the products, services, markets and distribution channels with which the organization implements the basic strategy.

- *Tactical modelling.* The relevant data is identified in detail for each functional area. This may include data used to derive strategic data. A tactical model is produced for each area.

- *Tactical objectives modelling.* The data required to measure the achievement of tactical objectives on this level is identified. Exception report requirements are noted as well as criteria for decision making by middle management.
- *Tactical refinement.* Normalization is applied to the tactical models and, as before, hidden entities may be identified. Models across different functional areas may be compared and related data may be grouped together.

Operations modelling stage

- This stage is concerned with the operational, day-to-day level of the organization. It firstly looks at current manual or automated systems and identifies the data used, as well as any interfaces that will be required. Each tactical area is then refined for its operational data.
- *Current systems modelling.* This cross-checks strategic and tactical data against the data currently used by the organization. Documentation, enquiries and computer files may need to be consulted. Data that was overlooked may be discovered.
- *Operational objectives modelling.* Data required for the day-to-day measurement of objectives are identified, as well as exception reports.
- *Operational refinement.* Operational data are obtained by refining a tactical area and *operational data models* are produced.

DESIGN PHASE

The design phase is built around the *design dictionary*, which is the central store (intended to be automated) for the data identified during the analysis phase. The data entered into the dictionary consists of detailed descriptions for each attribute, entity and association, including a description of their purpose or use within the organization, and the data types and lengths of attributes. Cross-references between elements are also made. A *strategic planning dictionary* is also maintained to record mission, objectives and so on, cross-referenced to design dictionary elements. There is tool support for interface design (see below).

GENERATION PHASE

The data models (or parts of them) are used to generate database systems.

- *Implementation strategies.* No specific assistance is provided for determining alternate strategies. Techniques from other methods may be imported for deciding on the different types of systems that might be implemented. Parts of the model may represent manual or automated systems, or data may be centralized or distributed.

- *Systems generation.* Parts of the data models are used as a basis for the generation of definition statements for database systems. Tool support is provided here.

TOOL SUPPORT

IE relies upon tool support for all its phases and the following functions receive help from tools:

- *Analysis phase.* This supports dictionary entries for data and the strategic plan, and shows data maps graphically. There is assistance for grouping related data into *subject databases* to produce an implementation plan for broad information systems areas.
- *Design phase.* An integrated version of the design and strategic planning dictionaries from the analysis phase is generated, and checks are made for consistency of definition (existence of homonyms or synonyms) and syntactical completeness.

   Application groups are defined from *subject databases*, and user interface designs are produced automatically from data definitions of application groups, allowing screen painting for input and report screen design, with assistance for including relevant data. It is possible to identify common data from different models and automatically produce integrated models.
- *Generation phase.* This generates database definition statements for application groups and provides an SQL-like language for users to access databases.

CASE STUDY

Strategic modelling

The user requirement in Fig. 11.5 contains a mission statement for the library: 'The aim of the library is to serve its members, and other libraries, by providing high-quality book services at a fair cost'. From this statement, we firstly identify *strategic data subjects*. These are member, library and book. These are capable of being refined into lower level entities such as different types of book (overnight, rare), library (private, public) and member (student, staff).

We next identify *relevant entities* from the data subjects by defining key identifying attributes (shown as underlined). The entities are:

Book type	Btype#
Book	B#, Btype#, ((Lib#)), ((M#))
Lib type	Ltype#,
Lib	Lib#, Ltype#
Member type	Mtype#
Member	M#, Mtype#

Associations between the entities are also noted, using foreign keys. For example, a book could be lent to many libraries and to many members. 'Many' associations such as these are shown as repeating groups, in double parentheses.

Strategic objectives modelling

This step identifies non-key data attributes of two types: firstly, descriptive attributes, such as the library name, but, more importantly, attributes related to the *objectives* of the organization. In this case, the library wants to incur only 'fair costs', and a measure of this might be the number of times a book was used. Thus we create a #uses attribute of book, as shown below:

Book   B#, Btype#, ((Lib#)), ((M#)), #uses

The strategic model obtained so far, consisting mainly of entities, may be shown diagrammatically in a data map, shown in Fig. 11.7. This shows associations conventionally as edges between entities. Further detail, such as relationship cardinality (using the 'crow's foot' notation for a 'many' relationship), is also shown.

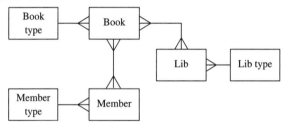

Figure 11.7 Data map of strategic model.

Strategic refinement

This applies *business normalization* to the entities, the first aim of which is to convert all entities into first normal form, which means ensuring that no entity attribute can have more than one value. We therefore check for multivalued attributes, or, as this is sometimes equivalently expressed, for repeating groups of attribute values. Where we find these, we remove them, creating new entities. In our example, entity book has two repeating groups, and the changes, including two new entities, lib-book and member-book (*intersecting entities*) are shown below:

Book	B#, Btype#, #uses
Lib-book	Lib#, B#
Member-book	M#, B#

Tactical modelling

After all the entities have been obtained from the mission statement, the tactical level is considered, where the different types of service provided by the library are determined. From the case study description, we can partition the requirement into member services (loan, return, reserve, renew), library services (swap-in and swap-out) and binding services (bind-in and bind-out). We will leave lib-type and member-type unrefined, as they are not elaborated in the user requirement. However, the strategic entity member-book can be refined into tactical entities loan, return, reservation and renewal, and lib-book into swap-in and swap-out. Reservation is refined into two entities, res-title and res-volume, which are examples of what IE terms *subtype* or *secondary* entities identical to entity subsets, discussed in Chapter 8. Book type may be refined into bind-in and bind-out subtype entities. For example, the book entities that are related as subtypes are:

Book	B#, Btype#, #uses
Book-type	Btype#, description
Bind-in	B#, date
Bind-out	B#, date

All these entities are treated similarly to the strategic entities above, creating a tactical model, as shown in the data map in Fig. 11.8, which, owing to the small size of the user requirement, has only required two levels of refinement to create what is a final model.

Design phase

Attributes, entities and associations are entered into the design dictionary. For example, for the book entity:

Entity name	*Entity content*	*Entity purpose*
Book	B#, Btype#, #uses	Records details about any books in circulation in the library, whether owned by the library or other libraries

Attribute	*Used in*	*Data type*	*Length*	*Purpose*
#uses	Book	Numeric integer	5	Records number of times a book is reserved, loaned and renewed

With automated support, dictionary definitions may be checked for consistency and different application groups established. The IE procedure for this is not very clear, but, for example, loan, reservation, renewal, return, book and

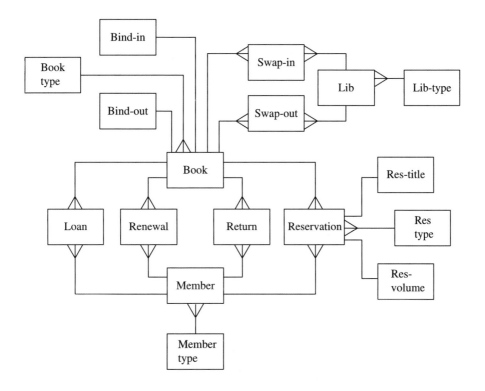

Figure 11.8 Final data map of case study entities from IE.

member (each of which are *subject databases*) are all related, and can therefore be clustered into an application group and chosen to be automated first, with binding and swaps left as manual systems for the time being.

Generation phase

With automated support, database definition statements for the application group defined above may be generated.

Structured systems analysis and design (SSAAD)

INTRODUCTION

There are a number of variants of this, and we shall refer to the common points as the *method*, drawing attention to important distinctions. The main sources for structured analysis are Gane and Sarson (1979) and de Marco (1979), and for structured design, Yourdon and Constantine (1979) and Myers (1975). The method does not consist of a prescribed set of phases, but is more a set of techniques to be used as the designer sees fit, although authors do make suggestions for some activities.

The aim of structured analysis is to produce a logical description of the data and procedures of the required system. Structured design is defined as 'the art of designing the components of a system and the interrelationships between these components in the best possible way' (Yourdon and Constantine, 1979). This is a rather high-level definition, and we can say that structured design aims to produce a physical design of an implementable system from a structured analysis description.

STRUCTURED ANALYSIS

Products

The products are *data flow diagrams*, *minispecifications* expressed in structured English or pseudocode, *decision tables* and *decision trees*, and the *data dictionary*:

- *Data flow diagrams.* 'The purpose of a *data flow diagram* (DFD) is to show, for a business area or a system or a part of a system, where the data comes from, where the data goes to when it leaves the system, where the data is stored, what processes transform it, and the interactions between data stores and processes' (Gane, 1990).

  On the diagram, *sources* and *sinks* (sometimes termed *external entities*) show sources and destinations of data that are outside the system; that is, they are objects about which we do not need to record information. *Data stores* represent places where data is stored in the system and *data flows* may be seen as pipelines through which groups of related data flow between data stores, processes and external entities. Finally, processes transform data in some way.

  The technique termed *levelling* is used for dividing a data flow diagram into parts for easier readability, analysis or for implementation purposes, and the principle is that processes are refined into successive levels of detail. The top level is usually termed a *context diagram* and shows only the external entities, their input and output data flows, and the relevant system or organizational area drawn as a single process.

  The next level, level 0, shows major sub-systems, external entities, data stores and data flow. The next level down, level 1, consists of a set of diagrams, where each diagram is a refinement (or 'explosion') of one of the level 0 sub-systems. Levelling of a process may continue until that process is a *functional primitive*, which usually means that its detailed process logic can be written in a page of structured English. Each diagram is numbered so that the relationships between diagrams and processes are easily traced. The principle of data conservation must also apply, which states that data at a lower level must be included in the data at a higher level.

A DFD aims to set a boundary to the system and is meant to be non-technical (Gane, 1990); that is it is meant to be understandable to business people who are familiar with the business area shown.

The relationships between the data and the processes are shown, but only on a simplified level. For example, exception or error processing should not be shown on a DFD, no timing (daily, weekly) is shown and important control structure such as sequence, selection and iteration of processes is also not shown. The DFD is meant as an overview of the required system.

- *Minispecifications.* These (also termed 'minispecs') describe the logic of functional primitives, that is the detail of the lowest level of processes from the DFD. Structured English is commonly used, incorporating sequence, selection and iteration.
- *Decision tables and trees.* These are used to diagrammatically illustrate complex conditions (selections) that are important and need checking by the user. Examples are given in Chapter 9.
- *Data dictionary.* The data dictionary (DD) is a central repository or 'encyclopaedia' which contains detailed components of an evolving specification. For structured analysis, it contains descriptions and definitions of data elements, structures, flows and stores.

  Each data flow from the DFDs is named and its components described, using data structure notations for hierarchical relationships, iteration and optionality. In addition, Gane and Sarson recommend that all data structures should be normalized. This applies to data stores and files also. Relationships between files should be shown.

Steps

Yourdon and de Marco suggest that one way to carry out analysis is to follow the steps shown in Fig. 11.9. These steps are based on the assumption that a new system will be based on an old system. The steps involve the initial production of what is termed a physical DFD. This is a DFD that models the physical information flow of the current system through the departments and individuals in the organization. Process names often refer to documents or machinery. The information may be on paper, over the telephone, and it may be used by people or a computer. Sometimes, the data flows may represent physical material flows, as well as information flows. This will be the case if we think we want to record information about such flows in the required system.

From this physical DFD, a logical DFD is produced in the second step, which abstracts the required data from its media, departments or individuals, and manual or computer systems. Step 3 takes place after various options

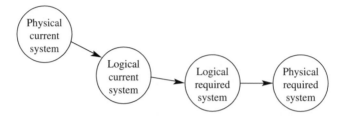

Figure 11.9 Recommended steps in structured systems analysis.

for improving the current system have been considered and step 4 considers the necessary detail for producing a new physical design.

STRUCTURED DESIGN

Structured design applies to the physical design level and is mainly concerned with producing detailed program designs, which are implicitly for third-generation programming languages. Input is from structured analysis and also from the selection of target hardware and software. The main techniques are building structure charts, coupling, cohesion, transform analysis, transaction analysis and module packaging.

CASE STUDY

Data flow diagram

A logical data flow diagram for the required system is shown in Fig. 11.10. This is a levelled DFD, with three levels shown, which we shall now briefly explain:

- *Context diagram.* This shows the main system required (library system), external entities, which are outside the system, and information input and output to the external entities.
- *Level 0 diagram.* This refines the main system process from the context diagram to show the four main sub-systems of membership services, book services, book use and book demand. The five data stores are (a) member, which records information about all library members, (b) book, which records information about all books, including the number of uses and whether a book is being bound or has returned from binding, (c) library, which records information about all external libraries, (d) lib-book, which records information about which books have been swapped in or out with which external libraries, (e) member-book, which records information about all books a member loans, reserves, returns or renews.
- *Level 1 diagram.* There are four level 1 diagrams, one for each of the four processes on the level 0 diagram, and each diagram shows the

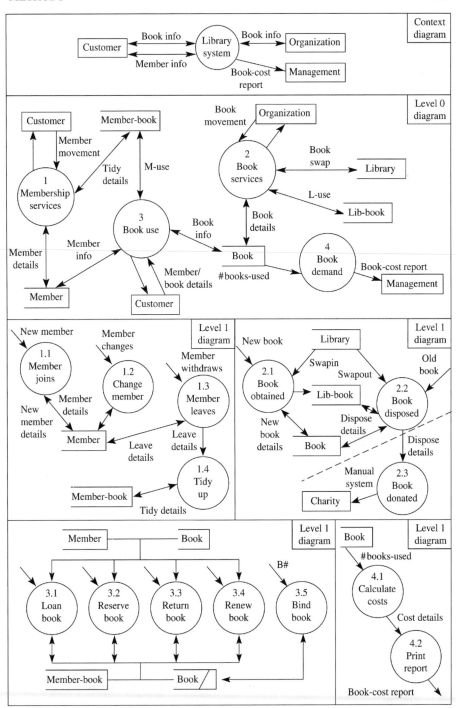

Figure 11.10 Structured analysis data flow diagram for library case study.

refinement of its 'parent' process. The membership services sub-system is refined into members joining, changing membership details, leaving and tidying-up; book services consists of obtaining, disposing of and donating books; book use refines into loaning, reserving, returning and renewing books to or for members, and binding books; and book demand provides a report on book costs.

Space does not permit us to show bind-in and bind-out processes, which are refinements of the bind 3.5 process, and similarly for the reserve-by-title and reserve-by-volume processes, as well as cancel reservation, which are refinements of the reserve book 3.2 process.

• *Human–computer boundary*. The boundary between the computer and the manual system is often indicated on the DFD. In this example, process 2.3 (book donated) represents the manual process whereby, after an unwanted book's record is modified, the book itself is donated to a local charity.

Minispecifications

The logic of functional primitive processes is produced in the minispecifications. In structured English:

> *Process 3.1*
> BEGIN
>   receive 'book' info
>   IF book does not exist
>   THEN
>   BEGIN
>   #uses = 0
>   . . .
>   END
> END

The process would contain exception processing and error messages, such as when we try to lend a book reserved by another member.

Data dictionary

The data dictionary contains data elements, data structures, data flows and data stores, and we shall show an example of each. Allowed ranges of values, or actual values permitted, may also be shown. We use indentation to show hierarchical relationships between elements for data structure, flow and store. There will also be extensive cross-references between data as well as between data and process.

element	B#
alias	Bnumber
description	primary key of Book
data type	7 characters AN
range	B1000–B999 999

structure   Book-line
                           B#
                           Book-description
                           #uses

flow   Book-cost report
                           Heading-book-totals
                           Book-line*

store   Book
                           B#
                           Btype#
                           #uses

JSD

INTRODUCTION

The JSD method of system specification was created in the UK by Michael Jackson (Jackson, 1983) and has been added to subsequently. In the 1983 book, there are six steps: (a) entity action, (b) entity structure, (c) initial model, (d) function, (e) system timing and (f) implementation.

Our description is based on this publication, as well as Cameron (1986) and more recent JSD courses, which describe three main stages for creating JSD specifications: *modelling, network* and *implementation*. The correspondence between the steps and the stages is:

Stage	*Step*
Modelling	Entity action
	Entity structure
Network	Initial model
	Function
	System timing
Implementation	Implementation

The modelling stage consists of defining an initial model of the objects and processes in the real world that the analyst judges should form the core of the desired system, and then elaborating that model; major products are the model process structure, operations table and context error table. The network stage specifies the links of the initial model to the real world, including input and output processes and a human–computer interface, and the product is the SSD, or system specification diagram. Finally, the implementation stage describes how the network processes may be organized so that the processes and data map into a physical implementation environment. This is shown on the SID, or system implementation diagram.

MODELLING STAGE

This stage creates a *real-world model* which contains entities, actions, model process structures and operations, which are refinements of actions. The actions are all *update* actions on entities. The initial model is produced first, consisting of an entity list, an action list and model process structures, which are then refined into elaborated models.

Initial model

- *Entities, actions, attributes.* Firstly, a list is made of all relevant object types, termed entities. The next step is to list all the actions that can take place on these entities (in JSD terms, entities *perform* or *suffer* actions). Next, the analyst decides which actions are performed or suffered by which entities, and lists all relevant attributes of both the entities and the actions.

- *Model process structures.* These describe diagrammatically the possible *sequence* of actions that can take place on an entity instance. A type of entity life history diagram is used, with the entity as the root node and the actions shown below it. Structures are built for all entities taking part in actions. It should be noted that (a) action sequence is explicitly modelled and is read from left to right, (b) the sequence of actions is on a *given instance* of the entity and not on *any instance* of the entity. The significance of this will be discussed in the case study example.

  In addition to the action sequence, selection and iteration are also shown, and Fig. 11.11 shows the three control components of model process structures. In the figure the box (*structure node*) labelled A is a *sequence node*. This is denoted by the occurrence of one or more unmarked nodes drawn below it, and the action sequence of these nodes is shown diagrammatically by left-to-right ordering. Node B is an *iteration node* and node C is a *selection node*. An iteration node is represented by having a single node below it which is marked with an asterisk. This node may execute zero or more times. A selection node is shown by the occurrence of one or more nodes below it, which are marked with a small circle. In the figure, one of E4 or E5 must execute, but not both.

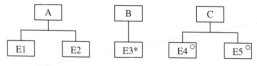

Figure 11.11 Sequence, iteration, selection and elementary nodes.

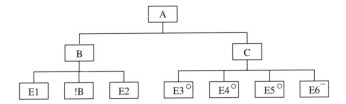

Figure 11.12 An example of a null and a quit node.

There are no conditions associated with a process structure. The structure specifies what action sequences are possible and not the circumstances in which particular sequences occur. The E nodes in the diagram are termed *elementary nodes*.

The E6 node in Fig. 11.12 is a null node, allowing for no action to be taken at this point. The !B node shown is a *quit node*. This node will check for a condition and if it is true the node B is exited and the next node in the sequence is actioned. In this case the next node is C.

Quit nodes are used in process structures to exit a branch of the hierarchy, typically for exceptions, such as when the 'normal' action sequence of an object may be suddenly terminated.

Elaborated model

- *Operations.* For each of an entity's actions, there is a set of *operations* that are performed on the entity attributes. The operations are refinements of the action and are drawn on model processes as boxes containing numbers. Each number represents one operation. The analyst will create a table specifying the operations against their *operation numbers*. The specification of operations is not precise, as it is written in natural language.
- *Resume points and text pointers.* Resume points are also shown in the process structure. A resume point is added to the start of each process structure and to the end of each elementary node. The eventual record that will represent the required attributes of each entity instance will also have a field called a *text pointer*. The text pointer records the resume point for the entity. This has an initial value of one. The text pointer is used to show the status of the entity instance with respect to its life history. The record of the attributes and text pointer of an entity instance is known in JSD as the *entity state-vector*.
- *Context errors.* At run-time, there may be errors in the input data to the actions of model processes or there may be certain rules, as we saw in Chapter 8, that must not be violated by the actions.

In order that the action data may be checked, a *context error table* is created. This is used to define rules (pre-conditions) on the actions in which an entity can take part. A context error table defines errors for each entity, resume point, action and relevant condition.

NETWORK STAGE

This stage is where the model processes, modelling the real world, have input and output functions added to them and their logic is specified in detail. The chief product is the system specification diagram (SSD), which is a type of data flow diagram.

All processes have their logic specified in the same diagrammatic notation as process structures, as well as using structure text for detailed specification.

First step (initial model)

This consists of showing all the model processes (only the entity node is shown) on the SSD, together with the data that flows between them. The logic of the processes, including the operations, is also specified in more detail as *structure text*. Data flow is shown using the *datastream and state vector*:

- *Datastreams*. The possible sequence of action messages from the real world can be considered as forming a queue to the model process. This is a datastream. Datastreams may also be used to connect the model processes to other types of process, the *function processes*, discussed below.
- *State vector*. A process will often want to know the values of the attributes of an entity instance. These are known as the entity state vector.

Second step (function processes)

The SSD so far only contains processes modelling the core organizational activities with their data flows, so this step adds function processes, which are the input and output processes that are required to transmit data to and from the system, together with data flows. There are three types of function process, input, information and interactive:

- *Input processes*. These read any input data for the model processes (*action messages*) and check that it does not contain context errors, using the information stored in the context error table. As well as dealing with the context errors, input processes check that the attributes of action messages are of the correct type (for example date, integer). These errors are called *message errors* and are checked against information specified with the action attributes. User interface details are also specified.
- *Information processes*. An information process sends messages to the outside world. Sometimes a process will inspect the state vector of some other process. This state vector inspection is represented in a network

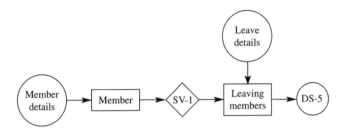

Figure 11.13 Information process, with state-vector inspection and output datastream.

diagram as a connection marked with a diamond, as in Fig. 11.13. The leaving members process produces a list of all members who have left since the last reporting time, by inspecting many instances of member state vector SV-1 and producing output on the DS-5 datastream.

- *Interactive processes.* A system may contain a function process that automatically generates action messages, input to model processes. For example, a stock control system might automatically generate orders for materials and parts.

Third step (system timing)

This step obtains information relating to time restrictions on the processes, such as the degree of synchronization between the real world and the system, affecting decisions to do with batch, on-line or real-time processing, the periodicity of reports (for example on request, daily, weekly) or time dependencies between processes themselves, such as terminal response time. Only narrative means are used to specify this.

CASE STUDY

Initial model

The entity list includes the following:

Entity	Definition	Attributes
Book	Books that are in the library	B#, Btype#, #uses
Member	Individuals who may use the library	M#, Mtype#
Library	External libraries who swap books	Lib#

The action list includes the following entries:

Action	Definition	Attributes
Lend	Someone borrows a book	B#, M#, date
Acquire	The library acquires a book	ISBN, title, Lib#, date
Join	An individual becomes a member	Name, address, date

Model process structures

An example is given in Fig. 11.14, where actions are represented by the leaves
of the hierarchy. Join, renew and leave and so on are actions performed by
(an instance of) the entity member. The actions on a process structure are
all performed or suffered by the same real-world object and are thus mutually
dependent. For example, in Fig. 11.15, renew depends on the book having
been obtained and lent.

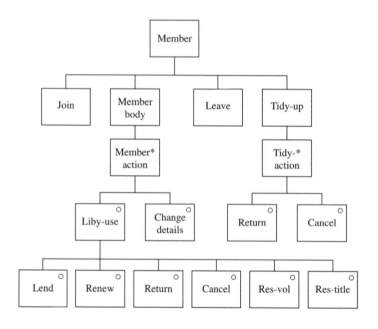

Figure 11.14 Model process structure for entity member.

However, there may be another set of actions in which the book instance
can take part. For example, the action res-vol (reserve book) is not constrained
by whether the book is on loan or being rebound, which means that res-vol
is independent of actions such as lend and should appear on a *separate*
process structure. However, res-vol is dependent on swap-in, acquire, swap-out
and sell, so these actions must also appear in this second process. The result
is the process book avail (Fig. 11.15).

The two process structures are said to represent different *roles* of the entity
book. This is the means by which JSD can model concurrent processes, as
an action in the process book-avail (for example, res-vol) may be executing
(on the same instance of a real-world book) at the same time as an action
(for example, return) in the process book.

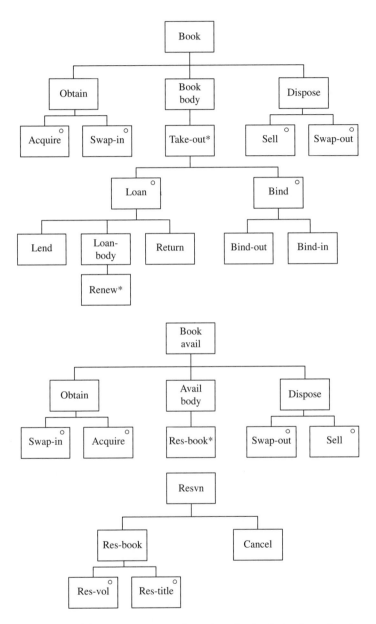

Figure 11.15 Model process structures for entity roles book, book avail and resvn.

Since res-vol appears on more than one process structure, it is said to be a *common action*. For the resvn (reservation) entity role, also shown in Fig. 11.15, all actions are common actions.

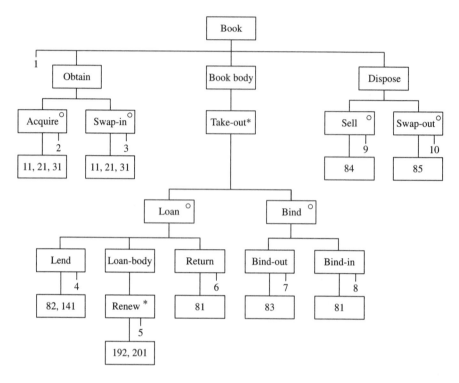

Figure 11.16 Model process structure for entity role book, with operations and resume
points.

Elaborated model

- *Operations and resume points.* Figure 11.16 shows the book process
  structure with operations and resume points, and Fig. 11.17 shows part
  of a matching operations table. A book with a text pointer of 2, for
  example, will have just been acquired by the library (see Fig. 11.16), that
  is acquire would be the last action of interest to the process structure,
  book, in which the book has taken part. The next actions that the book

Operations	
Numbers	Text
11	Store ISBN
31	Set library-no
201	Set member-no

Figure 11.17 A table of operations.

Entity role	Resume point	Action	Condition	Error Number/ OK	Error note
Book	1	Acquire		OK	
Book	1	Swap-in		OK	
Book	1	Lend		1	Library does not own book
Book	2	Acquire		37	Book already obtained
Book	2	Lend	Lend-date ≥ obtain-date	OK	
Book	2	Lend	Lend-date < obtain-date	43	Lend earlier than obtain
Book	6	Lend	Book-reserved-by = nil	OK	
Book	6	Lend	Book-reserved-by ≠ nil	888	Book is reserved

Figure 11.18 Context error table.

can take part in are lend and bind-out. If the book next suffers a lend (the book is lent to a member without having been reserved), its text pointer is changed to 4 and if the book suffers a bind-out the text pointer is changed to 7.

- *Context error table.* Figure 11.18 shows that for a book at resume point 6, receiving an action message relating to action lend, and under the condition that a member is trying to borrow the book which is reserved by another member, error 888, 'Book is reserved', will occur.

Network stage

- *Input processes.* These include the grouping of many actions for the convenience of the user. For example, a screen might allow the user to enter the details of many reservations being made by one member at once. Input processes specify all aspects of the human–computer interface.
- *Information processes.* An information process sends messages to the outside world. The network diagram in Fig. 11.19 shows a connection between an input process, the book model process and the inventory report information process to produce a book costings report. The process is reading the state vector SV-1 of book (obtaining values of #uses for each book instance) and writing to the datastream DS-5. Detailed logic of the inventory report process is specified in a process structure diagram and in structure text.

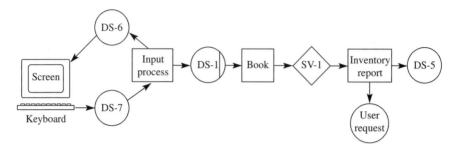

Figure 11.19 An input and information process connected to a model process.

The representation of 'screen' and 'keyboard' are for illustrative purposes only. They are not standard JSD symbols. The vertical bar on datastream DS-1 indicates that the datastream is a *control datastream*, which is a datastream that may be both read and written by a given process and is 'locked' to write operations of other processes in between the read and the write.

- *Interactive processes.* An example of this process type is cancel function, which automatically cancels any reservations made by a member on leaving. Figure 11.20 shows that it sends messages to the resvn and member processes.

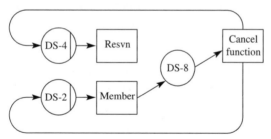

Figure 11.20 An interactive function – cancel function.

SSADM

INTRODUCTION

The SSADM method is maintained by the CCTA, a UK government agency (SSADM, 1990). The method originates from course material developed in the early 1980s by Learmonth and Burchett Management Systems (LBMS) with additional features.

The main variant of SSADM, intended for medium to large systems, is described here. The current version of SSADM is version 4 and a guide to this version may be found in Downs *et al.* (1992). The main phases and products (referred to as modules and products) may be seen in Fig. 11.21

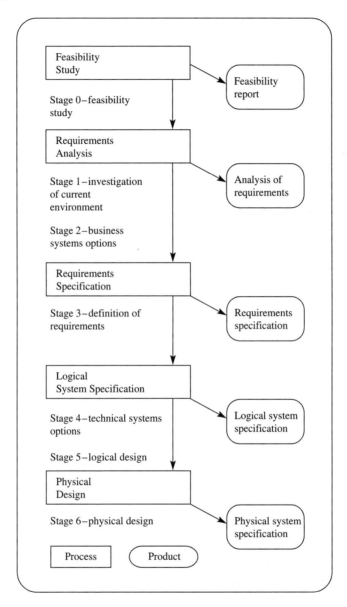

Figure 11.21 Version 4 modules of SSADM.

and the evolving requirements and specification are stored in what SSADM terms the requirements catalogue.

Some amendments have been made to version 4 by version 4.2, also referred to as version 4+ (SSADM, 1995). An outline of the basic version 4 will be given and then the differences due to version 4+.

Stage 0 – feasibility study

This assumes as a starting point that a project has been identified as the result of an exercise such as strategic planning, or something similar, and it sets out and evaluates different technical, organizational, financial and business options. The aim of the module is to establish whether the direction of the project and the requirements are feasible, and if it is therefore worth committing the necessary resources for project development. Feasibility study essentially consists of a shortened, higher-level version of the next two modules.

REQUIREMENTS ANALYSIS

This consists of two stages. In stage 1, requirements are defined by investigating the current environment and identifying problems or areas that need improvement. Stage 2 then develops a range of options that meet the defined requirements and selects one option as the basis for the desired system.

Stage 1 – investigation of current environment

The stage begins by creating an overview of the processing and data in the current environment (within the framework set by the feasibility report), and then documents problems, necessary improvements or new data or functions required. The intended users of the new system are also identified.

Subsequent steps analyse the processing and the data in more detail, finally producing a logical view of current processing. Data and processing are analysed in parallel, and the logical data flow diagram (DFD) and the process descriptions should refer only to entities. Products used are:

- *Data flow diagram.* This is the main product used for describing processes, and only update processes are shown. Enquiry or report processes will be shown later on the *enquiry access path* (see below). Physical DFDs are produced initially, which are then transformed to logical DFDs after the data has been analysed. The lowest level processes are described in narrative form on the *elementary process description.*

  A maximum of three DFD levels are recommended, with further process detail being shown in function definitions and entity–event modelling (see below). Exception or error handling should not be shown on the DFD.
- *Logical data structure.* This consists of a set of entities and relationships obtained by analysis of the data in the current system, using the entity modelling technique. The logical data structure (LDS) may also contain the most significant attributes.

Stage 2 – business system options

In this stage, several feasible high-level options for a proposed system are presented, which typically encompass the range of requirements from the mandatory to the optional. It is suggested that up to six 'skeleton' business system options are produced by the developers, with two or three being presented to the users. The selected option becomes the foundation for subsequent requirements specification.

A business system option (BSO) consists of a description of a proposed information system. It will typically be couched in terms of the existing environment, and each option should address the functional requirements, in terms of boundary, inputs and outputs, and principal transformations.

In addition, each option should also contain a description of how it will meet non-functional requirements, covering, for example: (a) priority and impact – the problems and requirements at present are noted together with the priority of the proposed system and its potential impact on the organization for example, to reduce library processing delay for a loan from four minutes to one minute might have the highest priority; (b) costs and time – costs and time of development and operation are estimated, as well as costs of hardware and software procurement and training; (c) technical points such as volume and volatility of expected data storage, as well as estimates of task frequencies. This will also cover options for handling processes on- or off-line, as well as for batch as opposed to real-time processing.

The system boundary is an important feature, as this will be drawn to distinguish computer and manual processes.

REQUIREMENTS SPECIFICATION

Using the option selected by business system options, a detailed specification of requirements now begins. The emphasis is on determining the desired system data, functions and events. Prototyping techniques are also suggested for the development of the human–computer interface.

Stage 3 – definition of requirements

The first two steps modify the previously defined DFD and LDS (which were of the current system only) to match the requirements in the selected BSO. All the attributes are specified on the LDS. In addition, non-functional requirements, such as security, access and archiving requirements, are defined.

The next step is to define *functions*. This involves identifying both update and enquiry functions and determining the events that are related to update functions. The input and output data for each function is then defined, using the *input/output structure* (see below). As most systems have on-line processing, system dialogues are identified in outline. As a check on the LDS, some functions have their input and output data analysed by *relational data analysis*, and the resulting relations are compared with the LDS entities.

The next step suggests prototyping the requirements with users to identify errors and to obtain any additional requirements. Procedures for managing prototyping sessions are provided and dialogues and report formats are emphasized.

Finally, using *entity–event modelling*, more detailed processing requirements are obtained. This is done by constructing an *entity life history* (ELH) for each entity from the LDS, and an *effect correspondence diagram* (ECD) is constructed for each event, showing the entities affected by that event. An *enquiry access path* is created for each enquiry showing the entities on a subset of the LDS that are to be accessed.

Methods used are:

- *Function definition.* A function 'is a set of system processing that the user wishes to carry out at the same time to support his business activity'. This technique builds functions from the DFD and enquiry processing requirements from the requirements catalogue. It then combines these and subdivides processes into separate functions. Functions are specified on forms.

- *Input/output structure.* This is based on JSP structure diagrams (Jackson, 1975), with data structure being shown in terms of sequence, selection and iteration. It may also be used to show on-line input and output dialogue data.

- *Relational data analysis.* This technique consists of the application of normalization to the input/output structures defined above. The main aims are to validate the LDS, to ensure that the data is logically easy to maintain and extend and to group the data together into optimum record types. The relations are a basis for defining databases or files in logical system specification.

   It is a bottom-up technique, as opposed to top-down entity modelling, and it may also be used in stage 1, where the input will be current system files, input/output documents and screens.

- *Specification prototyping.* This produces a live, 'dummy' system with which the user can experiment to refine the requirement for a user interface or to add other requirements.

- *Entity–event modelling.* This is used to define the DFD processes in more detail by including the effects of time on the system. This is done by considering entity events, where an event is 'something that triggers a process to update the system data'. *Entity life history analysis* constructs an ELH for each entity on the LDS, showing the updating events in the sequence in which they occur. Detailed operations are also added to each ELH as well as state indicators, which are equivalent to JSD resume points. The *effect correspondence diagram* takes the opposite view to the ELH and analyses the entities that are affected by each event. JSD diagrammatic notation is used.

- *Enquiry access path.* This shows, on a subset of the LDS, the entities and relationships involved in accessing the information required by an enquiry. The entry point is also shown. It uses JSD notation to indicate data structure.

LOGICAL SYSTEM SPECIFICATION

Stage 4 – technical system options

This assesses the different options for implementing a part of the specification and describes options, costs, benefits and constraints. Factors include internal and external constraints. External constraints consist of, for example, time, cost, business performance and any hardware or software restrictions set in the feasibility study. Internal constraints are, for example: (a) responsiveness – the responsiveness of the system is decided, considering synchronization issues such as real-time or periodic (monthly, yearly) and enquiry types, which might be *ad hoc* or scheduled; (b) sizing – numbers of entity instances indicate file sizes and process sizes, process frequencies are determined as well as number of lines in reports, and numbers of updates and reports; (c) security; (d) interfacing to other systems.

The aim is to select the best set of technical products that meet the requirements. A *technical environment description* for the chosen options is input to logical design.

Stage 5 – logical design

Dialogue design produces a design of the interface for on-line functions. Included are the dialogue specifications, command and menu structures. *Logical database process design* uses information from entity–event modelling to construct *update process models* and the enquiry access paths are used to construct *enquiry process models*. Only non-procedural specifications are produced in this stage. Processes have integrity checking and error processing added, and are consolidated into processing structures corresponding to an event.

PHYSICAL DESIGN

Stage 6 consists of physical design, and a classification framework is provided for types of physical processing and database management systems, enabling certain set procedures to be followed when translating logical designs to physical designs specific to one of these types of implementation environments.

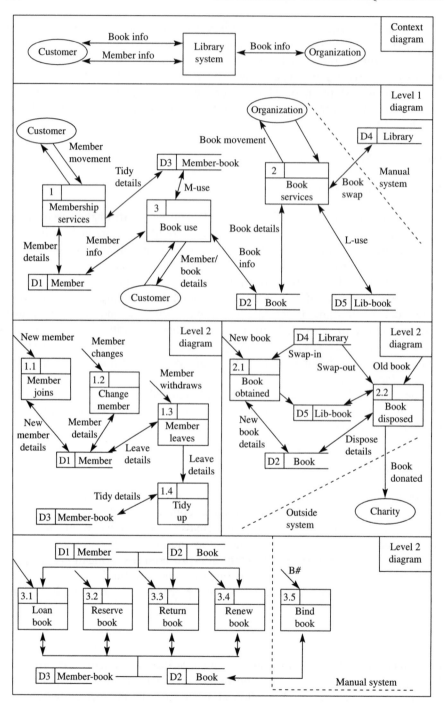

Figure 11.22 SSADM data flow diagram for case study process description.

In addition, the logical design may need to be refined to add any detail necessary for the physical environment. The techniques specified for this module are only very general, as it is intended that individual users will apply their own project-specific physical design techniques. This is to reflect the increasing use of packages and 4GLs.

CASE STUDY

Requirements analysis

- *Business system options*. The result of stage 2 might be that, to reduce costs, the library will not develop a totally computerized system to begin with, but will have a manual system for dealing with swap-ins and swap-outs (a card-index filing system could be decided upon later for recording book numbers in and out), as well as binding. Member services will be a batch system (additions and changes made at the end of the day), with the central book processes on-line. A decision has been made to keep only three months of data on-line at a time, using a simple archiving system. The book donated process will be excluded from the system.

Requirements specification

- *Data flow diagram*. Figure 11.22 shows levels 1 and 2 of the logical DFD of the case study produced in stage 3. The context diagram was set in stage 1. The diagrammatic notation uses rectangles for processes and ovals for external entities. In addition, as the DFD shows only processes that update data stores, and not enquiries or reports (which simply move data around the system), process 4 (book demand) is omitted. A decision was taken in business system options to exclude the donation of a book from the system. The diagram is, in other respects, identical to that of structured system analysis.
- *Logical data structure*. The logical data structure is an entity diagram of the type discussed in Chapter 8. Figure 11.23 shows this, which is similar to the final data map built for Information Engineering, but which does not show entity subsets directly. However, disjoint subsets, such as bind-in and bind-out, as well as res-title and res-volume, are shown as exclusive 1:1 relationships, indicated by an arc over the relationships. Only entities and their relationships are shown on the diagram, with attributes and relationship detail documented separately. Relationship names are normally present on the figure, but have been omitted to avoid diagram clutter.
- *Cross-checking*. At this point, the DFD and the LDS are cross-checked, to make sure that important data has not been omitted and that there

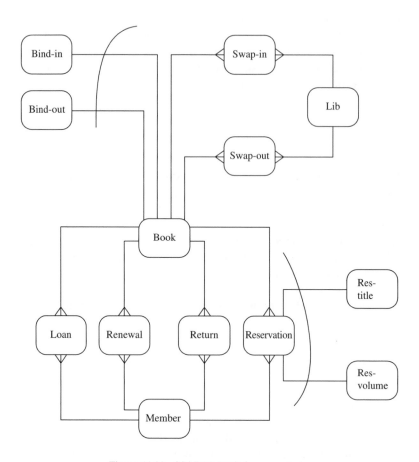

Figure 11.23 SSADM LDS for case study.

is correspondence between entities and data stores. The *logical data store/entity cross-reference* documents the entities involved in each data store. For example, the swap-in and swap-out entities on the LDS correspond to the lib-book data store, and details about loans, renewals, returns and reservations are stored in member-book.

The *process/entity matrix* documents, for each process, the type of access (update or retrieval) made to each type of entity. For example, the bind-in and bind-out types of book are updated by the bind book process 3.5.

- *Relational data analysis.* The set of normalized relations corresponding to the LDS in Fig. 11.23 is shown below. Subset relations are shown by a corresponding *type* relation, containing a distinguishing attribute. The date attribute of the book relation is set when a book is sent to or received from binding.

Relation	Attributes
Book-type	B-type#, b-description (bind-in/out)
Book	B#, Btype#, bind-date, #uses
Lib	Lib#
Member	M#
Swap-in	Lib#, B#, date
Swap-out	Lib#, B#, date
Loan	M#, B#, date
Renewal	M#, B#, date
Return	M#, B#, date
Reservation	M#, B#, Rtype#, date
Res-type	Rtype#, r-description (title/volume)

- *Enquiry access path.* If we assume that a simple enquiry for the number of uses of a book will satisfy the requirement for information to help with determining book costs, then an enquiry access path for obtaining this information is shown in Fig. 11.24. This shows that the key attribute of the book entity, B#, is used as the entry point and that a set of books is to be retrieved, indicated by the iteration symbol in the book box. Each book entity contains the attribute #uses.

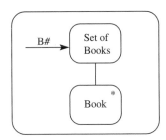

Figure 11.24   Enquiry access path for book use enquiry.

- *Entity life history.* Figure 11.25 shows the ELH for entities book, resvn and member, the first two of which have the same content as those in the JSD case study. However, one important difference is that in SSADM the ELH model *events*, while in JSD the process structure models *processes*. We may see the implications of this in the figure, for in the ELH for the member entity the tidy-up process is omitted, as it is not an event.

Another aspect of ELH specification that differs from JSD is that which is concerned with common actions and parallel processes. To model the fact that some member processes are in common with book processes (for example lend), JSD includes book actions on the member process structure (Fig. 11.14) as selections. SSADM simplifies this, as is shown in Fig. 11.25, by showing a book event on the ELH for member.

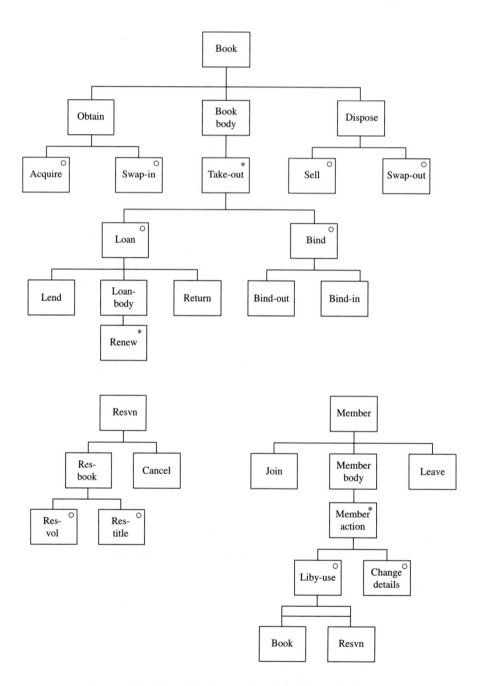

Figure 11.25 Entity life histories for book, resvn and member.

The requirement that a book may be reserved at any time, outside of the chronological event sequence of loan, renew and return, does not require a separate process as in JSD (see Fig. 11.15 for the process book-avail), but is modelled on the ELH for member as a parallel structure with book, shown by the double interconnecting line on Fig. 11.25.

- *Effect correspondence diagram.* Figure 11.26 shows the effect correspondence diagram for the lend event, where all entities affected by this event are detailed. The double-headed arrow between entities indicates that when one entity is updated, so is the other. Also shown is event data, which consists of the attributes input to the update process – in this example, member and book numbers M# and B#.

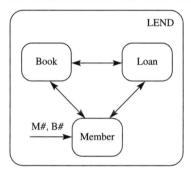

Figure 11.26 Effect correspondence diagram for lend event.

SSADM VERSION 4+

Several changes have been introduced by this more recent version of SSADM (1995) and a brief description of three major differences is given below.

Systems development template

In response to the fact that some SSADM users have felt that the stages in Fig. 11.21, now termed a default structural model, are too restrictive, it is suggested that systems development is viewed as a set of *concerns*, as shown in the systems development template in Fig. 11.27. Guidance is provided to assist users in combining the activities implied by these concerns into models of a systems development process suitable for given projects.

Business activity modelling

This is a new step which is added to stage 1. Its aim is to define requirements in a more comprehensive way than version 4, which was essentially limited to DFDs and LDSs of the current system. A business activity model consists of several components: *why* (why the organization is doing what it does),

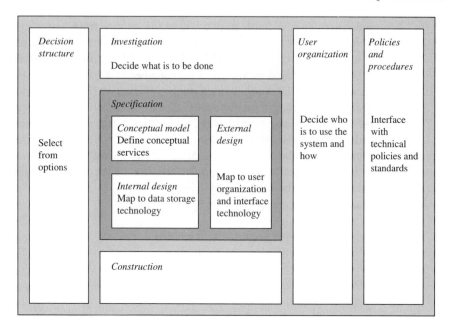

Figure 11.27　Systems development template – SSADM version 4+.

how (business rules that guide the organization), *what* (the organizational activities and their interaction with the environment) and *when* (business events). A generic business model is suggested as the basis of the *what* component. No particular technique is prescribed for building this model, although SSM (Checkland and Scholes, 1990) is an example.

3-schema specification architecture

SSADM now has a more structured view of a specification, seen in the *specification* component in Fig. 11.27, which is based on the ANSI/SPARC three-level database structure (ANSI/SPARC, 1975; Tsichritzis and Klug, 1977). The *conceptual model* consists of logical data model, enquiry and event processes, automated business activities and business rules; as it is on the conceptual level it is an abstract model. The *external design* component consists of the user interface (and possibly computer system context) while *internal design* consists of the logical and physical database design.

OMT

INTRODUCTION

The OMT (Object Modelling Technique) method contrasts with the previous, structured, methods as it is an *object-oriented* approach (Rumbaugh *et al.*,

1991). It has been introduced in Chapter 10 and there are three main phases: analysis, system design and object design. The analysis phase corresponds most closely to the requirements determination and analysis activities in which we are interested in this chapter.

OMT has a definite view of the purpose of analysis:

> *Analysis, the first step of the OMT methodology, is concerned with devising a precise, concise, understandable and correct model of the real world.*

and

> *The purpose of object-oriented analysis is to model the real-world system so that it can be understood.*

Finally,

> *The successful analysis model states what must be done, without restricting how it may be done, and avoids implementation decisions.*

The products of analysis are the object, dynamic and functional models.

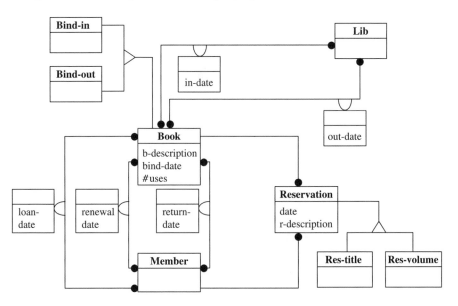

Figure 11.28 Object model for library case study.

CASE STUDY

Object model

The object model shows the classes in the application, together with their attributes, associations and relationships such as aggregation and generalization relationships. It is shown in Fig. 11.28, resembling the SSADM LDS in Fig. 11.23. The main differences are:

- *Generalization.* Classes bind-in, bind-out, res-title and res-volume are subclasses within generalization hierarchies.
- *Attributes.* These are shown in their class boxes in Fig. 11.28.
- *Link attributes.* These are loan-date, renewal-date, return-date, in-date and out-date, and are modelled instead of the corresponding entities in

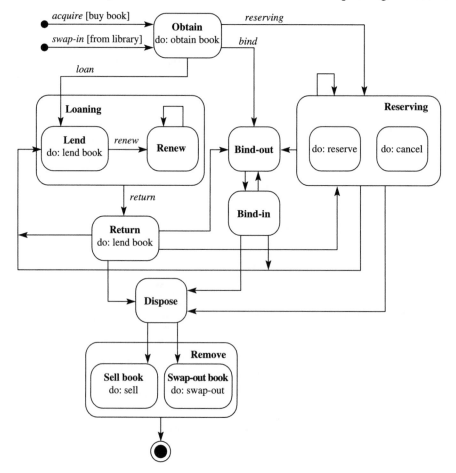

Figure 11.29 State diagram for class book.

Fig. 11.23, which were only modelled to 'carry' these attributes. This results in fewer classes and thus a simpler dynamic model.

Dynamic model

This model shows a set of state diagrams for the most important classes in the object model. A state diagram is a type of transition diagram, showing the events, transitions and activities for a particular object of a class.

Figures 11.29–11.32 show the state diagrams for the classes book, lib, member and reservation.

- *Book.* Figure 11.29 shows the state diagram for the class book. From an initial state, a book is brought into existence by one of two events: acquire or swap-in. From the obtain state, there are three transitions which may occur: bind, loan and reserving.
- *Bind.* If the bind event occurs then the book is in the bind-out state. When the book is returned from the binders it will make a transition to the bind-in state.
- *Loan.* If the loan event occurs then a transition is made to the lend state. After the book is lent, there are two possibilities: it may be returned or it may be renewed. If it is renewed it may be renewed indefinitely, or it may be returned. The return event is shown as one that is inherited by the lend and the renew states, as substates of the loaning superstate.

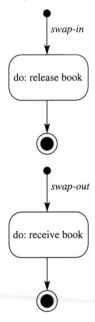

Figure 11.30 State diagram for class lib.

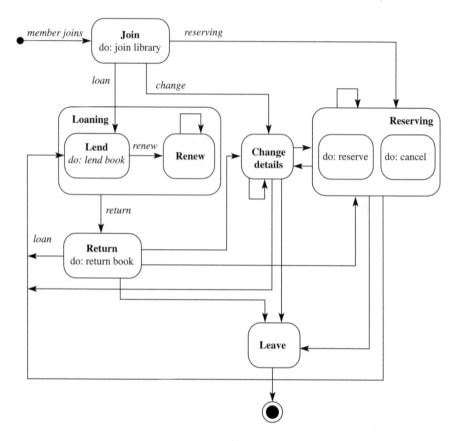

Figure 11.31 State diagram for class member.

When the loan event occurs for book, member is also affected as members borrow books. Thus Fig. 11.31 shows, for member, the loan event with common transitions and states for the behaviour shared with the book class.

- *Reserving.* Two types of events may occur here: a book may be reserved or its reservation may be cancelled, and the relevant activities are shown in the superstate containing the do: reserve and do: cancel activities. (These inherit the single event reserving. This can be refined on a more detailed diagram into two events). These events are also common to the reservation class, and Fig. 11.32 shows its allowable transitions and states.

Once the book has finished its binding, loaning or reserving activity, there are four possibilities: the book may be loaned, bound, reserved or disposed. If the book is to be disposed then there may be a transition to the sell book state or to the swap-out book state; both substates inherit the transition to the final book state.

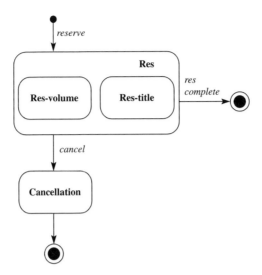

Figure 11.32 State diagram for class reservation.

- *Lib.* Figure 11.30 shows that swap-in and swap-out are the two events which affect the lib class. These also affect the book class, and this is shown by the common event names for book and lib.
- *Reservation.* Figure 11.32 shows that a reservation may be made and cancelled. Reservation and book interact and this is shown by the fact that the activity names, reserve and cancel, on Fig. 11.29 are also the names as those events which bring a reservation object into existence and which delete that object, as appearing in Fig. 11.32.

  A reservation may be either by volume or by title. After a book is reserved or cancelled, a transition is made to a final state with the event res-complete, allowing this to be treated as a 'subroutine', following Rumbaugh *et al.* (1991).
- *Member.* Figure 11.31 shows that after the initial transition to the join state, there are three possibilities: the member may loan a book, change details or make a reservation. We have discussed above the behaviour that results when loaning a book. As reserving also affects member then the behaviour shown is identical to that of book.

After a member has finished his or her loaning, changing details or reserving activity, there are four possibilities: loaning, changing details, reserving or leaving.

Functional model

This model uses a data flow diagram technique to show the computations performed by activities as well as the flow of data from input sources through

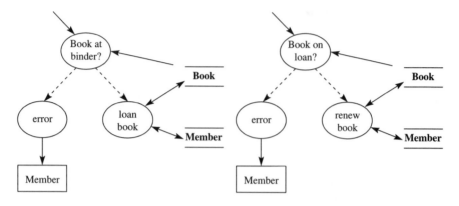

Figure 11.33 Partial functional model for library case study.

to output sources. The brief library case study does not emphasize either of these aspects of a set of requirements, but it is possible to show the use of control flow.

Figure 11.33 shows how control flow might be added to the DFD for SSADM, based on Fig. 11.22. This shows that execution of the loan book process is dependent on whether the book is at the binder's or not. Similarly, the renew book process is only executed if the book is already on loan.

Such control flows could be added to the DFD for all the processes which are dependent on the prior execution of other processes, a strong feature of this case study.

Comparison of methods

It is not our intention here to initiate an extensive comparison of methods, and fuller treatments may be found elsewhere. The well-known CRIS series of conferences and related publications provide many examples of method comparison (Olle *et al.* 1982, 1983, 1986, 1988; Verrijn-Stuart and Olle, 1994; Olle *et al.*, 1991). Other sources are Avison and Fitzgerald (1995), Davis (1990), Curtis *et al.* (1992), Maddison *et al.* (1983), Connor (1985), Fichman and Kemerer (1992), Iivari (1994), Jayaratna (1994) and Flynn and Fragoso-Diaz (1996).

In addition, our case study is chiefly suited to comparing methods for their technical model-building activities, and does not compare them for other important features such as project management assistance, procedures for validation and verification and suggestions for user participation.

However, the case study does allow comparison in terms of the *breadth* and *orientation* features. By breadth we mean the extent of the systems development phases covered by the method. This also considers necessary activities within the phases. For example, an analysis phase should have activities for modelling object, rule, process and HCI, as defined in Chapter

8. From the breadth we may determine the phase that has the most emphasis within a method, for example, requirements centred or logically centred. In addition, the orientation of a method is concerned with that aspect of the requirements, such as data or process, for which most support is provided.

We will use the phases and steps that we established in Chapter 6 for the comparison.

Results of comparison

BREADTH AND ORIENTATION

Information Engineering (IE)

This covers three phases, strategic planning, analysis and logical design (slightly), but only the object and data steps of each, and it is thus planning/conceptually centred. There is a lot of assistance for applying normalization and planning, and as IE basically produces what is often termed a corporate data model, it is a planning/data oriented method. IE also has a project management phase.

Structured systems analysis and design (SSAAD)

This covers the analysis and logical design phases, considering process as well as data, but is logically centred, as data and not entities are considered and the emphasis is on process detail. There are some techniques (such as decision tables and trees) provided for process, but little for data, so this is process oriented.

JSD

The model process structure part of JSD may be considered to be on the analysis level, while elaboration is in logical design. However, objects and data are considered even less than in SSAAD and JSD is logically/conceptually centred. The emphasis is firmly on the detail of process design and JSD is thus very process oriented.

SSADM

This covers the feasibility study part of requirements determination, the analysis phase (object, event and process) and logical design (data, process, HCI), so this is conceptually centred. There is some assistance for HCI modelling. There are many techniques (LDS, ELH, DFD) provided, as well as detailed assistance, so the method is data, event and process oriented.

OMT

This covers the analysis and logical design phases and is not addressed at the requirements determination phase; it is thus an analysis- and design-centred method. As an object-oriented method, there is an emphasis on objects, with a strong object model, but there is also an emphasis on processes, defined in both the dynamic and functional models. OMT is thus data, event, object and process oriented.

Table 11.1 summarizes this comparison. The advantage of using a practical example for comparison, as opposed to a more theoretical exercise, is that the similarities between the methods are clearly visible. It is hoped that the conclusion may be drawn that, where they cover the same steps in the same phases, they model the same thing in roughly the same way.

STRUCTURED AND OO METHODS

OO methods have only been in wide use for a few years and it may be premature to make judgements that compare them with structured methods. It is certainly too early to be able to evaluate claims made by OO method proponents concerning productivity, reusability and ease of maintenance, both of which require surveys over time on systems built using OO methods. We should also be careful, as pointed out by Iivari (1994), of assuming that all OO methods share the same characteristics.

A benefit of OO methods may be to achieve a less procedural and more modular specification, thus reducing complexity. Another may be to assist the modelling process by offering an integrated path from analysis through design to the implementation phase, as the concept of object is the same in every phase.

Fichman and Kemerer (1992) compared eleven structured methods for analysis and design with three OO methods for analysis and design. They reached three main conclusions. Firstly, OO methods are radically different from process-oriented methods, but are only incrementally different from data-oriented methods.

Table 11.1 Breadth of coverage of IE, SSAAD, JSD, SSADM and OMT

| Method | Strategic planning | Requirements determination | | Analysis | | | | | Logical design | | |
		Feasibility	Analysis	Object	Rule	Process	Event	HCI	Data	Process	HCI
IE	X			X					X		
SSADM		X		X		X	X	(X)	X	X	X
SSAAD						X			X	X	
JSD						X			X	X	
OMT				X	(X)	X	X	(X)	X	X	(X)

Secondly, there are two areas in OO methods which require improvement: (1) top-down refinement to reduce system complexity, as objects are too low-level, (2) as processes are grouped with their objects the specification of 'end-to-end' processes, that is the sequence of processes as they occur naturally in an organization, is hidden. Thirdly, despite the lack of empirical evidence to support many specific OO claims, the weight of opinion is that OO methods are a 'better idea' for systems development than structured methods.

Although OO methods are very recent, three leading methods (those of Rumbaugh, Booch and Jacobson) combined into the Unified Method in 1995. This poses an interesting contrast to structured methods which, after twenty years or so, often appear to emphasize their differences rather than their similarities.

Technical trends

Early methods were mostly concerned with the design level, and modern methods aim for a wide breadth, aiming to model as much as possible on the conceptual level, or higher levels, for the reasons explained at the beginning of this chapter. It is thus likely that methods will evolve into being *requirements centred*, emphasizing the requirements determination phase (and possibly strategic planning). This may involve prototyping trial systems to users from a specification.

Early methods were primarily process oriented and it is to be expected that methods will increase their set of orientations as they evolve. This means that they will provide modelling assistance for particular aspects of the user requirement and will be able to construct and present it in a variety of different ways. For example, future methods are likely to become *object oriented*, modelling a greater variety of objects on the conceptual level, and are likely to include the modelling or organizational rules on this level.

Problems addressed and solutions provided

The two major problems addressed by modern methods are the problems of quality and productivity. As we have discussed, a quality problem occurs when systems do not do what users require and a productivity problem is when systems are delivered late or over budget.

QUALITY

The main problem that methods address is the third quality problem, concerned with making errors in the analysis of information needs. Many delivered systems are not used and another large proportion require significant amendment, as they do not do what users thought they would do, because the designers made mistakes of this type. Two reasons for this are:

1. *Poor development methods.* Designers may make errors when developing systems due to lack of knowledge of suitable methods and techniques, as well as reliance on intuition. They may not know how to look for such typical errors, quoted in Davis (1990) as incorrect facts, omissions, ambiguities, inconsistencies and misplaced facts which occur in user requirements. In addition, there are inadequate methods for validating requirements with users, still mainly based on showing diagrammatic or narrative specifications.
2. *Designers cannot communicate.* Systems development is a team effort, requiring many designers to communicate together. The absence of commonly understood phase products or activities means that mistakes and misunderstandings may be made.

Both of these are compounded by the complexity of large systems.

The solutions provided are, firstly, for modern methods to emphasize the early phases more, including requirements determination and analysis, as this is where most errors are made, as we saw in the discussion in Chapter 6. Modern methods thus tend to be conceptually centred.

Secondly, knowledge has grown concerning more effective activities in the development process, including modelling techniques, approaches to validation and many others. By including this body of knowledge in a method, designer intuition may be reduced, so that fewer errors will be made in developing systems. Modern methods provide guidance and precise modelling techniques in an endeavour to capture more accurately, in a set of requirements, what users want.

Thirdly, there is a move towards methods that provide standard phase products, expressed in well-defined languages, or that use well-documented aids such as tables, matrices, diagrams and so on. If all the members of a development team are familiar with these expressive means then their ability to communicate together is enhanced.

PRODUCTIVITY

Problems

1. *Changing requirements.* Requirements may change after the project has started, causing work to be redone. A major reason for this is that *users do not know their requirements*. Users may not fully appreciate the nature of the system that the analysts are proposing to build for them, as they may be unsure about what they want. Alternatively, there may be disagreement over requirements between users. In addition, analysts can only express the nature of the eventual system in a computer-oriented way, mostly in the form of detailed diagrams, which do not allow users to fully comprehend their implications.

2. *Poor project control.* Many projects have no means of their status being measured at any given point, in relation to the amount of work completed or remaining to be done. Techniques for estimating required resources at the beginning of a project are inadequate, often giving rise to over-optimistic predictions for delivery dates and costs.

Solutions

1. *Allow users to refine their requirements.* Methods should not expect requirements to be fixed at the start, and it is suggested that, as users will never understand computer-oriented specifications, even after education, it is better to validate the requirements built by the analysts by using prototypes to demonstrate a part of the eventual system to the users and to allow them to learn their requirements in more detail. This feature is beginning to appear in methods, and SSADM contains suggested procedures for prototyping part of the HCI to users.
2. *Develop project control techniques.* The phase products defined in a method may be used as milestones to chart project progress, accompanied by sizing and estimating techniques, perhaps incorporated in a project management phase closely coupled to the method, to estimate required resources on a changing basis more correctly. There is some evidence of progress being made towards standardization in the United Kingdom in the emergence of the PRINCE project management method (CCTA, 1990) and also internationally as will be discussed in the next chapter.

It is also hoped that the improvements in quality resulting from the better definition of modelling and validation techniques mentioned above will reduce the amount of iteration required in the process, and hence reduce the productivity problem also.

ADVANTAGES OF METHODS

The main feature of modern methods is that they are based on the application of the principle of *abstraction* to the systems development process, concentrating on the early phases. They also emphasize their products, defining them more precisely than before, as well as providing assistance for phase activities. They may be compared with previous methods, for example, process-oriented methods, which emphasized activities. Method advantages include:

1. The development process is less complex as it is decomposed into distinct, simple phases. Each phase is concerned with one level of abstraction only, and its well-defined activities map the user requirement progressively from that level to the next. Guidance is provided for the activities, reducing designer intuition. Project control is also assisted.
2. The existence of high levels of abstraction in the early phases means that the users can be involved more fully in the development process, using

validation and prototyping, as the semantics of user requirements are not embedded in implementation detail. This can reduce error in determining requirements.

DISADVANTAGES OF METHODS

1. Methods may only address that part of the problem concerned with agreed documentation and modelling procedures. There are other problems (see Chapter 6), which may be caused by poor methods for defining the problem or assessing wider organizational issues, or the lack of talented development people.
2. Early phases of the process, if emphasized, will add to resources required during development. Although this will eventually decrease maintenance effort it often means that a system is delivered too late to take advantage of the business opportunity for which it was intended.
3. Many methods insist on documenting the smallest points, often referring to them many times in seemingly endless cross-reference lists. A lot of time may be wasted on trivial issues.
4. A view is that a method is only as good as the developer who is using it, as so many activities rely on experience and judgement. If good staff are in short supply, then a method will not help much.
5. Methods mostly emphasize the analysis and later phases, neglecting the requirements phase, where errors have the most impact.

CASE tools

INTRODUCTION

This section discusses the use of automated tools in systems development. Generally defined, a tool provides software support for precisely defined aspects of systems development methods. The term CASE tool is most frequently used to describe such tools, where CASE is an acronym for computer-aided systems or software engineering. A recent overview of the use of CASE tools may be found in Howard and Potter (1994).

There are many tools that are commercially available, with wide differences in their functionality, with tools for the technical activities of systems development as well as for related areas such as strategic planning, configuration management and project management. For technical activities, there are tools for diagramming (for example, entity modelling, data flow diagrams), code generation in the implementation phase, user interface modelling, prototyping, and reverse engineering in the maintenance phase. So-called upper-CASE tools support activities in the early phases and lower-CASE tools support the later phases.

Early tools such as STRADIS/DRAW, introduced in 1981, were only diagramming tools, providing drawing and printing facilities. In comparison, modern tools allow specification objects (for example, an entity instance) to be represented graphically and to be stored in a database, in such a way that the objects may be independently accessed by related tools, which may wish to use them for purposes such as cross-referencing or syntax checking. This feature excludes traditional development software, such as compilers, from being regarded as CASE tools.

TYPES OF TOOL

Introduction

Different classifications of CASE tools exist (Fuggetta, 1993). The one we adopt is based on Mair (1993), who identifies four categories or types of tool from the viewpoint of coverage of systems development: simple tools, work-benches, integrated CASE tools and open environments.

Simple tools

These aim to automate only one aspect of the development process, such as data flow diagramming or entity relationship modelling. Another characteristic is that they store data in their own, non-standard file structure, although some tools offer limited import/export facilities for communication with other tools.

Workbenches

A *workbench* consists of a family of tools that typically cover just one development phase. Individual tools generate products with a common format, which are stored in a database or *repository* used by all the tools. Output from one tool may thus be input to another. Typically the tools possess common features, such as interaction style and graphical symbols.
  Individual tools may be obtained singly or in different combinations. Workbenches may or may not support any particular method; if they do not they leave the designer to choose what tools to use within a project.

- *Analyst workbenches.* These support the requirements analysis and design phases and usually provide graphical editors for drawing diagrams with some degree of syntax checking for diagram consistency and completeness. There is usually a facility for non-graphical, textual entry to the repository and there may or may not be checking between textual and diagrammatic elements. Some analyst workbenches provide a limited code generation facility.
- *Programmer workbenches.* These support the design, implementation and testing phases. They provide a diagrammatic or semi-diagrammatic facility

for program, module or class design that allows code generation to take place. They usually also offer configuration control facilities and may allow host–target testing.

- *Project management workbenches.* These provide tools in the areas of project planning and control addressing activities such as resource allocation and scheduling. Support activities such as configuration management and process management (work group or work flow features for supporting teamwork within systems development) may also be included.

  They are characterized by strong reporting facilities and the ability to share data by import/export; their individual tools are thus generally not tightly coupled, perhaps due to the mostly textual, often unstructured nature of their input and the need for these tools to export data to non-workbench tools.

Integrated CASE tools

An integrated CASE (I-CASE) product consists of a tightly integrated set of tools that cover several phases of the development process, often including project management. They use a common repository and usually support a specific method. One of the first tools of this type was Excelerator, introduced in 1984, which was mainly based on the Yourdon approach to structured systems analysis.

Essentially, I-CASE tools integrate different workbenches together so that tools can share information with minimal duplication. Typically they aim to span the process down to code generation.

Open environments

The fourth type of tool, termed an open environment or IPSE (integrated project support environment), is a more advanced type, which, in addition to the features of I-CASE is intended to offer flexibility, in that facilities are provided to allow designers to configure their own method, method support and integration, allowing designers to integrate tools into the IPSE and use them in an integrated manner. However, not all products claiming to be IPSEs offer such comprehensive facilities. In addition, they are very expensive and probably only a few large organizations can afford them.

The open environment provides several theoretical advantages, in that tools already proven within an organization can be used and future tools may be adapted to work within the common environment. Two approaches to this are the repository approach and the meta-CASE tool.

- *Repository approach.* The repository approach considers the repository to be not only a central store for project-specific data, but also the source of the definitions of the types of product and product mappings that are allowed in the repository. These definitions, generally termed meta-data, may 'know' about many different types of product and mappings.

A repository therefore allows different software tools from different vendors to be integrated, allows those tools to store and retrieve data from the repository and provides physical data management and information presentation facilities.

- *Meta-CASE tool.* A meta-CASE tool enables the designer to build a customized CASE tool; as such, it extends the principle of an open environment. It is possible to decide on the systems development products required and then define their structure, content and formation rules (syntax and semantics) in a language definition schema, using a 'language definition language' provided by the meta-CASE tool. Their form of representation is similarly defined. Next, the mappings or translations between these products may be defined using the same language. For example, one could define an entity–relationship model and a relational data model and then define a mapping between them.

   The meta-CASE tool will provide facilities that allow the designer to create products that have been defined in language definition schemata and perform mappings between these products. It is also possible to include software support to assist the designer when performing various systems development activities.

TOOL COMPONENTS

A more detailed view of CASE can be obtained by considering some of the common types of components of workbenches or I-CASE tools. These are: diagramming tools, repositories, prototyping tools, code generators and project management tools.

Diagramming tools

These are typically used in the analysis phase and support a diagrammatic technique such as data flow diagramming or entity–relationship modelling. From the point of view of the user interface, in a typical Windows environment, there will be a main window that will contain the basic set of icons or graphical symbols used for drawing the diagram, and any one of these at a time can be selected using the cursor and mouse. The tool draws the symbol where the cursor is positioned which can then be moved to whatever position required. Other symbols may be selected to build more of the diagram.

The above describes the basic functionality; depending on the sophistication of the tool, further features are usually available. For example, when a symbol is selected, a sub-menu of different symbol types may be shown, with the user being asked to select one of the types. After a symbol is positioned, a dialog box may be shown asking for information to be given; the information might not be shown on the diagram, but may be stored in the repository.

There are usually a range of editing facilities available, such as cut, copy, paste and move. It is usually possible to select a group of symbols on a diagram and move them together; any lines connecting these symbols will often be extended or reshaped automatically when the final position of the group is selected. Full scrolling, magnification and printing facilities are usually available. If the method or technique assisted uses decomposition, there are facilities to assist in decomposing down and abstracting back up again.

Underneath the user interface, a tool will have access to knowledge concerning the rules of the diagrammatic technique. This is used when symbols are added to the diagram as there is usually a syntax-checking feature with accompanying warning messages to avoid illegal diagrams being built. There may also be more support in the form of advice or hints for building a diagram. Such knowledge may be kept in the tool or in the repository (see below).

The information in the diagrams will be represented in the repository in a form defined by the repository; for some tools, the physical diagrams are saved in the repository as well. Depending on the facilities available, it may be possible to map down from the diagram into more detailed phases of systems development.

Repositories

Repositories maintain all the information concerning the progress of a systems development project. They provide facilities for the following:

- *Data integrity.* This checks entries to the repository and establishes consistency between related objects.
- *Information sharing.* This allows tools and developers to share information without duplication.
- *Data–tool integration.* This feature defines a model (meta-model) of the types of information held in the repository for use by the tools.
- *Data–data integration.* This establishes a database management system that stores and retrieves data objects which represent the information handled by the tools.
- *Function support.* There may be rules, help or advice provided for users when they use different functions that access the repository. For example, it may be required to maintain consistency between different, related diagrams of a method.

Prototyping tools

Prototyping tools are useful for assisting in the determination of requirements and may help with eventual system acceptability. User-interface painters are required that can quickly build input and output screens and set up menus; these give users an early 'look-and-feel' for eventual system behaviour. Screen dialogues, menu navigation and data entry with error messages are also provided. Code for record, file screen and report descriptions can be generated automatically. An executable specification language is a form of prototyping tool where code can be generated directly from a specification.

To be effective, a prototyping tool needs to capture all the important requirements, produce a satisfactory user interface, provide realistic functionality and simulate the environment in which the application will operate.

Code generators

A code generator generates code from a specification or a program design that is intended for use in the working system. Depending on the features available, a skeleton or full set of code may be generated, including code for the database, files, screens and reports. Generated code may be source or object code.

Project management tools

This tends to be rather a mixed category of tools, as support tools such as configuration management and quality control are often included along with project planning and project control tools. Currently, there are many tools for project estimating and scheduling, but less for support or contractual features, such as risk management or calling for tenders for a project.

CURRENT TOOLS

Reviews are available of commercially available tools (Ovum, 1993; Howard and Potter, 1994), but they are quickly out of date. Tools in wide use in the UK include Systems Engineer, ADW, IEF, Oracle CASE, Maestro II, Software through Pictures, System Architect and Teamwork. Two examples of meta-CASE tools are ToolBuilder and Methods Factory.

PROBLEMS ADDRESSED

The main problem addressed by tools appears to be the third quality problem, concerning the errors made in analysing information needs. Tools address this problem by providing more effective techniques on well-defined phase products; in addition, tools may offer code generation. The problem of changing requirements is addressed using prototyping tools.

However, there is no firm evidence that tools deliver the levels of improvement in productivity and quality hoped for by earlier commentators such as McClure (1989). A recent survey (Flynn *et al.*, 1995) found that productivity was not improved but that quality was slightly improved. Alavi (1993) finds little evidence to substantiate the claims made for CASE and identifies two problems: firstly, software development is a group activity that very few CASE tools support, and secondly, more attention needs to be paid to organizational issues, such as training and changes to organizational work patterns.

However, it takes several years for the CASE culture to become established in organizations, and if its greatest impact is on maintenance it will be some years before benefits will show. The use of CASE may, over the medium and long term, also enable organizations to construct, on a conceptual level, precise descriptions of their systems and organizational practices. This may assist specification reusability for new applications.

CASE is not yet successful in producing what many users want – a fully integrated environment for systems development. This is because it cannot, for example, proceed from requirements to the generation of code for a complete system. The area of logical to physical transformation is a particular problem. The other areas where users will be looking for improvements are in the provision of better prototyping tools and tools which address the requirements phase, and for more attention to be paid to the organizational aspects of CASE tool use.

Summary

This chapter began by defining the notion of a method and introducing some common terminology. A brief chronological history of methods was then outlined, progressing from the pre-method era, through process-oriented, data oriented, object-oriented and future methods. Method trends in general were discussed.

Five methods: Information Engineering, Structured systems analysis and design, JSD, SSADM and OMT, were then compared for the way in which their model-building activities dealt with a simple case study. The conclusions introduced a comparison framework in terms of method breadth and orientation, also comparing structured methods to OO methods, and then some future technical trends were considered. The problems addressed by methods and the solutions they provide were then described, followed by method advantages and disadvantages.

The last section discussed the main features of CASE tools, describing four main types as well as CASE tool components. Problems addressed by tools and the solutions provided were discussed. Some predictions were made for the likely directions of CASE and required areas of improvement.

Discussion questions

1. What were the main trends that marked the change from the time referred to here as the pre-method era to structured methods?
2. What problems were addressed by the move from process-oriented to data-oriented methods?
3. List the three most important problems, in your opinion, that methods address. Why do you select these?
4. Compare the DFDs from SSAAD and SSADM. What are the differences, if any?
5. Compare the data map of IE with the output from relational data analysis of SSADM. Is there any overlap?
6. Compare the entity life history in JSD to that in SSADM for the case study example. Which of the two is easier to understand and why?
7. Compare the OMT state diagram for book in Fig. 11.29 and the JSD process structure for the same object in Fig. 11.15. What are the differences?
8. Compare the OMT state diagram for member in Fig. 11.31 and the JSD process structure for the same object in Fig. 11.14. Which diagram do you think is easier to understand?
9. Bearing in mind the problems addressed and solutions provided by CASE tools, summarize the three main advantages and disadvantages.

References

Alavi, M. (1993) Making CASE an organizational reality: strategies and new capabilities needed, *Information Systems Management*, **10**(2), 15–20.

ANSI/SPARC (1975) ANSI/X3/SPARC study group on database management systems, *Interim report*, FDT (Bulletin of ACM-SIGMOD), **7**(2).

Avison, D. E. and Fitzgerald, G. (1995) *Information Systems Development: Methodologies, Techniques and Tools*, 2nd edn, McGraw-Hill, London.

Baker, F. T. (1972) Chief programmer team management of production programming, *IBM Systems Journal*, **11**(1), 56–73.

Bamford, R. C. and Deibler, W. J. (1993) Comparing, contrasting ISO 9001 and the SEI capability maturity model, *IEEE Computer*, October, 68–70.

Bohm, C. and Jacopini, G. (1966) Flow diagrams, Turing machines and languages with only two formation rules, *Communications of the ACM*, **9**(5), 366–71.

Booch, G. (1991) *Object Oriented Design: With Applications*, Benjamin/Cummings, Menlo Park CA.

Cameron, J. R. (1986) An overview of JSD, *IEEE Transactions on Software Engineering*, **SE-12**(2), 222–40.

CCTA (1990) *PRINCE: Structured Project Management* (5 vols), NCC Blackwell, Oxford.

Checkland, P. and Scholes, J. (1990) *Soft Systems Methodology in Action*, Wiley, Chichester.

Coad, P. and Yourdon, E. (1991) *Object-Oriented Analysis*, 2nd edn, Prentice-Hall, Englewood Cliffs NJ.

Connor, D. (1985) *Information System Specification and Design Road Map*, Prentice-Hall, Englewood Cliffs NJ.

Curtis, B., Kellner, M. I. and Over, J. (1992) Process modelling, *Communications of the ACM*, **35**(9), 75–90.

Daniels, A. and Yeates, D. (1969) *Basic Training in Systems Analysis*, Pitman, London.

Date, C. J. (1995) *An Introduction to Database Systems*, 6th edn, Addison-Wesley, Reading MA.

Davis, A. M. (1990) *Software Requirements: Analysis and Specification*, Prentice-Hall, Englewood Cliffs NJ.

de Marco, T. (1979) *Structured Analysis and System Specification*, Prentice-Hall, Englewood Cliffs NJ.

Dijkstra, E. W. (1968) Go To statement considered harmful, *Communications of the ACM*, **11**(3), 147–8.

Downs, E., Clare, P. and Coe, I. (1992) *Structured Systems Analysis and Design Method*, 2nd edn, Prentice-Hall, London.

Fagan, M. E. (1976) Design and code inspections to reduce errors in program development, *IBM Systems Journal*, **15**(3), 182–211.

Fichman, R. G. and Kemerer, C. F. (1992) Object-oriented and conventional analysis and design methodologies: comparison and critique, *IEEE Computer*, October, 22–39.

Finkelstein, C. (1989) *An Introduction to Information Engineering*, Addison-Wesley, Wokingham.

Flynn, D. J. and Fragoso-Diaz, O. (1996) *Information Modelling: An International Perspective*, Prentice-Hall, London.

Flynn, D. J., Vagner, J. and Dal Vecchio, O. (1995) Is CASE technology improving quality and productivity in software development? *Logistics Information Management*, **8**(2), 8–21.

Friedman, A. L. and Cornford, D. S. (1989) *Computer Systems Development: History, Organization and Implementation*, Wiley, Chichester.

Fuggetta, A. (1993) A classification of CASE technology, *IEEE Computer*, December, 25–38.

Gane, C. (1990) *Computer-aided Software Engineering*, Prentice-Hall, Englewood Cliffs NJ.

Gane, C. and Sarson, T. (1979) *Structured Systems Analysis: Tools and Techniques*, Prentice-Hall, Englewood Cliffs NJ.

Horowitz, E. (ed.) (1975) *Practical Strategies for Developing Large Software Systems*, Addison-Wesley, London.

Howard, P. and Potter, C. (1994) *CASE & Methods Based Development Tools: An Evaluation and Comparison*, ButlerBloor Ltd, Challenge House, Sherwood Drive, Bletchley, Milton Keynes, MK3 6DP.

Humphrey, W. S. (1989) *Managing the Software Process*, Addison-Wesley, Reading MA.

Iivari, J. (1994) Object-oriented information systems analysis: a comparison of six object-oriented analysis methods, in *Methods and Associated Tools for the Information Systems Life Cycle* (eds. Verrijn-Stuart, A. A. and Olle, T. W.), Elsevier, Amsterdam, 85–109.

Jackson, M. A. (1975) *Principles of Program Design*, Academic Press, London.

Jackson, M. A. (1983) *Systems Development*, Prentice-Hall, Englewood Cliffs NJ.

Jacobson, I., Christerson, M., Jonsson, P. and Overgaard, G. (1992) *Object-Oriented Software Engineering: A Use Case Driven Approach*, Addison-Wesley, Wokingham.

Jayaratna, N. (1994) *Understanding and Evaluating Methodologies: NIMSAD – A Systemic Framework*, McGraw-Hill, London.

King, D. (1984) *Current Practices in Software Development: A Guide to Successful Systems*, Prentice-Hall, Englewood Cliffs NJ.

Lee, B. (1979) *Introducing Systems Analysis*, NCC Publications, Manchester.

Longworth, G. (1989) *Getting the System You Want: A User's Guide to SSADM*, NCC Publications, Manchester.

McClure, C. (1989) *CASE is Software Automation*, Prentice-Hall, Englewood Cliffs NJ.

Maddison, R. N., Baker, G., Bhabuta, L., Fitzgerald, G., Hindle, K., Song, J., Stokes, N. and Wood, J. (1983) *Information System Methodologies*, Wiley, Chichester.

Mair, P. (1993) *The Strategic Procurement of CASE Tools*, NCC Blackwell, Oxford.

Martin, J. and Odell, J. J. (1992) *Object-Oriented Analysis and Design*, Prentice-Hall, Englewood Cliffs NJ.

Myers, G. T. (1975) *Reliable Software through Composite Design*, Petrocelli-Charter, New York.

Nassi, I. and Shneiderman, B. (1973) Flowchart techniques for structured programming, *ACM SIGPLAN Notices*, **8**(8), 12–26.

Naur, P. and Randell, B. (eds.) (1968) *Software Engineering*. Report of a conference sponsored by the NATO Science Committee, Garmisch, Germany.

Olle, T. W., Sol, H. G. and Tully, C. J. (eds.) (1983) *Information Systems Design Methodologies: A Feature Analysis*, North-Holland, Amsterdam.

Olle, T. W., Sol, H. G. and Verrijn-Stuart, A. A. (eds.) (1982) *Information Systems Design Methodologies: A Comparative Review*, North-Holland, Amsterdam.

Olle, T. W., Sol, H. G. and Verrijn-Stuart, A. A. (eds.) (1986) *Information Systems Design Methodologies: Improving the Practice*, North-Holland, Amsterdam.

Olle, T. W., Verrijn-Stuart, A. A. and Bhabuta, L. (eds.) (1988) *Computerized Assistance during the Information Systems Life Cycle*, North-Holland, Amsterdam.

Olle, T. W., Hagelstein, J., Macdonald, I. G., Rolland, C., Sol, H. G., Van Assche, F. J. M. and Verrijn-Stuart, A. A. (1991) *Information Systems Methodologies: A Framework for Understanding*, 2nd edn, Addison-Wesley, Wokingham.

Orr, K. T. (1977) *Structured Systems Development*, Yourdon Press, New York.

Ovum (1993) *Ovum Evaluates CASE Products*, Ovum Ltd, 1 Mortimer Street, London, W1N 7RH, January.

Paulk, M. C., Curtis, B., Chrissis, M. B. and Weber, C. V. (1993) Capability maturity model, version 1.1, *IEEE Software*, July, 18–27.

Rachel, J. and Van Hasselt-Lim, C. (1995) Social views of technology development: the local life of methodologies, *Computer Bulletin*, 7(5), 2–3.

Ross, D. T. and Schoman, K. E. (1977) Structured analysis for requirements definition, *IEEE Transactions on Software Engineering*, **SE-3**(1), 6–15.

Royce, W. W. (1970) Managing the development of large systems, in *Proceedings of IEEE WESCON*, 1–9. (Reprinted in *Proceedings of the 9th International Conference on Software Engineering*, March–April 1987, Monterey CA, 328–38).

Royce, W. W. (1975) Software requirements analysis: sizing and costing, in *Practical Strategies for Developing Large Software Systems* (ed. Horowitz, E.), Addison-Wesley, London, 57–72.

Rumbaugh, J., Blaha, M., Premeriani, W., Eddy, F. and Lorensen, W. (1991) *Object-Oriented Modeling and Design*, Prentice-Hall, Englewood Cliffs NJ.

Shlaer, S. and Mellor, S. J. (1988) *Object-Oriented Systems Analysis: Modeling the World in Data*, Prentice-Hall, Englewood Cliffs NJ.

SSADM (1990) *SSADM Version 4 Reference manual* (4 vols), July, NCC Blackwell, Oxford.

SSADM (1995) *SSADM4+: Version 4.2*, NCC Blackwell, Oxford.

Stevens, W., Myers, G. and Constantine, L. (1974) Structured design, *IBM Systems Journal*, **13**(2), 115–39.

TickIT (1995) *TickIT guide to software quality system construction and certification*, issue 3.0, October, British Standards Institution DISC, 389 Chiswick High Road, London, W4 4AL.

Tsichritzis, D. and Klug, A. (eds.) (1977) *The ANSI/X3/SPARC DBMS framework: report of the study group on database management systems*, AFIPS Press, Montvale, NJ (also reprinted in *Information Systems*, **3**(3), 1978, 173–91).

Verrijn-Stuart, A. A. and Olle, T. W. (eds.) (1994) *Methods and Associated Tools for the Information Systems Life Cycle*, Elsevier, Amsterdam.

Warnier, J-D. (1974) *Logical Construction of Programs*, Van Nostrand Reinhold, New York.

Yourdon, E. (1978) *Structured Walkthroughs*, 2nd edn, Yourdon Press, Englewood Cliffs NJ.

Yourdon, E. (1982) *Writings of the Revolution: Selected Readings on Software Engineering*, Yourdon Press, Englewood Cliffs NJ.

Yourdon, E. and Constantine, L. L. (1979) *Structured Design: Fundamentals of a Discipline of Computer Program and Systems Design*, Prentice-Hall, Englewood Cliffs NJ.

Part Four

Standardization

Chapter 12 describes four recent standardization projects that focus on either the management of the components of the systems development process or an overview process level, appearing to represent a trend towards both the human and the technical problems of managing the process as a whole.

The first project, Euromethod, is an EC-sponsored programme for a standard, tailorable method for the development process, which covers, for example the technical nature of products as well as the human and administrative aspects of the process. SPICE is a proposal for an ISO standard for assessing the maturity of organizational processes that produce software, and hence emphasizes management of the process; the assessment may be used to improve the processes or to determine process capability.

ISO 12207 is a recent international standard that defines, on a high level, processes and roles of all aspects of systems development, while the last project, DSDM, is an industry-generated standard for rapid application development (RAD).

12
The movement to method standardization

Introduction

PROBLEM CONTEXT

A well-known researcher (Bubenko, 1986) has remarked that there are many hundreds, if not thousands, of systems development methods in existence. From the industry point of view, there are several disadvantages to this situation. For example, when organizations wish to contract external suppliers to develop software they are often faced with a bewildering set of different methods that those suppliers propose to use, making it difficult to understand what will be delivered.

Another problem is that method proliferation inhibits free movement of development staff and knowledge in the market, as skills which are generalizable are locked in to particular methods. Finally, it is an impossible task to try to improve software quality when there are so many different methods to be evaluated.

For these reasons, among others, there have been moves towards method standardization over the past decade. As we shall discuss below, the form that standardization is taking is towards a management view of the process, defining high-level activities that cover non-technical as well as technical areas. A likely explanation for this is that, on the technical level, no one method has emerged as superior. This has been accompanied by a slowdown in the rate at which new methods have emerged.

EXISTING STANDARDS

An example of standardization, briefly discussed in Chapter 11, is the ISO 9000-based set of standards that are applied to the development process and which are used, for example, by the UK Government's TickIT scheme (TickIT,

Standards

'Lloyd's Register launches software quality initiative', *Computing*, **7 September 1995**

Lloyd's Register is to offer a software certification service, to assure users of the quality of the products they buy. The Software Conformity Assessment will provide software buyers with independent certification that a product's development, verification and testing comply with industry standards and guidelines, including ISO 9001 and EN45000. Lloyd's Register will not provide insurance against the software's quality but will badge it with its stamp of approval.

Tony Darlinson, manager of software certification . . . said: 'We're allowing our logo to be used and putting our reputation at risk along with the software suppliers. We're confident in our abilities.' He added: 'A major problem with advanced and complex computer systems is that purchasers do not always know what they are buying.'

Geoff Quentin, chairman of the British Computer Society's Specialist Interest Group on Software Testing . . . welcomed the Lloyd's initiative. 'It's about time we started to behave professionally and produce things to a standard which other people can check.' 'It's what the market is forcing,' he said.

'IT staff set a new standard', *Computing*, **8 June 1995**

The 600 IT staff at Nationwide have helped the building society's technology division win the ISO 9000 quality standard. Four of the five divisions in Nationwide's IT department . . . spent three years working towards meeting the ISO 9000 requirements using the Department of Trade & Industry's exacting TickIT quality guidelines.

Bernard Simpson, Nationwide's group services director, said: 'We decided to develop the processes of our technology division to ISO 9000 to ensure that the society has systems in place to enable us to give customers the highest possible level of service.'

Nationwide has also been instrumental in pushing the British Standards Institution to expand the role of TickIT from software development to encompass every aspect of IT.

1995) to assess organizations. The two stories in the adjacent panel show how this standard may be used by an external certification organization such as Lloyd's Register as well as by an organization such as the Nationwide building society following self-certification.

EMERGING STANDARDS

In this chapter we discuss four emerging approaches to standardization: Euromethod, SPICE, ISO 12207 (software life cycle processes) and DSDM. Euromethod is a European, EC-sponsored initiative for a standard, tailorable method; SPICE is a proposal for an ISO standard for assessing the development process of an organization; ISO 12207 is a standard which defines, on a high level, processes and roles that cover all aspects of life cycle processes, from 'thinking' to 'retirement'; and DSDM is an industry-generated standard which describes a framework for rapid application development.

Euromethod

OVERVIEW

The aim of the Euromethod programme (CCTA, 1994; EM, 1994, 1997; Franckson, 1994) is, very generally, to improve the process of information systems development. The programme, funded by the European Commission, is concerned with the definition of a general development process to be used over organizational as well as over national boundaries, particularly within the European Union (EU).

Euromethod considers the relationships between the customer and the supplier to be at the heart of the development process, and it defines the deliverables (products) to be exchanged between them during all aspects of systems development, from call for tendering to system maintenance.

A particular influence has been the need to facilitate the process whereby an information system is required by a customer who is remote from several potential suppliers. A particularly relevant example, within the context of European integration, is where a public procurement body in one EU country is required to invite suppliers from any EU country to tender for the development of an information system.

HISTORY

Euromethod began in November 1989 when several EC member states agreed, in conjunction with the European Commission, upon initial requirements for a general method to support cross-border information system development. This was the start of Phase 1. Phase 2 consisted of an EC-funded feasibility study which ran for 8 months and started in May 1990. The outcome was a recommendation that Euromethod development should go ahead, based on a high-level structural model.

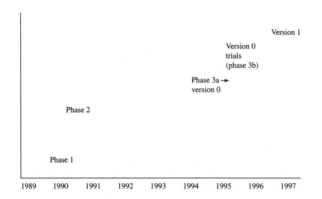

Figure 12.1 Historical development of Euromethod.

In the summer of 1992 what is now known as Phase 3a began, which has resulted in the initial version of Euromethod, version 0, delivered in June 1994 (EM, 1994). Phase 3b, consisting of public trials of Euromethod in member states, is ongoing with a draft version 1 currently available (EM, 1997). Initially, it is expected to be used on advertised public procurement projects, but it is unclear as to whether its use will be mandatory. Figure 12.1 shows this brief history.

Seven methods in use in Europe were selected as the basis for development of Euromethod in Phase 2. These were reputed to be the most widely used methods in their respective countries, and they were: SSADM from the UK, MERISE from France, SDM from the Netherlands, DAFNE from Italy, Vorgehensmodell from Germany, MEIN from Spain and Information Engineering. Information Engineering was a late entrant and was seen as providing an international perspective.

Funding has been undertaken by the European Commission separately from its IT research and development projects, and the programme sponsor is the Public Procurement Group, a European grouping of public procurement bodies. The programme is carried out by the Eurogroup consortium, consisting of ten partners from eight European countries, with the Sema Group (France) as the main contractor.

CONTEXT

Where

Euromethod is intended for use where there is a project concerning an information system where there is a customer, a supplier and a contract between customer and supplier which may be formal or informal.

An information system is considered as (EM, 1994: Overview):

that aspect of an organisation which provides, uses and distributes the information. It includes the associated organisational resources such as human, technical and financial resources. It is thus effectively a human system, possibly containing a computer system that automates selected elements of the information system.

When

Euromethod is designed for use within what it terms the *procurement process*. This term covers the information systems development process, from initial tendering through to maintenance. However, establishing the initial goal of the procurement is outside Euromethod. One use is to prepare a call for tender, whereby potential system suppliers are invited to, for example, submit bids to supply or maintain an information system. It may also be used to decide on project status or to approve final project deliverables. It is suggested that its full value is given when it is used throughout the whole process.

OBJECTIVES AND BENEFITS

Objectives

Three main problems are identified with the current development of information systems and Euromethod objectives are expressed in terms of these problems.

- *Relationships between customer and supplier.* These groups have different background and expectations with regard to outlook, culture, training and methods, which leads to confused and ambiguous relationships. With a widening of trade and relations between EC countries these problems might become critical, impeding the development of an open European market.
- *Differences between methods.* Many methods do the same thing or provide the same facility, but call them different names. In addition, the advantages or disadvantages of some methods compared with others may not be clear. To address this, Euromethod provides a framework consisting of a common set of concepts and requirements for potential method harmonization at a conceptual level. This level is chosen to avoid removing the competitive advantage of any existing method over other methods. The focus of this is the customer–supplier relationship.
- *Method flexibility and adaptability.* To improve the quality and efficiency of the development process, Euromethod identifies situational characteristics that occur within different types of systems development. It then suggests ways in which methods may be flexible so that they are easily adapted to those types of situations.

Benefits

Benefits are expressed in general terms and are largely seen to result in the expression of higher quality *requirements*. That is, the customer will express requirements more correctly that closely match the customer's real intentions.

Requirements are often not expressed satisfactorily because the customer expresses them in a vague or fuzzy manner. Alternatively, a solution may be provided to a perceived problem that may not be the best solution, or may even be addressing the wrong problem.

Another reason for poor requirements is due to the culture difference existing between customer and supplier. For example, customers may be frustrated by technical supplier jargon or the supplier may simply fail to understand the customer's requirements.

The focus in Euromethod on the customer–supplier relationship is seen as its main feature for addressing these problems. It is hoped that the result will be better information systems for customers, especially when developed in international tender situations. Benefits will also be felt by suppliers (that is, the information systems services industry in general), as they will understand customer needs and produce better proposals. In addition, their competitive position within European and international markets may also be improved.

EUROMETHOD PRINCIPLES

In the design of Euromethod a number of principles have been borne in mind that have affected its focus, determining the kind of real life situations to which Euromethod is most suited. The principles are: information system adaptation, variety of contracts, customer–supplier relationship, situation-driven, focus on decisions, focus on deliverables and method bridging.

Information system adaptation

An *IS-adaptation* is any change to an information system to fulfil the changing needs of the organization. It is wider in meaning than the term 'information systems development', as it refers to any kind of project concerned with information system change, such as systems development, procurement, maintenance, reverse engineering, feasibility study or system installation. In addition, it covers contractual and project management issues.

There are two fundamental types of activity within all these kinds of adaptation: production and management activities. Production activities perform the actual adaptation work through activities such as design, test and change study. Management activities control the production activities through project planning and control. Project planning is concerned with specifying the components, timing, resources and procedures of the project. Project control monitors the progress of the project, its quality, direction and resource utilization compared with the project plan.

Euromethod views IS-adaptation as constituting the *process* side of performing changes to information systems; while, on the *product* side, as the notion of an information system is broad, products may consist of organizational, human and technical elements.

Variety of contracts

Euromethod is intended to apply to any IS-adaptation that can be characterized by an initial and a final state, and it can thus be reapplied at any of the stages during the life of a given information system. Figure 12.2 shows some examples of typical IS-adaptations occurring to an information system.

Where an adaptation is regulated by a contract, at the outset of this adaptation contract the IS and the knowledge on the IS, expressed as products, constitutes what is termed the *initial state* of the IS. The desired state of the IS and the related products that express the knowledge on the IS comprise the *final state*.

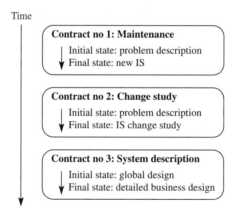

Figure 12.2 A series of contractual arrangements during the life of an information system.

Customer–supplier relationship

This relationship is of central importance to Euromethod, as it supports the contractual relationships between a customer and a supplier of an IS-adaptation. Figure 12.3 shows this relationship. Two levels of the relationship are shown: the *contractual* and the *project* levels.

A focus of Euromethod is the contractual level, starting with the call for tender, through to contract signing, the production of deliverables and ending in contract termination. It is interested in what it terms *transactions*, which involve decisions between customer and supplier on the contractual level. It

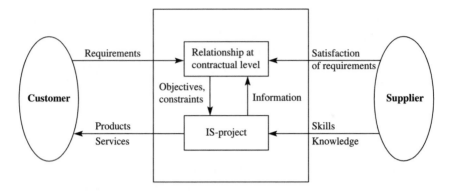

Figure 12.3   Two levels of customer–supplier relationship.

seeks to enhance this relationship, as well as to bridge the cultural difference between the parties involved on the contractual and project levels. This is shown in Fig. 12.4.

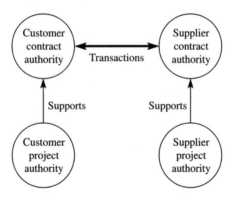

Figure 12.4   Key roles in an IS-adaptation.

Focus on decisions

The procurement of an information system, an IS-adaptation, is viewed as consisting of three main types of transactions which take place between customer and supplier, as shown in Fig. 12.5. Transactions exchange products and take decisions on the basis of information contained in those products.

The *tendering process* starts with the call for tender and usually ends with contract signing with the chosen supplier. The *production process* is where the IS-adaptation itself is performed and the *completion process* is where the contract is technically and commercially terminated.

Euromethod provides a set of specific types of transactions which are used to build a simple and general model of the tendering and completion processes for a given IS-adaptation.

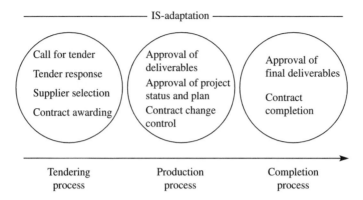

Figure 12.5 Customer–supplier transactions in IS-adaptations.

For the production process, in contrast, a set of general types of transactions are used to build a tailored model. This model focuses on *decision points* where transactions occur and key decisions are taken by the customer which will determine the properties of the new information system.

The main decision points and their sequence are approved or defined by the customer, as well as the related transactions. Some assistance is provided for determining the correct type of products to be delivered to support a given decision.

Focus on deliverables

The focus is on the 'what' of a deliverable rather than on the 'how'. That is, Euromethod specifies the nature and content of the deliverables as these are more important for the customer than the way in which they are produced by the supplier. As the deliverables constitute a vital part of the contractual customer–supplier relationship then the activities which produce them may be secondary even for the supplier.

Deliverables are the key planning elements to support decision making and progress management.

Figure 12.6 shows the principal types of deliverable, where a distinction is made between target and project domains. The target domain is that part of an organization for which an IS-adaptation is performed, while the project domain is that temporary organization, often referred to as the 'project', that has been set up to adapt an information system of an organization.

Target domain deliverables concern the information system to be adapted, and include descriptions (for example, specifications or designs) of the system as well as operational items (for example, code or hardware). The delivery plan describes the approach to the production process while the project domain deliverables concern the progress of production scheduling, including more detailed plans as well as reports on progress and problems.

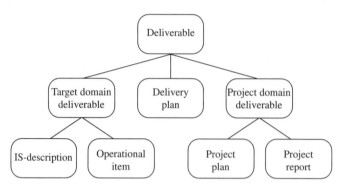

Figure 12.6 Principal types of deliverable.

Situation driven

Euromethod provides for an IS-adaptation strategy and plan to be developed based on situational factors. These are factors in the problem situation which are used to predict the risks and determine the appropriate problem-solving strategies for reduction or containment.

Guidelines are provided for identification of important situational factors, assessment of complexity, uncertainty and risk, and the definition of an IS-adaptation strategy which will address the problem situation. The strategy places specific requirements on the delivery plan of the contract.

Method bridging

Euromethod may be viewed as a high-level method framework as it is intended that, for any particular IS-adaptation, the production process will use specific process and product models from available IS-development methods, such as SSADM, Information Engineering or Merise.

Euromethod has produced sets of guidelines which bridge between its own concepts and those of 'external' methods, and the guidelines can be used to relate such methods being used in an IS-adaptation to the Euromethod deliverables and transactions that are prescribed in the delivery plan.

MORE INFORMATION

The Eurogroup consortium who are developing Euromethod are: Sema Group (France), BT (UK), Cap-Volmac (Netherlands), CGI (France), Datacentralen (Denmark), EMSC formed by Bull (France), Olivetti (Italy), Siemens (Germany), Eritel (Spain), Finsiel (Italy), Instituto Nacional de Administrao (Portugal) and Softlab (Germany).

Up to date information on Euromethod is available from the address given in the references (EM, 1994, 1997). Within the UK, the CCTA are members of the Euromethod Programme Management Board, a body set up to validate Euromethod project deliverables. The CCTA organize Euromethod trials in the UK, they produce periodic bulletins describing Euromethod project progress (CCTA 1994) and also have documentation on various aspects of Euromethod.

SPICE

OVERVIEW

Aims

The SPICE (Software Process Improvement and Capability dEtermination) project is intended to assist:

- the software industry to make significant gains in productivity and quality
- software acquirers (purchasers) to select suitable software suppliers and to reduce the risk associated with large projects and purchases of software

The drive behind this has come largely from acquirers who require large, critical software-intensive systems, particularly in the defence and telecommunications sectors (Rout, 1995).

The main aim of SPICE is to provide a standard framework for assessing the software processes of an organization. This assessment may be used either to improve those processes or to determine process capability.

SPICE is a current project of the International Organization for Standardization (ISO) which is intended to deliver an international standard for software process assessment (ISO 15504)

Benefits

The benefits of SPICE are stated as follows:

- *Benefits for the software industry*
  1. There will be only one process assessment scheme for software suppliers. At present, there are many similar schemes in use.
  2. Software suppliers will have the means to maintain a continuous process improvement programme.
  3. Management are provided with assistance for aligning software development with the business goals of the organization.
- *Benefits for software acquirers*
  1. Software acquirers are helped to determine the capability of software suppliers and can assess the risk in selecting one supplier over another.

The need for SPICE is due to the fact that the activities concerned with software are increasing their proportion of organizational spending. Modern software systems and projects are becoming more complex and more closely embedded within the organizational fabric. This makes it difficult for organizations to identify risks and improve quality and productivity.

Managers need more specialized expertise, based on a comparison with industrial best practice, to help them understand the capability of an organization to develop systems. In addition, they need to understand how to identify risks and possible improvements in the software processes of an organization (not necessarily their own).

SPICE consortium

The SPICE consortium comprises over 50 international participants, including software acquirers and suppliers. The SPICE standard has been developed from their experience in the area of software development and is also being validated in trials with a variety of organizations and projects. In the UK, BT and the Defence Research Agency are participants.

Software process assessment – its characteristics

SPICE has a broad view of a software process, as it is not only a development process but may be any process, such as managing or acquiring, which is concerned with software.

The focus is on process, as product quality is perceived to be determined by process quality.

Software process assessment is viewed as a disciplined examination of a process against a set of standard criteria, with the emphasis on determining the capability of the process to perform within quality, cost and schedule goals.

HISTORY OF DEVELOPMENT

In June 1991, an ISO study report (ISO/IEC, 1992) found that there was international consensus on the need for a standard for process assessment. As a result, the SPICE project was established in June 1993 (Dorling, 1993) to build on the results of this study.

A nine-part working draft standard was produced in June 1995, and a trialling period commenced in January 1995 to test the proposed standard. A draft Version 1.0 of the standard was produced in November 1996 and trials are continuing.

SPICE FRAMEWORK

Figure 12.7 shows the framework that has been developed for software process assessment. It consists of three components: process assessment, process capability determination and process improvement.

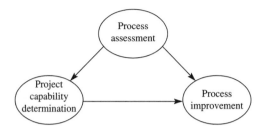

Figure 12.7 SPICE framework, showing main components.

Process assessment

Process assessment examines organizational processes against the SPICE standard and reports on the way in which those processes are carried out, in terms of how well they achieve quality, cost and schedule goals. Typically, an assessment will be carried out by or on behalf of any software supplier that wishes to understand and evaluate its processes.

Process improvement

This uses the results of an assessment typically to improve current processes. An assessment might be used by or on behalf of a software supplier for this purpose.

Process capability determination

This component uses assessment results to check whether the capability of processes in an organization match the requirements of a particular project. This is for the situation where a software acquirer wishes to determine the suitability of the processes of a software supplier for a specific project.

Assessment results are intended to be repeatable and comparable over similar contexts. This is achieved using a qualified assessor, a standard assessment instrument and guidance available in the documentation.

DOCUMENTS

Figure 12.8 shows the parts that comprise SPICE products, consisting of nine documents. Part 1 is an entry point to SPICE. It describes how the parts fit together and provides guidance for their selection and use. It explains the requirements in the standard and how they should be applied to the conduct of an assessment, the construction and selection of supporting tools and the construction of extended processes. These are processes which are not defined in the process model of the standard.

Part 2 presents a process model or architecture that defines the fundamental activities which are essential to software engineering. It structures them into

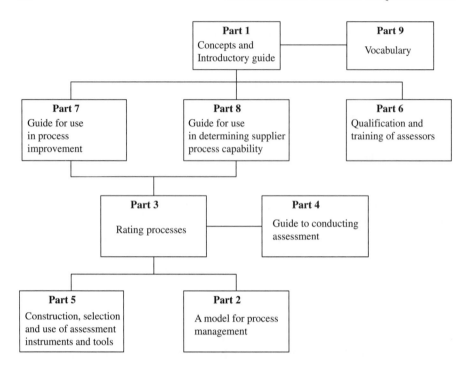

Figure 12.8 SPICE document set.

increasing levels of process capability that reflect the ways in which processes can be implemented in an organization.

Part 3 defines a framework for conducting assessments, setting out the basis for rating, scoring and profiling process capabilities.

Part 4 offers guidance on the conduct of team-based software process assessments. The guidance is general for any type of organization and allows the use of different methods, techniques and tools when performing assessments.

Part 5 defines how an assessment instrument should be constructed from a set of standard framework elements. This will assist an assessor when performing an assessment. Guidance is also provided concerning the selection and usability of different types of assessment instrument.

Part 6 describes the competence, education, training and experience of assessors relevant to conducting process assessments. Mechanisms are described that can be used to demonstrate competence and to validate education, training and experience.

Part 7 describes how to define the inputs to and use the results of process assessment for the purpose of process improvement.

Part 8 describes how to define the inputs to and use the results of process assessment for the purpose of process capability determination. This is applicable either for an organization when determining its own capability or for an acquirer wishing to determine the capability of a potential supplier.

Part 9 defines the terms used in the standard.

PROCESS ASSESSMENT

Context

Inputs to process assessment are: scope (that is, the processes to be assessed); constraints; the individual or organization with the responsibility for carrying out the assessment; and any process definitions to be included which are variants of the processes defined in the SPICE process model, discussed below. The SPICE process model is the process standard against which a process is assessed. An assessment instrument is used which conforms to SPICE guidelines.

Process assessment outputs are a process profile and an assessment record. For each assessed process a process profile is built, giving a rating for each of five capability levels in terms of process ability to achieve quality, cost and schedule goals. The assessment record is important because it describes the context of the assessment to aid comparability of assessments.

Process model

The SPICE process model, shown in Fig. 12.9, defines a set of fundamental activities that are essential for good software engineering.

Left branch

The left branch of the model consists of a hierarchy on three levels. At the bottom are *base practices*, which are unique software engineering or manage-

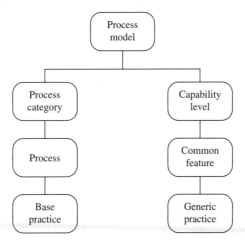

Figure 12.9 SPICE process model.

ment *activities*. These are grouped into *processes*, which in turn are grouped into five *process categories*. The level of description has been chosen to describe what activities are performed rather than how they are performed.

For example, the five process categories are: customer–supplier, engineering, project, support and organization. An example of two processes in the customer–supplier process category are *establish contract* and *assess customer satisfaction*, while a process in the engineering category is *integrate and test software*. A process has a *purpose*, which is the reason for performing it.

Right branch

The right branch consists of activities termed *generic practices*. These are more general than left branch processes and consist of activities which manage a process and improve its capability to perform. When they are applied to any process this is termed *institutionalization* of that process.

Generic practices are grouped into *common features*, which are then grouped into capability levels. The basis for grouping is the way in which the practices improve a process; that is, the type of institutionalization they bring about.

Each capability level is characterized by a type of institutionalization which is expressed in the descriptive name of the capability level. For example, the type of institutionalization of capability level 4 is *Measured*, and generic practices and common features which address this are grouped into this level.

Two examples of generic practices, their common features and capability levels are: *standardize the process* (Defining a standard process – level 3), and *establish quality goals* (Establishing measurable quality goals – level 4).

Capability level hierarchy

The six capability levels and their names are:

- Level 0 – Initial (not-performed)
- Level 1 – Performed (performed-initially)
- Level 2 – Managed (planned-and-tracked)
- Level 3 – Defined (well-defined)
- Level 4 – Measured (quantitatively-controlled)
- Level 5 – Optimizing (continuously-improving)

Each of the six capability levels in the process model defines a major enhancement in capability to that provided by its predecessor(s) in the performance of a process. The capability levels provide a rational way of progressing through enhancements to a process.

Level 0 is characterized by the fact that either base practices are not performed or there are no identifiable products. Level 1 is the next step up, as base practices are performed but they are not rigorously planned and tracked, and performance depends on individual knowledge and effort.

On level 2, the distinction is that base practice performance is planned and managed. Products are reviewed for adequacy and version control is applied. Level 3 is characterized by the fact that base practices are planned and managed using approved versions of standard documented processes.

On level 4, measurable process goals are established for each defined process and measures of performance are collected and analysed. Level 5 is where a quantitative approach is taken to setting targets and monitoring process output and progress, and results are fed back into procedures for continuous process improvement.

ASSESSMENT PROCEDURE

The *assessment instrument* is used during the performance of an assessment to assist an *assessor* in obtaining reliable and repeatable results. It may be a manual or a computer instrument, a questionnaire or a survey.

Guidance is provided with a set of assessment indicators to help assess the process under review, to make consistent judgements about institutionalized practices and to analyse and present the results. Requirements are given for the way in which to conduct assessments so that results will be reliable and repeatable. An assessment should be conducted by a qualified assessor or a team containing a qualified assessor.

PROCESS PROFILE

Base practice

When a process is assessed, its base practices are compared against the standard base practices for that type of process described in the SPICE process model.

A process has a capability level of 0 (Initial) when none of its base practices exist. If the process exists, then all of its base practices are rated in terms of whether they are adequately performed at capability level 1.

A four-point scoring scale is used, where a practice is rated as not adequate, partially adequate, largely adequate or fully adequate. Adequacy is defined by whether or not the practice satisfies the *purpose* of the process.

Generic practice

For levels 2 to 5 all generic practices that institutionalize the process are rated. Depending on the type of institutionalization addressed by the generic practices the process will be assessed on each of these four levels.

The rating of each generic practice is a judgement, within the process context, of the extent to which an institutionalized generic practice satisfies the process purpose.

A process profile thus shows process ratings on levels 1 to 5 of the capability levels, where each level consists of a rating of the adequacy of its generic practices. Base practice adequacy is effectively being rated on level 1 as there is only one generic practice on this level.

For example, a process might be 40 per cent largely adequate and 60 per cent fully adequate on level 1, but 20 per cent not adequate and 80 per cent partially adequate on level 2, with 0 per cent scores on higher levels. A profile is produced for each process being assessed.

PROCESS IMPROVEMENT

When process assessment results are used for process improvement it is suggested that improvement actions should be aligned to business goals, and cultural and management issues should be addressed. The capability levels are intended to suggest progressively the types of improvement to be considered.

PROCESS CAPABILITY DETERMINATION

The aims of process capability determination are to determine the extent to which the processes of an organization can satisfy the requirements of a specific project and to estimate any risks to the successful outcome of the project.

Process capability determination may be used where a software acquirer needs to evaluate the process capability of a supplier before making contractual arrangements with the supplier for a project. It is envisaged that a target capability is defined in terms of process capability levels, and the capability of the supplier to meet the target is determined by comparing supplier assessment results with this target. Risks that may be involved with this supplier for the project are also ascertained.

Another use is where a supplier may want to ascertain its own process capability before responding to an acquirer's proposal.

Capability determination is thus envisaged as supporting a market-place where acquirers may have different levels of requirement for different software projects and different levels of supplier exist, some of whom may be able to offer a range of capabilities.

TRIALS

Trials to validate the products in organizations before the standard is issued are a part of SPICE. The trials seek to establish usability and coverage of the standard, to establish assessment repeatability and to begin a process of data collection, to provide evidence, over the long term, that SPICE has a positive influence on software projects.

SOURCES

The sources for this description of SPICE, an ongoing project, are Dorling (1993, 1995), ISO/IEC (1992, 1995a, 1996), Kuvaja *et al.* (1995), Rout (1995), Rout (1995) and the SPICE project web address ESI (1997), containing up to date project details.

ISO 12207 – software life-cycle processes

OVERVIEW

Aim and motivation

ISO standard 12207 (ISO/IEC, 1995b) is concerned with defining a high-level architecture of software life-cycle processes, covering all processes from thinking about the need for software to 'retirement' of a software system.

The drive to establish the standard has been motivated by the fact that, although software has become an integral part of many scientific and business disciplines, there is a lack of a uniform framework that can be used by software practitioners to create and manage software. A standard framework may focus the development of environments or methods for developing and managing software and may also remove barriers between international trade.

FOUNDATIONS

Basic criteria

The life-cycle process architecture is composed of *key processes* and their interrelationships. The processes have been identified on the basis of two criteria: *modularity* and *responsibility*.

Processes are modular in the sense that they are maximally cohesive and minimally coupled. That is, each process is self-contained and relies upon other processes for only specialized functions.

Responsibility is an important concept, as each process is considered to be the responsibility of a certain party in the life-cycle. The key activities of roles such as supplier, acquirer, operator, maintainer and project manager are covered. This is contrasted with a textbook approach, which has a functional view on processes, refining them into work areas such as development, project management and quality.

Life-cycle processes

There are three broad types of process: *primary, supporting* and *organizational.* Primary processes are acquisition, supply, development, operation and maintenance; these cover major life-cycle functions. These are shown in Fig. 12.10.

Supporting processes are documentation, configuration management, quality assurance, joint review, audit, verification, validation and problem resolution. Organizational processes are management, infrastructure, improvement and training; these may be invoked by an organization at a high level to establish, implement and improve a life-cycle process.

A process is defined in terms of activities which are in turn defined in terms of tasks. A task is expressed in the form of a requirement, self-declaration, recommendation or permissible action. Certain standard verbs (for example, shall, should and may) are used in task descriptions and differentiate between tasks.

Quality perspective

The architecture emphasizes the principles of total quality management as it provides an integrated set of processes covering the entire life-cycle and it

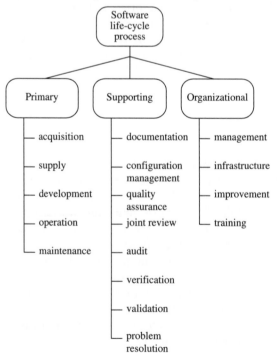

Figure 12.10 Software process life-cycle processes.

specifies that each process should have a 'plan-do-check' cycle. In this way, quality is built in to the processes in an appropriate manner at different stages and assigned to the roles performing those processes.

In addition, a quality assurance process provides for 'external' activities to ensure that products and services conform to their requirements.

Contractual framework

Task descriptions are expressed in contractual language to facilitate the application of the standard in a contractual manner. If the standard is applied internally within an organization it may be regarded as self-imposed tasks; with another organization the tasks may form the basis of a contract; another scenario is where an organization makes public a minimum set of tasks to which suppliers must comply.

Open architecture

To be responsive to the rapidly changing software engineering discipline, the standard is based on an open architecture approach, achieved by avoiding prescriptive activities. For example:

- Activities and tasks are expressed as 'what to do' and not 'how to do'. This allows an acquirer to specify, for example, a desired product, while leaving a supplier to produce this product in any way suitable.
- The standard is usable with any life-cycle model or with any analysis, design or programming language. No time-dependent sequence is suggested. These choices are left to the user of the standard to decide depending on the project and available technology.
- Any sector or culture (national or organizational) may use the standard.
- No documentation standards are set. The standard may state that certain outputs are required from a process but it does not define their content or format.

The standard is seen as a set of building blocks which, although they are well-defined, are for users to assemble together in ways that are cost-effective for the relevant project and organization.

PRIMARY PROCESSES

- *Acquisition process.* This defines the behaviour (activities and tasks) of the acquirer, who contractually acquires software (product or service). Activities include: definition of need to acquire product or service, preparation of and call for tender, supplier selection, supplier monitoring, acceptance and completion.
  Responsibility: *acquirer.*

- *Supply process.* This defines behaviour of the supplier, who contractually agrees to supply software. It may be initiated by a decision to prepare a response to a call for tender or by entering into a contract with an acquirer. Activities include: initiation, preparation of response, contract, planning, execution and control, review and evaluation, delivery completion.
  Responsibility: *supplier.*

- *Development process.* This concerns the development of new software or the maintenance of existing software. Activities include: system requirements analysis, system design, software coding and testing, software integration, system qualification testing, software acceptance and report.
  Responsibility: *software developer.*

- *Operation process.* This covers the operation of the software and its integration into the wider system, and operational support to users. Activities include: process implementation, operational testing, system operation and user support.
  Responsibility: *operator.*

- *Maintenance process.* This covers the activities that take place when a system undergoes modifications, to, for example its purpose, organizational context, hardware, software or documentation. Activities include: problem and modification analysis, modification implementation, maintenance review, migration and software retirement.
  Responsibility: *maintainer.*

SUPPORTING PROCESSES

Supporting processes contribute to the success and quality of the project. They are invoked as needed by any process and are the responsibility of the organization performing that process.

- *Documentation process.* This records the information produced by a life-cycle process.
- *Configuration management process.* This keeps track of system components, including modification and delivery.
- *Quality assurance process.* This provides a framework for establishing that products or services comply with acquirer requirements and contract.
- *Verification process.* This checks that products or services are complete and correct, depending on system criticality.
- *Validation process.* This checks that the final system does what users wanted.
- *Joint review process.* This provides the framework for reviewer–reviewee interaction for reviewing project status or products.

- *Audit process.* An auditor checks the products or services of an auditee for compliance with requirements or plans.
- *Problem resolution process.* This provides the mechanism for resolving problems as they arise during life-cycle processes.

ORGANIZATIONAL PROCESSES

These processes typically cut across projects as they are on a corporate level. They assist and help to implement and improve processes.

- *Management process.* This defines the generic activities of the management of any life-cycle process. For example, initiation, execution and control.
- *Infrastructure process.* This establishes the infrastructure needed for a process, such as hardware, tools, standards and facilities.
- *Improvement process.* This consists of activities such as data collection, assessment and measurement which seek to improve a life-cycle process.
- *Training process.* This identifies, acquires and develops personnel resources and skills required on management and technical levels.

TAILORING

Characteristics of projects and infrastructure of applicable life-cycle processes are suggested and, based on this, guidance is provided to tailor the standard to particular situations.

SOURCES

This section is based on the discussion in Singh (1994) and the ISO standard document (ISO/IEC, 1995b).

DSDM

Dynamic Systems Development Method (DSDM) offers a contrast to the standards discussed above, as it is not under the auspices of a standards body or an organization such as the EC which can legislate for standard procedures to be followed.

DSDM is a UK industry-generated, high-level method for rapid application development (RAD), undertaken jointly by a consortium of UK software suppliers and purchasers formed in January 1994.

PROBLEMS ADDRESSED

The main problem addressed is that the systems development process is frequently too slow and that it emphasizes the perspective of the software developer rather than other parties, for example users, project managers and quality assurers.

The basic approach of DSDM is what is termed *incremental prototyping*. It criticizes traditional development methods on two counts. Firstly, the 'total solution' approach, where requirements are effectively frozen at the start of development, often results in a system that is not what is required, as users have modified their requirements due to learning throughout the process. This is characterized by the fact that each stage of a waterfall life-cycle is completed before going on to the next stage, and no previous stage can be revisited.

Secondly, if it is permitted to revisit earlier life-cycle stages to take account of changing requirements, then the necessary undoing of work already done generally results in a system that is delivered too late.

DSDM produces a prototype system which is planned to produce, in its first step, '80 per cent' of what the user wants. It then iterates previous steps to include improvements for the next version. This incremental approach thus produces part of a system followed by later parts. According to some users, most time savings come from the fact that the analysis stage is completely left out, saving up to 40 per cent of the development period time.

DSDM recognizes that not all projects may be suitable for this approach. For example, it is suggested (Soft, 1994) that there are two factors which must be present. Firstly, the functionality of the application must be clearly visible at the user interface. The prototyping emphasis obviously demands that application logic can be demonstrated to users on screen.

Secondly, it is necessary to be able to work with a clearly defined user group who have the power to make decisions; again, this is necessary so that a group is available and willing to participate with developers in frequent requirements and review sessions with prototypes. If decisions on requirements or prototype characteristics cannot be made in joint user–developer sessions, but instead must be sent away for management review, then this will delay the development process.

PRINCIPLES

The first version of DSDM in February 1995 ('A radical break', *Computing*, 2 March 1995) provided a high-level framework for developing systems founded on 13 key principles. The more recent second version in December 1995 is based on nine principles. These are:

- Active user involvement is imperative.
- DSDM teams must have the power to make decisions.
- The focus is on frequent delivery of products rather than the way they are produced.
- Every deliverable is fit for its business purpose. Traditional methods focus on satisfying a requirements document, while losing sight of the fact that requirements are often inaccurate.

- Iterative and incremental development is a powerful way to develop systems. If systems grow in stages there is more chance for users to give developers feedback. Although iteration is part of software development, DSDM makes it explicit. Revision is not seen as delaying development.
- All changes are reversible.
- The high-level purpose and scope of the system under development should be agreed or frozen at a level which makes it easy for further investigation during development.
- Testing is integrated throughout the life-cycle.
- A collaborative and cooperative approach between all stakeholders is essential.

DSDM METHOD

Figure 12.11 shows an outline of the method proposed by DSDM. After the initiation of a business study and feasibility determination, a functional prototype begins an iterative cycle of identification, creation and review. After final review, different design prototypes may begin a similar cycle, ending with an implementation cycle where the system is implemented and users are trained in system use. After implementation another design or functional prototype may begin its cycle.

Specific techniques are not proposed by DSDM. For example, any type of development technique, such as structured or object-oriented techniques, may be used. Instead, it emphasizes more human factors, such as project organization, team structure and effective interaction with users, as the areas which influence the development of a successful system.

In addition to the dynamic view above, DSDM contains guidelines for the deployment and use of a set of responsibilities and techniques at all of the main steps. For example, it makes suggestions for project management, team structure, user involvement, prototype management, skills and responsibilities, estimating, risk assessment, change control, configuration control, development environments, method tailoring, testing, quality assurance and software procurement.

SOURCES

The information on DSDM was obtained from the following: 'A radical step', *Computing*, 2 March 1995; 'A radical break', *Computing*, 9 November 1995; Millington and Stapleton (1995); DSDM (1997); Soft (1994) and Stapleton (1997).

Summary

In this chapter we have outlined four current proposals for standards for the systems development process. Two of these – ISO 12207 and DSDM – are

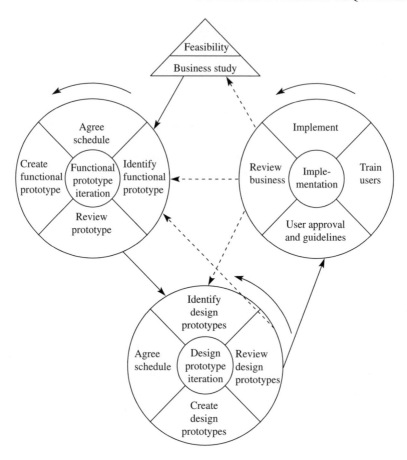

Figure 12.11   DSDM overview.

already defined, while Euromethod and SPICE are undergoing customer trials. At the time of writing all of these proposals are too new for any definite opinion to be formed with regard to their eventual penetration and acceptance in industry.

However, their significance should not be underestimated, as they represent a concerted attempt to bring 'civilization' to the information systems 'jungle' that has existed for a long time. What is also significant is the trend away from technical to non-technical aspects of systems development. This may be interpreted as a view that no improvement of a technical nature in methods or tools is likely, for the moment, to bring about the quality and productivity gains required; instead, reliance is being placed on management principles applied to the systems development process, in all its aspects, as a way to deliver these benefits.

Discussion questions

1. Map the methods discussed in Chapter 11 into Euromethod. What methods have the broadest and the narrowest Euromethod coverage?
2. To what extent are the activities of Euromethod and SPICE identified by the ISO 12207 standard?

References

Bubenko, J. A. (1986) Information system methodologies – a research view, in *Information Systems Design Methodologies: Improving the Practice* (eds. Olle, T. W., Sol, H. G. and Verrijn-Stuart, A. A.), Elsevier, Amsterdam, 289–318.

CCTA (1994) *Euromethod update, October 1994*, available from CCTA, Rosebery Court, St Andrews Business Park, Norwich, NR7 0HS.

Dorling, A. (1993) SPICE: Software Process Improvement and Capability dEtermination, *Software Process Journal*, **2**, 209–24.

Dorling, A. (1995) History of the SPICE project, in *Proceedings of 2nd International SPICE Symposium, Software Process Assessment: Theory and Practice*, 1–2 June, Brisbane, Queensland, Australia.

DSDM (1997) *Dynamic Systems Development Method*, DSDM Consortium, The Coach House, Church Hill, Ashford, Kent, TN23 3EG, or http://www.dsdm.org

EM (1994) *Euromethod Version 0*, BT Tallis Consultancy, 515 Gower Street, London WC1E 6BA.

EM (1997) *Euromethod*, http://www.esi.es/Euromethod

ESI (1997) European Software Institute, SPICE project overview, http://www.esi.es/ or http://www-sqi.cit.gu.edu.au/spice/

Franckson, M. (1994) The Euromethod deliverable model and its contribution to the objectives of Euromethod, in *Methods and Associated Tools for the Information Systems Life Cycle* (eds. Verrijn-Stuart, A. A. and Olle, T. W.), Elsevier, Amsterdam, 131–49.

ISO/IEC (1992) *The need and requirements for a software process assessment standard, study report issue 2.0, JTC1/SC7 N944R*, June.

ISO/IEC (1995a) *Software process assessment – Part 1: concepts and introductory guide*, working draft V1.00, June.

ISO/IEC (1995b) *ISO/IEC 12207, International standard: information technology – software life cycle processes*, August.

ISO/IEC (1996) *Software process assessment – Part 1: concepts and introductory guide*, Version 1.00, May.

Kuvaja, P., Bicego, A. and Dorling, A. (1995) SPICE: the software process assessment model, in *Proceedings of 2nd International SPICE Symposium, Software Process Assessment: Theory and Practice*, 1–2 June, Brisbane, Australia.

Millington, D. and Stapleton, J. (1995) Developing a RAD standard, *IEEE Software*, September, 54–5.

Rout, T. P. (1995) SPICE: a standard framework for software process assessment, in *Software Process Improvement and Practice*, 1, Wiley, Chichester, 57–68.

Singh, R. (1994) ISO/IEC draft international standard 12207, software life cycle processes, in *Methods and Associated Tools for the Information Systems Life Cycle* (eds. Verrijn-Stuart, A. A. and Olle, T. W.), Elsevier, Amsterdam, 111–19.

Soft (1994) *Software Futures*, December, APT Data Services, Sutton Row, London.

Stapleton, J. (1997) *DSDM – The Method in Practice*, Addison-Wesley, London.

TickIT (1995) *TickIT guide to software quality system construction and certification*, issue 3.0, October, British Standards Institution DISC, 389 Chiswick High Road, London, W4 4AL.

Part Five

Soft Approach to Information Systems

Part 3 was concerned with a description of methods and techniques which are representative of what has come to be known as the *hard* approach to systems development. Broadly, this means that the methods and techniques assume that a problem to be solved has a logical or mathematical basis, and that a computer system, which has its functions specified very clearly and in great detail, is in most cases a suitable solution.

Part 4 briefly described some recent standards or proposals which are broadly concerned with the *management* of hard approaches within the overall process of systems development.

Part 5 will present a complementary approach to the hard approach, termed the *soft* approach. This goes further than the rather narrow view often attributed to the hard approach, as it is concerned with what may be broadly termed the environmental effects of information systems. That is, it is concerned with the relationship between such systems and social, economic, legal and psychological aspects of the environment, usually the organization, for which they are ostensibly designed.

First, Chapter 13 will set the scene by showing how methods belonging to the soft approach have evolved to meet some of the well-known problems that occur in information systems built with hard methods. Hard and soft approaches will be contrasted and several soft approaches will be considered, including SSM and some recent work in requirements engineering. Chapter 14 describes how research into the theory of organizations has produced results that may be applied to develop further the theoretical basis, as well as the practical use, of the soft approach, by determining key organizational characteristics as a prelude to information systems development.

Finally, Chapter 15 covers a range of topics mostly concerned with the effects that information systems have on society, discussing information systems evolution, organizational effects of investment in information systems, legislation, and unauthorized computer access by human and software threats.

13

Hard and soft approaches

Introduction

In this chapter we reconsider the problems found in information systems, and discuss how, even after the improvements to systems development detailed in preceding chapters, many problems still exist. We go on to suggest that certain of these problems occur because key problems are not addressed by a group of methods, termed *hard approaches*, to systems development.

Methods belonging to the *soft approach* are then described, showing how these address the problems raised by the deficiencies of the hard approach. Finally, we discuss how both hard and soft approaches are valuable if viewed from the perspective of a contingency framework, where the organizational situation determines the type of approach that is most suitable.

Problems with information systems

Despite the improvements brought about by the techniques, methods and tools we have considered since Chapter 6, there are still problems with information systems.

SUCCESSFUL AND UNSUCCESSFUL SYSTEMS

We may define a successful system as follows:

A successful system is one that meets its targets of quality and productivity.

The quality target is that the system meets its requirements, while the productivity target is that the system is developed on time and within budget.

An unsuccessful system, on the other hand, is one that fails to meet either its quality or its productivity targets. It may be useful to distinguish several types of unsuccessful system:

1. The system is never delivered to the user.
2. The system fails one or both of its targets and is rejected by the user.
3. The system fails one or both of its targets but is accepted by the user.

These definitions cannot be very precise, as, for example, initial targets are often modified as systems development proceeds. In addition, much of the evidence concerning successful or unsuccessful systems rests on folklore concerning systems development problems, where verification is rather difficult for commercial (and personal survival!) reasons.

PROBLEM REPORTS

Early problems of productivity and quality are discussed in the Garmisch conference where the term software engineering first appeared (Naur and Randell, 1968). A report in the USA (*Washington Post*, 1 December 1989) states that Federal agencies incurred costs of $17 billion for 1989 versus $9 billion in 1982 for computer applications. 'Invariably these systems do not work as planned, have cost overruns in the millions and even hundreds of millions of dollars, and are not developed on time. Congressional interest . . . has increased.'

More recently, Collins *et al.* (1994) discuss the ethical aspects of three well-known system failures. Firstly, the flaws in the main mirror of the $4 billion Hubble Space Telescope that severely crippled its ability to perform as planned; the flaws were due to the fact that computer testing of the mirror used bad input data. The second failure occurred due to a bug in exception-handling software in a telephone switching system operated by American Telegraph & Telephone (AT & T), causing long-distance communications to be disrupted for about nine hours. Lastly, the case of the USS *Vincennes*, a warship which in July 1988 shot down a climbing Iranian airliner on the mistaken assumption that it was a descending, hostile F-14 fighter.

The Home Office's Phoenix national criminal records database was criticized for failing to report previous convictions of a defendant in a Bolton court case ('Phoenix crime system fails to inform police', *Computing*, 2 November 1995). According to Assistant Chief Constable Sweeney 'This is a national problem. The shortcomings of Phoenix are a great inconvenience to all agencies involved in the criminal justice system'. A spokeman for Phoenix claimed that 'a national database covering all convictions was prohibitively expensive'.

In a report on a fashion of the early 1990s, business process re-engineering (BPR) ('Facing the firing squad', *Computing*, 2 November 1995), Julian Stainton, chief executive of Western Provident Assurance was scathing about the role of technology and was quoted as saying: 'I spent £10m on IT, we had hardly any noticeable improvement in service and productivity actually fell'.

There are many stories and reports which are similar to the above. Neumann (1995, 1996) is an important source of 'risks to the public' from computer systems. Business reports in the USA (McFarlan, 1981) indicate major quality and productivity problems with commercial systems, and, in the UK, the literature contains similar problem reports (Fawthrop, 1990). Although one of the main goals in introducing computer technology is job reduction, with resulting gains in efficiency, this goal is not often achieved (Fairbairn, 1989). It is suspected that unsuccessful systems may also lose customers and eventually threaten organizational survival.

OTHER EVIDENCE

It may be argued that reports of the type above are anecdotal and possibly distorted, representing a minority of systems only. However, there is a growing accumulation of evidence, from various sources, that unsuccessful systems are widely encountered. The following are examples.

Government reports

- A study (NEDO, 1983) in the United Kingdom of 15 organizations, reported in Winfield (1991), showed that only about half of the organizations found job reductions after computer systems were introduced. In some cases, many computer-oriented jobs were created.
- A report concerning the investment decisions of organizations in computer technology (Kearney, 1985) revealed that up to 20 per cent of the investment might be wasted, for example, software paid for but never delivered or software delivered but never used.
- A Department of Trade and Industry report (DTI, 1985) found that time-scale overruns occurred in 66 per cent of projects, while 55 per cent were over budget.
- For 'front-office' applications, a 1986 survey (DTI, 1986) showed that, of 20 pilot office automation projects begun in 1982, only half worked as the users expected, were fully accepted or brought positive benefits to the organization, and 20 per cent were rejected.
- A study (DTI, 1988) estimates that poor quality software costs £1 billion annually to UK companies, in making corrections before and after delivery, overruns and high maintenance costs. These are direct costs and do not include indirect costs such as lost business, lower effectiveness, damage to reputation or missed opportunities.

Industrial surveys and reports

- Capers Jones (1995) presents a view of project success or failure from inside industry and suggests several contributory factors.

- A survey of 252 companies (KPMG, 1990) showed that 'runaway systems' (systems with poor quality and productivity) concerned over 30 per cent of all major projects. The major effects of these systems were loss of time, reduction in staff morale, loss of money, reduced customer satisfaction and a negative market image.

Academic research

- Brynjolfsson (1993) discusses how investment in IT and delivered computing power has increased since 1970 in the USA but, at the same time, productivity (that is worker productivity), especially in the service sector, has not followed this pattern, but has in fact stagnated. In a review of researchers' findings on the relationship between IT investment in manufacturing and services and worker productivity, he concludes that no firm judgement can be made at the moment, on account of problems such as suspected mismeasurement and time lags in measuring productivity.
- Robinson (1994) gives an account of a notorious failure concerning a new system for the London Ambulance Service, and Myers (1993) analyses the reasons for a failed information systems project.
- Kemerer and Sosa (1991) discuss major failures in information systems.
- Lyttinen and Hirschheim (1987) estimate that up to 50 per cent of information system projects may be failures.
- Harrington (1991) describes research into organizations in the North East of the UK, where 60 per cent of the firms had major problems within two years of a computer-induced change in their structure.
- In a survey of 10 small companies setting out to implement computer systems (Wroe, 1985), it was found that only four managed to proceed to the implementation phase.
- Finally, Eason (1988) refers to studies in the UK in the 1980s which indicate that up to 40 per cent of systems may never be delivered, or may fail and be rejected. In addition, a significant proportion (again, up to 40 per cent) had only a marginal effect, with an unforeseen and possibly negative impact. This suggests that only 20 per cent of systems have a positive effect on organizations.

OTHER INDICATIONS

Another indication is to study the rate at which the proportion of the organizational software budget consumed by maintenance has risen from 40 per cent in 1973 (quoted in Boehm, 1975), through 70 per cent in 1984 (King, 1984) to an estimated 80 per cent in 1990 (Pressman, 1992). This means that in many installations there may soon be no resources available to build new systems. It is suspected, although there is no direct evidence, that this maintenance backlog is chiefly due to changes to installed systems that do not meet user requirements (Pressman, 1992).

A recent analysis (Humphrey, 1988) by the Software Engineering Institute, based at Carnegie-Mellon University in the USA, evaluated approximately 150 of the leading software producers in the USA. Five levels of software maturity of the development process used by the organizations were defined, where level 1 (the lowest level) was considered a chaotic process, with problem areas of progress planning and change control, and level 2 was a repeatable process with rigorous controls, but with problems in the design/code inspection and software process training areas; 12 per cent of organizations were on level 2, with 86 per cent of organizations on level 1.

CAUSES OF PROBLEMS

The main information systems problems and their causes, discussed in previous chapters, are summarized below. Table 13.1 shows why some problems are still outstanding, as the methods (including tools and techniques) that we have been considering only address some of the problems.

Table 13.1 Quality and productivity problems addressed by hard approach methods

Problem	Solution provided
Q1	–
Q2	–
Q3	Methods, tools
Q4	–
P1	Prototyping, group sessions
P2	–
P3	–
P4	–

Quality

1. *Wrong problem.* The wrong activities to assist are chosen, as the problem is not defined correctly or the system may conflict with organizational aims or strategies.
2. *Neglect of wider organization.* Wider social or psychological factors may be neglected, such as the degree of decentralization or centralization of the organization, or the factors of acceptability and usability.
3. *Incorrect analysis.* The right activities are identified, but errors may be made in analysing information needs due to poor development techniques.
4. *Wrong reasons.* Technology push or political pull.

Productivity

Productivity problems are caused by changing requirements, due to:

1. *Users change their minds.* Users refine their requirements as the project progresses, or there may be conflict between users.
2. *External events may occur that change the requirements.* Changes in external factors such as technology, legislation, the market or the political environment often change requirements.
3. *Implementation may not be feasible.* There may be implementation implications contained in requirements that are not feasible and that are recognized only during implementation and testing.

Another cause is:

4. *Poor project control.* Inadequate project resource estimation and tracking techniques.

EXTENT OF PROBLEM

Although there are anecdotal reports of problems with particular systems, and we have referred to a small number of studies concerning problems in general, it is not so easy to reach a general conclusion regarding the extent of these problems overall, or over the majority of information systems. There are many success stories, and we therefore have to be cautious as to how we interpret the findings. For example, the view may be held (Bjorner, 1987) that productivity problems do not exist and that systems development comes too cheaply, as the estimates made at the beginning of projects are unrealistically optimistic and not properly founded on experience of similar projects. This is perhaps an unrealistic view, as it assumes that there is time available to build a perfect system. However, users generally have only a limited time window of opportunity in which to build a system before, for example, a competitive advantage is lost.

As noted in Angell and Smithson (1991), it is important to maintain a balanced view concerning the systems failures that do occur, against the undoubted possibilities of the technology if used effectively (Clemons, 1991). Such a balanced view is likely to be informed by a good understanding of the problems that may occur when applying the technology, as well as the progress being made towards finding solutions that address those problems.

It is possible that the 40 per cent of systems that fail do so due to productivity and quality problems, where quality is defined on the basis of requirements consisting of functionality only. If so, then the 40 per cent that are accepted, but are marginal at best in their effect, may have quality problems according to the broader definition we have discussed. Organizational problems due to the effect of systems may only emerge after a period of time has elapsed.

Hard approach

Two of the most significant problems that still remain in systems development are the first two quality problems:

1. *Methods solve the wrong problem*
2. *Methods neglect the wider organizational context*

Methods that do not address these problems are often termed *hard approaches* to systems development, a typical example being the avalanche model discussed in Chapter 6. In contrast, *soft approaches*, discussed below, focus on these problems.

UNDERLYING ASSUMPTIONS

An assumption made by the hard approach is that the problem to be solved is logically based and has a solution in a computer system, thus limiting the range of problems that can be addressed to those that possess a mathematical or logical solution. A second assumption is that the computer-based solution may be placed in the organization without taking account of the social and psychological context within which the system will interact (Dobson and Strens, 1994).

A consequence is that only the computer system is regarded as important, shown by the fact that many methods emphasize only the tasks and objects of a technical system, expressed in forms such as flowcharts, data flows and so on. The hard approach neglects the important issues of defining the right problem and wider organizational factors, drawing requirements too narrowly.

Soft approach

This section discusses soft approaches, describing the problems addressed and their general characteristics.

PROBLEMS ADDRESSED

There are several reasons why methods should take into account the wider impact of information systems on organizations. Firstly, the impact may be negative, as has occurred with hard approaches, and improvements are required (Bjorn-Andersen *et al.*, 1986; Fitzgerald, 1994). Secondly, a new system may require a radical restructuring of the work process to take account of, for example, a changing environment or to allow the full exploitation of information technology (Child, 1987; Hammer and Champy, 1993). Thirdly, there is a strong influence from the workplace democracy movement in Scandinavia (Bjerknes *et al.*, 1987), which maintains that in a democracy people should have a say in the technology they use at work.

With regard to the first quality problem, soft approaches allow for problem situations that may be investigated by a variety of problem definition techniques and emphasize the determination of key organizational policies and goals. A computer system will not necessarily result from this approach.

For the second quality problem, soft approaches focus on wider issues in the social context which may influence the nature of a problem solution, such as organizational structure, employee job satisfaction or professional ethics. Approaches may also take into account factors of usability and acceptability, which are less explicit and which should also be assessed when determining quality. These may be described as follows:

1. *Usability.* The intended users, with their inherent skills and capabilities, should be able to work with the system and use it as intended.
2. *Acceptability.* The minimum requirement for this is that the system should present itself to users in such a way that it does not threaten aspects of user work held to be important. Ideally it will be perceived as being an active agent in assisting users to accomplish their desired work-related goals. It is often found that, as many information systems bring about considerable change in organizational working practices, there is resistance to change. Although new working conditions may appear acceptable when viewed from one perspective, nevertheless, to the existing employees, who may be cautious about change, they may represent a threat.

An issue that should be considered is: do the users want the system? It may often be the case that users have the system imposed from above (for example, head office) or outside (for example, a takeover) or they do not want it, as it may, in their view, lead to inefficiencies or redundancies.

An example of where psychological factors were not taken into account is described in Harrington (1991), where a manufacturing firm found that productivity was worse after the introduction of a computer system compared with the old manual system. A study revealed that the relationships between the department personnel had changed. They had previously been a cohesive group, but after system introduction they worked only in isolated units and consequently missed the personal contact they had had while carrying out their jobs.

A conclusion we may draw from this discussion is that the notion of quality defined at the beginning of the chapter, that a system should meet its requirements, may not be enough, as requirements may be too narrow and the system may not have the beneficial effect on the organization that was intended.

FOCUS ON REQUIREMENTS

Requirements determination was identified in Chapter 7 as having four stages: problem identification, feasibility study, requirements acquisition and requirements modelling and the main characteristic of soft approaches is their focus on *requirements acquisition.*

Several assumptions concerning requirements acquisition are held by the hard approach. These are that users:

1. Know their requirements
2. Can easily envisage a system built from their requirements
3. Communicate their requirements easily to developers

According to this 'dairy' metaphor of requirements acquisition, users, ruminating on their needs, 'produce' their requirements in a private and independent manner and only need to be 'milked' by developers, in a process which is mechanical and one-way, requiring a minimum of interaction from both parties.

There are advantages in adopting this metaphor for both parties, in that the time spent on difficult meetings between two cultures is minimized. However, the metaphor is inaccurate, considering the nature of requirements sought by soft approaches, and even those sought by hard approaches (Potts, 1995).

Dobson and Strens (1994) state that requirements and their origins, such as organizational goals and employee values, located in the social context of a system, are emergent and not objectively available. This means that they are often deeply embedded in the situation in the form of, for example assumptions and may have to be debated before they can be articulated and emerge as requirements.

As the 'dairy' metaphor is inappropriate, many soft approaches attempt to involve users much more actively in requirements acquisition. A further impetus is given by the fact that many systems are now innovative, in that they either consist of new products or provide new product support and are not based on existing systems. It is essential that users be fully involved in determining requirements for such systems. Traditional approaches such as the latest version of SSADM (1995) propose the use of the SSM (see below) in the early phases.

A variety of terms are used to refer to this type of user involvement, such as user participation, joint application design, user-centred design and participative design (Holtzblatt and Beyer, 1993). We shall now look at several soft approaches and describe how they address the two quality problems discussed above (Goguen and Linde, 1993).

SOFT SYSTEMS METHODOLOGY

The first approach we shall consider is the Soft Systems Methodology (SSM) due to Checkland and co-workers (Checkland, 1981; Checkland and Scholes, 1990). The approach has an underlying theme, which is that reality is socially constructed by humans and is not a 'given'. The implication for requirements is that they are not objective and are unlikely to be fixed for long, as they are made up of the different views of different individuals and are continuously evolving. They are partly shaped by, for example, the goals and personalities of key organizational participants and partly shaped by environmental and organizational factors, such as the competitive environment, the main organizational task and organizational structure, which often restrict the choice of a desired system. Finally, any one of several systems might be suited to a given situation.

Determining requirements consists of initiating a discussion, bargaining and construction process whereby a requirement emerges. Out of such discussions could also emerge, in addition to the rather narrow technical system specification, plans for modified organizational structure, task or even

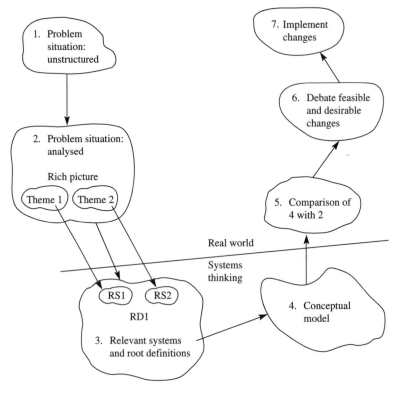

Figure 13.1 Stages in soft systems methodology.

objectives and environment. Problem situations are thus viewed as fuzzy, not structured, and solutions are not apparent.

Aims and stages

The methodology may be seen, in outline, in Fig. 13.1. Its aim is to analyse a problem situation, in terms of different viewpoints, with a view to designing systems that will improve the problem situation.

Stages 1 and 2 constitute an expression phase, which aims to avoid premature positions about the nature of any perceived problem. Instead, the emphasis is on the *problem situation*. Many different viewpoints on the situation are gathered from different individuals, and a *rich picture* is drawn, which is a graphical illustration of the problem situation. At this point, *problem themes*, which are apparent problems, are identified and described succinctly in natural language.

Stage 3 begins to propose problem solutions. Each problem theme is taken and a *relevant system* is stated. This is a notional system which might solve the problem or part of the problem. It is high level and should only be named. The relevant systems are used to form one or more *root definitions*, which are concise descriptions of human activity systems that capture a particular view. The root definition can be expressed on various levels of detail, and six criteria are provided to check it for completeness.

Stage 4 builds a *conceptual model* (not the same as in Chapter 8) of the activity system needed to achieve the transformation described in the root definition. This is an account of the activities that the system must do, and is process oriented. The activities are ordered in time sequence and also include the flow of resources.

An important stage is then to check conceptual models, and a set of criteria is provided for this that check for completeness and contradictions. It is also possible to use other notions from systems thinking that are deemed relevant by the designer, in an attempt to avoid being over-prescriptive about the methodology.

Stage 5 then compares the conceptual model with parts of the problem situation in stage 2, not to establish correctness but to stimulate debate with the participants with regard to possible changes to improve the problem situation. Four different approaches are identified: ordered questioning (asking questions about the situation based on the model), event reconstruction (reconstructing events in the past and comparing with what would have happened had the system implied by the model been implemented), general comparison (features of the model that differ from the current situation are used to raise strategic rather than detailed queries) and model overlay (a conceptual model of the existing system is made and overlaid with the conceptual model being proposed – the overlay may reveal a mismatch).

Stage 6 indicates three types of possible change: structural, procedural and attitudinal. Structural change includes changes to organizational groupings, reporting structures and so on. Procedural change involves direct changes to the dynamic element – activities concerned with, for example, reporting and informing. Attitudinal changes refer to changes in expectations or notions of good or bad within the organizational context. Again, the nature of this stage is to generate discussion of change. After agreement has been reached on the change required, steps are taken in stage 7 to implement the change.

Summary

SSM directly addresses quality problem 1, and the emphasis is placed on this. However, as the method expects users to be involved in discussions, disagreeing and changing their minds, productivity problem 1 is also addressed.

CLIENT-LED DESIGN

Stowell and West (1994) describe the client-led design approach, which provides philosophies, skills, concepts and approaches for problem definition, emphasizing the need for users to be in control of the development process. Problem definition is influenced by the soft systems approach, and is intended to lead into subsequent stages of development.

MULTIVIEW

Multiview (Avison and Wood-Harper, 1990) incorporates an initial stage based on soft systems but is additionally a methodology in the sense that it recommends a contingency approach, taking into account, for example skills of developers and the problem situation; some aspects of the methodology may be effective in some situations, but are not advised in others. As for client-led design, it includes subsequent stages of systems development.

PARTICIPATIVE SYSTEMS DESIGN

Participative Systems Design is defined as 'handing responsibility for the design of a new work system to the employees who eventually will have to operate it' (Mumford, 1981). Two themes will be apparent from this definition. Firstly, design should be undertaken with the *participation* of the relevant employees and, secondly, design should emphasize that a new 'work system' is to be produced. The term design does not have the low-level connotations of the systems development process.

For this second theme, the method adopts the *socio-technical approach*, which pays attention not only to the 'technical' system but also to the 'social' system, consisting of employees and the wider organization, as well as the harmony between the two systems. A similar approach is the user-centred approach described in Eason (1988) or usability design (Gould *et al.*, 1991).

Participation

Participation can result in, for example, creating a greater degree of freedom in the working environment or controlling the pace of work. Four arguments are put forward to support the notion of participation in the design of computer systems (the notion of computer system includes the social as well as the technical system):

1. *Ethics.* People have a basic right to control their own destinies, and this applies in the work situation as elsewhere.
2. *Expediency.* If people do not have a say in the decisions of others, they may repeal or subvert the decisions as soon as those others leave the scene.
3. *Expert knowledge.* People who are the experts on topics such as task design are the people who do the jobs.
4. *Motivating force.* Participation is a motivator and will increase the productivity and efficiency of the eventual system.

Three different levels of participation are proposed: (a) consultative participation, which leaves most design decisions to computer specialists, with system objectives and the eventual form of the system being greatly influenced by users; (b) representative participation, where a design group is formed involving users to design the new work system to fit in with the new technology; (c) consensus participation, where users are involved continuously throughout the design process.

Recommending the use of participation is psychologically based, deriving from the human relations school. The argument is that if employees participate in design, psychological factors such as job satisfaction or positive attitudes towards the system will be improved. Therefore, system quality will be good as the system will win acceptability. Figure 13.2 shows this.

This view thus emphasizes people and the way that their behaviour affects organizational factors. Psychological or social psychological research studies human characteristics such as attitudes, beliefs, value systems and conflicts,

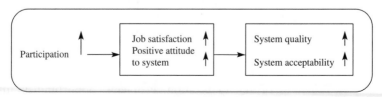

Figure 13.2 Relationship between degree of participation, human and organizational factors.

and seeks to understand the effects of these characteristics on general organizational factors, such as productivity, adaptability and the quality problems mentioned above. It is also possible that participation will enable the correct problem to be defined, as the users are experts.

Socio-technical approach

The second theme in the method, found in step 4 below, is the emphasis on a socio-technical approach. This means 'a design philosophy that produces productivity, quality, coordination and control; but also provides a work environment and task structure in which people can achieve personal development and satisfaction' (Mumford, 1981). The aim of the approach is 'to produce technical and social structures which have a high capacity to achieve technical and social goals and which reinforce each other in the achievement of these goals' (Mumford, 1981).

A socio-technical system is any unit in the organization composed of a technological and a social sub-system having a common goal or task to accomplish. The technical system consists of the tools, techniques and procedures in the production process for transforming inputs into outputs, and can thus include human as well as computer procedures.

The social system is the network of roles, relationships and tasks that interact with each other and with the technical system. For example, the manager of the organizational post room discussed in Chapter 3 may be manager X, who has 30 people working for him or her. He or she is under manager Y and is advised by manager Z. Of the 30 employees, there are two groups of 15, one group responsible for the sorting task, who pass letters and packets on to the other group for depositing. The overall aim of manager X is to deliver all letters and packets within one working day.

The scope for change is theoretically very wide in the social system, and can include considerations of the roles required for the new system, responsibilities of role holders, and organizational goals and policies. However, the method described below is limited to a consideration of job satisfaction.

Method

The participative systems design method is shown in outline in Fig. 13.3. It may be seen as being based on the socio-technical approach, as its two main objectives are, firstly, an increase in organizational effectiveness in the technical system and, secondly, an increase in job satisfaction in the social system.

Step 1.   *Analysis of the required system.* The first task describes key objectives and functions of an organization. Problems, opportunities, interest groups, system boundaries and objectives, and principal unit operations are established. Unit operations are sub-systems, and detailed

Figure 13.3 Participative systems design method.

activities together with information requirements are broadly specified.

The second task identifies job satisfaction needs. Questionnaires may be used to elicit from users the kind of satisfaction they would like to receive from their work environment.

Step 2. *Analysis of the existing system.* The extent to which the current system diverges from the required system is determined. A form of discrepancy analysis is suggested using variances occurring in unit operations. Existing job satisfaction will be determined.

Step 3. *Agreeing objectives.* A set of objectives is produced that will overcome the discrepancies found in step 2. Tasks are to identify interest groups and their objectives, from a technical as well as a social point of view. Through a negotiation process, an agreed list will be produced.

Step 4. *Designing the organizational system.* This step consists of applying the principles of the socio-technical approach, discussed above. A more detailed account (Mumford, 1983) breaks the process down as follows, taking agreed technical and social objectives as input from step 3.

Task 1. Determine social (work organization, job design) and technical and administrative (hardware, software, work procedures, information flow) alternative solutions.

Task 2. Those technical and social alternatives that are compatible with each other are put together. Impractical alternative combinations are rejected.

Task 3. For each of the combined alternatives estimate and rank in terms of ability to meet technical and social objectives.

Task 4. (a) Determine technical constraints, estimate the technical resources required and perform a technical cost/benefit evaluation.

(b) Determine social constraints, estimate the social resources required, for example experts, knowledge and facilities, and estimate social costs and benefits.

Task 5. Rank solutions in terms of availability of required resources, costs/benefits and constraints and make a choice of the best socio-technical solution.

Step 5. *Implementing the system.* This step is concerned with the smooth introduction of the new work system into the working practices of the organization, so as to ensure minimum disruption and system acceptability. This may involve changing organizational structures and office layout, job evaluation, user training and so on.

Summary of method

The method combines a participative approach, starting with problem definition, with a socio-technical approach. Quality problem 2 is addressed by the emphasis on participation, also addressed by the socio-technical approach. Quality problem 1 is also addressed as user needs and wants should emerge more clearly in problem definition, as well as in the process of stating and evaluating alternatives.

USER FACTORS LIFE-CYCLE

This approach (Mantei and Teorey, 1989) is one that integrates new stages, shown in italics in Fig. 13.4, into the conventional life cycle. Iteration is shown between many of the stages. The central theme of this method is the inclusion of psychological principles and measurement techniques to assist in determining correct requirements, designing the user interface and evaluating the system. The stages based on this theme are as follows:

1. *Market analysis.* This stage begins the life-cycle and adopts a marketing approach, whereby market data is obtained from potential users to determine what 'product' to develop, using techniques such as focus groups (groups of about ten people who generate product ideas), market surveys (measuring existing user behaviour that is related to the proposed product) and surveying current users (getting product ideas).

2. *Product acceptance analysis.* This is a structured prototyping session whereby a prototype system demonstrates actual use. Techniques used in the sessions are facading (a mock demonstration of the system is videoed and shown to users, who are then asked in a questionnaire to comment on different system characteristics) and focus groups, who have a demonstration of the prototype and are asked questions.

3. *Task analysis.* This is based on engineering models of how users view and accomplish their current tasks, and results in a very detailed (keystroke

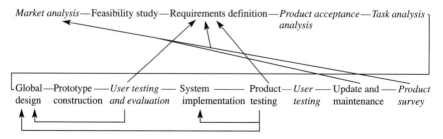

Figure 13.4 Development stages in User Factors Life Cycle (UFLC).

level) description. It aims to understand how users think about their work so that the design of the new system will not violate the user's approach. Techniques used are protocol analysis (users speak out loud what they are thinking or planning and a psychologist records and analyses this) and memory organization analysis (parts of user memory that are difficult to verbalize in an interview are probed for).

4. *User testing and evaluation.* This checks the system interface for usability and acceptability. In user testing, users are studied while they accomplish a variety of system tasks. One way in which this is done is called usability testing. Testing is done in a simulated work environment and users are given everyday tasks to perform in sessions which are videoed. Another approach is to test users on what they have learned about the system. In evaluation, the user's attitude towards the system is obtained, as well as determining whether or not the system meets functional requirements. The two techniques of facading and focus groups described above are used.

5. *User testing.* This is similar to user testing and evaluation, except that it takes place on the actual system, not a prototype.

6. *Product survey.* This obtains user responses to the installed system. The system may require changes or a major redesign. Techniques suggested are the customer hot-line, on-site observation and user surveys.

Summary

The method emphasizes user interface design, marketing techniques for determining requirements and adopts a structured approach to testing and evaluation. It therefore addresses quality problems 1 and 2. Prototyping addresses productivity problem 1.

QUALITY FUNCTION DEPLOYMENT (QFD)

Quality function deployment (QFD) (Hauser and Clausing, 1988; Haag *et al.*, 1996) is an approach to design, manufacture and marketing that is founded on the belief that the tastes and desires of customers should determine the design of products. Customer needs and desires are identified not only by close contact with customers, preferably in their place of work, but by coordinating the skills of a variety of experts, such as marketing, design and manufacturing people within the organization.

Originally developed in a Japanese shipyard in the 1970s, the approach is used for a variety of organizations, including those that produce software. A central concept is the *house of quality*, a diagrammatic concept for integrating customer requirements and their relative weightings with suggested product characteristics; also included may be customer evaluations of similar products, technical difficulty of product characteristics, competitive products and estimated costs. The effects of each requirement on other requirements and on factors such as cost are determined. Discussion and negotiation are required to understand and trade off many of these characteristics.

An important aspect of QFD is its emphasis on how a particular requirement should be implemented; this is useful to test feasibility and to give a feel for what a requirement will eventually look like. A component from a house on the early 'what' level may form a house on a more detailed 'how' level.

QFD is an abstract concept only, requiring detailed procedures to be put into effect, although its use is often described within a joint application design group or workshop consisting of users or user representatives and developers. It applies particularly to requirements acquisition, as it proposes a simple method, as well as a philosophy, for understanding customer requirements.

QFD may be seen as a way of implementing a total quality management (TQM) system within the requirements process, which contrasts to traditional zero defect-based approaches aimed at minimizing negative qualities, such as defects (Zultner, 1995). Instead, it emphasizes the prevention of dissatisfaction, rather than its detection and correction, by seeking an understanding of customer needs and transmitting these downwards to implementation.

It may be especially suited to organizations that produce generic software; that is, software for customers outside the organization whom the design group may never meet – for example, any organization which produces a software product for sale. In this situation, there are typically many different types of customer whose needs must be balanced; for example, end users, retailers, other software organizations and suppliers of software components.

USTM

Macaulay (1993) makes a case for a more active role for the user in the process of organizational change brought on by systems development. She focuses on the social process that constitutes the interaction between the participants in the earliest stages, where requirements are scoped and captured. The traditional approach to these stages is regarded as viewing the user in too passive a light, and also disregards the fact that there are several types of user, all of whom have different roles to play with regard to requirements, such as manager, trainer, developer and technical author, as well as the user who actually uses the system in their day-to-day work.

A linear communication structure is identified as prevailing in the traditional approach between all these users, with an attendant loss of communication, and it is proposed that improvements result if users participate in a shared perception of requirements.

The stakeholder concept is described, where a stakeholder is one who has a stake in the change being considered, and a range of stakeholders are identified, from project manager through user to software designer. It is argued that an approach to requirements capture involving the elicitation of the views and needs of many stakeholders must be managed to prevent chaos, and a cooperative requirements capture approach is outlined based on the user skills task match (USTM) method.

The method organizes stakeholders in a series of two-day face-to-face meetings, with aims and tasks set out in a handbook. Meetings are led by a facilitator, who is an expert at applying the method and who manages group interactions. There are seven stages to USTM: business case, work groups, users, objects, tasks, interactions and consolidation. In the business case stage, the proposed system is justified, while in the next two stages, work groups in the context of the proposed system and generic system users are identified. The objects and tasks stages identify system components while the interactions stage identifies object, task and user interactions. The final consolidation stage reassesses the business case.

Advantages stated are that the method employs user language and terminology; participation by stakeholders ensures that important views are heard; and a managed process creates a climate which aids the development of a consensus view of the requirements. The disadvantages are that senior staff have to attend a time-consuming series of meetings.

KJ METHOD

Takeda *et al.* (1993) state that 'the most important step in system development is to analyze, understand and record the problem that the sponsor is trying to solve'. They introduce a problem recognition method, the KJ method, which is used in the Japanese business community for consensus making between participants in ideas generation.

The method consists of four steps in which members participate in a team structure. In the first step a participant writes down on an index card something relevant to the situation under discussion. Only one thing should be on the card and no judgement of importance should be made. In the second step, all the cards are shuffled and placed on a desk, read by the team and then grouped together. This should be done subjectively and a new card may be created to represent the essence of a group. Groups may also be grouped.

In step 3, card groups are arranged on a large piece of paper and each group is enclosed by an outline. The spatial relationships of cards and groups is important and should be carefully handled. Proximity represents relatedness while distance represents unrelatedness. Special lines should be drawn between cards and groups to represent semantic relationships such as dependence and opposition. This is termed an A-type chart. In step 4, an essay on the subject of the A-type chart is written, termed B-type writing. It is possible to revise the A-type chart.

The advantages of the KJ method are that the language of the cards is understood by both sponsor and developer and the bottom-up nature of the method is suited to the requirements process. The method is supported by a software tool with virtual cards which can also record the editing actions and hence the outward manifestation of the thinking process of the developer.

AMORE

Wood *et al.* (1994) discuss the problem in requirements acquisition whereby requirements for systems do not just exist in the form of natural language documents, but may be in a mixture of formats recorded on a variety of media, such as informal technical notes, technological surveys, written notes from meetings, and audio and video records of meetings. They argue that current methods only focus on formal or semi-formal textual and graphical notations, leading to the obscuring of important information and the loss of full traceability from requirements to more structured models.

AMORE is then described, which is a multimedia software assistant that can store requirements information in a variety of formats, including textual, graphical, digital audio and video, and which makes use of a structuring mechanism for organizing what may be thousands of individual requirement elements. The structuring mechanism is a levelled hierarchical diagram with an object dictionary. Requirements are located at primitive nodes, with the raw information from which they are derived located at preceding nodes, assisting traceability. Knowledge is provided in AMORE to assist the developer in eliciting requirements as well as browsing and editing.

ETHNOGRAPHY

Ethnography is a social science approach originally developed by anthropologists to understand social mechanisms. The approach involves an anthropologist spending a considerable amount of time living in a society and making an ethnographic record of its detailed practices. The record is subsequently analysed and the society characterized in social order terms such as structure, role and class. Two aspects of such studies are that no presuppositions about the society are made and the ethnographer does not impose any value judgments (Sommerville *et al.*, 1993).

The approach is applied to the requirements process to address the problems that occur when system design pays insufficient attention to the social context of work (Hughes *et al.*, 1995). It contrasts with, for example, workshops or groups which discuss requirements away from the work setting. Ethnography tries to make visible the real world aspects of a social setting by presenting life as seen by those who work in a domain such as an organization. Of particular appeal to some developers is the fact that by focusing on activities as social phenomena, ethnography can reveal needs and activities that users may be unable or unwilling to articulate due to organizational power relationships.

Hughes *et al.* (1995) discuss two problems with the application of ethnography to the requirements process: time and presentation. The time that ethnographic studies have typically taken (sometimes years) poses a problem and the authors describe how they have adopted a 'quick and dirty' approach involving short, focused studies to gain a general picture of the situation. The studies consist of ethnographers studying the setting in which users work. The study duration is relative to the size of the task.

The second problem is that of presenting the results of the study. Typically, an ethnographic record is structured according to the fieldworker involved, but Hughes *et al.* describe how they use the notion of *viewpoint* as a central presentation concept. In this context, a viewpoint is the view or perspective of an individual in a setting that is relevant to the situation under investigation. Viewpoints are chosen as they highlight the multiple and sometimes conflicting perspectives that individuals possess and facilitate the process of informing the requirements by setting these perspectives side-by-side.

It is emphasized that viewpoints are *emergent properties*, in the sense that they emerge from the requirements process and not from the application of some predetermined categories. Viewpoints are formed by an iterative process of collaboration between ethnographers and developers.

A software tool is described which supports three generic types of viewpoint. The *setting of work* viewpoint describes the physical, spatial location of work, the participants, the work they do and the resources they use. The *social and organizational perspectives on work* viewpoint highlights the day-to-day experience of work from the perspectives of the participants in the work setting. The third viewpoint, *flow of work*, focuses on sequences of work activities, information flows and end-to-end processes.

ORDIT

ORDIT (Dobson and Strens, 1994) is concerned with the nature of the debating processes whereby the requirements that arise from the social context of a system are brought to the surface. Requirements may arise, for example from ethics, power structures and values. Three principles are set out to distinguish ORDIT from classical soft systems approaches such as SSM: responsibilities, composition and architecture.

The communications gap between user and developer is recognized and the concept of *responsibility* is put forward as a 'boundary object'; that is, a place where the worlds of the user and the developer can meet. An organization is viewed as a network of responsibilities that users hold, and which are seen as an effective source of user requirements, as users know their responsibilities within the organization for their work.

The responsibility of a work role is central to a generic model of organizations in terms of three hierarchical levels: responsibilities, obligations and activities. *Responsibilities* are on the highest level and are relationships between *agents* for states of affairs (for example, legal liability) who have certain *rights* along with their responsibilities. On the next level, *obligations* are discharged by agents in *roles* by virtue of their responsibilities. On the lowest level, obligations are refined into *activities*, which is how obligations are carried out by *agents* using *resources*.

The model allows three basic questions to be formulated concerning what each role needs (a) to know, (a) to do and (c) to audit, which facilitate the identification of data and functions for an information system. It is stated that responsibilities, as they make the social context more explicit, are a better starting point than activities for forming requirements.

The notion of composition is rooted in a criticism of traditional methods which decompose a problem into a solution, but then cannot show how this decomposition is a solution to organizational objectives. In contrast, the hierarchical levels in ORDIT, based on the triple of agent, action and resource, can be used to link lower level activities with objectives.

It is acknowledged that the choice of an architecture or method for requirements determination is a political statement, as one architecture can often satisfy only one perspective in the organization. ORDIT views organizations in terms of relationships, as described above, and its emphasis is on exploring possible solutions at the same time as specifying the problem, with the expectation that requirements are gradually refined from an initial set into a more systematic set.

The method is designed to analyse organizational change and may generate requirements for a system or as a consequence of a system being introduced. It is based on four concurrent subprocesses: scoping, modelling, requirements and options. These are viewed as a road map and can be visited in any order, more than once with no specific start or end point.

Scoping establishes the organizational territory and important stakeholders as well as boundaries to the proposed system. Requirements consists of an exploration of possible futures through interaction and iteration with stakeholders and involves a two-way transfer. Firstly, the developer builds a set of responsibility-based models using information communicated from the stakeholders. Secondly, the developer transfers these models to the stakeholders for them to validate and explore different possibilities. The options subprocess considers different socio-technical system options emphasizing the perspectives on which they are based, such as efficiency, return on investment and customer satisfaction.

USER-CENTRED DESIGN

Brun-Cottan and Wall (1995) describe their user-centred design approach and emphasize the need to *re-present* users and their work in a way that users find accurate, and they describe the use of video to provide a view of a user site. Advantages of video are the permanent record of detailed events and the ability to present users with structured accounts of their work in a recognizable form. Disadvantages are the time involved in making the video record, viewing and analysing the record and retrieving and structuring the video clips.

APPRENTICESHIP MODEL

Beyer and Holtzblatt (1995) discuss an ethnographic approach based on the apprenticeship model, where the apprentice (developer) spends time in the work situation observing the master (user) learning how the master does their job. This is viewed as a useful model for the relationship between user and developer as it promotes an attitude of inquiry and learning on the part of the developer. Advice is also given concerning other roles which the developer may inadvertently fall into. The understanding of work structure and the articulation of developer understanding back to the user is emphasized, although no specific concepts or methods are suggested for this.

USER-CENTRED MODELLING

Flynn and Davarpanah Jazi (1994) describe an approach based on a diagrammatic, user-centred modelling tool which has been developed to correspond to the user view rather than the developer view of the organization. Intended for the later stages of requirements acquisition, the tool addresses the user–developer communications gap by allowing users to build their own models of information and activity flows in their organization.

Soft approach – conclusions

PROBLEMS ADDRESSED

One of the characteristics of soft approaches is that they all address quality problems 1 and 2, as well as the first two productivity problems caused by changing requirements. This is shown in Table 13.2. In addition, they adhere to the systems paradigm noted above (Wood-Harper and Fitzgerald, 1982), as they all take the view that the computer system interacts with other systems, receiving inputs and producing outputs. It is a goal that all systems are in equilibrium.

Table 13.2 Problems addressed by different approaches

Problem	Solution provided
Q1	soft approaches
Q2	
Q3	hard approaches
Q4	–
P1	soft approaches
P2	
P3	–
P4	–

CRITICISMS OF SOFT APPROACHES

1. *They only cover a small part of the life cycle.* SSM stages 1 to 6 only cover early requirements determination activities, as we have defined them, and participative systems design (PSD) steps 1 to 4 cover the same area (but in more detail). Other approaches only cover part of the requirements phase. However, as we have seen in user factors life-cycle (UFLC), and also in the Multiview method (Avison and Wood-Harper, 1990), a solution is to combine new methods with a soft approach by adding new stages and the required iteration.

2. *They require more resources.* More emphasis on the early stages will increase the time and cost requirement, and experts such as psychologists or group discussion leaders will need to be hired or trained. User participation sounds a good idea, but user availability is often limited, as is the time in which to develop a system. However, these efforts should result in a better system, recovering the extra costs by savings in the maintenance phase, which often consists of changes due to errors or misunderstanding made earlier in development.

3. *Participation may not improve system quality.* Empirical work (Tait and Vessey, 1988; Flynn and Ade, 1996) on the effects of participation is inconclusive; it has not been shown definitely that participation has the positive effect claimed. This may be due to the fact that participation is not a significant factor, relative to other factors.

4. *They have not been tested sufficiently in practice.* Both the Checkland and Mumford methods have been used in systems development projects, but not on a large scale. However, there is no documented evidence that traditional hard approaches have a higher success rate than soft approaches.

5. *Concepts like usability are hard to operationalize.* Such factors do not currently have an agreed definition, cannot therefore easily be measured and are thus hard to 'sell' to user management (compared to tangibles like project cost).

6. *Quality problem 1 is not really addressed.* Although SSM and PSD provide for discussion, this does not guarantee that the real problem will be determined. This may be due to user bias or bounded rationality. In PSD, although users may be expert at their current tasks, this does not mean that they are expert at the requirements for new tasks, possibly with new technology.

7. *Impact of new technology on old requirements.* Approaches generally appear to be weak in the area of proposing how new technology may bring benefits to organizations. For example, the ethnographic approach may succeed in describing current work and may elicit user requirements very well, but requires additional concepts so that user requirements may be changed to take into account how technology may change future work.

SOFT APPROACH CHARACTERISTICS

It is perhaps too early in the development of methods belonging to the soft approach to list more than a few characteristics.

1. Development of information systems in organizations will increasingly require solutions to problems of a wider nature than those traditionally addressed. This reflects the increasing penetration of information systems into the less routine areas of the organization. The breadth of knowledge of the systems designer is thus likely to grow. An emphasis will be on theory for guiding the particular type of development method to be used in a given situation, based on a more analytical approach to the organizational situation. Methods will have phases concerned with social and psychological factors in the problem situation, in conjunction with the more traditional phases characteristic of the hard approach.

2. An emphasis on user participation is necessary, as it will always be important that the correct requirements are obtained, and, equally importantly, validated with the user in an effective way. User participation in development work will thus grow.

   Although opinion is generally positive concerning the benefits of user participation there are known disadvantages, such as the extra resources in terms of time and user commitment required, and perhaps the scarce resources of trained developers. The type and extent of user participation may vary widely, and Keil and Carmel (1995) suggest that there may be a limit to the extent of participation beyond which no significant benefits are experienced. More research into the effects of participation is required, especially as there are reports that some types of participation may have negative effects (Flynn and Ade, 1996).

3. Different types of user participation are apparent from the soft approaches described above. For example, some approaches are based on the ethnographic principle of observing users in their work setting, for example ORDIT, the apprenticeship model, user-centred design and user-centred modelling. However, approaches such as USTM, QFD and the KJ method prefer workshop sessions. Other approaches (SSM, PSD, UFLC, client-led design, Multiview, AMORE) appear to allow for both.

4. Some approaches address the issue of providing a 'gateway' down to later development phases, such as ORDIT, USTM and user-centred modelling, while others focus only on the requirements phase.

Contingency approach to method use

If we study the different characteristics of the methods and their respective approaches, one possible conclusion is that the methods have developed to suit different situations. For example, some methods, such as SSADM and participative systems design, assume that a current system always exists, which can be used as a basis for analysis and design of new systems. Other methods, like the Checkland methodology, do not make this assumption. An example of this approach (Davis, 1982) describes how a multidimensional set of factors concerning the uncertainty of the desired system, type of users and type of designers may be evaluated and used to select the most appropriate requirements determination strategy.

We outline here a contingency framework that may be useful for determining the situation in which it is best to use a particular method or approach. The framework is based on two variables, both concerned with different aspects of uncertainty inherent in the situation – requirements uncertainty and process uncertainty:

1. *Requirements uncertainty.* This is the extent to which the requirements are known and fixed. In some very stable situations, requirements are very clear, with no ambiguity, and all parties agree. In addition, they will not change once development work begins. However, where there is a great deal of uncertainty, there may be no agreement on requirements, with several interested parties holding radically different views. Requirements may also be liable to change once development begins.

2. *Process uncertainty.* This relates to the degree of knowledge that we have concerning the problem to be solved. In some cases, where the problem is based on logic or mathematics, such as an accounting system or a system that analyses data statistically, the degree of knowledge concerning the solution is high and we may often use standard solutions. In other cases, where the problem is of a novel type or where the eventual system is likely to have a major effect on the organizational situation, we may not know, with a high degree of certainty, the best way to solve the problem.

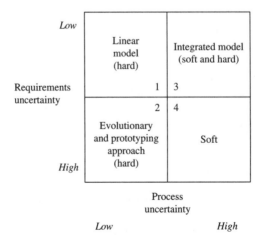

Figure 13.5 Contingency framework for organizational situation and IS methods.

These two variables may be combined to give four types of organizational situation, shown in Fig. 13.5, and we may use this to assist in determining the method most suited to the situation to produce an information system.

Where requirements and process uncertainty are low, the simple linear model may be the most appropriate. Where the requirements become more uncertain, but where process uncertainty remains low, a combination of the evolutionary and prototyping approaches may be the most appropriate.

Where requirements are known, but where the type of solution is uncertain, an integrated approach consisting of both soft and hard approaches will probably be most appropriate. Soft approaches are most suited to a situation where uncertainty for both requirements and process is high, as they involve extensive discussion and propose evaluation of solutions for their effect on the organization.

Summary

We began this chapter by stating that there are problems of quality and productivity concerned with the development of information systems and that these problems have been only partially addressed by the methods considered up to now. These methods were representative of the hard approach to systems development. We then described characteristics of the soft approach, which addresses problems omitted by the hard approach, and discussed several methods, including soft requirements engineering methods.

Some criticisms were made of the soft approach, and some of its characteristics were described. Finally, it was suggested that a complementary approach, involving a contingency framework, which attempted to 'fit' different types of method to different organizational situations was a likely future development as shown by Euromethod in Chapter 12, and a framework based on two organizational factors – requirements uncertainty and process uncertainty – was briefly discussed.

Discussion questions

1. Based on systems you know or drawing on case studies you may find in textbooks in the library, try to construct the way in which quality and productivity targets are set for development projects. What sort of evaluation procedures are used to establish quality and what techniques are used to estimate the resources (users, designers, time, money, equipment, software) that will be needed?
2. If you work in a computer department, what proportion of the department budget is consumed by maintenance?
3. Of the development methods with which you have had experience, have you found that they take user factors such as usability and acceptability into account? Do they do this explicitly or implicitly?

4. Which of the hard approach assumptions do you think causes most problems in information systems?
5. Do the soft approaches adequately address all the problems raised by the assumptions of the hard approach?
6. To what extent do the soft approaches discussed cover the life-cycle? What do these approaches have in common?
7. Try the contingency framework out on development situations of which you have experience. Is it easy to use? Does it predict the right type of method to use? Could you improve it by, for example, increasing the number of variables?

References

Angell, I. O. and Smithson, S. (1991) *Information Systems Management: Opportunities and Risks,* Macmillan, London.

Avison, D. E. and Wood-Harper, A. T. (1990) *Multiview: An Exploration in Information Systems Development,* Blackwell, London.

Beyer, H. R. and Holtzblatt, K. (1995) Apprenticing with the customer, *Communications of the ACM,* **38**(5), 45–52.

Bjerknes, G., Ehn, P. and Kyng, M. (1987) *Computers and Democracy: a Scandinavian Challenge,* Gower, Aldershot.

Bjorn-Andersen, N., Eason, K. and Robey, D. (1986) *Managing Computer Impact: An International Study of Management and Organisation,* Ablex, Norwood NJ.

Bjorner, D. (1987) On the use of formal models in software development, in *Proceedings of the 9th International Conference on Software Engineering,* Monterey CA, 17–29.

Boehm, B. W. (1975) The high cost of software, in *Practical Strategies for Developing Large Software Systems* (ed. Horowitz, E.), Addison-Wesley, London, 3–14.

Brun-Cottan, F. and Wall, P. (1995) Using video to re-present the user, *Communications of the ACM,* **38**(10), 61–71.

Brynjolfsson, E. (1993) The productivity paradox of information technology, *Communications of the ACM,* **36**(12), 67–77.

Capers Jones, T. (1995) *Patterns of Software Systems Failure and Success,* Thomson, London.

Checkland, P. (1981) *Systems Thinking, Systems Practice,* Wiley, Chichester.

Checkland, P. and Scholes, J. (1990) *Soft Systems Methodology in Action,* Wiley, Chichester.

Child, J. (1987) Organizational design for advanced manufacturing technology, in *The Human Side of Advanced Manufacturing Technology* (eds. Wall, T. D., Clegg, C. W. and Kemp, N. J.), Wiley, Chichester, 101–33.

Clemons, E. K. (1991) Evaluation of strategic investments in information technology, *Communications of the ACM,* **34**(1), 22–36.

Collins, W. R., Miller, K. W., Spielman, B. J., and Wherry, P. (1994) How good is good enough? An ethical analysis of software construction and use, *Communications of the ACM*, **37**(1), 81–91.

Davis, G. B. (1982) Strategies for information requirements determination, *IBM Systems Journal*, **21**(2), 4–30.

Dobson, J. and Strens, R. (1994) Organisational requirements definition for information technology systems, in *Proceedings of the First International Conference on Requirements Engineering*, 18–22 April, Colorado Springs, Colorado, IEEE Computer Society Press, Los Alamitos CA, 158–65.

DTI (1985) *Benefits of Software Engineering Methods and Tools: A Study for the Department of Trade and Industry*, PA Computers and Telecommunications. Available from Library and Information Centre, Department of Trade and Industry, 1–19 Victoria Street, London SW1H 0ET.

DTI (1986) *Profiting from Office Automation* (2 vols). Available from Library and Information Centre, Department of Trade and Industry, 1–19 Victoria Street, London SW1H 0ET.

DTI (1988) *Software Quality Standards: The Costs and Benefits. A review for the Department of Trade and Industry*, April, Price Waterhouse. Available from Library and Information Centre, Department of Trade and Industry, 1–19 Victoria Street, London SW1H 0ET.

Eason, K. (1988) *Information Technology and Organisational Change*, Taylor & Francis, London.

Fairbairn, D. (1989) Senior management's perception of information technology and information systems' function, in *Information Management and Planning: Database 87* (eds. Feldman, P., Bhabuta, L. and Holloway, S.), Gower Technical, Aldershot, 27–32.

Fawthrop, A. (1990) The systems engineering approach within British Telecom, in *SE90 (Proceedings of Software Engineering 90, Brighton)*, (ed. Hall, P. A. V.), Cambridge University Press, Cambridge, 514–28.

Fitzgerald, B. (1994) Whither systems development: time to move the lamppost? *Proceedings of the Second Conference on Information Systems Methodologies* (eds. Lissoni, C. *et al.*), 31 August–2 September, Edinburgh, British Computer Society, Swindon, UK, 371–80.

Flynn, D. J. and Davarpanah Jazi, M. (1994) Organisational and information systems modelling for information systems requirements determination, in *Proceedings of 13th International Conference on Entity–Relationship Approach*, 13–16 December 1994, Manchester, UK, 79–93.

Flynn, D. J. and Ade, S. (1996) *A survey on the research into user participation*, Technical Report, Department of Computation, UMIST, May.

Goguen, J. A. and Linde, C. (1993) Techniques for requirements elicitation, in *Proceedings of the IEEE International Symposium on Requirements Engineering*, 4–6 January, San Diego CA, IEEE Computer Society Press, Los Alamitos CA, 152–64.

Gould, J. D., Boies, S. J. and Lewis, C. (1991) Making usable, useful productivity-enhancing computer applications, *Communications of the ACM*, **34** (1), 74–85.

Haag, S., Raja, M. K. and Schkade, L. L. (1996) Quality function deployment usage in software development, *Communications of the ACM*, **39**(1), 41–9.

Hammer, M. and Champy, J. (1993) *Reengineering the Corporation: a Manifesto for Business Revolution*, Nicholas Brealey Publishing.

Harrington, J. (1991) *Organizational Structure and Information Technology*, Prentice-Hall, London.

Hauser, J. R. and Clausing, D. (1988) The house of quality, *Harvard Business Review*, May–June, 63–73.

Holtzblatt, K. and Beyer, H. (1993) Making customer-centred design work for teams, *Communications of the ACM*, **36**(10), 93–103.

Hughes J, O'Brien, J., Rodden, T., Rouncefield, M. and Sommerville, I. (1995) Presenting ethnography in the requirements process, *Proceedings of the Second IEEE International Symposium on Requirements Engineering*, 27–29 March, York, UK, IEEE Computer Society Press, Los Alamitos CA, 27–34.

Humphrey, W. S. (1988) Characterizing the software process: a maturity framework, *IEEE Software*, **8**, 73–9.

Jayaratna, N. (1994) *Understanding and Evaluating Methodologies – NIMSAD: A Systemic Framework*, McGraw-Hill, London.

Kearney, A. T. (1985) *The Barriers and Opportunities of Information Technology: A Management Perspective*, Institute of Administrative Management/Department of Trade and Industry, London.

Keil, M. and Carmel, E. (1995) Customer–developer links in software development, *Communications of the ACM*, **38**(5), May, 33–44.

Kemerer, C. F. and Sosa, G. L. (1991) Systems development risks in strategic information systems, *Information Software Technology*, **33**(3), 212–13.

King, D. (1984) *Current Practices in Software Development: A Guide to Successful Systems*, Prentice-Hall, Englewood Cliffs NJ.

KPMG (1990) *Runaway Computer Systems – A Business Issue for the 1990s*, October. Available from KPMG Peat Marwick McLintock, 1 Puddle Dock, Blackfriars, London, EC4V 3PD.

Lyttinen, K. and Hirschheim, R. (1987) Information systems failures – a survey and classification of the empirical literature, *Oxford Surveys in Information Technology*, **4**, 257–309.

Macaulay, L. (1993) Requirements capture as a cooperative activity, *Proceedings of the IEEE International Symposium on Requirements Engineering*, 4–6 January, San Diego CA, IEEE Computer Society Press, Los Alamitos CA, 174–81.

Mantei, M. M. and Teorey, T. J. (1989) Incorporating behavioral techniques into the systems development life cycle, *MIS Quarterly*, **13**(3), 256–73.

McFarlan, F. W. (1981) Portfolio approach to information systems, *Harvard Business Review*, **48**, 142–59.

Mumford, E. (1981) Participative systems design: structure and method, *Systems, Objectives, Solutions*, **1**(1), 5–19.

Mumford, E. (1983) *Designing Human Systems for New Technology: The ETHICS Method*, Manchester Business School, Manchester.

Myers, M. (1993) A disaster for everyone to see: an interpretive analysis of a failed IS project, *Proceedings of the 4th Australian Conference on Information Systems*, 596–611.

Naur, P. and Randell, B. (eds.) (1968) *Software Engineering*, Report of a conference sponsored by the NATO Science Committee, Garmisch, Germany.

NEDO (1983) *The Impact of Advanced Information Systems*, National Economic Development Office, London.

Neumann, P. G. (1995) *Computer-Related Risks*, Addison-Wesley, New York.

Neumann, P. G. (1996) http://catless.ncl.ac.uk/Risks/I.J.html (where I = volume no. and J = issue no. of Software Engineering Notes. Six issues annually – 1996 is volume 21). Alternatively email risks-request@csl.sri.com with single text line 'info'.

Oakley, B. (1988) The issues of today, in *Software Engineering (Proceedings of Software Tools 88 Conference, London)*, Blenheim Online Ltd, London, 1–4.

Potts, C. (1995) Invented requirements and imagined customers: requirements engineering for off-the-shelf software, in *Proceedings of the Second IEEE International Symposium on Requirements Engineering*, 27–29 March, York, UK, IEEE Computer Society Press, Los Alamitos CA, 128–30.

Pressman, R. S. (1992) *Software Engineering – A Practitioner's Approach*, McGraw-Hill, New York.

Robinson, B. (1994) Social context and conflicting interests in participant understanding of information systems failure, in *Proceedings of the Second Conference on Information Systems Methodologies* (eds. Lissoni, C. *et al.*), 31 August–2 September, Edinburgh, British Computer Society, Swindon, UK, 235–47.

Sommerville, I., Rodden, T., Sawyer, P., Bentley, R. and Twidale, M. (1993) Integrating ethnography into the requirements engineering process, *Proceedings of the IEEE International Symposium on Requirements Engineering*, 4–6 January, San Diego CA, IEEE Computer Society Press, Los Alamitos CA, 165–73.

SSADM (1995) *SSADM4+: Version 4.2*, NCC Blackwell, Oxford.

Stowell, F. and West, D. (1994) *Client-Led Design: A Systemic Approach to Information System Definition*, McGraw-Hill, London.

Tait, P. and Vessey, I. (1988) The effect of user involvement on system success: a contingency approach, *MIS Quarterly*, **12**(1), 91–107.

Takeda, N., Shiomi, A., Kawai, K. and Hajime, O. (1993) Requirement analysis by the KJ editor, *Proceedings of the IEEE International Symposium on Requirements Engineering*, 4–6 January, San Diego CA, IEEE Computer Society Press, Los Alamitos CA, 98–101

Winfield, I. (1991) *Organisations and Information Technology: Systems, Power and Job Design*, Blackwell Scientific Publications, Oxford.

Wood, D. P., Christel, M. C. and Stevens, S. M. (1994) *Proceedings of the First International Conference on Requirements Engineering*, 18–22 April, Colorado Springs CO, IEEE Computer Society Press, Los Alamitos CA, 53–6.

Wood-Harper, A. T. and Fitzgerald, G. (1982) A taxonomy of current approaches to systems analysis, *The Computer Journal*, **25**(1), 12–16.

Wood-Harper, A. T. and Flynn, D. J. (1983) Action learning for teaching information systems, *The Computer Journal*, **26**(1), 79–82.

Wroe, B. (1985) Towards the successful design and implementation of computer based management information systems in small companies, in *People and Computers: Designing for Usability* (eds. Harrison, M. D. and Monk, A. F.), Cambridge University Press, Cambridge.

Zultner, R. E. (1993) TQM for technical teams, *Communications of the ACM*, **36**(10), 79–91.

14

Socio-organizational factors and information systems

Introduction

The soft approach described in the previous chapter is based on the belief that information system success should not only be assessed in terms of functional or technical factors, concerning the ability of the system to perform a given task. In contrast, it emphasizes that notions of success should take into account *social* and *psychological* factors in the organization, such as job satisfaction, organization goals, system usability and user acceptability.

For example, jobs should be designed which maximize variable factors, such as job satisfaction, and systems should be designed to achieve organization goals. Work has also been carried out into matching personal factors of individuals and different aspects of information systems. Factors studied include cognitive style, Jungian personality factors and leadership styles.

An aspect of this emphasis is the belief that increased user participation, particularly for obtaining user requirements, will increase user acceptability, as users are given the system that they want. An information system should thus be designed to match the personal preferences of users with regard to the types of information required and the way in which information is acquired, stored and retrieved. Wider matters are frequently addressed, such as the nature of users' work and the ways in which they construct meaning in a given work setting.

There is always the possibility that a user-centred approach may suggest a system that, although it is what users want, may not necessarily be the best for the users or for the organization. Although one must be careful of developer arrogance, this situation may arise due to, for example, simple economic factors (the desired system may be too costly), user bias (Moynihan,

1989) or the fact that a competent user may be an incompetent analyst (Avison and Wood-Harper, 1991).

This situation may also be due to the fact that the proposed system will not 'fit' with certain social factors, generally termed *organization structure*, that have been studied systematically in the social sciences and that provide the basis for generic organizational knowledge. For example, Goodhue (1988) suggests that information systems result in individual performance improvements only when there is correspondence between system functionality and the task requirements of users.

This knowledge may provide assistance when attempting to identify important social factors in an organization and consists of an improvement over the largely intuitive approach to social factors present in the requirements engineering approaches discussed in the previous chapter. Many approaches, for example, do not identify important social factors.

Knowledge of these factors is helpful in several areas, and in this chapter we consider several approaches to identifying aspects of structure and then show their practical use within systems development, for example in contingency approaches to selecting or tailoring a systems development method, identifying norms in requirements engineering and designing information and information flows.

Finally, we discuss the work on critical systems thinking of Jackson (1992), which serves to tie together many of the themes of this and the preceding chapter, as well as suggesting an exciting direction for information systems in the future.

Organization structure and information systems

STRUCTURE

Those social factors that constitute organization structure, which we shall refer to as *structure*, may be described as follows: when the actions of different actors, sharing common social situations, tend to be the same or similar, and when the actions of the same actors in the same types of situations tend on different occasions to be the same, then these two aspects constitute structure.

Structure may be seen as an enduring set of rules which influence people's behaviour. Some elements of structure are:

1. *Roles*. For example, secretary, accountant, cleaner (rather than the people in these roles).
2. *Organizational groupings*. Product teams or functional units such as marketing, production or finance departments.
3. *Hierarchies*. Manager–employee relationships found in organizations.
4. *Degree of centralization and decentralization*. The extent to which information either flows centrally, to and from one decision-making point, or flows to and from many decision-making points.
5. *Norms*. Organizational goals, ethics and values.

Fit with structure

This structural viewpoint is also accompanied by an open systems perspective. Organizations are seen as being capable of change, in response to environmental inputs, in order to survive and to achieve their goals. There are influences on organizations which cause individuals in the organizations to set up different types of structure (either consciously or unconsciously). The structure aims to 'fit in' or 'match' with the environmental influences so that the organization can perform at its best.

An example might be where a supermarket, criticized by consumer groups for excessive secrecy with regard to the country of origin of its products, responds by opening a customer relations department with a well-publicized telephone number, avoiding a boycott of its products. Structure has thus changed, with a new department, and new roles have been created.

If we apply this notion, it follows that an information system that we wish to introduce into an organization must fit in with the prevailing structure if the organization as a whole is to perform well. A well-known error is to design an information system that is too complex. For example, a system for a small organization that gathers large quantities of data concerning employee productivity may never be used, as the owner may estimate productivity at a glance.

An example is given (Harrington, 1991) where a firm found low morale in the workforce affecting productivity after the implementation of a computer system. On investigation, it was found that the new system had changed the reporting structure and some departments had increased responsibilities while others had decreased; this change was responsible for creating new conflicts.

ORGANIZATION THEORY

Organization theory is concerned with the processes and structure of an organization and their relationship to the organizational environment. We shall consider *contingency approaches* to organization theory, so named as they suggest that various aspects of organizations are contingent upon (that is, influenced by or closely linked with) key factors in the organizational environment. They are important as they are an advance on the 'one best way' school of thought about organization structure and management (Morgan, 1997).

Butler (1991) describes different contingency approaches, using the general terms *contextual variable* (independent variable) to refer to an influencing factor on an organization and *structural variable* (dependent variable) to refer to an element of structure that is influenced. He identifies three broad types or streams of contextual variables which we term (a) technical, (b) environmental and (c) normative which will be discussed in more detail below.

Contingency approaches suggest types of organization structure, and their relevance is that we should design information systems to 'fit' or match these types, as inappropriate systems may be rejected by the organization or may fall into disuse. The approaches also suggest important contextual variables which may be useful when we wish to tailor a systems development approach to the situation, or seek to discover and understand normative variables, such as goals and ethics, that are an important part of requirements.

In addition, contingency approaches are *predictive models* of organizations, as they predict that a given element of organization structure is closely linked with a given contextual variable, for example a type of technology or an aspect of the environment. They may thus provide guidance concerning the structures that *should* be in place in an organization, given certain contextual variables. This may help when deciding requirements for the wider organizational system, especially when re-engineering.

We shall also briefly consider a *political* perspective on organizations, concerned with the nature and effect of power within organizations and how this may affect both the approach to information system development and the type of information system required. We finish this section with some practical recommendations.

Task-technology

Goodhue and Thompson (1995) describe an empirical study which investigated the 'fit' between tasks and the technology intended to support those tasks. A model, termed the Technology-to-Performance Chain (TPC), was proposed, suggesting that for 'an information technology to have a positive impact on individual performance, the technology must be utilized and the technology must be a good fit with the tasks it supports'. Over 600 individuals in 26 different departments of two companies, using 25 different information technologies, were surveyed.

Technologies were viewed as the tools used by individuals to carry out their tasks; in the research, this covered computer systems and user support services as training and help lines. *Tasks* were defined as the actions carried out by individuals in turning inputs into outputs. *Task-technology fit* was the degree to which a technology assisted an individual in performing his or her portfolio of tasks. Performance impact was measured by asking individuals for their perceptions concerning the impact of technology on effectiveness, productivity and performance in their job.

The TPC model was built on previous research focused on utilization theory and task-technology fit. Utilization theory, in its simplest form, states that increased use (utilization) of technology leads to improved performance, on the assumption that technology will only be used if it results in benefits. Goodhue and Thompson discussed how, for reasons concerned with involuntary use and the prevalence of poor technology, performance may not necessarily improve. Task-technology fit research has claimed that such a fit results in improved performance; again, the authors described how technology must be utilized before performance can be affected. Utilization was therefore perceived as complex, based on factors such as habit and social norms as well as fit.

The results of the research found strong evidence that performance was predicted by the degree of both task-technology fit and utilization. As for performance, both task-technology fit and utilization were measured by asking individuals for their perceptions concerning these factors. However, individuals' perceptions of task-technology fit were not found to be linked to their utilization of the technology. This may be because, whether they like using technology or not, many individuals may have to use it.

Technology

TYPES OF TECHNOLOGY

Woodward (1980) conducted empirical work in 100 manufacturing organizations, and her team found a relationship, for successful organizations, between technology and structure. By the term technology she meant the way in which an organization produced its products.

It is suggested that an advantage of using technology as the contextual variable is that it simplifies a great mass of environmental factors which may affect an organization, as the effect of such factors is 'filtered' by the technology of the organization.

In terms of their technology, organizations were located on an eleven-point scale, reflecting the degree to which the technology was controllable and predictable. From this scale, they were categorized into three main groups.

1. *Unit and small batch production* (for example, bespoke suits, custom furniture, machine tools)
2. *Large batch and mass production* (for example, car assembly lines, bakeries, mass-produced clothing)
3. *Process production* (for example, chemical plants, oil refineries)

The elements of structure considered were the degree of functional specialization, degree of clarity of duties, extent of written or verbal communications, span of control, number of hierarchical levels of management, and various employee ratios such as the proportion of managers to non-managers.

Relationships between technology and structure

Two types of relationship between technology and structure were found. Firstly, there was a linear relationship, where factors such as levels of management and span of control of the chief executive increased from group 1 to group 3. Secondly, there was a 'curvilinear' relationship, where structure was similar for organizations at the extremes (groups 1 and 3), but different in the middle (group 2).

For example, organizations at the extremes were found to be *organic*, meaning that they had ill-defined reporting responsibilities, continual job redefinition (low job specialization) and extensive coordination by lower managers rather than top managers, while organizations in the middle were *mechanistic*, with clear vertical management hierarchies, high job specialization and coordinated operations from the top.

Successful organizations

It was found that the most successful organizations, in a particular technology group, were those that were closest to the mean for the elements of structure of that group. Put another way, given an organization's technology, successful organizations had similar structures. To back up this finding, it was also observed that successful organizations, which were in the process of changing from one type of technology to another, changed their structure in the appropriate manner.

The results demonstrated that classical, 'scientific' management principles had limited applicability, as they were only found in the structures of successful large batch and mass production organizations, involving clear definitions of duties, unity of command and an emphasis on paper communications. It was not therefore the case that there was 'one best way to manage', as organizations were different. This classical view was possibly due to the work experience of early authors and managers such as Henri Fayol (Fayol, 1949) and Frederick Taylor (Taylor, 1911).

CONTROL SYSTEMS

Factors other than technology

However, it was felt that technology might not be the only important factor linked to structure, as the relationship was not so strong for the large batch and mass production group. At the scale extremes, it was hypothesized, the physical work flow restricts organizational choice and organizations tend to have a homogeneous structure, whereas between extremes, technology defines limits within which organization structure can be decided.

Between these extremes, the next stage of the research found that a *control system* was an 'intervening variable', and decisions such as the separation of planning and control from execution were key decisions that would influence organizational structure. In turn, the control system would be influenced by the nature of the technology and top management policy (Woodward, 1970).

This is shown below, and it modifies the earlier assumptions, which resemble the viewpoint of technological determinism, to make explicit the influence of management choice on structure. The notion of choice had been implied in the concept of success, as some organizations were below average in success, so factors other than technology had taken a hand in shaping structure.

Technology and top management policy → control system → organization structure

Control system components

When an organization makes a decision to manufacture a product, a control system comes into existence, consisting of the components of planning (including objectives setting), execution and control. Objectives have to be determined and the sequence of activities intended to achieve the objectives must be planned. Plans are then executed and information is generated to enable the results to be assessed. Finally, corrective action may need to be taken, or the objectives modified in the light of the results obtained. The control system is thus the framework within which individuals operate, determining the discretion they have in organizing their own activities.

DIMENSIONS OF CONTROL SYSTEMS

Control systems were conceptualized along two basic dimensions, from personal to mechanical and from unitary to fragmented.

Personal to mechanical

In the simplest type of system, the owner–employer decides what the organization requires and sees that it is done. As the organization increases in size and complexity, hierarchical control becomes more difficult to exercise, line management can no longer have enough knowledge of the specialist processes required and the three control system components become increasingly differentiated. To avoid losing control, management build into the organization impersonal processes of control which regulate and influence work behaviour of employees. Such processes may be administrative, covering, for example, production planning, or they may be mechanical, as in control of machine tools or a process plant.

A scale was thus envisaged, from completely personal hierarchical control to completely mechanical control, with impersonal or administrative control in between these two extremes.

Unitary to fragmented

Many control procedures can exist within an organization, perhaps set by different departments, and they can be linked or fragmented. Some organizations make considerable efforts to link standards from different departments set by different specialists into a single integrated control system.

Types of control system

The two dimensions are combined to form four types of control system: A1 – unitary and mainly personal control, B1 – fragmented and mainly personal controls, B2 – fragmented and mainly impersonal administrative or mechanical controls, and A2 – unitary and mainly impersonal administrative or mechanical controls.

Relationship to technology

Table 14.1 shows the links that resulted when the types of control system were related to the technology categories of the 100 original organizations. It may be concluded that unitary control dominates unit and process types of production. For large batch and mass production there were no clear links, as all types of control category are used, and this accounts for the fact that these organizations differ widely in structure.

Table 14.1 Control system types found with different technology categories (%)

Category	A1	B1	B2	A2
Unit and small batch	75	25	–	–
Large batch and mass production	15	35	40	10
Process production	–	–	5	95

SUMMARY

For organizations to perform at their best, structure needs to fit technology, as only successful organizations were found to have the appropriate structure. Woodward found this for the technology scale extremes; for large batch and mass production the links were not clear.

It was clear that the contingency relationship was not one whereby technology *determined* structure, as there were organizations (the unsuccessful ones) which did not have the appropriate structure for their technology type. In addition, the control system was an intervening variable, influenced by top management policy, which was also linked to structure. This made more explicit the influence of management choice on structure.

In retrospect, the concept of the control system as an intervening variable between technology and structure is not very useful, as control systems may be considered to be part of organizational structure.

Task

REFINEMENT OF NOTION OF TECHNOLOGY

Perrow (1970) refined the Woodward concept of technology into that of *task*. He identified two basic dimensions of the task that affect the degree of organization structure: (a) task variability and (b) search behaviour, and he defined the technology of an organization as the combined effect of both factors.

Task variability

This is the variability of occurrence of unexpected stimuli, such as unfamiliar situations or problems, that lead to search behaviour. It is the extent to which problems requiring solutions arise in the task. When search behaviour is required for most tasks, variability is high, and when most jobs are familiar and task search is only rarely required, it is low.

Search behaviour

This occurs as a response by individuals to the unfamiliar or problem stimuli that arise during the performance of the task. Some problems that arise may have known solutions. In this case, 'analyzable search' takes place, involving reference to sources such as standards manuals, where information is typically in a rational form.

However, when little understood problems arise, it is difficult to find the correct solution, as rational task knowledge is low. Therefore 'unanalyzable search' must take place, characterized by thinking for long periods of time or acting on intuition.

Both task variability and task problem response may be seen as types of task uncertainty.

CATEGORIES OF TECHNOLOGY

Perrow then combined the two dimensions, the degree of variability of stimuli and the degree to which search procedures are analyzable, to form four categories of technology, shown in Fig. 14.1.

Craft technologies (1) exhibit little task variability, but problem solutions are not well understood, for example in a fine glass factory. Where the degree of task variability is high and where problems cannot be rationally solved, non-routine technologies (2) may be found in, for example R&D departments of organizations.

Routine technologies (4) have little task variability and use analysable search for the few problems that arise. This might occur in a factory manufacturing a standard product such as parts for wooden furniture.

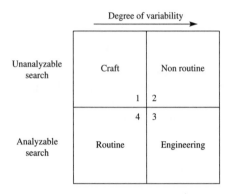

Figure 14.1 Perrow's categories of technology.

Engineering technologies (3) possess a higher degree of variability because more problems occur, but the problems are usually easily solved by recourse to standard sources, for example a lawyers' conveyancing practice.

ORGANIZATION STRUCTURE

Technology is thus seen by Perrow (1970, 1972) as a key influence on organization structure. He hypothesized that organizations, wittingly or unwittingly, wish to maximize the fit between their structure and their technology. He then went on to define four important variables of organization structure, which concerned two levels of management, the technical and supervision levels, consisting of (i) middle and lower management and (ii) supervisors.

	Discretion	Power	Coordination	Interdependence		Discretion	Power	Coordination			
Technical	Low	Low	Plan			High	High	Feedback			Unanalyzable search
				Low					High		
Supervision	High	High	Feedback			High	High	Feedback			
				Decentralized 1	2	Flexible, polycentralized					
				Formal, centralized 4	3	Flexible, centralized					Analyzable search
Technical	Low	High	Plan			High	High	Feedback			
				Low					Low		
Supervision	Low	Low	Plan			Low	Low	Plan			

Low   Task variability ⟶   High

Figure 14.2 Task-related interaction for the four technology categories.

The variables were: (a) discretion possessed in carrying out group tasks, (b) power of each group to utilize scarce resources and organizational strategies, (c) how activities are co-ordinated, either by planning or by feedback, and (d) degree of interdependence between the two groups. Figure 14.2 shows how these structural characteristics are related to the four categories of technology discussed above.

- *Craft* (1). The supervisory level has high discretion and power, with coordination achieved through feedback. The technical level is weak, depending on reports from supervisors, and has little power or discretion.
- *Non routine* (2). Discretion and power are high for both groups, coordination is through feedback rather than by planning and group interdependence is high, meaning that both levels work closely together, as there is not enough information about production to enable the technical level to control the supervisors.
- *Engineering* (3). Great discretion exists in choosing tasks and planning is all important, with little interdependence between the two groups. Coordination is achieved by feedback of information for problem solving. Discretion and power by the supervisors are minimal.
- *Routine* (4). In these, the technical group has power over the supervision level, as they plan the work. There is low discretion for both, as problems do not generally occur, and planning is the coordinating force, as events can be foreseen. This approaches the model of a typical bureaucracy.

SUMMARY

Perrow's work is useful as it refines Woodward's one-dimensional scale of technological predictability into two dimensions. He also differentiates between two types of role, technical and supervision, showing how, for each of the four technology types, their activities vary. Implications for information systems will be discussed at the end of the chapter.

Environment

The environment of an organization, in terms of actors such as customers, competitors and suppliers, as well as resources, is an important source of contextual variables. There are various strategies that organizations may pursue in response to different types of environment that are linked to different structures for successful organizations.

ENVIRONMENTAL DIMENSIONS

Butler (1991) identifies three dimensions of the environment: heterogeneity–homogeneity, variability–stability and interdependent–autonomous.

Heterogeneity–homogeneity

A homogeneous environment is one in which an organization has only to deal with a small number of similar environmental elements, for example a single product firm with one group of customers and a small number of suppliers. In contrast, a heterogeneous environment is one where a large number of similar environmental elements exist as the organization produces a variety of products or services.

The implications for structure are that, in a heterogeneous environment, the organization must differentiate by creating separate units to cope with different segments of the environment, where each unit has discretion to cope with its own mini-environment (Lawrence and Lorsch, 1967). This brings with it the problem of creating integration between the different units, so that, for example, resources are not duplicated and the variety of ideas concerning problem solving are not too different.

Variability–stability

In some environments, there can be sudden changes in demand, for example as experienced in government social services departments, due perhaps to the political climate or ideas concerning approaches to care (Didrickson, 1989). The structural approach to variability is to decentralize decision-making, creating a structure which is organic as opposed to mechanistic and which requires coordination and integration to ensure that conflict is minimized and different parts of the organization work in the same direction.

Interdependent–autonomous

Interdependence between environmental elements and the organization occurs when the organization needs to coordinate its actions with other organizations. For example, local government must coordinate transport policy with several different types of organization, including consumer groups and bordering local authorities. Such interdependence requires extra decision-making capacity and increases uncertainty from the environment. For a good fit, such a situation is linked to a 'fuzzy' structure where, for example, there is elasticity as to who does what job as well as the extent to which procedures may be adapted to varying situations.

TASK UNCERTAINTY

Galbraith (1973) argues that task uncertainty is a key environmental variable which constrains organizations, where the degree of task uncertainty is defined as the difference between the amount of information needed to be processed and the amount of information actually available for processing. This approach focuses on information as an environmental resource.

Organizations have two basic alternatives for coping with a high degree of task uncertainty: reducing their need for information and increasing their capacity to process information. Strategies for reducing information needs are (a) creating slack resources (for example, carrying a high quantity of stock to cover any likely demand) or (b) creating a matrix organization to reduce diversity. A matrix structure is where an organization is structured along functional as well as, for example, product lines and an employee occupying a cell of the resulting matrix has a functional responsibility as well as a product responsibility. This requires an integrating department to coordinate activities for each product.

There are also two strategies for increasing information-processing capacity: (a) increasing the number of information systems and (b) creating new horizontal relations, lowering decision-making to the point where information is located. An interesting feature of this model is that information needs are perceived as a major organizational influence.

Norms

COMPARISON DIMENSIONS

Norms provide standards of desirability by which an organization is scored and scores itself (Thompson, 1967); that is, they serve as standards against which organizational behaviour may be evaluated and, as such, form part of organizational *culture* (Harris, 1979). Butler (1991) suggests that there are two dimensions of comparisons that are useful when trying to classify norms: clarity–ambiguity and comparability–uniqueness.

The clarity–ambiguity dimension concerns the extent to which the standard is clear or ambiguous. For example, standards of manufacturing output are relatively clear while the performance of a charity is not. Assessment clearly becomes more difficult along the ambiguity axis. The comparability–uniqueness dimension refers to the availability of similar organizations against which comparisons may be made. It is relatively easy, for example, to compare secondary schools on the basis of league tables, as there are many comparable schools. A charity may again be used as an example at the uniqueness end of the dimension if it is viewed as providing a unique service. The two dimensions allow four types of norm to be identified, as shown in Fig. 14.3.

Efficiency norms are for use in clear situations where comparability is possible and these can be applied in the competitive market-place. *Moral* norms are the most difficult to measure as they normally concern the achievement of an absolute value. *Instrumental* norms may apply, for example, to government agencies such as Customs and Excise, where there is no other organization of the type available for comparison. Although targets can be set and easily measured, such as the number of drugs-related smuggling offences detected, it is difficult to assess the progress being made towards total elimination. *Referent* norms apply typically in professional organizations, such as a legal firm, where professional work is difficult to assess but where there are peers available for comparison.

IDEOLOGY

Norms and ideology

Many important norms are set by powerful forces in the institutional environment, for example, government, investors, shareholders and trade unions. These define the essential values of the organization and the goals required to achieve these values. Such external norms may be contradictory, and the organization needs to translate these into internal norms; that is, an *ideology* to underlie its decision-making that is consistent with external norms.

Daft (1989) suggests, with the competing values approach, that some norms imply an external orientation while other imply an internal orientation. From Fig. 14.3, efficiency goals are externally oriented, focusing on factors such as profit and customer relations and are found in commercial organizations. In contrast, instrumental norms are internally oriented, emphasizing internal targets and procedures, found in government bureaucracies. Referent norms are externally oriented, using, for example, peer group evaluation, while moral norms are internally oriented, as in charities.

It is often the case that organizations have to respond to different norms and must prioritize them in their ideology.

Ideology and structure

Butler (1991) suggests that an organization with a fuzzy structure requires what is termed a robust ideology, which is one that consists of all four types

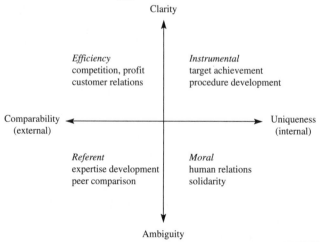

Figure 14.3 Four types of norm along two dimensions.

of norm. In contrast, organizations with crisp structures tend to focus on a narrow set of ideas.

Power

The approaches to understanding and analysing organization structure discussed above are all based on the assumption that organization structure is contingent on factors such as the environment or technology.

MANAGEMENT CHOICE

However, these may not be the only influencing factors. This has already been suggested in Woodward's work, where the poor degree of fit between structure and the large batch and mass production category, shown by the fact that all four types of control system can occur, led her to suggest that there must be an element of choice, on the part of management, which leads to the adoption of a particular type of control system.

It was discussed how such an organization could either integrate planning, execution and control with line supervisors or differentiate the tasks, having a production control department responsible for planning and control, with a higher status than the production department, which would be responsible only for execution. She found that, historically, this decision had mainly been based on whether the line supervisors had the necessary skill and judgement to combine these functions. However, there was also the suggestion that differentiation had occurred because it was management's belief that it was an appropriate way to rationalize the task. Clearly, in this case, management is exercising a choice.

SUCCESS

If the notion that technology influences structure for successful firms is considered more deeply, what about the unsuccessful organizations? Why has technology not affected them similarly? This implies that an organization may or may not choose a structure that will lead to success.

This is especially so when we look a little more closely at the nature of success, as there are different types of success for different organizations and organizational groups. For example, some organizations aim for growth, others for profit increase or debt reduction. Perceptions of success thus vary between and within organizations, which raises the question – which idea of success prevails?

The answer to this question introduces the notion that the type of 'success' adopted by an organization may be strongly influenced by the different power groups in the organization. This implies that we should consider the different types of access that groups have to power-related resources such as information, skill and ability to offer rewards and sanctions, and different types of rationality that may underlie the choice, and emphasizes the point (perhaps too easily lost sight of) that organizations are created by humans and not by impersonal forces. It is possible that different types of structure may be required to achieve different types of success.

Technology – or any other influencing variable – does not therefore set up organizational structure as a given, which then sets the boundaries for organizational behaviour. A particular technology may lead to a consensus (a state of uniform beliefs) between those with the necessary power that a certain course of action (resulting in structure) is appropriate. The outcomes are then a function of both the technology constraints and the beliefs of key powerful or influential organizational participants. Such beliefs could be, for example, derived from previous job experience or management theory, or both. This theory, however, neglects to mention that one choice may constrain another. For example, the original choice for the technology may constrain the later choice for structure.

Organizational outcomes will usually depend on negotiation between the different key actors (organizational participants), as there will always be different solutions to problems, or short-term versus long-term views (Hirschheim and Newman, 1988; Robey et al., 1989). These participants will possess different degrees of power, which will affect the negotiations. For example, Woodward described how the development, production and marketing departments had most status in the unit and small batch, large batch and mass production, and process production technologies, respectively. She did not, however, go on to say how this high status was used to influence structure.

Research into the effect of power distributions and beliefs on organizational structure is an interesting area (Newman and Noble, 1990). An example of the usefulness of a knowledge of power distribution in organizations may be found during requirements determination, where conflicting requirements between different groups may be evaluated in terms of their relative power.

Power is also seen as important, in a more direct way, by those who identify top management support for information systems as a key factor in eventual system success (Sanders and Courtney, 1985). Different groups may also experience an increase in power after computerization (Markus, 1983; Attlewell and Rule, 1984), which may affect their attitude towards the potential system at an earlier stage.

SUMMARY

Organizations are humanly constructed and their structure is set by a complex interaction of impersonal forces, such as technology or uncertainty, and personal forces, such as the exercise of choice over different notions of success by the power holders in an organization.

Practical recommendations

The following recommendations are given for three areas of concern: (a) organization structure, (b) information system and (c) requirements determination.

APPROPRIATE ORGANIZATION STRUCTURE

Do not assume that an information system will necessarily be the best solution to an apparent problem. Establish firstly the key aspects of organizational structure, together with such influencing factors as environmental characteristics, technology and task, and then consider whether they are matched, according to the criteria discussed in this chapter. If not, then changing structure may reduce the problem. It will always be necessary to take into account the views of power holders in this process. When applying Woodward's work, it may be useful to use the control system types to represent the relevant structural characteristics.

Knowledge of the power structure in the organization, in terms of departments, groups or managers with the most power is useful for a number of purposes, for example, resolving conflicting requirements and determining priorities. There will always be the possibility that a good 'fit' will be rejected by a power holder if it is felt inappropriate.

APPROPRIATE INFORMATION SYSTEM

Environment – roles and information flows

Butler identifies types of organizational structure which contain certain roles and role relationships, which are important as they receive and transmit information. For organic organizations, information should be designed to flow laterally between low-level managers, while in mechanistic organizations information should flow vertically upwards to top management, and then downwards in the form of instructions to employees.

Galbraith has similar findings: where uncertainty increases, a possible response is a structural change, introducing a matrix structure (for example, mixed groups of production, marketing, R&D and finance) or lateral relations.

To be successful, organizations which specialize their functions in the face of uncertainty should integrate their specialist departments using either (a) an integrating department or (b) teams of mixed specialists. Information systems to support these structures are control systems, used chiefly for conflict resolution.

To summarize, the developer should (a) note the type of structure associated with the relevant variables in the environment, (b) ensure that information will flow to match the structure between the specified role holders and in the right direction.

Technology – organization structure and information systems

Environmental authors do not give any detail concerning the information required for organizational structure. For example, they don't say whether it should be computer information, or what activities the information should support.

Woodward (1970, 1980) gives a typology of four control systems to match organizational technology. The control system types have implications for how the activities of planning, execution and control are carried out, and whether information systems should be computerized.

For type A1, the control system is personal, where the entrepreneur plans, directs execution and controls the organization intuitively, and computer systems do not play a key role in providing or analysing information. Planning and coordination are too unpredictable to be formalized and verbal communication is best. Control reports (feedback) may be limited to simple periodic summaries, for example, weekly units completed.

For type B1, growth has been accompanied by differentiation, so control is fragmented and is increasingly hard to coordinate personally. Information systems may be used to assist the control activity, by producing feedback reports concerning different factors such as time, cost and quality, from differentiated parts of the organization for top management to assist with planning and execution.

For type B2, two structures are possible, both characterized by many computerized reports containing impersonal controls, contrasting targets with what has been achieved: (a) line/staff where staff groups carry out planning and control, and where line groups carry out execution, and both need their own control reports; (b) matrix, where managers have their own control system and need control reports for planning and execution. For both structures, control systems are fragmented and it may not be appropriate to attempt to replace them by centralized controls, as this may reflect the power distribution between different departments, particularly where line and staff conflict occurs.

For type A2, planning and execution are usually built into the production process, and control systems are highly integrated. This implies a need for a centralized database holding the overall plan and many information systems producing control reports for the execution activity, to check progress against the plan. Some control and adjustment may also be carried out automatically.

Woodward emphasizes whether control systems should be integrated, who should receive control reports for execution or planning, and whether computerization is needed. Thus, she gives guidelines for centralized databases, information systems (transaction processing systems and management reporting) and role holders to receive information. We may note that centralized databases are suitable for only one of the four types.

As computer systems were relatively much more costly and less techno-logically advanced when the research was carried out, we may allow the scope of computerization to be wider. For example, in type A1, even the smallest corner shop may now have a PC with a transaction processing system for sales. However, it is unlikely that such a system will be extended to, for example, contain sales targets for different sales staff, as the owner will prefer to set these personally.

Perrow's (1970, 1972) categories of technology and matching structural characteristics are useful refinements of Woodward's types, as they pay more attention to task uncertainty and distinguish two types of role. For example, the craft and non-routine categories may be seen as refinements of Woodward's unit and small batch type, as the roles for planning are different between the two. In the craft technology, the supervisory level is stronger than the technical level, while in the non-routine technology, both levels are strong.

The engineering category is a refinement of the large batch and mass production type, emphasizing control reports for planning, while the routine category is a refinement of the process production type, where control reports are not so important, as events can be foreseen. Information systems can be integrated for the routine category for planning, whereas all other categories plan by feedback.

Norms–control systems

Using knowledge of the norms present or expected to be present in a given organization will help design the correct type of control system.

REQUIREMENTS DETERMINATION

Depending on the organization type this may be used as a guide for the type of norms in the situation and how explicit or implicit they are likely to be. This will help in requirements determination when trying to understand the reasons why a certain system is required.

Critical systems thinking

INTRODUCTION

In a discussion on the application of critical social theory to information systems, Jackson (1992) suggests how information systems development should mature so as to deal more effectively with a broader range of organizations and problem situations. He makes the point that development methods traditionally are based on a hard viewpoint, originating from scientism, and that the aspects of organizations that have been the subject of this focus are technical systems only.

Critical social theory is based on the ideas of Habermas (1972), who maintains that there are three pre-eminent interests of human beings. The *technical interest* is based on the importance of work as a means to achieve goals and bring about material well-being, which leads individuals to attempt to predict and control natural and social affairs. The *practical interest* is in the processes of inter-subjective communication, whereby individuals secure and expand the possibilities for mutual understanding among other individuals also involved in social systems. Finally, the *emancipatory interest* of individuals is concerned with freeing themselves from constraints involved in power relations and learning to control their own destiny.

At present, Jackson maintains, methods primarily support only the technical interest. In the future, they should change so as to support the practical and emancipatory interests also. A short description of Jackson's discussion will be given below, which he presents in terms of four aspects of critical thinking about information systems.

CRITICAL AWARENESS

Critical awareness is directed at understanding the theoretical underpinnings of methods, assumptions underlying different views of organizations and the nature of the fit between the two. Also involved are the assumptions and norms that underpin an existing or proposed system design or requirement.

Many current methods have been criticized by a variety of authors for assuming images of the organization as a machine, with information as a commodity. Methods belonging to the hard approach are based on scientism (Klein and Lyytinen, 1985) which conceives information systems too narrowly as consisting only of technical systems to be engineered, ignoring social factors and the need to share and create meaning. Jackson notes that although several alternative methods have been put forward, for example based on user participation or ethnography, little critical review has taken place concerning method underpinnings or situations which fit a method. Considering a specific fit between a method and a problem situation, the success of the Checkland SSM in a problem situation where the conditions for genuine, open debate are absent is questioned.

The work of Bloomfield (1992) discusses the 'social within the technical' concept whereby developers employ techniques, that they believe to be neutral, which embody ideas about management, decision making and power that are sociologically impoverished. The movement to make the assumptions underlying system designs more explicit may be seen in the previous chapter where organizational goals and their links to requirements were discussed. The principle of user involvement may also include this if all affected users can debate the design. In this chapter, the discussion above concerning types of organizational norm may be helpful by relating these to specifications.

Further work describing different methods or types of theoretical underpinning may be found in, for example Churchman (1971), Jayaratna (1994) and Hirschheim and Klein (1989), who identify four paradigms – functionalism, social relativism, radical structuralism and neohumanism – to which development methods may belong.

SOCIAL AWARENESS

One aspect of this concerns the organizational and societal climate which allows some approaches to flourish and others to wither. For example, methods which emphasize development teams may be influenced by the movement to adopt Japanese business methods, and object-oriented methods may be proposed as they are connected to object-oriented programming and database technologies.

Another aspect concerns the social implications of the use of a particular method. For example, the use of a hard method might skew a system to emphasize only explicit, readily available information belonging to one stakeholder at the expense of other types of information or other stakeholders. The effect of social change on the nature of information systems may also be considered.

COMPLEMENTARISM

Method

The essence of complementarism is that several viewpoints may coexist concerning a given situation, each of equal validity. At the level of a systems development method, this means that there may be several different views of a problem situation in an organization, requiring guidance to select different types of approach to elicit the richness of the situation. It is not clear as to whether, in this plurality of approaches, several are meant to be applied at the same time or selection of the most appropriate one is to be made, based on the situation that is being studied.

This concept relates to the practical use of a method, and an application has already been seen in contingency approaches mentioned in previous chapters, such as those discussed in Euromethod in Chapter 12, where the emphasis is on tailoring a general method rather than selecting from different methods. Some requirements engineering approaches discussed in the previous chapter allow different viewpoints to be built at the same time. The earlier discussion in this chapter concerning types of organizational structure is also relevant to the selection of an appropriate method, where, broadly, there may be benefit to be gained from applying a soft approach in an organic as opposed to a mechanistic organization.

Theory

At this level, complementarism is concerned with the nature of methods, and recommends that they be designed to take into account the plurality of viewpoints that may occur in the problem situation, so that they either explicitly address one type of problem situation or address several aspects in a complementary way. No one type of approach or aspect of a problem situation is seen as superior to any other. For example, it is suggested that methods may be designed to address each of the three interests defined by Habermas.

HUMAN WELL-BEING AND EMANCIPATION

Broadly, hard methods only serve the technical interest of individuals and soft methods serve the practical interest, but few methods serve the emancipatory interest, which seeks to further individual well-being. A central feature of critical systems thinking is that methods should explicitly seek to further the emancipatory interest.

This requires methods which actively seek, for example, to design jobs for individuals that enrich their lives and allow them greater autonomy (Klein and Hirschheim, 1987).

Summary

Information systems, if they are to be successful, should be designed to match organization structure, consisting of important social factors. Approaches that emphasize psychological factors and tailor systems to an individual or to a problem run the risk of bias or may have a short life, because, for example, the manager who requests a system may not be there when the system is delivered. The structural approach taken in this chapter, in contrast, suggests basing information systems on relatively enduring, structural, characteristics.

Several models were described that explained the influence of different contextual variables on organizational structure. Many of these models conceptualize a 'fit' or 'match' between such variables and different aspects of structure for organizational success.

Butler and Galbraith described environmental contingency approaches, which were based on the influence of various kinds of complexity or uncertainty on structure. Woodward described a technological model that attempted to match technology and structure as well as a typology of control systems. Perrow refined technology into task variability and search response and showed how these variables combined to produce four types of organization and corresponding structure. Butler proposed four types of norm that organizations may adopt.

Practical recommendations for different aspects of systems development were made, with the aim of achieving a match between a system and the different aspects of structure identified by the models. The models provide a source of organizational knowledge concerning important social factors and their links with contextual variables, as well as information systems, that can be useful.

There still is only a small amount of research specifically on the organizational factors that are appropriate for introducing different types of system. One example is the work of Child (1987) concerning the organizational factors for introducing computer-based manufacturing machines and processes. In addition, the effect of the introduction of such systems on organizations and their structures requires more research.

There are other factors, which we have not been able to cover in this chapter but which are also held to influence information systems (Swanson, 1987). Among these are environmental instability (Huber, 1984), the need to have rational objectives (Robey, 1981), task complexity (Culnan, 1983), and environmental analyzability (Daft and Weick, 1984).

The notion of human choice in determining structure within organizations was emphasized, and with it the importance of power in allowing such choice to be exercised, underlining the fact that organizations are socially constructed, by both impersonal and personal forces. Finally, Jackson described critical systems thinking and its application to information systems which tied together many themes from this and preceding chapters and also suggested an agenda for information systems for the future.

Discussion questions

1. Explain the difference between social and psychological factors within organizations that are relevant to the study of information systems.
2. Why do we need to know about social factors when we are considering developing an information system for an organization?
3. Compare the different notions of environmental uncertainty. How do they affect organizations?
4. What are the two separate notions of structure that Woodward conceived? Are they related?
5. 'Woodward produced a contingency theory of organizations, based on technology as the independent variable.' What is the meaning of this statement and how important is the notion of a successful organization?
6. Describe the basis for Perrow's technology categories and explain how they may be seen as refinements of Woodward's production categories.
7. Discuss how power and choice are related and how these concepts modify an impersonally determined view of organization structure. How useful to the systems designer is a knowledge of the prevailing power distribution in an organization?

References

Attlewell, P. and Rule, J. (1984), Computing and organizations: what we know and what we don't know, *Communications of the ACM*, **27**(12), 1184–92.

Avison, D. and Wood-Harper, A. T. (1991) Information systems development research: an exploration of ideas in practice, *The Computer Journal*, **34**(2), 98–112.

Bloomfield, B. (1992) Understanding the social practices of systems developers, *Journal of Information Systems*, **2**, 189–206.

Butler, R. (1991) *Designing Organizations: A Decision-Making Perspective*, Routledge, London.

Child, J. (1987) Organisational design for advanced manufacturing technology, in *The Human Side of Advanced Manufacturing Technology* (eds. Wall, T. D., Clegg, C. W. and Kemp, N. J.), Wiley, Chichester.

Churchman, C. W. (1971) *Design of Inquiring Systems*, Basic Books, New York.

Culnan, M. J. (1983) Environmental scanning: the effects of task complexity and source accessibility on information gathering behaviour, *Decision Sciences*, **14**(2), 194–206.

Daft, R. L. (1989) *Organization Theory and Design*, 3rd edn, West Publishing Company, St Paul MN.

Daft, R. L. and Weick, K. E. (1984) Toward a model of organizations as interpretation systems, *Academy of Management Review*, **9**(2), 284–295.

Didrickson, J. (1989) A framework for performance management in a local authority social services department, *MBA dissertation*, University of Bradford Management Centre.

Fayol, H. (1949) *General and Industrial Management* (Translated by C. Storrs), Pitman, London.

Galbraith, J. (1973) *Designing Complex Organizations*, Addison Wesley, Reading MA.

Goodhue, D. L. (1988) IS attitudes: towards theoretical and definition clarity, *DataBase* **19**(3/4), 6–15.

Goodhue, D. L. and Thompson, R. L. (1995) Task–technology fit and individual performance, *MIS Quarterly*, June, 213–36.

Habermas, J. (1972) *Knowledge and Human Interests*, Heinemann, London.

Harrington, J. (1991) *Organizational Structure and Information Technology*, Prentice-Hall, London.

Harris, M.L. (1979) *Cultural Materialism*, Random House, New York.

Hirschheim, R. and Klein, H. K. (1989) Four paradigms of information systems development, *Communications of the ACM*, **32**(10), 1199–216.

Hirschheim, R. and Newman, M. (1988) Information systems and user resistance: theory and practice, *The Computer Journal*, **31**, 398–408.

Huber, G. P. (1984) The nature and design of the post-industrial organization, *Management Science*, **30**(8), 928–51.

Jackson, M. C. (1992) An integrated programme for critical thinking in information systems research, *Journal of Information Systems*, **2**, 83–95.

Jayaratna, N. (1994) *Understanding and Evaluating Methodologies: NIMSAD, a Systemic Framework*, McGraw-Hill, London.

Klein, H. K. and Hirschheim, R. (1987) Social change and the future of information systems development, in *Critical Issues in Information Systems Research* (eds. Boland, R. J. and Hirschheim, R. A.), Wiley, Chichester, 275–305.

Klein, K. H. and Lyytinen, K. J. (1985) The poverty of scientism in information systems, in *Research Methods in Information Systems* (eds. Mumford, E., Hirschheim, R., Fitzgerald, G. and Wood-Harper, A. T.), Elsevier, Amsterdam, 131–61.

Lawrence, P. R. and Lorsch, J. W. (1967) *Organization and Environment*, Harvard University Press, Cambridge MA.

Markus, M. L. (1983) Power, politics and MIS implementation, *Communications of the ACM*, **26**(6), 430–44.

Morgan, G. (1997) *Images of Organization*, 2nd edn, Sage Publications, London.

Moynihan, E. (1989) Systems analysis and design without users, *Computing*, 12 October 1989.

Newman, M. and Noble, F. (1990) User involvement as an interaction process: a case study, *Information Systems Research*, **1**(1), 89–113.

Perrow, C. (1970) *Organizational Analysis: A Sociological View*, Tavistock Publications, London.

Perrow, C. (1972) *Complex Organizations: A Critical Essay*, Scott, Foresman and Company, Glenview IL.

Robey, D. (1981) Computer information systems and organizational structure, *Communications of the ACM*, **24**(10), 679–87.

Robey, D., Farrow, D. and Franz, C. R. (1989) Group process and conflict in system development, *Management Science*, **35**, 73–85.

Sanders, G. L. and Courtney, J. F. (1985) A field study of organizational factors influencing DSS success, *MIS Quarterly*, **9**(1), 77–93.

Swanson, E. B. (1987) Information systems in organization theory: a review, in *Critical Issues in Information Systems Research* (eds. Boland, R. A. and Hirschheim, R. A.), Wiley, Chichester, 181–204.

Taylor, F. W. (1911) *Shop Management*, Harper, New York.

Thompson, J. D. (1967) *Organizations in Action*, McGraw Hill, New York.

Woodward, J. (1970) *Industrial Organization: Behaviour and Control*, Oxford University Press, Oxford.

Woodward, J. (1980) *Industrial Organization: Theory and Practice*, 2nd edn, Oxford University Press, Oxford.

15

Society and information systems

Introduction

Previous chapters in Part 5 have looked at information systems mostly from the viewpoint of the considerations needed to be taken into account in system development and design by social, psychological and economic factors within the organization. In contrast, this chapter will discuss issues raised by the effects of information systems on individuals, organizations and society, covering the security and reliability problems discussed briefly in Chapter 1.

The first section is concerned with the social effects of information systems on organizations, considering several evolutionary models of organizations, followed by a brief discussion of the implications for centralization and organization size of increasing investment in information systems. The notion of software as a resource is then considered, where software has its value estimated and is treated as any other organizational asset.

Several issues are then considered, emphasizing the impact of systems on the economy, the home, crime and how reliability is affected. The Data Protection Act 1984 is discussed, with its implications for privacy of personal data and organizational behaviour with respect to data security. Two further aspects of security are examined – human threats such as hacking, involving a discussion of the Computer Misuse Act 1990, and software threats such as viruses.

Information systems evolution

In this section, we look at the effect of information systems on the organization as a whole. To do this a number of evolutionary models are presented; they discuss the stages through which organizations pass as computerization increases.

NOLAN MODEL

The Nolan model (Nolan, 1979) was developed in the 1970s by empirical research in a number of large US organizations, and describes six stages through which an organization evolves as it spends an increasing amount of money on computerization of its activities. The six stages are:

1. *Initiation.* The emphasis in the first stage is on computerizing functional activities, with the aim of cost reduction.
2. *Contagion.* Users now have overcome their unfamiliarity with the computer and the demand for new applications rapidly increases. Computer services may be free to users. The IT department expands to meet demand in a haphazard fashion with little planning or control.
3. *Control.* Senior management move to control expansion by limiting or cutting the IT budget. Costs and benefits of systems are made more visible, by installing management techniques in the IT department. Emphasis is placed on methods and documentation.
4. *Integration.* Existing systems are integrated usually via database technology. User accountability for their systems becomes accepted as a principle and the function of the IT department is to service users.
5. *Data administration.* Database experience has been gained and a data-oriented approach to systems development is adopted. This consists of a data administration function that controls organizational data, allied to an emphasis on common data for planning new, integrated systems. Users are responsible for the appropriate use of the technology.
6. *Maturity.* In the last stage, the technology is completely integrated with the organizational objectives, and there is joint user and IT department accountability for IT resources.

The model may be used in several ways. For example, information about many organizations may be gathered and used to determine the approximate degree of maturity that has been reached. Within an organization, the model may be used to determine the degree of maturity of different aspects of the organization, such as its extent of planning or user participation, which is a useful starting point for planning new systems, giving clues about the degree of staff expertise or the level of computer awareness in a user department.

The model has several weaknesses, as it has not been verified by later research and takes no account of outsourcing. Examination of the model suggests that, particularly for the first two stages, it is a historic model only. In addition, there is some confusion about accountability in the last three stages.

HIRSCHHEIM MODEL

A three-stage model is presented which is claimed to overcome some of the deficiencies of the Nolan model (Hirschheim *et al.*, 1988). The stages are:

1. *Delivery.* The focus in the IT department is inward, concentrating on technical problems and issues with hardware and software. It is important to achieve management credibility by delivering a product (not necessarily what users want) within budget and on time.
2. *Reorientation.* It now becomes important to forge good relationships with user departments, as systems are used in more and more parts of the organization. The emphasis is on delivering what users want.
3. *Reorganization.* User departments have become aware of the benefits that can be obtained from successful systems and top management moves to planning for integration of organizational and technological issues.

This model is very much an intuitive model, as it is not based on empirical research, as is the Nolan model, and it is a two-step model to achieving planning.

THREE-ERA MODEL

This model (Ward *et al.*, 1990) focuses on only one aspect of the organization and its use of computers, which is the broad type of activity supported. The model is:

1. *Data processing (DP) era.* Most information systems only automated the operational activities of organizations. The aims were reduction and productivity gains.
2. *Management information systems (MIS) era.* This era emphasized user-initiated enquiry systems and information analysis for assisting management activities. Technologically, these management systems shared a common base of information with DP systems. The aim was to enhance management effectiveness or to improve the quality of product or of service.
3. *Strategic information systems (SIS) era.* The current era is characterized by the aims of improving organizational competitiveness by changing the ways in which objectives are achieved, or by changing objectives. New types of system may incorporate more intelligence than before or they may process a wider variety of information than traditional data.

The authors add that, broadly, the DP era dates from the 1960s, the MIS era from the 1970s and the SIS era from the 1980s. However, it is possible for different computerized parts of an organization to be in different eras.

SUMMARY OF EVOLUTIONARY MODELS

The models described above are not claimed to be very precise, but they may be useful tools for applying to different departments or functions within an organization, to determine the rate at which computerization has proceeded. For example, it is common to find that the accounting function is ahead of departments such as production, in terms of computerization. Different rates of computerization can obviously affect the potential for integration.

Information systems and organizational structure

There are few studies of how the use of information technology affects organizations as a whole, but in Gurbaxani and Whang (1991) this topic is developed, in a theoretical manner, concentrating on two aspects of organizational structure: the degree of centralization and the organizational size.

Two kinds of costs are outlined, termed internal and external coordination costs. Internal coordination costs are those that are incurred in the endeavour to keep the behaviour of organizational employees in line with the objectives set by senior management, shareholders and so on. For highly centralized organizations, decision information costs are high, as information is more easily and quickly accessible to employees at the bottom of the organizational pyramid, and it therefore has to be channelled upwards to management for them to make decisions.

For highly decentralized organizations, what are termed agency costs are high, as the organizational leaders have to constantly monitor employee behaviour to ensure that they adhere to objectives. The aim is thus to minimize both decision information costs and agency costs.

For organizational size, external coordination costs are important. These are costs incurred when carrying out transactions in the external market, such as transactions with suppliers or customers. Costs are for writing and enforcing contracts, searching for information, transportation and so on. However, there may come a point when costs may be reduced by performing the transactions within the organization, and this may be achieved by mergers of the vertical integration type, where an organization acquires, for example, a key supplier.

The conclusions of the study are that information technology does not have a decisive effect on the degree of centralization, as both decision information and agency costs may be reduced. Other factors, such as those discussed in Chapter 14, are important for deciding the degree of centralization or whether a hybrid (mixed) structure is appropriate.

For organizational size, the authors find that if information technology is reducing internal coordination costs, there is a trend, other factors being equal, to larger organizations, measured both vertically (the range of value chain the organization spans) and horizontally (the number and corresponding share of different markets in which the organization sells its goods or services). This is also due to economies of scale being made possible by new technology.

However, organizations must balance their internal coordination costs with their external coordination costs, because in order to grow larger, reducing external costs, internal costs may be increased, so possibly deriving no overall benefit. Some organizations therefore may choose not to grow larger and may instead establish close contacts with customer or supplier organizations, if they do not wish to incur the larger internal costs of a larger organization. Depending on current cost structures, as well as other factors, organizations may grow larger or smaller.

Software as a resource

Although development budgets often run into millions of pounds and the software produced is maintained at even greater cost, it is not current accounting practice to show software as an asset on the organization balance sheet. This means that software is not audited, costed or depreciated, as are other assets, but, more importantly, it is not budgeted to be replaced when it is of no use. However, in an interesting paper, Rigby and Norris (1990) describe a project that involved them in developing a cost model for the software owned by British Telecom in the UK.

The basic idea underlying the approach is that of the 'software death cycle', as opposed to the traditional life-cycle concept. The emphasis is thus on the cost of keeping an existing system productive, rather than on the cost of developing a new system.

The steps suggested are:

1. *Audit software.* This consists of identifying items such as which programs and in what computers and locations they are held, program support environment (for example, operating system environment), associated documentation, licensed (how many licences) or developed software, and current or disused software. An advantage from this audit is that software ownership can be established, which is useful for assigning costs later.
2. *Assess value.* It is obviously difficult to put an objective value on an item of software, and the factors that should be considered range from financial to goodwill factors. Two extremes are suggested. Firstly, there is commercial software that has been bought to do a job or that has been developed to be sold, and its value can be partially estimated by determining whether or not it earns money. However, the costs, particularly of developed software, such as development costs or maintenance costs, are

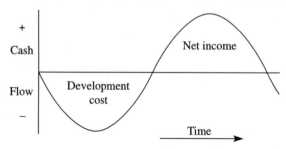

Figure 15.1 Cash flow model of software ownership.

not so easy to determine. At the other extreme, there is strategic software, which performs an essential function within the organization. The value of this is often unrelated to the actual cost of development or potential market value, and is usually highly subjective.

After a value has been assigned, it should be possible to draw a model of income/cost over time, and an actual situation, relating to a program product that was developed and sold commercially, is shown in Fig 15.1. Ideally, when the costs outweigh the benefits the software should be retired.

The figure shows that the initial costs are development costs (time and money taken to develop the software with no income) and the net income is income from sales minus the cost of support for the product.

3. *Establish value system.* Once the value has been assessed, a planning system for the software is suggested. This is done using two key variables – the present and predicted values of the software – to show how the software currently fits onto a planning grid based on the business portfolio analysis model, often termed the 'Boston matrix'. This is shown in Fig. 15.2 and is basically another way of representing the information in Fig. 15.1.

A product at the beginning of the curve in Fig. 15.1 has only a low present value but a high predicted value, and is thus a 'wild cat', which has valuable potential. A product that has crossed from negative to positive income is a 'star', and should be strongly supported. 'Cash cows' graze around the top of the curve and represent money in the bank, while 'dogs' are going downhill with no long-term value and should be removed.

It should be noted that a problem with this simple model is that the predicted value of the software relies heavily upon business judgement, and no method is given for taking subjective views of the current value of the software into account.

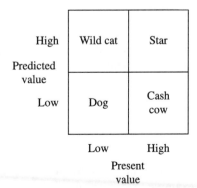

Figure 15.2 Boston matrix for assessing software value.

The economy

'UK teleworkers lose out to cheap foreign labour', *Computing*,
6 July 1995
Advances in telecommunications technology mean teleworkers in
the UK are losing jobs to overseas workers in cheaper labour
markets. Richard Nissen, managing director of UK teleworking
bureau The Virtual Office . . . warned: 'Around 200,000 jobs may
be lost by the end of the century.'

The combination of cheaper labour, the latest telecoms technology
and international phone connections at local-call prices has made
export of work cost-effective. British Airways (BA) outsources
some work to India where skilled labour is one tenth of the price
in the UK. BA's ticket-handling department redirects booking
queries to India where teleworkers process queries.

The home

'Barclays trials home banking', *Computing*, **13 July 1995**
The UK's largest retail bank, Barclays, is to launch a home PC
banking service which will allow its 10 million personal customers
to carry out a wide range of transactions via computer . . .
customers will be offered Windows-based software developed by
Barclays and Visa which will enable them to pay bills, request
statements and balance enquiries, carry out fund transfers and
establish standing orders via PC. . . . The initial service will . . .
update customer information on a daily basis.

Computers in the economy and the home

The stories in the panel above give an indication of how computers and
information systems may make a significant impact on daily life. The first
story shows how teleworking offers cost reductions to firms in the provision
of services. Unlike manufacturing, where plant has to be physically relocated,
services may be provided at the end of a telephone or fax. The second story,
concerning home banking, shows how consumers may soon be expected to
take over part of the work of bank staff!

Computers and crime

There are several general aspects to computers and crime and some are
discussed below. For example, recent research concerning computer crime
('Computer crime arrested', *The Sunday Times*, 24 March 1996), claims that

almost 75 per cent of companies suffering computer failure will themselves fail within 18 months, and that computer-related theft cost UK firms more than £1 billion in 1995; worldwide, computer-related crime is expected to cost £130 billion by the year 2000. According to the article, at least 60 per cent of computer-related crime is caused by insiders.

Reliability

The problem of system reliability is extremely important, often involving life or death or the safety of large financial transactions. Concern is increasing that, as software begins to play a larger part in these systems, with an attendant reduction in human supervision, the chance of system failure is increasing. The consequences of such failure for human life, confidence in financial institutions or markets, or the environment, for example, may be far-reaching.

Reliability is concerned with the correctness of an implementation with respect to a specification. For example, there should be no bugs in code written from a specification. Typical environments in which problems may occur are: spaceflight, missile and air defence, naval weapon systems, military and commercial aviation, surface transport (rail and bus), cars, robots (at least six cases of robot-induced death have occurred), financial systems and medicine.

For example, there have been reports of serious failure in safety-critical software which controls instrument panels on BA planes (*The Guardian*, 8 September 1990) and signal centres for British Rail (*The Guardian*, 23 July 1990). Another example concerns the loss of the Phobos I spacecraft (quoted in *Software Engineering News*, October 1988), where a mistaken 'commit suicide' command caused the spacecraft's solar panels to point the wrong way, preventing the batteries from charging, and ultimately causing a loss of power to the spacecraft.

A similar problem occurred with the Mir space station (*The Times*, 20 August 1997).

Privacy

The issue of privacy is concerned with the extent to which information concerning individuals that is stored in files or databases is accessible to individuals or organizations other than those who originally collect or supply the information. This has been an issue for several years, but it has come into sharp focus recently, with technological advances making it easier to access information. The next panel contains three stories which give different perspectives on the problem. The next section describes the Data Protection Act, as well as briefly mentioning two EU directives, which may offer some protection against this problem.

Data Protection Act

INTRODUCTION

The Data Protection Act 1984 is concerned with the privacy and security of certain types of 'automatically processed information' – broadly, data held in computer systems. The main aim of the Act is to protect the information rights of the individual, by restricting the availability of sensitive personal data, such as data concerning the individual's health, as well as allowing access rights to the individual about whom data is recorded. In addition, the Act allows data to be transferred freely, for purposes such as trade, between the UK and other European countries that have ratified the Council of Europe Convention on Data Protection.

The Act only applies to automatically processed information; it does not cover data that is only processed manually. Legal requirements are set out concerning the registration availability and transfer of what is defined as 'personal data'. This is information recorded on a computer about living, identifiable *individuals*, and not, therefore, organizations. Information includes opinions as well as facts.

The 'data user' is the user (often an organization) of the data who is legally responsible for data acquisition and who controls the content and organization of the data. The 'data subject' is the individual to whom personal data relates. Obligations are placed on data users, as well as 'computer bureaux', who are people or organizations who broadly process personal data for data users.

The Act therefore has implications for those who design and operate information systems that contain personal data.

REGISTRATION

The data user is advised to appoint a Data Protection Officer, who is responsible for properly registering personal data and describing the purpose for which it is to be used and who is the person to whom an individual would make a subject access request concerning his or her personal data. It is a criminal offence not to register such data. It is also a criminal offence if a registered data user knowingly or recklessly operates outside the descriptions contained in their register entries.

Registration of personal data and its use is accomplished by applying for a register entry with the Data Protection Registrar, who is an independent official reporting directly to Parliament. The Registrar's duties include:

1. Establishing the Register of Data Users and Computer Bureaux and making it publicly available.
2. Considering complaints about alleged breaches of the Act and, where appropriate, prosecuting offenders or serving notices on registered data users or computer bureaux.

Privacy

'France warns CSA to restrict data sharing', *Computing*, **27 June 1995**
A rising tide of complaints about abuse of data held by the Child Support Agency (CSA) has led Data Protection Registrar Elizabeth France to warn Government departments to put their houses in order.

. . . 'Every disclosure of information by the CSA should be properly justified,' she warned. . . . But France's comments reflect her concern at the prospect of information being shared by departments such as the Inland Revenue and the DSS.

'Industry must face up to civil liberties', *Computing*, **9 November 1995**
Complaints from civil liberties groups about the allegedly damaging effect of IT on the quality of life are not uncommon. But it is surprising to hear one of the UK's leading scientists add his voice to those expressing concern. Bill O'Riordan, ICL's chief scientist and a noted authority on technological change and its social impact argues . . . that the time has come for an urgent discussion of the role technology plays in society.

'I think we have come to the point where we may have to protect society from the revolution for which we have been responsible,' said O'Riordan. . . . According to O'Riordan, many technological developments – particularly those involving database and monitoring technology – represent profound threats to people's liberties. He is particularly concerned about . . . the development of in-car traffic management systems. . . . O'Riordan said: 'It will be possible to plot individuals' journeys. People seem to be oblivious to the fact that something which can receive data can also transmit positional data.'

He added: 'Real-time positional information on individuals can allow unscrupulous governments to infer exactly what an individual is doing. If they can instantly find out who is at a meeting, then they can work out the reason for that meeting...'

3. Encouraging the development of codes of practice to assist with compliance to the eight principles, discussed below.

EXEMPTION FROM REGISTRATION

Some personal data is exempt from registration under the Act. Such data need not be registered and the Registrar has no power over the data. The exemptions are:

1. Data held by an individual concerning his or her personal, family or household affairs.
2. Information that the law requires to be made public, such as the electoral register maintained by an electoral registration officer.
3. Data to safeguard national security.
4. Data for payroll, pensions and accounts purposes, but the data may be held only for certain specified purposes and there are restrictions on how it is made available to others.
5. Data concerning unincorporated members' clubs.
6. Data for mailing lists. The data must be held only for distribution purposes and there are four conditions that must be met.

PRINCIPLES

There are eight principles that should be used as a guide when developing and operating information systems. They are intended to protect the rights of the individuals about whom personal data is recorded. All principles apply to data users, but only the eighth principle applies to computer bureaux.

First principle

> The information to be contained in personal data shall be obtained, and personal data shall be processed, fairly and lawfully.

This means that the person who provides information should not be deceived or misled with regard to the purpose for which the data will be used or disclosed.

Second principle

> Personal data shall be held only for one or more specified and lawful purposes.

To comply with this principle it is necessary to register under the Act and process data in accordance with the purpose registered.

Third principle

> Personal data held for any purpose or purposes shall not be used or disclosed in any manner incompatible with that purpose or those purposes.

The use or disclosure of data must, for compliance with this principle, only be in accordance with the registered purpose.

Fourth principle

> Personal data held for any purpose or purposes shall be adequate, relevant and not excessive in relation to that purpose or those purposes.

The intent of this principle is that the data held shall be the minimum that is necessary and sufficient for its purpose.

Fifth principle

> Personal data shall be accurate and, where necessary, kept up to date.

Data is only considered to be inaccurate within this principle if it is incorrect or misleading with regard to a fact, as opposed to an opinion.

Sixth principle

> Personal data held for any purpose or purposes shall not be kept for longer than is necessary for that purpose or those purposes.

This concerns the length of time that data may reasonably be held for the registered purpose. Personal data held for historical, statistical or research purposes may be kept indefinitely, as long as the data is not used so as to cause damage or distress to any data subject.

Seventh principle

> An individual shall be entitled:
> (a) at reasonable intervals and without undue delay or expense –
>   (i) to be informed by any data user whether they hold personal data of which that individual is the subject; and
>   (ii) to access any such data held by a data user; and
> (b) where appropriate, to have such data corrected or erased.

Section 21 of the Act and Registrar's Guideline Number 5 set out the rights of subject access in more detail. 'Reasonable intervals' between access requests will depend upon the type of data and how frequently it is updated. 'Appropriate' in relation to data correction or erasure is concerned with compliance with the other principles.

Eighth principle

> Appropriate security measures shall be taken against unauthorised access to, or alteration, disclosure or destruction of, personal data and against accidental loss or destruction of personal data.

The issue of security applies here, to both data users and computer bureaux, and covers:

1. Unauthorized access, either physically into the computer premises or into the hardware or software.
2. Alteration, disclosure or destruction of data without the authorization of the data user.
3. Accidental loss or destruction of data because of unreliable hardware, software or back-up and recovery procedures.

Particular consideration should be given to security needs in the light of the sensitivity of the data and the harm that could result from any of the above breaches. Consideration should also be paid to the physical security of the computer installation, to software security measures and to the reliability of staff accessing data. This might include staff selection on the basis of competence, as well as sound induction and adequate system training.

SUBJECT ACCESS

Access rights

An important part of the Act relates to the access rights of data subjects; that is, those individuals about whom personal data is recorded. The data subject has the responsibility to apply for 'subject access', and must specify the registered entry under which access is being requested. This is because data users may register a number of purposes under different subject entries.

All information, current and historical, held under a registered entry about the individual should be provided. The data user must respond to a subject access request within *40 days* of having received the request. The period starts when the data user can identify the data subject and locate the relevant data. The data user may charge a fee for access to each registered entry, and there is a statutory maximum.

Exemptions from subject access

Data held for certain purposes is exempt from subject access. For example:

1. Data held for the purposes of crime prevention, or tax or duty assessment or collection.
2. Government department data concerned with the making of judicial appointments.
3. Data consisting of information that might form the basis of a claim of legal professional privilege, that is concerning lawyer–client confidentiality.
4. Data held only for the preparation of statistics or the carrying out of research.
5. Back-up data, that is, data held only for replacing other data if it is lost.
6. Data held by credit reference agencies. This is available under the Consumer Credit Act 1974.
7. Data that incriminates the data user.
8. Data exempt from registration.

In addition, the relevant Secretary of State may, with an order, exempt certain personal data from subject access. Currently, the following orders have been made:

- *Health.* 'Health data' is defined as data relating to the mental or physical health of the data subject. Furthermore, the data must have been collected by or on behalf of a health professional, such as doctors, dentists, chemists, nurses, opticians and clinical psychologists. Data users may be, for example, employers, insurance companies, health authorities or GPs. Subject access rights are removed either where subject access would be likely to cause serious harm to the health of the data subject or where another individual would be identified. Before data users take a decision on a subject access request they must consult the 'appropriate health professional', who might be, for example, the most recent GP of the data subject.
- *Social work.* Access rights of data subjects are removed where disclosure would either cause serious harm or where another individual is identified. Data users here are primarily health and local authorities, or institutions concerned with care such as the NSPCC. As for health data, subject access rights are removed either where subject access would be likely to cause serious harm to the health of the data subject or where another individual would be identified. There is no requirement for another professional to be consulted before disclosure or non-disclosure.
- *Others.* Data relating to adoption records and children's special educational needs is exempted, as is data designed to protect the public from financial loss by persons involved in financial services or company management. A schedule of financial and other bodies and functions is included.

Response to requests

A response from the data user to a request for personal data is always required. If personal data concerning the individual making the request is not held, or if there is subject access exemption, then the statement may be made that no data is held that the data user is required to disclose.

Where data is held that must be disclosed, a copy must be supplied within 40 days. This period begins when the data user has:

1. The information reasonably needed to identify the data subject.
2. Information reasonably required to locate the data.
3. Consent from other individuals to disclose data identifying third parties (where such individuals are referred to in the personal data of a data subject).

The response may be in any form (for example, handwritten or typed) intelligible to the data subject. Exam marks have a special status in connection with the 40 day limit for response to access requests, and the time limit is five months from the request or 40 days after the day on which exam results are announced, whichever is the earlier.

INACCURATE DATA

If an individual considers that data held by a data user is incorrect, he or she may apply to the Data Protection Registrar or the courts for an order requiring the data user to erase or correct the inaccurate data. Data can only be corrected concerning a matter of fact, not opinion. The onus of proof for accuracy is with the data user.

Data subjects may claim compensation through the courts from a data user if they have suffered damage through inaccurate personal data being held, or if they have suffered damage due to loss or unauthorized disclosure of data. The onus of proof lies with the data user or bureau concerned.

TIMETABLE

The timetable for introduction of the measures of the Act was as follows:

> 12 July 1984 – Royal Assent
> 12 September 1984 – compensation through the courts available for loss or unauthorized disclosure of personal data
> 11 November 1985 – registration began.
> 11 May 1986 – compulsory registration began for data users and computer bureaux
> 11 November 1987 – rules on 'subject access' and the Registrar's supervisory powers came into force

OTHER ASPECTS

Individuals may complain to the Registrar if they feel that they have been affected by an alleged breach of the principles of the Data Protection Act. The Registrar may mediate if the complaint is justified. Further action is to issue various types of notice, or finally to prosecute the data user in the criminal court if the notices are ignored.

The Data Protection Tribunal exists to consider appeals by data users or computer bureaux against the Registrar's decisions. It can overturn the Registrar's decision and substitute its own. There is the right of appeal, on questions of law, to the High Court.

An example of the type of protection that can be necessary is described in the next panel.

SUMMARY

The Act gives basic protection to individuals against data users for misuse of their personal data. It is not clear, however, whether the eighth principle can be enforced as, whenever security violations occur (see next section), the Act could be contravened by the data user if not enough consideration has been given to system security.

EU LAW

The European Commission is becoming increasingly active in legal matters concerning computers, and two directives are relevant to the UK Data Protection Act. The European Directive on Data Protection, adopted in July 1995 and to be implemented within a year in member states, has as one of its measures an extension of data protection from electronic media to all forms of storage; that is, manual files are now included.

The European Draft Directive on the Legal Protection of Databases was adopted in 1996 and one of its effects will be to replace copyright control on non-creative databases (for example telephone directories) with a new right, lasting less than the 70 years from author death which currently applies to copyright.

Security

INTRODUCTION

The following sections deal with security of computer systems. This traditionally covers a wide spectrum of topics, all concerned with the vulnerability of a computer system to accidental or intentional threat.

One of these topics has already been considered indirectly, as the Data Protection Act sets out a framework that requires protective measures to be taken against unauthorized access, alteration, disclosure or destruction of personal data, as well as its accidental loss or destruction.

Privacy

'Wrong suspect settles his case for \$55,000', *New York Times*,
6 March 1988
Terry Dean Rogan, who was arrested five times in Michigan and
Texas for crimes he did not commit, has settled a lawsuit against
the City of Los Angeles for failing to remove his name from a
crime computer's file. . . . The murders and robberies he was
charged with were ultimately traced to an Alabama jail inmate,
Bernard McKandes. Mr McKandes was found to have assumed
Mr Rogan's identity after Mr Rogan apparently discarded a copy
of his birth certificate.

Security

'Electronic blizzard brings down US planes', *Monitoring Times*,
May 1990
The scene is Libya, 1986. High in the sky, an armada of 33
high-tech US fighter planes begin their attack. But something is
wrong. One plane, carrying two crew members, crashes. Of the
surviving 32 planes – including five F-11s – seven are unable to
get off even a single shot. The probable reason: an electronic
blizzard that, according to Pentagon officials, came not from the
Libyans but from high-powered US military transmitters that filled
the night sky with electronic signals designed to jam Libya's
anti-aircraft defenses, hunt down targets, guide weapons, and
communicate.

   According to Air Force Colonel Charles Quisenberry, during the
Libyan strike, US weapons 'were interfering with each other . . .
some of this interference can actually affect the aircraft's flight
controls'.

There are three types of security consideration (Elbra, 1990) for a computer
system, organizational, physical and logical security. Organizational security
covers standards for staff procedures and monitoring of deviations from those
standards. The main aim is to prevent breaches of security which might lead
to fraud, theft, damage and so on. One aspect of this relevant to computer
systems concerns change control, which regulates any changes made to software
systems.

Physical security is broadly concerned with threats to the fabric of the
computer system; the most common causes in the UK being fire/explosion,
power/lightning, water and industrial action. However, an increasing problem
of this type is due to inadvertent electromagnetic interference from devices

Hacking

'Rude remark prompts tube system probe', *Computing*,
21 September 1995
London Underground is fighting to clean up its computer systems
after one of its own trainees hacked in and posted an offensive
message on the digital displays located above tube platforms around
the capital . . . a message appeared on displays at Piccadilly,
Elephant & Castle and Regent's Park underground stations
declaring 'All signalmen are w****s'. The message went unnoticed
by tube staff for more than 12 hours before being removed.

A London Underground spokesman told Computing: '. . . It
seems one of the trainees obviously had more experience than the
others. He managed to hack into the computer, bypass the input
codes and put a message on the dot matrix displays. . . . The
trainee is no longer an employee.'

'2 men accused of "hacker" crime', *Milwaukee Journal*,
24 February 1989
. . . a Milwaukee County prosecutor has charged two Milwaukee
men with fraudulently obtaining free long-distance telephone
service. Working independently, using home computers and similar
software programs, the men are alleged to have obtained calling
codes for customers of an independent long-distance telephone
company, Schneider Communications. They then used the codes
to bill their personal calls to Schneider's customers. . . .

' "Mad Hacker" jailed for computer war' (appeared in *Daily
Telegraph*, publishers have been unable to trace the copyright owner)**
A computer operator who called himself 'The Mad Hacker' became
the first in Britain to be jailed for the offence yesterday. Nicholas
Whiteley, 21, of Enfield, north London, was sentenced to 4 months
with a further 8 months suspended for criminally damaging
computer disks and wreaking havoc on university systems. . . .
Whiteley declared war on computer experts, using a computer in
his bedroom to swamp university computers with masses of useless
material including threats and boasts about his brilliance. One
said: 'Don't mess with me because I am extremely nutty.' He was
found guilty last month of 4 charges of causing damage to magnetic
disks in mainframe computers at the Universities of London, Bath,
and Hull. The judge said some of the computers stored important
and confidential data relating to medical and scientific research.

such as cellular phones, nearby radio antennae or other sources. An example is shown in the panel on p. 400.

We shall only discuss logical security here, which is broadly concerned with threats to the software in the computer system. The two topics we shall consider are threats posed by humans (by hacking) and threats posed by software (for example by viruses).

Human threats

HACKING

The term hacking originally referred to the activities of 'compulsive' programmers whose sole interest was in generating large quantities of roughly formed program code, in a manner that resembled a woodcutter hacking logs from a felled tree. However, more recently, the term has been used to describe unauthorized access to computer systems (as hackers are chiefly concerned with 'loggin'!).

Modern computer systems make it possible to gain access over telecommunications lines, using direct dial-up lines (perhaps for salespeople to access a computer while they are in the field, or for diagnostic support), specialized data transmission services or personal computers linked to a network. Older, standalone systems required a prior breach of physical security. Although computer systems have a first line of defence, which is usually a set of confidential log-in and password identifications, these in the main have not proved to be successful against the determined 'hacker' as shown in the previous panel.

COMPUTER MISUSE ACT 1990

Introduction

In the third extract in the previous panel, Whiteley had been found guilty under the common law relating to criminal damage. However, similar prosecutions under common law have failed, and the Computer Misuse Act received Royal Assent on 29 June 1990 and came into force on 29 August 1990. The background to the Act is that there is increasing reliance on computers, for operational as well as information storage purposes, and unauthorized computer access is becoming a matter of major concern to computer users. This is because losses are incurred by system owners whose systems are violated, and confidence in computer systems may be undermined.

Three new offences are introduced by the Act; these are described below.

Unauthorized access offence – Section 1(1)

A person is guilty of an offence if:

(a) he causes a computer to perform any function with intent to secure access to any program or data held in any computer
(b) the access he intends to secure is unauthorized; and
(c) he knows at the time that he causes the function that that is the case.

This concerns any unauthorized and deliberate access to a computer that causes the computer to perform a function, and it is intended to deter disgruntled employees (who account for approximately 70 per cent of the problem) or a hacker. Electronic or physical eavesdropping is thus not covered, unless the computer is induced to perform a function. The intent to commit the offence need not be directed at any specific program, data or computer.

The maximum penalty is a fine of £2000 or a prison sentence of up to six months, or both.

Ulterior intent offence – Section 2(1)

A person is guilty of an offence under this Section if he commits . . . the 'unauthorized access offence' with intent:

(a) to commit an offence . . . ; or
(b) to facilitate the commission of . . . an offence (whether by himself or by some other person).

This section is concerned with unauthorized access to a computer to commit a further offence. For example, access might be gained to learn confidential information of a personal, commercial or security nature, for blackmail, fraud or espionage purposes. This is regarded more seriously and hence attracts a higher penalty. The maximum penalty is an unlimited fine or a prison sentence of five years, or both.

Unauthorized modification offence – Section 3(1)

A person is guilty of an offence if:

(a) he does any act which causes an unauthorized modification of the contents of any computer; and
(b) at the time when he does the act he has the requisite intent and the requisite knowledge.

The 'requisite intent' is an intent to modify the contents of any computer that might (a) impair computer operation, (b) prevent or hinder access to a program or data in any computer, (c) impair the operation of any program or the reliability of any data.

This is intended to prevent the introduction of viruses into programs, Trojan horses and similar software threats (see below), which may impair operation, hinder access or damage data. Such threats can interfere with networks containing hundreds or thousands of computers, delaying or damaging ongoing work, can introduce large elements of uncertainty into the question of reliability of computer-generated results, can corrupt data or can make programs unworkable. The maximum penalty is five years imprisonment or an unlimited fine, or both.

This offence was introduced partly to remove the uncertainty of court judgements concerning damage to data or programs that had been considered under the Criminal Damage Act. If a modification results directly in physical damage, such as damage to a disk head, then the Criminal Damage Act 1971 will apply.

Other details

In all cases, there has to be proof that the offence was caused with intent; that is, the unauthorized access was deliberate. This therefore will not affect individuals who accidentally gain access to, for example, an unauthorized computer or who unknowingly introduce a virus into a system that is contained in a program on their floppy disk.

UK legislation normally only has jurisdiction within the UK. However, where an offence has been committed involving a computer in the UK, even if the offender is abroad, then it may be possible to prosecute under the Act.

The Act was introduced as a private member's bill by Michael Colvin MP and later supported by the Government. Powers are also available for a suspected hacker to be monitored by police, dependent on a permit issued by the Home Secretary.

Software copyright

The Act may also be used under Section 1 to prevent the illegal copying of software. Also covered under Section 1 are unauthorized uses such as printing calendars and using the computer as a calculator for private accounts. A consequence of the Act is that the infamous *Hacker's Handbook* has had to be withdrawn from publication, as it might incite an offence under the Act. However, the Act already has its critics and the next panel gives an example.

Conclusions

The first line of precautions that can be taken against the problem of illegal access involves keeping numbers of dial-up lines or other communications addresses secret. Secondly, the security practices available on the computer

Hacking

'New hacking law "too hard to enforce"', *The Guardian*, 29 August 1990

Peter Sommer, author of the Hacker's Handbook, who opposed the need for new legislation, said he feared that . . . it would make it more difficult to prosecute malevolent hackers. 'They are creating more difficulties for this offence than before,' he said. The new and untried legislation might be open to challenges on the definitions used in the wording of the Act.

Scotland Yard's four-strong computer crime squad will be enlarged to cope with the extra work expected. . . . Over the last five years the Department of Trade and Industry has recorded 270 computer crime cases. Only five were brought to court. . . . Although estimates of the annual cost of computer crime have ranged up to £1 billion, most is fraud committed by employees using computers for crimes that would otherwise have involved paper forgeries. . . . But cases of hackers breaking into systems and damaging computer files are increasingly common.

system should be followed, although these are often rather rudimentary and basically involve keeping log-in aids and passwords secret and unavailable to unauthorized individuals. If passwords are long (for example, eight characters) and regularly changed, this makes access much more difficult.

Hacking is a growing problem and it is clear that the means by which authorized users identify themselves to systems are too easily violated. It is not clear whether modern legislation, such as the legal requirement in the Data Protection Act for data users to protect personal data from unauthorized access, will bring about any increase in security measures.

Software threats

INTRODUCTION

This section discusses the threat posed by viruses and similar types of software to the security of a computer system. These types of software are introduced into a computer system illicitly, and are either directly introduced or are hidden in software (a 'host') that is otherwise innocent.

The main types of software that pose this threat are:

1. *Virus*. This is defined (Cohen, 1984) as a program that can infect other programs by altering them to include a copy of itself. The virus may change in the 'reproduction' process. Another name for a virus is a 'worm'.

2. *Time bomb.* This is activated when a particular date or time occurs, for example on 1 April.
3. *Logic bomb.* This is activated by a given combination of events either in the host or some other source (such as system software or data).
4. *Trojan horse.* This is similar to a virus, but it does not reproduce itself in other software. It is hosted by seemingly innocent software.

TYPES OF DAMAGE

The damage that can be done by such software ranges from minor irritants, such as displaying a Christmas tree at log-on on 25 December, to serious inconvenience or loss, such as slowing or temporarily stopping a system or deleting all data from hard disks.

A well-known case in the USA concerned Robert T. Morris, a student, who in spring 1990 was found guilty under the US 1986 Federal Computer Fraud and Abuse Act. The actual charge against Morris was access without authorization. On 2–3 November 1988 Morris gained access via the Internet to several thousand computers, many of which are for military or research use, at up to 600 institutions, and introduced a virus, known as the Internet virus or worm. It caused no actual damage, although many systems were saturated with multiple copies of the virus program, but owing to its unauthorized presence in a top-security environment many computers were shut down for up to 48 hours and many hours were spent tracing the origin of the problem.

However, there are cases where actual damage to data has been done. Some examples are given in the next panel.

There are several ways in which viruses may be introduced into a computer system. In addition to those mentioned above, a common route is via public domain software (for example, games software) which may be obtained either by post or from bulletin boards on networks cheaply or for free. Such software often contains a Trojan horse which will infect software in the host computer.

PROTECTION

There are programs ('vaccines') that can detect many of the better known software threats, and these may be installed on a computer to scan all types of input. However, new viruses are constantly being produced (Simons, 1989). Consultants also may offer their services as virus experts. Traditional remedies against data loss include keeping back-up copies of all data. Care should be taken in screening staff (who may insert such software during program development) and in obtaining software only from reputable sources.

As discussed in the previous section, Section 3 of the Computer Misuse Act 1990 provides penalties for unauthorized modification of programs or data, and it remains to be seen whether this acts as a sufficient deterrent for those who manufacture and introduce software threats.

Software threats

'Black Baron shot down by virus ruling', *Computing*, 1 June 1995
An unemployed man, who goes under the guise of the 'Black Baron', has become the first person in the world to be convicted of writing and planting computer viruses. . . . Christopher Pile admitted 11 charges under the 1990 Computer Misuse Act and a separate charge of inciting others to spread computer viruse.... Prosecuting counsel Brian Lett told the court that a virus on one computer had cost one unnamed firm £500,000, but added that the total damage to UK business could amount to more than £1m.

Pile was brought to court following a police investigation into computer viruses named 'Queeg' and 'Pathogen' – expressions from the cult BBC2 comedy *Red Dwarf*. Chris Hook, managing consultant at the National Computing Centre, said: '. . . There is now a realization that viruses can damage the economy of the country.'

'US companies plagued by PC infections', *Computing*, 4 April 1991
Every large US business will be suffering from one new computer virus infection a month by the end of the year, according to a new survey. Already, more than one quarter of all US businesses with at least 400 PCs have one or more systems infected. . . . In the first quarter of 1990, just 9% of US businesses said they had found viruses in their PC systems. . . . But the second half of 1990 showed a rapid increase with 16% reporting virus attacks in the third quarter, rising steeply to 25% in the last three months of the year. . . . 13% of the companies reported at least one attack which disabled 25 or more PCs.

CONCLUSIONS

It is difficult to estimate the seriousness of the problem. Viruses in safety-critical systems (railways, aeroplanes) may have serious consequences. More effective means, apart from the deterrent of the Computer Misuse Act, need to be developed to combat these problems.

Summary

This chapter has explored several wider issues raised where information systems have been introduced into society. Within organizations, we considered several evolutionary models of how organizations change with respect to the type of applications built and the extent of planning that exists, the effect on organizational size and degree of decentralization of information systems and the question of how to estimate the value of the software resource that many organizations currently have.

Some examples of the impact that systems are beginning to have on the economy, the home and on crime in general were then briefly discussed, as well as issues of system reliability, and then the Data Protection Act 1984 was described within the context of the privacy issue and its main points outlined. Its main aim is to protect the information rights of the individual by placing certain obligations on those who process personal data. Under the heading of human security threats, the topic of hacking was considered and the Computer Misuse Act 1990 was briefly discussed. This seeks to prevent unauthorized access to computer systems.

For software threats, the types of damage that can be done by software such as viruses, for example damage to data or programs, were then described. Protection measures were then briefly discussed.

Discussion questions

1. Compare the three evolutionary models of information systems discussed. Are they making the same point, in more or less detail, or not? What is the point they are making?
2. If you keep a mailing list for your football or cricket club on your PC, do you have to register as a data user under the Data Protection Act 1984?
3. Do you need to use the Data Protection Act 1984 to find out the detail of your latest exam results?
4. At what points in the analysis and design of a new information system does the Data Protection Act 1984 have implications for your work?
5. Name the three offences under the Computer Misuse Act 1990. Which offence will you breach if you (a) introduce a computer game on to the hard disk of the computer at work or in college and then play that game, (b) copy an item of copyright software from that computer and bring it home, (c) introduce a time bomb into the system's software to exclusively occupy the only printer every hour for five minutes?

References

Cohen, F. (1984) Computer viruses, in *Computer Security. A Global Challenge (Proceedings of the 2nd IFIP Conference IFIP/Sec '84, Toronto, Canada)* (eds. Finch, J. H. and Dougall, E. G.), Elsevier, Amsterdam, 143–159.

Data Protection Act 1984, *Guidelines*. Available from Data Protection Registrar, Springfield House, Water Lane, Wilmslow, Cheshire SK9 5AX.

Elbra, T. (1990) *A Practical Guide to the Computer Misuse Act 1990*, NCC Blackwell, Oxford.

Gurbaxani, V. and Whang, S. (1991) The impact of information systems on organizations and markets, *Communications of the ACM*, **34**(1), 59–73.

Hirschheim, R., Earl, M. J., Feeny, D. and Lockett, M. (1988) An exploration into the management of the IS function: key issues and an evolving model, in *Proceedings of the Joint International Symposium on IS*.

Hook, C. (1989) *Data Protection Implications for Systems Design*, NCC Publications, Manchester.

Kenny, A. D. (1989) *Managing Software: The Businessman's Guide to Software Development*, Blackwell Scientific, Oxford.

King, D. (1984) *Current Practices in Software Development: A Guide to Successful Systems*, Prentice-Hall, Englewood Cliffs NJ.

Nolan, R. L. (1979) Managing the crises in data processing, *Harvard Business Review*, **46**(2).

Rigby, P. J. and Norris, M. T. (1990) Implications of assessing software as a financial asset, in *SE 90 (Proceedings of Software Engineering 90, Brighton)* (ed. Hall, P. A. V.), Cambridge University Press, Cambridge, 435–63.

Simons, G. (1989) *Viruses, Bugs, and Star Wars: The Hazards of Unsafe Computing*, NCC Blackwell, Oxford.

Ward, J., Griffiths, P. and Whitmore, P. (1990) *Strategic Planning for Information Systems*, Wiley, Chichester.

Glossary

abstract system – a system (see *system*) that consists only of ideas and that does not do anything; a conceptual system only, as opposed to a physical system

abstraction – this is the process of modelling some aspect of the real world, with certain unwanted detail removed. Different levels of abstraction may exist, depending on the level of detail we wish to consider or omit

acceptability – a property of an information system such that it does not challenge or threaten aspects of users' work held to be important. Ideally, such a system should be perceived by all users as assisting in the accomplishment of work-related goals. This property is usually interpreted fairly broadly and concerns the wider organizational effects of information systems

analysis – in the traditional approach to systems development, the phase where the user requirement is analysed using a precise but abstract language

application – the area of an organization that is being considered for computerization; the problem domain of an item of software. For example, an order entry or video game application

application portfolio – the set of information systems in an organization. These may be current, under development or proposed

attribute – a descriptor of an entity. For example, date of birth and age are descriptors of the entity person

building – the term applied to the activity of representing the real world in models such as entity, process or rule models

business analysis – the analysis of the business activities of an organization, emphasizing, for example, critical success factors and application portfolio contents, product life-cycle or organizational value chain

CASE (Computer Aided Software (or Systems) Engineering) – an approach to the systems development process that automates key development activities with the aim of improving system quality and productivity

conceptual modelling – an approach to requirements analysis that emphasizes the non-procedural and integrated modelling of structure, rule and process

contingency approach – in the context of systems development, an approach recognizing that different development methods are appropriate to different organizational circumstances

critical success factor (CSF) – used in business analysis (see above), this is a key factor perceived to be essential for meeting objectives in any part of the organization

data flow diagram (DFD) – a graphical method for specifying processes and data flow in an organization

data-oriented – a data-oriented method places emphasis on the analysis, on an abstract level, of data for a system. Compare with *process-oriented*

data processing (DP) system – see *transaction processing system*

decision support system (DSS) – a type of information system that typically applies mathematical techniques to the analysis of information and the generation of solutions to assist management in decision-making activities

documentation – a general term relating to any sort of description of an information system in whole or in part

entity – a class of objects that are of interest in the application, for example, car or department. An *entity instance* is an individual object belonging to a class, for example, a car YOB 1 or a marketing department

entity life history (ELH) – a diagrammatic method that describes the allowable update processes and their sequence that may occur on an entity instance

entity modelling – a diagrammatic method for describing entities, attributes and relationships

event – this is an important occurrence that provides information or initiates a process. It is often shown on the DFD or process decomposition

executive information system (EIS) – similar to a decision support system (see above) but aimed at more senior management

functional requirements – a description of system requirements that only considers the information and processing required

generalization hierarchy – at its simplest, this consists of a single entity and its generalization into lower level entities. For example, person is a generalization of man and woman. There may be many levels in the hierarchy so that, for example, man is a generalization of lower level entities such as father

hard approach – this approach to systems development assumes firstly that there is a problem to be solved that is logically based and that has a computer solution, and secondly, that the computer solution can integrate well into the organization, without having taken account of wider social or psychological factors

implementation and testing – the penultimate phase of the traditional approach to systems development where a system is constructed and tested

information architecture – a phase product of strategic planning, this is a non-redundant, centralized description of the information and processes that need to be represented in the system to support the organization's information needs. It is usually in the form of entity models, data flow diagrams and so on

information needs – the information needed by the organization to achieve its objectives, as well as the information required to generate that information

information system – an information system provides procedures to record and make available information, concerning part of an organization, to assist organization related activities

information systems development – see systems development process

information systems strategy – a plan for the desired organizational activities and the information systems required by those activities

information technology strategy – a plan for the computer technology that will deliver the information systems strategy

iteration – the process of repeating an activity more than once; within the context of systems development, redoing earlier work to incorporate changes

linear model – the traditional approach to systems development, whereby phases are executed completely in a strict sequence

logical design – in the traditional approach to systems development, the phase where the computer-based system is first designed

maintainability – the maintainability of a system is concerned with the ease with which the system may be changed, due to a change in requirements or technology

maintenance – the last phase of the traditional approach to systems development, where changes to the existing system are made

management information system (MIS) – this consists of a transaction processing system (see below) with additional procedures for presenting system information to management

method, methodology – an integrated set of procedures, methods and techniques for systems development

mission – within business analysis, the highest-level formal statement of the long-term aims of an organization

model – an abstract representation of the real world. The term may also be used to refer to a language or set of symbols for representing the real world, as in the entity model

non-functional requirements – a broad description of system requirements that take into account the anticipated effects the system will have on the organization. For example, required characteristics of the human computer interface, expected training needs or desired organizational benefits

normalization – in the context of the relational data model, a technique for separating structured data into 'normalized' relations. The technique is designed to address efficiency problems for update and retrieval

open system – a system that interacts with its environment by receiving input and producing output

participation – generally used to mean an emphasis on the inclusion of the user at different points in the systems development process to improve the quality of the final system

participative systems design (PSD) – a systems development method (see above) that employs user participation

phase – a major part of the systems development process. A **phase task** is an activity within a phase, and a **phase product** is a specification produced by a phase task

physical design – in the traditional approach to systems development, the phase where the desired hardware, software and human processes are added to the system design, and where the detail of the organizational context in which the system will operate is considered

physical system – a system that has a real world existence and that exhibits behaviour; a system that does something

process – an activity of interest that occurs in the application

process control structure – the three ways in which a process may be structured are: (1) sequence: the order of processes relative to one another (2) selection: the conditions under which a process may execute (3) iteration: whether a process may occur once or many times

process decomposition – a graphical method for describing the hierarchical refinement of processes

productivity – the notion of productivity is that of developing a system on time and within budget. The two main reasons for productivity problems are changing requirements and poor project control

quality – the notion of quality is that of developing a system that meets the requirements of the users. There are four main reasons for poor quality: the wrong problem is defined; the wider organizational context is neglected; analysis is incorrect; or systems development is undertaken for the wrong reason, such as technology push or political pull

reliability – this concerns the ability of a system to behave consistently in its intended environment, and it is an important property of safety-critical systems

relational data model – a technique for modelling data based on the mathematical theory of relations. It is sometimes used in the analysis phase to model data in a 'bottom-up' manner

relationship – within the context of entity modelling, this is an association between entities, but it may also be used to refer to an association between an entity and an attribute

requirements acquisition – the stage within the requirements determination phase where the requirements are obtained from the user

requirements modelling – the last stage within the requirements determination phase where the user requirements are analysed from a narrative into a more structured form

requirements-centred – a general description of modern development methods that emphasize the early phases of requirements determination and analysis

requirements determination – the first phase of the systems development process, where the problem is defined, system feasibility is identified, and the user requirement (see below) is obtained

reverse engineering – the process of producing higher level documentation from the lower level products of an existing system, such as program code, database definition statements or file structures

rule – defined within the analysis phase to be a restriction over the structure component specified in the conceptual model. It is a non-procedural restriction over an object or objects of interest

soft approach – an approach to systems development that regards the hard approach (see above) as being too narrow. It allows for problem situations that may be investigated using a variety of techniques, and it also takes into account the wider organizational context by focusing on social and psychological issues related to the development and impact of an information system in an organization

soft systems methodology (SSM) – a method that is an example of the soft approach (see above) to systems development

specification – a general term used to refer to a description of a system (in whole or in part). It may be expressed in a variety of ways on different levels of abstraction, such as natural language, graphical forms or structured text

state space approach – this approach considers a (discrete) system state, at any instant, as being defined by the relevant objects that exist in the system at that instant. An update process transforms the system from one state to another

state transition diagram – a diagrammatic method for describing transitions between system states, often used for specifying interactive dialogue in human computer interfaces

strategy – this describes how an organization will achieve its long-term objectives

strategic – this term may be applied to planning (see below), the highest level of decision-making, or the highest level of information (see Chapter 5)

strategic plan – a general term used to refer to an overall plan for an organization or part of an organization involving the use of information technology. The plan usually refers to organizational aims and the information systems necessary to support those aims, together with a description of the management structure and technology that will be required to implement the plan

system – an assembly of related parts that act together as a whole; something that may be decomposed into the following components: input, output, process, boundary and environment

systems development process – the process of developing an information system starting from understanding user requirements, through implementing a system that meets those requirements, to maintaining that system when changes occur

systems life cycle – another term for the systems development process, intended to emphasize the fact that, taking the maintenance phase into account, a system effectively goes through many cycles of analysis, design and implementation

tool – an automated, software aid to an activity within the systems development process

transaction – a self-contained event that is a fundamental unit of the main area of concern of an organization. For example, a bank withdrawal or a concert seat reservation

transaction processing system (TPS) – this is a system that provides procedures to record and make available information concerning the occurrence of transactions (see above) in the application

usability – a property of an information system such that the users can work with the system and use it as intended. This is usually interpreted as relating to the design and use of the human computer interface

user requirement – this is the user perception of a system that the user wants, interacting with the organization, together with the expected benefits that the user hopes will materialize from the use of the system. It is the set of functional and non-functional requirements that the user has of a system and its interaction with the user organization

validation – the activity that checks that a phase product of the systems development process is correct in terms of the user requirement. The term usually implies that users are involved in checking that the phase product has captured the requirement correctly

verification – the activity that checks that a phase product is internally (syntactically) correct. It is usually performed by designers. For example, checking a DFD that all data flows have names, or that no flows exist between data stores

Author Index

R L Ackoff 53
S Ade 350
K Agusa 146, 148
N Ahituv 23
M Alavi 288
I O Angell 332
R N Anthony 93, 95
ANSI/SPARC 164, 270
P Attlewell 374
D E Avison 226, 276, 338, 350, 360

F T Baker 228
G Baker 291
R C Bamford 234
P Barnard 145
V Basili 116
C Batini 165
N Bassiliades 186
C M Beath 22, 111
R Bentley 357
P Beynon-Davies 15
H R Beyer 335, 349
L Bhabuta 291, 292
A Bicego 323
G Bjerknes 334
N Bjorn-Andersen 333
D Bjorner 332
M Blaha 224, 292
B Bloomfield 378
B W Boehm 117, 118, 160, 330
C Bohm 228
S J Boies 355
M Boman 103
G Booch 232

M L Brodie 164
F Brun-Cottan 348
E Brynjolfsson 12, 15, 330
J A Bubenko 129, 297
R Butler 361, 369, 371–2, 375

J R Cameron 249
T Capers Jones 15, 329
E Carmel 351
S Castano 147
CCTA 281, 299, 307
S Ceri 189
J Champy 333
P Checkland 61, 270, 336
P P Chen 165
J Child 333, 381
M B Chrissis 292
M G Christel 358
M Christerson 224, 291
C W Churchman 53, 379
P Clare 203, 290
D Clausing 343
E K Clemons 332
P Coad 223, 232
I Coe 203, 290
F Cohen 405
W R Collins 328
D Connor 276
L Constantine 228, 243, 244, 292
D S Cornford 33, 226
J F Courtney 374
J Crinnion 127
M J Culnan 381
W Curtis 37, 202, 276, 292

R L Daft 372, 381
O Dal Vecchio 290
A Daniels 227
R Darimont 163
C J Date 231
M Davarpanah Jazi 349
A M Davis 23, 89, 199, 201, 202, 276, 280
G B Davis 33, 96, 352
V De Antonellis 147
T de Marco 117, 194, 199, 201, 229, 243
W J Deibler 234
J Didrickson 370
E W Dijkstra 228
J Dobson 333, 335, 347
A Dorling 308, 315
E Downs 258
DSDM 321
DTI 14, 329

M J Earl 23, 409
K Eason 15, 330, 339, 354
S Easterbrook 146
F Eddy 224, 292
P Ehn 354
T Elbra 400
K El Emam 142
R Elmasri 165
EM (Euromethod) 299, 300, 306
Ernst and Young 12
ESI (European Software Institute) 315

M E Fagan 121, 228
D Fairbairn 329
D Farrow 383
A Fawthrop 329
H Fayol 89, 364
M Feblowitz 144
D Feeny 409
R G Fichman 223, 276, 278
B Fields 163
C Finkelstein 117, 236
B Fitzgerald 333
G Fitzgerald 226, 276, 291, 349
D J Flynn 143, 145, 165, 184, 202, 203, 276, 288, 349–51, 358
F T Fodemski 161
O Fragoso Diaz 165, 202, 276
M Franckson 299
C R Franz 383
A L Friedman 33, 226
A Fuggetta 283

J Galbraith 370, 375
C Gane 121, 194, 229, 243, 244, 245
T Gilb 124
J A Goguen 335
D L Goodhue 360, 362
P A Gough 146
J D Gould 339
S Greenspan 144
P Griffiths 409
J A Gulla 146
V Gurbaxani 387

S Haag 343
J Habermas 378
J Hagelstein 292
O Hajime 357
K Hales 110
T A Halpin 103, 164, 165
M Hammer 333
J Harrington 41
M Harrison 371
M L Harris 145, 163
J R Hauser 343
I T Hawryszkiewycz 119
D J Hickson 96
S A Higgins 161
K Hindle 291
C R Hinings 96
R A Hirschheim 15, 40, 330, 374, 379–80, 385
K Holtzblatt 335, 349
C Hook 409
E Horowitz 226
P Howard 110, 111, 118, 160, 282, 287
G P Huber 381
J Hughes 346–7
W S Humphrey 15, 234, 331

J Iivari 223, 276, 278
N Iscoe 37
Y Ishihara 143
ISO 164, 186, 308, 315, 319

M A Jackson 148, 229, 249
M C Jackson 360, 377
I Jacobson 223, 232, 233
G Jacopini 228
N Jayaratna 226, 276, 379
P Johanneson 129
P Jonsson 224, 291

T Kasami 161
C B Kavan 24

K Kawai 357
M Keil 351
A T Kearney 329
M I Kellner 203, 290, 330
C F Kemerer 15, 223, 276, 278
K E Kendall 134, 137
J E Kendall 134, 137
A D Kenny 409
S J H Kent 148
K Kimbler 162
D King 226, 330
H K Klein 378–80
A Klug 164, 270
D R Knight 143
KPMG 14, 330
H Krasner 37
P Kuvaja 315
M Kyng 354

M Lacity 40
P R Lawrence 370
A L Lederer 15
B Lee 227
M Lefering 148
J C S P Leite 148
C Lewis 355
C Linde 335
O I Lindland 161
F H Lochovsky 164
M Lockett 409
G Longworth 124
W Lorensen 224, 292
J W Lorsch 370
P Loucopoulos 164
H C Lucas, Jr 45, 95
K Lyttinen 15, 330, 378

L Macaulay 344
I G Macdonald 292
J Madey 163
R N Maddison 276
N H Madhavji 142
N Maiden 147
P Mair 283
T S E Maibaum 162
M M Mantei 342
M L Markus 374
J Martin 233
F Maryanski 186
P Massonet 163
B Matthews 147
R K McClean 129
C McClure 288

F W McFarlan 329
F McGarry 129
S J Mellor 223
K W Miller 355
D Millington 321
H Mintzberg 44, 68, 89, 93
D E Monarchi 223
G Morgan 361
E Moynihan 359
E Mumford 338–341
G T Myers 228, 243, 292
M Myers 15, 330
J Mylopoulos 144, 189

I Nassi 228
P Naur 227, 328
S B Navathe 164, 165, 189
NEDO 329
P G Neumann 15, 329
S Neumann 23
M Newman 374
G M Nijssen 103, 164
B Nixon 145
F Noble 374
R L Nolan 385
M T Norris 388
B Nuseibeh 146
J O'Brien 356
J J Odell 233
A Ohnishi 146, 148
A P Oliveira 148
T W Olle 226, 231, 276
M H Olson 33
J Over 290
Ovum 287
Open University 53, 61
L Orman 139
K T Orr 229
J Over 203
G Overgaard 224, 291

J Page 129
R Pajerski 129
C Pancake 223
D L Parnas 163
M C Paulk 234
J Peckham 186
C Perrow 367–9
L F Pitt 12
C Potts 335
C Potter 110, 111, 118, 160, 282, 287
J Prasad 15
W Premeriani 224, 292

R S Pressman 110, 112, 330–1
D S Pugh 89
G I Puhr 223
J M Punshon 163

W J Quirk 162

J Rachel 234
M K Raja 356
B Randell 227, 328
S J Ray 161
B Regnell 148
P J Rigby 388
D Robey 354, 374, 381
B Robinson 15, 330
A Rochfeld 164
R Rock-Evans 83, 110, 165, 193
T Rodden 356–7
C Rolland 292
D T Ross 229
M Rouncefield 356
T P Rout 307, 315
W W Royce 230
J Rule 374
J Rumbaugh 204, 208, 223, 232, 270, 275
K Ryan 144, 147

A Salek 146
G L Sanders 374
T Sarson 121, 194, 229, 243
C Sauer 15
P Sawyer 357
L L Schkade 356
J W Schmidt 189
J Scholes 65, 270, 336
K E Schoman 229
H Seki 161
J A Senn 132
A Shiomi 357
S Shlaer 223
B Shneiderman 228
H A Simon 28
G Simons 406
J Sims 14
R Singh 319
S Smithson 332
Soft 320
H G Sol 291, 292
A Solvberg 161
I Sommerville 346, 356–7
J Song 291
P G Sorenson 163
G L Sosa 15, 330

B J Spielman 355
SSADM 164, 165, 233, 258, 259, 269, 335
J Stapleton 321
S N Stevens 358
W Stevens 228
N Stokes 291
F Stowell 338
R Strens 333, 335, 347
A G Sutcliffe 147
E B Swanson 22, 111, 381

P Tait 350
N Takeda 345
F W Taylor 364
T J Teorey 165, 342
J D Thompson 371
R L Thompson 362
TickiT 234, 297
J P Tremblay 163
D Tsichritzis 164, 270
C Tully 291
M Twidale 357

D B Urfrig 129

J Vagner 290
F J M Van Assche 292
C Van Hasselt-Lim 234
A Van Lamsweerde 145
A J Van Schouwen 148
A A Verrijn-Stuart 276, 291, 292
I Vessey 350
I Vlahavas 186
L Von Bertalanffy 53

S Waligora 129
P Wall 348
B Wangler 129
J Ward 386
R Warhurst 203
J-D Warnier 229
R T Watson 24
C V Weber 292
K E Weick 381
A Wesslen 162
D West 338
S Whang 387
P Wherry 355
P Whitmore 409
L Willcocks 40
G Willumsen 161
I Winfield 329
R Winter 164

J J V R Wintraecken 165
D P Wood 346
J Wood 291
A T Wood-Harper 338, 349–50, 358, 360
J Woodward 363–4, 374–7
P Wright 145
B Wroe 330
C-H Wu 145

D Yeates 227
E Yourdon 223, 226, 228, 229, 232, 243, 244
E S K Yu 144

P Zave 148
M Zelkowitz 129
R Zicari 164
R E Zultner 344

Subject Index

abstraction 56, 181–2
acceptability 6
aggregation 182, 206–7
analysis 103–5
analyst
    systems/business analyst, analyst
        programmer 38
application 5, 46–8
association 206–8
attribute 173–5, 205

back-office application 12
Big Brother 22
Boston matrix 389
business process re-engineering 328
business systems 45–8
cardinality constraint 169–72, 174–5,
    208
CASE tools 282–8
    meta-case tool 285
changing requirements 21
classification of systems 61
Computer Misuse Act 402–5
conceptual model components 164
conceptual modelling 103–4, 164–5
context diagram 246
contingency approach to methods 351–3
control system 58, 66, 73–4, 364–6
cost/benefit analysis 12
crime, computers and 390–1
critical systems thinking 377–80

database system 31
data dictionary 248–9

Data Protection Act 392–9
data flow diagram (DFD) 194–7, 247,
    264
data processing (DP) system 35
decision, levels of 93
decision support system (DSS) 28
decision table 201–2
decision tree 199–201
domain knowledge and reuse 147–8
DSDM 319–21
dynamic model 220–1

effectiveness 11
efficiency 11
entity 166–7
    sub-/supertype 176–8
entity diagram 180
entity life history (ELH) 267–9
entity modelling 165–82
environment
    system 55
    organization and 369–71
environmental uncertainty 370
ethnography 346–7
Eurobells⌂ 68, 148–59, 180, 196
Euromethod 299–307
event 72, 214
evolution of information systems 384–6
evolutionary approach 123–5
exhaustion 178, 212
exclusion 178, 212
executive/enterprise information system
    (EIS) 28–9
expert system 31

failure, information system 12–18, 327–8
feasibility study 101, 133–6
flowchart 199
front-office application 12
functional activity 7
functional information 9, 94–5
functional model 221
functional requirements 145

Gantt chart 136
Garmisch software engineering
    conference 328
generalization 176–7, 181, 211–12
group sessions 344–5
groupware system 31

hacking 402
hard approach 333
hierarchical organization 56
human computer system (HCS) 76, 106,
    108

identifier 174
ideology 372
implementation and testing 108–110
incremental approach 124
information
    and meaning 41
    internal/external 9
    formal/informal 41–4
    functional 9, 94–5
    management 9
    paradigms of 41
    strategic managerial/operational 94–5
    value of 44–5
information base 76
    representation 78–9
Information Engineering 236–43
information needs 5
information system 3
information systems evolution 384–7
information technology (IT) department
    37
inheritance single, multiple 178, 211–12
input/output 55, 69
input system 76–7
interview and questionnaire 137–8
ISO 12207 315–19
iteration 118
iterative approach 118–20

job satisfaction 340
JSD 249–58

knowledge-based system 31

languages 148
law, computers and 391–405
levels, conceptual, external, internal 164
linear model 112–13
link 206
link attribute 209–10
logical data structure (LDS) 266
logical design 105–6

MacAdam's takeaway 3
maintainability 22
maintenance 110–12
management activities 7
    classical model 89
    Mintzberg model 89–91
management information 9
management information system (MIS) 28
management system 66–7, 74, 88
message system 76
method
    advantages/disadvantages 281–2
    contingent 351–3
    definition 225–6
    history 226–35
    standards 234–5
methodology 226
methods
    AMORE 346
    Apprenticeship model 349
    Client-led design 338
    DAFNE 300
    DSDM 319–21
    Ethnography 346–7
    Information Engineering 236–43
    JSD 249–58
    KJ method 345–6
    MEIN 300
    MERISE 300
    Multiview 338
    OMT 204
    ORDIT 347–8
    Participative Systems Design (PSD)
        338–42
    QFD 343–4
    SDM 300
    Soft Systems Methodology (SSM)
        336–8
    SSADM 258–70, 300
    Structured systems analysis and design
        (SSAAD) 243–9
    Systemscraft 127

User-centred design 348–9
User-centred modelling 349
User Factors Life Cycle (UFLC) 342–3
USTM 344–5
Vorgehensmodell 300
minispecification 248
model
    analytic/descriptive/normative/optimiz-
        ing/predictive 61–2
    avalanche 230
    linear 112–13
modelling languages 148
multiple relationship 178–9, 209

N-ary relationship 179
natural language processing 143–6
non-functional requirements 145
norms 371

object 69, 204–5
    class 205
    model 213
object-oriented methods 232–3
office information system 31
OMNIS model 67, 81–2, 158–9
OMT (Object Modelling Technique) 204,
    270–6
organization 5–6, 7–9, 11, 69–73, 339–40,
    359–62
output system 77
outsourcing 40

participation 339, 350
participation constraint 172–3, 175, 208–9
participative systems design (PSD) 338–42
perception-driven paradigm (of
    information) 41
PERT diagram 136
phase task/product 100, 226
physical design 106–8
power 373–4
privacy 391
problems
    analysis problems 187–8
    hard approach problems 328–33
    information systems problems 18–22,
        328–32
    requirements determination problems
        139–42
    soft approach problems 350
    systems approach problems 63–4
problem definition stage 101, 132–3
process 70–72

primitive (create/change/delete) 70–71
query 80
report 71, 80
support 71
process component 191–2
process control structure 191–2
process decomposition 192–4
productivity 21–2, 115–16, 139–41, 280–1,
    332–3
project control 332
property 69
prototyping 125–7, 320–1

quality 19–21, 114–15, 141–2, 279–80, 331

rapid application development (RAD)
    125–7, 320–1
real-time system 29
reliability 22, 391
relationship 167–9, 206–8
requirements acquisition 102, 136–9,
    147–8, 149–67
requirements engineering 142–8, 233
requirements modelling 102, 139, 143–5,
    158–9
requirements determination 101–102,
    131–9
    problems 139–142
requirements model 102
requirements validation 145–7
resource-driven paradigm (of
    information) 41
reverse engineering 282
role name 167
rule 72, 182–6, 212
    definition 182
    framework 185
    language 185–6
    problems 183–4
rule component 164, 182

security 22, 399–402
simulation system 75
social factors 333–51
socio-technical approach 340–2
soft approach 333–5
    characteristics 349, 351
    criticisms 350
    solutions 351–3
soft systems methodology (SSM) 336–8
Software Engineering Institute 331
software process 315
software threat 405–7

SPICE 307–15
SSADM 258–69
  version 4+ 269–70
standards 234–5
  CMM 331
  DSDM 319–21
  Euromethod 299–307
  ISO 9000 297–9
  ISO 12207 315–19
  Spice 307–15
  TickiT 297–9
state (OO) 214
  diagram 215–19
state space approach 60
state transition diagram 197–9
statement of requirements 136, 148, 157
structure (organization structure) 360–2,
  368
  impact of information systems on
    362–3, 387–8
structure component 164
structured systems analysis 229
subset 176
success, information system 12, 327
successful/unsuccessful systems 12–18,
  327–8
system
  boundary 55
  classifications 61
  definition 53
  design 59
  sub-system 56
  types
    abstract/physical 54
    closed 55
    control 58
    continuous/discrete 60
    deterministic/non-deterministic/
      predictable/non-predictable/
      stochastic 57–8

    open 54
  system state 70
systems development process 6, 99
  avalanche approach 230
  contingency approach 351–3
  evolutionary approach 123–5
  hard approach 333
  incremental approach 124
  iterative approach 118–20
  prototyping approach 125–7
  socio-technical approach 340–2
  soft approach 333–51
  traditional approach 99–100, 112–13,
    128–9
    problems 113–18
  user validation approach 120–3
  waterfall approach 230
systems life cycle 6, 99, 315–19
Systemscraft method 127

task 362–3, 367–9
  uncertainty 367–8, 370
technology 362–9
tendering process 304
tool
  types 283–4
  components 285–7
  disadvantages 288
transaction 26
transaction processing system (TPS)
  26

uncertainty 44–5, 59, 102
usability 6
user 333, 336–49
user factors life cycle (UFLC) 342–3
user requirement, definition 128
user validation approach 120–3

validation 120, 142